Policy Perspectives
on Educational Testing

Evaluation in Education and Human Services

Editors:

George F. Madaus, Boston College, Chestnut
Hill, MA, U.S.A.
Daniel L. Stufflebeam, Western Michigan
University, Kalamazoo, MI, U.S.A.

**National Commission on Testing
and Public Policy**

Gifford, B.; *Test Policy and the Politics of
Opportunity Allocation: The Workplace and
the Law*

Gifford, B.; *Test Policy and Test Performance:
Education, Language, and Culture*

Gifford, B., and Wing, L.: *Test Policy in
Defense*

Gifford, B., and O'Connor, M.; *Changing
Assessments, Alternative Views of Aptitude,
Achievement, and Instruction*

Policy Perspectives on Educational Testing

edited by

Bernard R. Gifford

University of California at Berkeley

Kluwer Academic Publishers
Boston Dordrecht London

Distributors for North America:
Kluwer Academic Publishers
101 Phillip Drive
Assinippi Park
Norwell, Massachusetts 02061 USA

Distributors for all other countries:
Kluwer Academic Publishers Group
Distribution Centre
Post Office Box 322
3300 AH Dordrecht, THE NETHERLANDS

Library of Congress Cataloging-in-Publication Data

Policy perspectives on educational testing/edited by Bernard R.
  Gifford.
      p.   cm. — (Evaluation in education and human services)
    Includes bibliographical references and index.
    ISBN 0–7923–9238–8
    1. Educational tests and measurements — United States.
  2. Education and state — United States. 3. Minorities — Education —
  United States. I. Gifford, Bernard R. II. Series.
  LB3051.P59 1992
  371.2'6'0973 — dc20   92–5610
                                                                       CIP

Copyright © 1993 by Kluwer Academic Publishers

Printed on acid-free paper.

Printed in the United States of America

Contents

Contributing Authors

Anne E. Cunningham is a visiting professor at the University of California, Berkeley. Her research interests are in the area of literacy and assessment in early childhood education. Dr. Cunningham received her Ph.D. in developmental psychology from the University of Michigan in 1987. She received the 1988 Outstanding Dissertation of the Year Award from the International Reading Association and a Spencer Fellowship for 1989 to 1991 from the National Academy of Education.

Bernard R. Gifford is Chancellors Professor of Education, in the Division of Mathematics, Science and Technology Education, Graduate School of Education, University of California at Berkeley, where he served as Dean between 1983 and 1989.

Between 1989 and 1992, he was with Apple Computer, Inc., serving as the company's first Vice President for Education. While employed at Apple, Gifford wrote a well received column on Education, technology and public policy, for the *Chronicle of Higher Education* and *Education Week*.

His latest books are *History in the Schools: What Shall We Teach?* (Macmillan, 1988), *Test Policy and the Politics of Opportunity Allocation: The Workplace and the Law* (Kluwer Academic Press, 1989), *Testing Policy and Test Performance: Education, Language, and Culture* (Kluwer Academic Press, 1989). He also co-edited (with Linda C. Wing) *Test Policy in Defense: Lessons from the Military for Education, Training and Employment* (Kluwer Academic Press, 1992) and (with Mary Catherine O'Connor), *Changing Assessments: Alternative Views of Aptitude, Achievement and Instruction* (Kluwer Academic Press, 1992). The four volumes on testing policy were originally sponsored by the Ford Foundation funded National Commission on Testing and Public Policy, which Gifford chaired between 1987 and 1990.

A 1971 Ph.D. in radiation biology and biophysics from the University of Rochester Medical School, where he was an Atomic Energy Commission Fellow in Nuclear Science and was also elected to *Phi Beta Kappa*, Gifford spent a post-doctoral year at Harvard University, where he was a Kennedy Fellow at the John F. Kennedy School of Government, as well as a Loeb Fellow at the Graduate School of Design. Gifford was awarded an Honorary Doctorate of Humane Letters from Long Island University in June of 1988.

Before becoming a full-time academic in 1981, as Vice President and Professor of Political Science & Public Policy at the University of Rochester, Gifford served as Resident Scholar at the Russell Sage Foundation (1977–1981) and as Deputy Chancellor of the New York City Public Schools (1973–1977). Prior to joining the NYC public schools, Gifford served as President of the New York City RAND-Institute (1972–1973), jointly established in 1969 by the RAND Corporation and New York City Mayor John Lindsay, to conduct systematic policy studies of the City's municipal operations.

An active participant in the public policy arena, Gifford currently serves on the Board of Trustees of the Children's Television Workshop, the producers of Sesame Street, the University of Rochester, and the National Center for Family Literacy. He also has served as a Trustee/Director of the American Associaton for the Advancement of Science (AAAS), The German Marshall Fund of the United States of America, New York University, and the Congressional Black Caucus Foundation.

Arthur R. Jensen is the author of *Genetics and Education, Educability and Group Differences, Educational Differences, Bias in Mental Testing, Straight Talk About Mental Tests* and more than three hundred articles in scientific and professional journals — writings that have placed him among the dozen or so most frequently cited contemporary psychologists. He is recognized for his research contributions in the fields of human learning, differential psychology, psychometrics, and behavioral genetics. After receiving his Ph.D. from Columbia University and doing a clinical psychology internship at the University of Maryland Psychiatric Institute, he spent two years as a research fellow in the Institute of Psychiatry of the University of London. He was later Guggenheim Fellow and a Fellow of the Center for Advanced Study in the Behavioral Sciences. Since 1958, he has been on the faculty of the University of California, Berkeley, where he is a professor of Educational Psychology.

Lyle V. Jones, while a student at Reed College, enlisted in the Army Air Corps (1943 to 1946). He received B.S. and M.S. degrees in psychology in 1947 and 1948 and a Ph.D. degree at Stanford in 1950. In 1950 to 1951, he was an NRC postdoctoral fellow with L. L. Thurstone at the University of Chicago, where he remained as a faculty member in psychology. He joined the faculty at the University of North Carolina in 1957, where he currently is Alumni Distinguished Professor of Psychology and Director of the L. L. Thurstone Psychometric Laboratory. He served from 1969 to 1979 as Vice-Chancellor and Dean of the Graduate School at the University of North Carolina at Chapel Hill. He has been a visiting faculty member at the Universities of Illinois, Texas, and Washington and twice was a fellow at the Center for Advanced Study in the Behavioral Sciences. He serves on several national advisory boards and committees that are concerned with psychological testing. Many of his publications are pertinent to the psychological measurement of human preferences and values, of the effects of brain damage and aphasia, and of educational achievement, especially for black students.

P. David Pearson is the Dean of the School of Education at the University of Illinois in Urbana-Champaign. He has been active in professional organizations, serving the International Reading Association as a member of the Board of Directors, The National Council of Teachers of English as a member of its Research Committee, The National Reading Conference as president and The National Conference of Research in English as president. He has published several books, *Teaching Reading Comprehension* and *Teaching Reading Vocabulary*, with Dale D. Johnson for Holt, Rinehart & Winston, which are now in their second edition. Also, he conceived of and edited the *Handbook of Reading Research*, published by Longman; the second edition was recently published. He has also published materials for teachers and children in his role as an author for the *Silver, Burdett & Ginn Reading Program*. He served two terms as coeditor of *Reading Research Quarterly*, from 1978 to 1985. Professor Pearson received his B.A. in history from the University of California, Berkeley, taught elementary school in California, completed his Ph.D. in education at the University of Minnesota, and taught there for several years before moving to Illinois. His current research interests center on reading comprehension instruction and assessment.

Maria Pennock-Román was born and raised in Puerto Rico. (She had a truly bilingual upbringing and schooling since her first language was Spanish, most of her elementary education was in English, and her high school studies were in Spanish.) She majored in theoretical mathematics and minored in psychology at Cornell University. Later, she received an M.S. in statistics and a Ph.D. in quantitative psychology, both degrees from the University of California, Berkeley. She has held postdoctoral fellowships from the Ford Foundation-National Research Council Program for Minority-Group Scholars and the Rockefeller Foundation Fellowship Program for Minority-Group Scholars. Currently, she is a research scientist at Educational Testing Service (ETS) in the Division of Cognitive and Assessment Research. Before joining ETS, she was on the faculty at the University of Pennsylvania Graduate School of Education where she taught courses in psychological and educational measurement and statistics.

Charles W. Peters is currently a reading consultant for Oakland Schools in Waterford, Michigan. In this capacity he provides professional and staff development in a variety of areas related to the language arts for the 28 school district he serves. He received his Ph.D. in reading at the University of Wisconsin-Madison. He has taught at the middle school, high school, and university levels. He has published widely in a number of leading educational journals as *Reading Research Quarterly, Educational Psychologist, Journal of Reading, Reading Teacher,* and *Educational Leadership*. He has coedited two book and contributed numerous chapters to others. His most recent article on assessment appears in *Perspectives on Assessment* (R. Smith and D. Birdyshaw eds.) He has received the Outstanding Dissertation of the Year Award from the International Reading Association and the Professional Service Award from the American Educational Research Association. He was a member of the 1990 NAEP Item Writing Panel and a member of the Steering and Planning Committee for the 1992 NAEP. He is currently a member of the English Language Arts Advisory Group of the New Standards Project. He is past codirector of the project between the Michigan Department of Education and the Michigan Reading Association to revise statewide objectives and tests in reading.

Sheila Valencia is Associate Professor of Education at the University of Washington, Seattle where she teachers courses and conducts research on reading and writing instruction and assessment. She received her undergraduate and master's degrees in education from the State University of New York at Buffalo and her Ph.D. in Reading Education from the University of Colorado, Boulder. She has held faculty positions at The Center for the Study of Reading at the University of Illinois, Urbana-Champaign and the University of Colorado, Boulder. Dr. Valencia began her career as a classroom teacher in New York City and upstate New York, and later spent six years as district reading supervisor in Northglenn, Colorado.

Over the past 6 years, Dr. Valencia's work has focused on literacy assessment. She was co-director of the research and development project for the Illinois Goal Assessment Program in Reading at the University of Illinois, Urbana-Champaign and has served on numerous national and statewide assessment task forces and committees. Currently, she is a consultant to the New Standards Project, the IEA International Reading-Literacy Study, and several state reading assessment projects. She serves on the Task Force on Assessment, an advisory group to the National Council on Educational Standards and Testing, the International Reading Association Issues in Literacy Assessment Committee, and the Joint NCTE/IRA Task Force on Literacy Assessment Issues. Dr. Valencia has written extensively on literacy assessment, with articles appearing in *Educational Leadership, Reading Research Quarterly, The Reading Teacher, Applied Measurement in Education*, and several edited volumes.

Karen K. Wixson is a professor of education at the University of Michigan. Prior to receiving her Ph.D. in reading at Syracuse University, she was a remedial reading and learning disabilities teacher. She conducts research and publishes widely in the areas of reading assessment and instruction, and her awards include the IRA Elva Knight Research Award, the AERA Professional Service Award, and the MRA Reading Researcher Award. Recent projects include: coauthor of a diagnosis and remediation text for Harper Collins; coeditor of a current volume from Teachers College Press on *Improving Basal Reading Instruction*; and past codirector of the project between the Michigan Department of Education and the Michigan Reading Association to revise statewide objectives and test in reading. She served on the NAEP Objectives Panel in 1990, two special NAEP Committees in 1992, the Oral Reading and the Metacognitive Assessment Committees. She is currently a member of the Language Arts Advisory Group of the New Standards Project.

POLICY PERSPECTIVES
ON EDUCATIONAL TESTING

1 INTRODUCTION

Bernard R. Gifford

In the 1980s, the American public came to grips with a crisis in education and its potentially devastating effects on the nation's economic and social life. The federal government's publication, in 1983, of *A Nation at Risk: The Imperative for Educational Reform* riveted attention on our schools and provided a vocabulary for public debate. Over the next several years, educators and policymakers sought to document the extent of the crisis, to gauge its potential impact, and to develop educational strategies that would boost achievement. In this setting, educational reform was hoisted high on the nation's political agenda. Parents, business leaders, and a broad range of public and private organizations issued urgent calls for accountability — that is, "more educational bang for the buck." State education departments and legislatures took measures designed to ensure that tax dollars expended for education resulted in measurable achievement.

This period turned the spotlight on educational assessment — the procedures, practices and tools that educators use to gauge the progress of students, as individuals and groups, and to answer the question: Which educational strategies are likely to result in improved outcomes for these students? Political leaders gave unprecedented attention to test data, calling press conferences to publicize good results or to explain disappointing outcomes. Technical terms like *criterion-referenced norms* began ot find their way into the popular media.

The chapters in this volume shed light on a range of issues within the field of educational assessment, with an emphasis on those issues that have sparked public policy debate in recent years. They were submitted

3

at the invitation of the National Commission on Testing and Public Policy. It was my pleasure to chair that commission from its inception in 1987 until shortly after the publication of its major report in 1990 entitled, *From Gatekeeper to Gateway: transforming testing in America*.[1]

To appreciate the setting in which the commission was created and these articles were written, it may be helpful to consider the historical context in which today's debate took shape.

The Historical Context

We Americans have always held our public schools accountable for instruction, but not for achievement. For most of the first two centuries of American public education, teachers were held responsible for teaching, and students (and their parents) were held responsible for learning.[2] Today, schools are held accountable not only for the delivery of services, but also for students' performance; not only for teaching, but also for learning. A student's failure is considered to be an institutional failure — at least in theory.

We very much take for granted the notion that schools are accountable for results, but in fact this notion is relatively new.[3] It dates back a mere quarter of a century, to the passage in 1965 of the *Elementary and Secondary Education Act* (ESEA). Most of the dollars allocated under ESEA were Title I funds, providing financial assistance to local education agencies for the education of children from low-income families. As Walt Haney pointed out in his review of the history of testing in American education, "With the federal funding came strings, in the form of a provision for the evaluation of the effectiveness of Title I-funded programs."[4] These "strings" constituted a demand for accountability: local education agencies would receive funding only if "effective procedures, including provisions for appropriate, objective measurement of educational achievement, will be adopted for evaluating at least annually the effectiveness of the programs in meeting the needs of educationally deprived students."[5]

The vast majority of Title I programs — more than 90 percent — met this legal obligation by administering norm-referenced tests to participants.[6] In this way, Title I legislation was responsible for the significant growth of standardized testing in American schools during this period. As Haney notes, that was ironic in at least two ways: first, because at this time educational researchers were questioning the wisdom of using norm-referenced tests for program evaluation, preferring the use of criterion-referenced tests; and second, because developments in the schools soon raised doubts about whether widespread testing in schools was doing more to retard rather than advance the interests of disadvantaged students.[7]

ESEA created a legal framework for what was to come. But in the mid-1960s, the call for accountability was not yet a top-down demand originating with governors, legislators, or business leaders. It was for the most part a grassroots movement by parents and others in the civil rights community, demanding that government respond to children's educational needs. The legislation authorizing Chapter 1 funding, for example, required schools that received these funds to set up Parent Advisory Committees and to publicize test scores so that parents and other taxpayers could gauge the impact of the program.

Over the next several years, this bottom-up approach to accountability was turned on its head. By the early 1970s, articles on accountability were appearing with regularity in the educational literature, offering definitions of the term and promoting the idea that those involved in teaching and learning must answer for children's outcomes — but not so much to parents as to the legislative bodies that allocate tax revenues to education and to the government agencies that provide funding.

A leading proponent of this position was Leon M. Lessinger of Georgia State University, who wrote in 1971: "A growing number of people are becoming convinced that we can hold a school — as we hold other agencies of government — to account for the results of their activity." He called this notion "a most radical departure from present-day practices," adding that "educators are put in the position of reporting results for funds expended."[8] In the same year, Raymond Bernabi noted that: "Eventually, attempted and achieved student learnings will be related to instructional efforts. When that occurs, teacher accountability will be established."[9] In 1972, Frank Jennings wrote, "It is essential...that the school and other 'people-changing' institutions be available for public audit of their performance."

The concern with accountability raised in the early 1970s proved to be more than that season's educational fashion. It created an environment in which process measures of school effectiveness (such as teacher/student ratios or hours of instruction) gave way to outcome measures (such as the percentage of students scoring at or above grade level on a standardized reading test). From 1972 through 1985, the number of state testing programs grew from one to thirty-four. By 1989, every state had a mandated testing program of some kind.[10]

Underlying all of these accountability policies is an assumption that we question too rarely: that student progress is both measurable and controllable. This idea has been traced back to the work of logical positivist philosophers and behavioral psychologists such as A. J. Ayer, Edward Thorndike, James Watson, Ivan Pavlov, and most notably, B. F. Skinner.[11] Their work promoted not only the idea that progress toward predetermined educational goals can be predicted and measured, but also that those abilities that lend themselves to precise measurement have greater educational value than those that do not.

This approach stands in stark contrast to a more humanistic approach to education, which emphasizes those kinds of thought processes and creative abilities that most standardized tests can neither predict nor detect. Some researchers see, in the history of American education, a pattern of alternating dominance between the humanistic versus the positivist/behaviorist approach. The humanistic approach seems to have been in ascendency in the 1890s, the 1930s, and the 1960s; the positivist/behaviorist view in the 1920s, the 1950s, and the 1970s.

That tension is palpable in American education today. The *Nation at Risk* trauma of the early 1980s intensified calls for public audits of education: over a two year period from 1982 to 1984, some twenty national reports appeared dealing with some aspect of public education, virtually all critical and negative in tone.[12] But the crisis also prompted educators and policy-makers to reexamine their own assumptions and to move toward a broader view of accountability. A number of educators commented on the tendency to blame teachers for students' poor achievement. David P. Ericson and Frederick S. Ellett, Jr. wrote: "In assigning blame, there has been finger-pointing in many directions. But like the fabled roads of the Roman Empire, they all seem ultimately to lead to one place: the teaching profession."[13] At about the same time, the concept of shared accountability received greater attention in the educational literature, reflecting a growing consensus that the problems faced by many of our students are so severe that schools alone cannot solve them.

Focus on Fairness

The expansion of state-mandated testing programs in the 1980s brought new attention to the differential performance on standardized tests of various populations and prompted new concern about equality of opportunity, and about the possibility that "excellence" would become a code word for a retreat from equity.

The increasing reliance on testing prompted concern about the use of standardized tests to allocate educational and employment opportunities, and about the fact that some test uses result in unfair treatment of individuals and groups. It intensified concern about cultural bias. And it raised questions about how the pressure to improve scores might be affecting classroom practice, particularly in early childhood programs.

These were among the issues taken up by the National Commission on Testing and Public Policy. The commission recognized the importance, usefulness, and inevitability of testing in our society. It acknowledged the role played by tests in telling us "how our organizations and institutions are doing, what our children are learning and how well, and who among us are likely to make the most of opportunities that cannot be provided to all."[14] But the commission also concluded that assessment information should play an important but supportive role in decision making, and that the critical factor in responsible practice is an active weighting and balancing of different forms of information. In other words, the commission took the position that accountability includes testing, but must not be reduced to testing.

At this date, the pendulum appears to be swinging once again toward the identification of accountability with assessment. The centerpiece of the Bush Administration's plan to create "better and more accountable schools" for today's children is the establishment of national standards, called *New World Standards*, linked to "a new (voluntary) nationwide examination system" called *American Achievement Tests*.[15] This system of nationwide testing has reopened the debate. In this context, the theoretical questions raised in these chapters are live issues. Their authors offer insight into some of the concepts and controversies that will inform public policy debate for some time to come.

An Overview of the Issues

Cognitive skills tests administered to large populations in the United States often provide data that makes it possible to compare the average performance of different subgroups. In its report, the commission addressed differential test performance at length, pointing to a substantial body of research that establishes fairly consistent differences in average test scores of minority and nonminority groups.

Studies of both educational and employment tests have found substantial differences between average scores of black and white Americans: typical findings show that only about 16 percent of black Americans score above the median score of white Americans. Hispanics, American Indians, native Pacific Islanders, some Asian Americans, and other minorities also tend to score significantly lower than their majority peers on many tests.

Researchers report that minority children tend to receive significantly lower scores on all kinds of tests, ranging from kindergarten entry tests to standardized tests used to gauge progress in elementary and secondary schools, to the minimum competency tests used to determine grade promotions and high school graduation. Minority adults tend to score lower on most major types of high-stakes tests, including college admissions tests; rising juniors tests (required for promotion to upper-division status at college and for entry into undergraduate-level professional preparation programs); graduate admissions tests; and licensing and certification exams.

Differential test performance has been grist for the nurture versus nature mill for nearly a century. In its report, the commission positions itself squarely on the side of "nurture," emphasizing two broad reasons for differential test performance: first, like other methods of predicting behavior, tests are culturally bound and almost always reflect the dominant culture both in form and content; and second, group differences in test scores are consistent with broad social, economic, and educational inequities.

The commission also highlighted research showing that gaps in test performance are not borne out by large group differences in actual performance in the classroom or on the job. "The crucial point," the commission concluded in its report, "is that the limited power of tests to predict success in either schools or the workplace, coupled with test score gaps larger than performance gaps, mean that using test results alone to classify people will result in higher rates of misclassification for lower scorers, particularly for minority groups who tend to score poorly on the tests. This is true regardless of whether the test score gap between minorities and non-minorities arises from economic and educational disadvantages, from biases in the tests, or from an interaction of these factors."[16]

Four of the five chapters collected in this volume discuss the impact of testing on various subgroups of the population: blacks, Hispanics, young children, and children considered to be of "below average" ability. While these chapters were all submitted by invitation of the commission, they do not necessarily reflect the commission's conclusions. Taken together, they represent a broad range of views on differential test performance.

Black/White Differences in Test Performance

In "School Achievement Trends for Black Students," Lyle Jones provides an historical perspective on black/white differences in test performance, tracing the debate as far back as the turn of the century. He reviews early polemics, which focused largely on army qualification tests and IQ tests, shedding light on the black/white comparisons reported recently by the National Assessment of Educational Progress (NAEP).[17] He observes that politicians were so sensitive about the disclosure of such differences that NAEP initially planned not to disclose subgroup scores. They were released only after leaders in the black community argued that the data were important for making policy decisions.

Jones compares black/white NAEP test score differences over time, from 1970 to 1984, and finds that the gap has been narrowing for each of the three age groups tested (9, 13, and 17). Reading test score differences decreased from about 19 to 11 percent; math test score differences decreased from about 23 to 15 percent. He bolsters his argument with Scholastic Aptitude Test (SAT) data that also show the gap narrowing. At the same time, Jones points to international data that are much less encouraging. According to cross-national studies of educational achievement, American students on average lag behind their counterparts in other industrialized countries.

Jones states, "While it is reasonable to conclude that most achievement tests are not biased in any psychometric sense, it is undoubtedly true that majority and minority subgroups have different opportunities to master the test content." He proposes policies that he thinks will equalize opportunities for effective schooling, such as increasing the number of days children attend school; making learning more active and group-centered; instituting career-long education for teachers; teaching "how-to-learn" conceptual skills; and offering instruction in the scientific way of thinking, as opposed to the separate disciplines of biology, chemistry and physics.

Hispanic Students' SAT Performance

In "The Status of Research on the Scholastic Aptitude Test (SAT) and Hispanic Students in Postsecondary Education," Maria Pennock-Román addresses head-on the controversial question of whether the SAT is biased, or simply a bearer of bad news.

Citing 1987 College Board data, she shows that Hispanic students' SAT performance consistently lags behind that of non-Hispanic (NH) white students. The differences are 87 (Verbal), 89 (Math) for Puerto Rican students; 68 (Verbal), 65 (Math) for Mexican-American students; and 60 (verbal), 57 (Math) for Latin American students. The gap narrows when grades and courses are held constant; however, marked differences persist. The same is true with respect to language. Pennock-Román observes that, "Among students who learned English as their first language, the means for Latin American students are only 28 (Verbal) and 34 (Math) points lower than for NH white students. This pattern is also found for Mexican-American and Puerto Rican students and at every category of language backgroud." Pennock-Román believes that if researchers were able to control for such variables as the quality of the high school and other subtle socio-economic factors, the mean differences would diminish even further.

Psychometricians generally agree that a student's score on an aptitude test underestimates her true abilities when that test is not administered in her native language, but according to Pennock-Román, that does not mean that the SAT is unfair to these students. She writes: "In the context of college admissions, where English is the language of instruction, language background may affect college performance in the same way and to the same degree that it affects test performance." In other words, a test that underpredicts ability, nevertheless, remains an apt prediction of that students' ability to meet the challenges of an English-speaking environment, whether a test, a classroom discussion, or an essay.

Pennock-Román describes the specific items on which Hispanics and NH whites exhibit differential performance. Hispanics do better than their total scores would suggest on vocabulary questions that present true Spanish cognates, as well as on reading comprehension questions that refer to passages in which their culture is discussed. They perform worse than would be expected on homographs, some analogies, and questions that contain false Spanish cognates. After using a method of statistical analysis known as the Mantel-Haenszel technique, Pennock-Román found that if one subtracts the number of questions on which Hispanics perform worse than expected from the number on which they perform better than expected, only slightly more questions favored NH whites over Hispanics.

Pennock-Román attributes NH white students' higher SAT scores to their higher level of participation in a college preparatory curriculum. She points to a need for programs that will encourage Hispanic students to take more college preparatory classes in high school. Pennock-Román reviews the successes of a project designed by the Hispanic Higher Educational Testing System/Education Coalition, and the College Board. Together, they developed a kit to help students prepare for the Preliminary Scholastic Aptitude Test, which included materials for a one-semester course on the basic skills needed to perform well on the PSAT. A survey of students in the pilot project found a strongly positive response to the course: the number of students who said they planned to take the PSAT increased from 58 percent to 86 percent. Pennock-Román also found an increase in the students' understanding of basic test-taking skills (like how to budget one's time), and of concepts that frequently crop up in test-taking situations (like the difference between a synonym and an antonym).

Intelligence Reconsidered

In "Psychometric *g* and Achievement," the controversial psychometrician, Arthur Jensen, also addresses differences in test performance by individuals and groups. He presents his views in the context of his discussion of *psychometric g* — the scientific representation of genetically determined intelligence. Jensen returns to the debate about the definition and, therefore, the origin of intelligence. He now argues that the word "intelligence" has been so badly abused and distorted by the popular culture that it no longer has analytic value. Instead, careful thinkers ought to return to a more specific term, *psychometric g*. Although the paper contains a number of ambiguous statements, Jensen apparently still believes that psychometric *g* is genetically determined: he argues that the average intercorrelation of about .50 among "mental tests" is due to this psychometric *g*. In other words, about half of a student's score on one test can be explained by whatever caused a similar score on another test; for Jensen that "whatever" are genetic endowments.

Jensen's numerous critics charge that *g* is an artifact of the overlapping contents of ability tests, and that the ability test scores are determined by socio-economic factors. Jensen counters: "*g* is a psychological reality that cannot be ignored, and whatever processes underlie individual and group differences in *g* are the main source of the wide range of differences in observed scholastic performance."

He marshalls scientific evidence from his own research and the work of others to defend the reality of *g*, primarily by showing mathematical and statistical analyses of the intercorrelations between various ability tests. He tries to persuade readers that sophisticated statistical analyses allow us to judge whether *g* represents the same innate abilities in different *people*, or merely similarities between different *tests*. Jensen, again, argues that *g* represents the former.

In his conclusion, Jensen considers various policy options. He favors examining test *utility*, as opposed to test *validity*. He opposes banning tests that have an adverse impact on minorities because that violates employers' rights to make their own cost-benefit analyses. He also opposes the government's discontinuation of psychological tests, arguing that the alternatives would be more costly to taxpayers.

In a move that may surprise some of his critics, Jensen cites recent research showing that by using SAT scores, college admissions officers only slightly improve their ability to predict the academic performance of college freshmen; for all practical purposes, they do just as well when they base their predictions exclusively on grade-point averages and teacher evaluations. He argues that college admissions offices should not require SAT scores, and that the same type of utility analysis could inform policymakers' decisions about whether to use other tests for selection purposes.

Although Jensen locates individual differences mainly at the neurological, rather than behavioral or psychological level, he still offers educators some suggestions "that might reduce the untoward effects of g differences." Rather than reduce the variance among individuals, by focusing more resources on under-achieving students and less on over-achievers, Jensen advocates strategies that will "increase absolute levels of achievement in certain knowledge and skills sufficiently to allow a larger percentage of the population to become self-sufficient and productive." Direct instruction, a compensatory model by which the teaching is aimed directly at the particular knowledge or skill in which the student is deficient, is the best method to accomplish that. In addition to this, Jensen suggests that children's readiness for schooling be evaluated before they enter first grade, to reduce the frustration for those whose "mental age" is lower than average. Jensen also refers educators to findings that "the lower the aptitude, the more the learner will benefit from instruction that reduces the information load per unit of instruction time." Jensen adds that instruction that is heavily dependent on rote exercises is more useful than conceptually-oriented teaching for students with below-average g.

How Testing Drives Educational Policy

Anne Cunningham's chapter, "Eeny, Meeny, Miny, Moe: Testing Policy and Practice in Early Childhood," examines the effects of educational testing on children ages four through eight. In the process, she offers a fascinating case study of how the political side of testing can drive educational policy. She observes that testing programs at higher grade levels has encouraged teachers, principals, and state legislators to "pass the buck" to earlier grades by setting minimum competency standards for grade advancement. (A fourth grade class composed of students who have all passed certain tests to enter that grade will presumably score higher on standardized tests than a class selected strictly by age.) Schools (or states) that want to claim credit for high student test scores for each grade level can boost the averages by restricting enrollment in each grade to children who have already demonstrated their ability to meet previous test cut-off scores.

The "buck stops here" at kindergarten entrance requirements. With respect to Georgia, for instance, Cunningham states, "The decision to perform mass screening of kindergarten children's present level of academic skills was made to help both children and teachers in meeting the educational requirements established by the Georgia Department of Education for students in kindergarten, third grade, and high school." Although minimum competency tests for school entrance is not the only way to boost test scores, in the short run, it is the most inexpensive method. Standardizing the curriculum, or teaching-to-the-test, is another apparently cost-effective means to raise test scores without spending much money.

Cunningham discusses four undesirable consequences of current early childhood testing policies:

- *Grouping by ability.* Teachers sort students into three groups in the hope of realizing "economies of scale." Rather than students re-ceiving individual instruction, which would be quite time-consuming, the expectation is that students in each group will share enough skills to benefit from receiving the same lessons. Cunningham writes, "Despite the lack of research documenting the positive effects of homogeneous grouping and a fairly substantial body of research outlining its educational and social costs, we have in fact observed more homogeneous grouping of children in primary grades."
- *Increasing the entrance age for kindergarten.* On average, older children receive higher test scores than younger children in the same grade. A quick short-term boost in test scores can therefore be realized by raising entrance age requirements. In 1958, four year olds whose birthdates were after December 1 could not enroll in kindergarten. In the 1970s, most districts required that children be five years old by October first. Now in some parts of the country, the requirement is that children be five by June 1.
- *Increasing kindergarten retention.* The number of children "held back," to either repeat kindergarten or enter a special "pre-first grade" class, has increased 67 percent since 1984.
- *Increasing reliance on IQ-type tests for placement.* The most popular

test of whether a child is prepared to enter kindergarten is the
Gesell School Readiness test, which researchers have found is
almost identical to the Stanford-Binet IQ test in item content. The
main difference is that the Gesell test is less psychometrically
reliable than most IQ tests. The little research done on the Gesell
test's validity indicates that *"for every potential failure accurately
identified, a successful child was falsely identified."* In that regard,
Cunningham cites some provocative work done by Samuel Meisels.

Meisels argues that criteria and norms used to evaluate the success of
medical screening programs ought to be applied to educational screening
programs. The risks associated with particular rates of false positives and
false nagatives[18] need to be understood before readiness screening programs are implemented. Furthermore, standardized screening tests should
be only the first step of a student's diagnosis. Just as medical doctors look
to the particular symptoms and etiologies of individual patients before
making a final decision as to treatment, educators cannot, on the basis of
a generic test score alone, have enough information to place a particular
student.

Cunningham argues against the practice of using achievement testing
for screening entry into first grade; against the practice of retaining
children in kindergarten or readiness rooms; and against the use of the
Gesell test to dictate the pace of education of individual children. She
supports more individualized classroom instruction and more formal ties
between the home and school throughout the entire period from preschool
through elementary school. And finally, she urges policymakers to disentangle curriculum from testing objectives and to build curricula that
stresses conceptual rather than rote learning.

Innovative Assessment Strategies

Several authors represented in this volume allude to newer types of
assessment, but this topic is most thoroughly addressed by Charles W.
Peters and his associates in "Changing Statewide Reading Assessment: A
Case Study of Michigan and Illinois." Like Cunningham, Peters et al.
look at instruction first, and then consider how testing can systematically
capture information about how effective that instruction has been.

Their chapter is devoted to the innovative reading assessments they
have developed in Illinois and Michigan. They make a strong case for
grounding new assessments in state-of-the-art research on instruction. For

example, their approach to assessing reading was based on research that shows how children actually learn to read. They took a broad approach. By asking children to describe their own reading habits, and thereby finding out what children know about a particular topic before testing them with a reading passage, they could take the children's prior knowledge into account.

Peters et al. argue that educators ought to abandon most current reading achievement tests because they are based on assumptions about reading acquisition skills that have been disproven by recent research. They note that in the past, educators viewed reading as a "series of hierarchical skills, starting with the recognition of letters, sounds, and words and proceeding to the understanding of sentences and larger units of text." This understanding fostered the development of reading tests that "dissected reading into its most atomistic elements and provided an index of performance on each element."

In contrast, new studies reveal that reading is the "process of constructing meaning through the dynamic interaction among the reader, the text, and the context of the reading situation." The student's prior knowledge of the subject matter, the organization of the text, knowledge about reading processes, and attitudes and motivation are among the key factors in determining the student's learning and performance in reading.

The authors describe new Michigan and Illinois reading assessment tests whose design, construction, and interpretation are based upon theoretical knowledge of the reading process. The basic components of the tests are:

1. the reading selections;
2. constructing meaning items;
3. items evaluating metacognitive knowledge about the reading process;
4. reading habits and attitudes items; and
5. items assessing students' familiarity with the topics of the reading selections.

In conclusion, the authors discuss how their recommendations for new reading tests and test policies were debated and eventually adopted in Michigan and Illinois. They stress the importance of involving educators from all levels of the system during the early stages of planning. They also emphasize the value of holding workshops for teachers to place the reconceptualization of reading assessment into an appropriate curricular framework.

In describing this innovative approach to assessment, Peters et al. do not shy away from discussing its political ramifications. In fact, they stress the importance of building support and promoting acceptance of new forms of assessment. This is a tough challenge, and all of the affected groups have to be involved in the process from the outset if they are to "buy into the new procedure when the time comes."

These are but some of the issues addressed in this volume; needless to say, the articles touch on many more. Taken together, they are meant to provide an informative, insightful guide to the assessment issues, including testing, that loom so large on today's educational landscape.

Acknowledgments

The impetus for the Commission on Testing and Public Policy grew out of a series of conversations with Lynn Walker, Deputy Director of the Human Rights and Governance Program, and Peter Stanley, Vice-President, Programs in Education and Culture, at the Ford Foundation. I want to acknowledge their long-standing commitment to informing public debate about complex public policy issues through disciplined inquiry. Lynn and Peter have proved to be challenging advisors, but they have never sought to channel the thinking of the Commission member (or its many advisors and consultants) in any particular direction.

I am also indebted to Linda Wing, who served as the Associate Director of the National Commission on Testing and Public Policy during its most formative stage, and on whose shoulders so many of us stood. Commission members Antonia Hernandez and Edward E. Potter also proved to be thought-provoking counselors, especially when they lined up on opposite sides of an issue.

George Madaus was the principal author of *From Gatekeeper to Gateway*, the Commission's report, and proved to be heaven-sent. He has done extraordinary work under difficult circumstances.

Notes

1. *From Gatekeeper to Gateway: transforming testing in America.* Report of the National Commission on Testing and Public Policy (Chestnut Hill: Boston College), 1990.
2. See R. J. Havighurst, "Joint Accountability: A Constructive Response to Consumer Demands," *Nations Schools* (May 1972), 46–47.
3. M. L. Mickler notes that the term "accountability was not applied to education

prior to 1966." See her "Accountability: Perceptual Changes Over a Decade," *Educational Horizons* (Spring 1984), 90.

4. W. Haney, "Testing Reasoning and Reasoning about Testing," *Review of Educational Research* (Vol. 54, No. 4, Winter 1984), 620.

5. Public Law 89−10: *The Elementary and Secondary Education Act*, 1965.

6. Haney (1984), 620.

7. Haney (1984), 620.

8. Cited in Mickler (1984), 92.

9. Cited in Mickler (1984), 90.

10. *From Gatekeeper to Gateway*, 16.

11. K. S. Keefover, "Accountability—A Historical Perspective," in *The Educational Forum* (Spring 1983), 365.

12. E. G. Buffie, "Accountability: The Key to Excellence," in *Childhood Education*, November/December 1984, 107.

13. D. P. Ericson and F. S. Ellett, Jr., "Teacher Accountability and the Causal Theory of Teaching," *Educational Theory* (Summer 1987), 295.

14. *From Gatekeeper to Gateway*, 35.

15. *America 2000: An Education Strategy* (U.S. Department of Education, 1991), 11.

16. *From Gatekeeper to Gateway*, 14.

17. Every four years the U.S. Department of Education tests reading, math and science skills of children in elementary and secondary public schools. The tests are done on national samples at several grade levels, and scores are used only for tracking these skills over time. Currently, there are no interpretations by region or state of the NAEP data.

18. If a particular medical test indicates that an individual has a disease, but in fact the individual does not have that disease, then the test result is called a false positive. If a medical test indicates that an individual does not have a disease, but in fact the individual does have that disease, then the test result is called a false negative. Those labels (as well as true positives and true negatives) describe the accuracy of all diagnostic tests.

2 SCHOOL ACHIEVEMENT TRENDS FOR BLACK STUDENTS

Lyle V. Jones

Achievement tests traditionally have been used by teachers for ascertaining the extent to which students have mastered curricular content. Performance on tests has often served as a primary determinant of grades assigned by the teacher. Presumably, grades have provided incentives for learning as well as for good test performance.

The use of tests to assess achievement levels for large groups of U.S. students is a phenomenon of more recent vintage. Tests were employed for this purpose for a short period in the 1920s, but it was not until 1969, with the establishment of the National Assessment of Educational Progress (NAEP), that periodic information about group achievement levels has become available on a regular basis. NAEP results continue to be reported for (probability samples of) all students in the nation at ages nine, thirteen, and seventeen, and also for selected subgroups defined by "background variables" such as region of the country, type of community, level of parental education, gender, and ethnic origin.

The primary purpose of this chapter is to review evidence from NAEP and other sources on achievement trends for this nation's black students and to discuss interpretations of the evidence and implications for educational policy. Achievement trends for minorities other than blacks are also of interest, but evidence for other minorities is scanty. NAEP has not consistently reported results for other minority groups. Also, for Hispanic students, interpretation of trends is made difficult by uncertainties about the students who are so classified and about their facility with English, a problem compounded by the changing composition of the Hispanic population due to shifting patterns of immigration and emigration.

19

To place in perspective the findings concerning achievement of U.S. black students, some evidence is provided about achievement of all U.S. students compared with students in other countries. This chapter also discusses questions about the appropriateness of the form and content of assessment tests, the propriety of disseminating results about minority performance, and policies that might lead to the further improvement of educational outcomes for black students.

The Origins of Group Testing

The large-scale group testing of intellectual skills has a relatively brief history, despite its widespread adoption in American educational institutions in recent years. The practice originated in the United States in 1917 when a panel of psychologists, led by American Psychological Association President Robert M. Yerkes, developed the Army Alpha, a group-administered paper-and-pencil test of intelligence. Included on the panel was Lewis M. Terman, whose Stanford-Binet Intelligence Scale had just been published. The design of the Army Alpha test was strongly influenced by Arthur S. Otis, at that time a graduate student at Stanford, who had just introduced and developed multiple-choice and other "objective" types of test items suitable for group-administered testing. (The Stanford-Binet test was and remains today an individually administered test of intelligence.)

Between 1917 and 1919, the Army Alpha test was administered to nearly two million men in the U.S. armed forces. The Army Beta, a non-language test, was simultaneously developed to be administered to illiterates and to soldiers who had failed the Army Alpha.

A report on the army testing program was published in 1918 (Terman 1918), and comprehensive results were later provided in a volume of nearly nine hundred pages (Yerkes, 1921). One chapter of that volume is entitled "Intelligence of the Negro." There, and in other chapters, comparative distributions of Alpha test scores are shown for black and white officers and for black and white enlisted men, with an emphasis in each comparison on the conclusion that "the negro group appears markedly inferior to the white" (531). Among the authors of the report were some who, in earlier published papers, had expressed the belief that measured intelligence depended largely on hereditary factors. There is no doubt that they had designed the army tests with the belief that the tests would measure innate intelligence (see Gould, 1981, 198–199).

The publication of the Yerkes report led William Bagley, a psychologist at Columbia University, to criticize the assumption of a hereditary determination of measured intelligence (Bagley, 1922). With Terman's response (Terman, 1922a) the nature-nurture debate was joined; it soon reached a broader audience through a series of articles in *The New Republic* by the renowned journalist Walter Lippmann (1922). Lippmann rejected the concept of "fixed intelligence," seeing in it a revival of the doctrine of predestination. Tests might be useful for classification in the army, he opined, but if classification is equated with categorization (without some adaptation of instruction), the tests then serve as an "engine of cruelty" that would lead to a hereditary caste system. The effect of the reply to Lippmann by Terman (1922b) may have been to ensure the continuation of the controversy in both academic and lay publications over a period of several more years.

The nature-nurture debate took on a more moderate tone in 1928, with the appearance of a yearbook published by the National Society for the Study of Education (Terman, 1928). Terman had chaired the committee of psychologists who contributed to this volume. Some contributions leaned toward environment and some leaned toward heredity as the primary determinant of intelligence; most admitted the importance of interactions between the two.

In the 1930s, a new debate arose. The question was whether intellectual ability was better measured as a unitary construct, intelligence, or as a number of component intellectual abilities (Thurstone, 1938). For several years, debate about a multiple-factor account of intellectual abilities versus a unified construct of intelligence overshadowed the nature-nurture controversy.

In 1940, another yearbook from the National Society for the Study of Education (Stoddard, 1940) cited evidence from "the Iowa studies" of substantial gains in IQ as a consequence of environmental stimulation and concluded that heredity plays a minimal role. Goodenough (1940) and McNemar (1940) discounted the Iowa studies on technical grounds; Woodworth (1941) provided a balanced review that was intended to still the debate.

Questions about the extent to which IQ can be changed arose again in the mid-1960s in the context of President Johnson's War on Poverty, especially with the initiation of Head Start, designed in part to increase the readiness for schooling of disadvantaged young children, many of whom were minority children. The publication by Jensen (1969) of a treatise supporting the heritability of racial differences in IQ thus raised political as well as scholarly issues and led to a storm of controversy in scholarly articles and books and also in the public media. A balanced review of the issues, with authors selected by the Social Science Research Council (Loehlin, Lindzey, and Spuhler, 1975), concluded that the apportionment of the relative contributions of heredity and environment, as applied to differences among ethnic groups on intelligence tests, constituted an intrinsically unsolvable problem. More recently, a number of other balanced treatments have appeared, (for example, Wigdor and Garner, 1982; Neisser, 1986; Reynolds and Brown, 1984; Scarr, 1981; Yando, Seitz, and Zigler, 1979). It now is clear that some early intervention programs can foster higher IQ scores as well as better adjustment to family and school, but little is yet known about the relation between program characteristics and the extent of improvement (see Consortium for Longitudinal Studies, 1983; Garber, 1988; Zigler, 1979; Zigler and Hodapp, 1986, 162–180).

The use of tests for ability grouping in the schools came under legal attack in *Larry P. v. Riles*, decided in 1979 (see Wigdor and Garner, 1982, 110–116). The judgment enjoined California schools from using any standardized intelligence tests without securing prior approval of the court. Plaintiffs had presented evidence that black school children were disproportionately placed in classes for the educable mentally retarded, based upon IQ test scores, and the court accepted this evidence prima facie, shifting to the defendants the burden of proof to rebut a presumption of racial discrimination. The defense failed to argue strenuously against the allegation of racial bias in the tests, and the court found for the plaintiffs.

In a 1980 case, *Parents in Action on Special Education v. Hannon*, the outcome was very different. The Wechsler Intelligence Test for Children and the Stanford-Binet were judged to be substantially free of bias. The court allowed their use for placing Chicago school children (see Wigdor and Garner, 1982, 113).

Regardless of the merits of the argument that intelligence tests are culturally biased, *Larry P* dramatized the stigmatic effect of assigning labels based on test scores and the deleterious educational consequences for children so labeled. Since *Larry P*, a consensus has emerged regarding appropriate uses of tests in the schools. As stated by Sandra Scarr, "Low scores are indicators for action — instructional action to fit educational needs of the child. They are not excuses for labeling and discard" (Scarr, 1981, 436). This view is consistent with conclusions and recommendations of Wigdor and Garner (1982) and with those of many other commentators on the use of testing in the schools. It also seems consistent with the position presented six decades earlier by Lippmann (1922).

The Issue of Test Bias

When a test is used to select among candidates for a job or for an educational opportunity, the test is considered to be biased if it exhibits differential predictive validity for identifiable subgroups of candidates. When subgroups are composed of black candidates or white candidates, there is compelling evidence that tests in common use for personnel selection are not biased against the minority group, a conclusion supported by a number of reviews of the relevant research literature (for example, Hunter, Schmidt, and Rauschenberger, 1984; Jensen, 1980; Reynolds, 1982; Reynolds and Brown 1984; Vernon, 1979).

When a test is used to assess mastery of subject matter rather than to predict success on a criterion, the test employed is biased if it measures different constructs for identifiable subgroups of examinees, or if it measures the same construct but with differing degrees of accuracy (Reynolds, 1982, 194). When subgroups are made up of black or white examinees, factor analysis often is employed to determine whether the same constructs are being measured in both groups. Typically, for tests in common use, neither factor structure nor reliability appears to differ for blacks and whites (Reynolds, 1982, 194−200).

A test item displays content bias if the average item difficulty is greater for one group than for the other when the true distributions of ability for the two groups are the same. Items in widely used commercially available tests typically have been screened by panels of judges and by pretesting in an effort to ensure that items will be discarded if they display differential difficulties for groups defined by gender or ethnicity. While an occasional item may survive the pretest even though it retains some content bias, the effect of bias on total test score is usually negligible (Reynolds, 1982, 188−194).

While it is reasonable to conclude that most achievement tests are not biased in any psychometric sense, it is undoubtedly true that majority and minority subgroups have had differential opportunity to master the test content (see Jones, 1987; Samuda, 1975; Williams et al., 1980). This raises an important issue about the interpretation of subgroup differences in test scores. Whenever average performance levels are displayed separately for black and white students, as they will be presented here, some readers may incorrectly infer that a "reason" for performance difference resides in the ethnic difference, that is, that ethnicity causes the difference. Such an inference is unwarranted. Black and white student populations differ in many respects. Black students are less likely than white students to attend effective schools, to come from affluent families or from families with parents or siblings with education beyond high school, to be counseled to enroll in advanced high school courses, and so on. These differences often masquerade as ethnic-group differences. They are likely candidates as causal agents for white/black differences in performance.

Disseminating Information About Achievement by Ethnic Group

If one were to conclude that achievement tests are biased against minority students, it would be unfair to report average scores for minority groups, at least without a correction for bias. Having concluded that achievement tests are not systematically biased, should results be reported for ethnic subgroups?

In 1965, as the design for NAEP was being formulated, it was anticipated that no information about a student's race or ethnic origin would be recorded as part of the data base; the aim was to prevent reporting by ethnicity in keeping with perceived political sensitivities of that time. Between 1965 and 1969, when the first NAEP assessment was conducted, leaders in the black community successfully petitioned for the identification of student ethnicity and for the reporting of results by ethnic group, arguing that average achievement differences among groups constituted policy-relevant information.

As recently as the late 1970s, the College Board declined to report average Scholastic Aptitude Test (SAT) scores by ethnic group, although the relevant data were recorded in the files. The motivation for this policy seems to have been one of fear that such reports might be misinterpreted by the media and the public. The policy was reversed in response to complaints that information of public interest was being kept secret.

It is increasingly recognized that freedom of information, when balanced by the maintenance of privacy for individual records, is a desirable policy in a free society. Reporters need to be held responsible for honest reporting and for integrity in the interpretation of reported results. The failure to release public information, however, is now illegal in most jurisdictions and is generally considered to be antithetic to the public interest. These principles should apply to information about achievement levels of minority students as they do to other forms of public information.

International Comparisons for Mathematics and Science

International studies of school achievement yield comparisons of overall U.S. achievement levels with those of other nations. Before discussing average achievement levels for U.S. black and white students, it is reasonable to ask how all U.S. students compare with students in other countries in order to provide a link between the average performance of U.S. black students and an international standard of performance. International comparisons are available for mathematics and science, subjects of special concern in the United States in recent years (see Jones, 1981; Committee on Research in Mathematics, Science, and Technology Education, 1987; National Science Board Commission on Precollege Education in Mathematics, Science, and Technology, 1983).

Mathematics: Evidence from IEA

The International Association for the Evaluation of Educational Achievement (IEA) coordinated studies of mathematics achievement in many countries in 1964 and again in 1982. Results for the United States from the more recent effort are reported by Crosswhite et al., 1985; McKnight et al., 1987; and Travers and McKnight, 1985.

When considering results from the IEA mathematics study, it is important to acknowledge difficulties with the execution of that study that bear upon the interpretation of results, especially those related to low levels of participation among sampled schools, classrooms, and students (see Jones, 1988b). While these difficulties impose a demand for caution about conclusions from the study, especially those that pertain to change in achievement levels from 1964 to 1982, the conclusions that are cited below, nevertheless, appear to be relatively robust and trustworthy.

Common items were administered to samples of eighth-grade students in the United States in 1964 and in 1982. Overall, eighth-grade performance was lower in 1982 than in 1964 by an average of 3 percent fewer correct answers. An even greater performance decline, a 6 percent drop, was found for items on arithmetic and for items on geometry. "Declines were somewhat greater for more demanding comprehension and application items than they were for computation items" (Crosswhite et al., 1985, xi), a finding consistent with NAEP results at age thirteen.

For the eighth-grade population, McKnight et al. (1987) report 1982 results for each of twenty countries. U.S. eighth graders present average scores near the median average score of the twenty countries for arithmetic, algebra, and statistics and present average scores below the lowest quartile for geometry and measurement.

Common items were administered by IEA in 1964 and 1982 to a sample of twelfth-grade college preparatory students in the United States who were enrolled in mathematics classes that required two years of algebra and one year of geometry as prerequisites. Overall, average performance in 1982 was six percentage points higher than in 1964 due to a large increase (35 percent) on a single item on sets and relations, and to greater numbers of correct answers to items on elementary functions and calculus. (U.S. enrollments in high school calculus courses were considerably greater in 1982 than in 1964, and thus some elevation of knowledge of calculus could have been expected.)

For twelfth-grade college preparatory students, McKnight et al. (1987) show results for thirteen nations. The U.S. score average is in the lowest quarter of those nations for algebra, geometry, number systems, and elementary functions/calculus and is below the median for the remaining topics, probability/statistics and sets and relations.

It might be hypothesized that the lower achievement of U.S. twelfth graders compared with the achievement of those in other countries results from larger proportions of U.S. adolescents remaining in the school population. However, even for 1964 IEA mathematics data, "The percent of adolescents in secondary schools does not explain all the differences between the achievement of students from the United States and students from other developed countries" (Austin, 1985). Also, between 1964 and 1982, high school retention rates increased sharply for some other countries. For example, at age seventeen, 92 percent of Japanese youth are in school, compared with 82 percent of U.S. youth (McKnight et al., 1987, 16, table 1). Further, "It is *not* the case. . .that for advanced mathematics, the U.S. enrolls a. . .larger proportion of students than other countries. In fact, we rank about average in terms of the proportion of students who take advanced mathematics courses" (McKnight et al., 1987, 61). It appears that differential retention rates cannot explain 1982 IEA findings.

Mathematics: Evidence from Comparisons with Japan

Harnisch et al. (1985) present results on a sixty-item mathematics test given in 1981 to seventeen hundred high school students in Japan and to ninety-six hundred high school students in Illinois. The test consisted of items on algebra, geometry, modern mathematics, data interpretation, and probability. Results are reported separately by age of student: fifteen, sixteen, or seventeen and older. "For all three age groups. . ., the Japanese exceeded the Illinois students by two standard deviations. . . .The average Japanese student outranked about 98 percent of the Illinois sample. At the upper ranges, the differences are still more striking. Only about 1 in 1000 Illinois students attained scores as high as the top. . .ten percent Japanese students" (Harnisch et al., 1985, 280).

Stevenson, Lee, and Stigler (1986) studied the mathematics test performance of younger children from Minneapolis and from Sendai, Japan, selected as a Japanese city comparable to Minneapolis. At each of the kindergarten, first, and fifth grades, between two hundred and three hundred children were selected, and a common mathematics test was individually administered. Test content was based on the common content of mathematics textbooks used in the two cities. The test for kindergarten contained items assessing basic concepts and operations included in the curricula from kindergarten to the third grade. The test for elementary children was derived from materials from the mathematics curricula through grade six.

Average Sendai scores were higher than Minneapolis scores for each age group with mean differences of nearly one standard deviation at the younger two ages and about 1.3 standard deviation at grade five. "The highest average score of an American fifth-grade classroom was below that of the Japanese fifth-grade classroom with the lowest average score" (Stevenson et al., 1986, 231).

Science: Evidence from IEA

In the first IEA science study, data were collected in the United States in 1970 for school children in the fifth, ninth, and twelfth grades. In the second IEA science study, data were collected from U.S. students enrolled in the same grades in 1983 and in 1986. Doran and Jacobson (1987) summarize the changes in performance of the U.S. students between 1970 and 1986, and for twelfth graders, provide preliminary comparisons of the U.S. students with students from other countries.

Sampling procedures utilized in the IEA science assessment are described by Jacobson, Doran, and Muller (1985); evaluations of the sampling were conducted and reported in two papers by Wolf (undated, a; undated, b). As in the IEA mathematics study, nonresponse bias may be a serious problem, especially for results that pertain to changes in U.S. science achievement over time. Based upon 1986 data for U.S. students at grade five, compared with U.S. students at grade five in 1970, Doran and Jacobson (1987) report "no change to slight growth." The same comparison at grade nine yields "no change to slight decline." At grade twelve, students recently enrolled in physics courses scored (on a "bridge test" composed of items on all science topics) "slightly better" than their 1970 cohorts. On the same test, the performance of U.S. twelfth graders who had not recently enrolled in science was "no different" from their cohorts in 1970. The nonscience twelfth graders had the same mean score as that of all ninth-grade students on a subset of sixteen science items that were common to the two test batteries (Doran and Jacobson, 1987).

U.S. students not taking science in grade twelve performed at a level about ten percentage points lower than the average for comparable students in nine countries in an international comparison group. For twelfth graders who were taking a second year of biology, chemistry, or physics, U.S. students performed at an average level from ten to thirty percentage points lower than the averages for the other countries (Doran and Jacobson, 1987). Advanced twelfth-grade science students in the United States "have not done well in comparison with students in the last year of the secondary school in Japan, England, and nine other countries" (W. J. Jacobson, pers. com. July 28, 1987).

Science: Evidence from Comparisons with Japan

IEA science achievement findings for the United States and Japan show increasing differences favoring Japanese students from grade five to grade nine to grade twelve. The largest differences favoring the Japanese students appear on "science process" items (Jacobson et al., 1986).

In studies of reasoning skills of students in grades seven, eight, and nine for thirty-five hundred students in North Carolina and forty-four hundred students in Hiroshima, average test scores for the Japanese students were appreciably higher than for the North Carolina students. A large difference was found even at grade seven, suggesting a cumulative differential influence of education on reasoning skills in the earliest elementary grades (Jacobson et al., 1986).

General Conclusions from the International Studies

The average level of achievement of students in the United States for mathematics and science is below that of most other developed nations. This conclusion should be kept in mind when comparing subgroups of U.S. students with the U.S. average or with one another. Subgroups with achievement levels below the U.S. average would exhibit even lower levels relative to an international standard.

Trends in School Achievement for Black and White Students

What have been the recent trends in average levels of school achievement for black children in the United States? Before attempting to answer this seemingly straightforward question, some of its hidden complexity needs to be recognized. A definition of "black children" is required, and the definition must not change from one year to another. Furthermore, because the answer to the question may be different depending on the age or grade of students, and depending on subject matter, each of these must be specified. (The progress of students through school grades can differ from time to time due to changes in school policies. For this reason, comparisons over time by age are more satisfactory than comparisons by grade.) A meaningful answer to the question for a particular age and subject matter demands that results be available from comparable achievement tests on comparable national samples of students for two or more years during a target time span. The tests selected should exhibit high construct validity for the subject matter being assessed. It is highly desirable that the tests used at different times be identical both in content and format. (Methods have been developed for equating scores on tests that are not identical in item content, but results from these methods are sensitive to violations of assumptions that rarely are totally satisfied by empirical data.)

NAEP was designed to assess changes over time in achievement levels of U.S. children at ages nine, thirteen, and seventeen. For each NAEP assessment, about twenty thousand students were assessed at each age. At each age, exercises were designed to assess skills and knowledge that were expected to have been taught in school by that age. Exercises were presented by professional test administrators to large national probability samples of students. They were administered aurally by tape recording, as well as visually by printed form, to minimize performance differences attributable to different levels of reading skill. Most exercises were in a multiple-choice format, and all exercises included an "I don't know" alternative, designed to reduce guessing. The results presented here are based on exercises common to adjacent assessment years, suitable for detecting change from one assessment to the next.

Since 1970, NAEP has sampled children attending school rather than all children at a given age; thus, even these best available data might be misleading for the total population to the extent that school dropout rates differed appreciably from year to year.

Other relevant sources of data, in contrast to NAEP, exhibit greater problems of noncomparability. Test scores are available for a national sample of high school seniors in 1972 from the National Longitudinal Study and a national sample of high school seniors in 1980 from High School and Beyond. While some of the tests in these two studies were identical, some were not, and conditions of test administration and format were different on the two occasions. Also, annual average scores for black and white students on the SAT are available for 1976, and more recently. But students in the SAT sample are self-selected; they individually choose whether or not to take the test, and the samples, therefore, may not be comparable from year to year. Despite these difficulties, evidence from these sources is referred to below in addition to evidence from NAEP.

Prior studies of NAEP results show that, for a typical age and the typical achievement area assessed, average performance differences between white and black school children declined from 1969 to the early 1980s (for example, Burton and Jones, 1982; Humphreys, 1988; Jones, 1984; Jones, Burton and Davenport, 1984; Matthews et al., 1984). While these studies emphasized trends in differences in performance between black and white students, it is also of interest to examine trends in average achievement test scores separately for black and white students. Both sets of comparisons will be discussed here. Within age, results will be presented by subject matter for reading, mathematics, and science, the three subject areas most frequently assessed.

Detailed descriptions of the sources of data and the methods employed to adapt results to a common format for presentation here, along with tables of those results, are provided in Appendix A.

Findings at Age Nine

Reading. NAEP reading results are available for school years 1970–1971, 1974–1975, 1979–1980, and 1983–1984. The average percentages of correct answers, shown separately for black and for white nine-year-olds, appear by birth year in figure 2–1 (and in table A1, Appendix A). In this and other figures showing NAEP results, the vertical scale shows the average percentage of exercises that were correct (scaled to the earliest assessments by the methods in Appendix C, and for reading, Appendix B). In each figure, the lines represent the trend of average percentage that were correct and are labeled for black students and white students.

For black children born in 1961 (assessed in 1970–1971), the average percentage of correct response to the reading exercises was about 50 percent. For black children born in 1970, the average had risen to about 60 percent but then declined by about 2 percent for children born in 1974. The difference in average performance between white children and black children declined from about 17 percent on the first reading assessment to 10 percent and 12 percent on the most recent assessments.

Mathematics. Mathematics achievement was assessed by NAEP in 1972–1973, 1977–1978, 1981–1982, and 1985–1986. For nine-year-olds, result by birth year for white and black students (table A2, Appendix A) are shown here in figure 2–2. The average performance of black nine-year-olds improved steadily from 23 percent for those born in 1963 to 26 percent for those born in 1968, 28 percent for those born in 1972, and 32 percent for those born in 1976. The gap between average performance of white and black nine-year-olds narrowed from about 18 percent to less than 9 percent over that period.

Science. Science was assessed by NAEP in 1969–1970, 1972–1973, 1976–1977, 1981–1982 and 1985–1986. Results for nine-year-olds are shown in table A3 (Appendix A) and in figure 2–3. For nine-year-old blacks, the average percentage correct was about 46 percent for the first three cohorts; it then increased to about 50 percent for those born in 1972 and to 53 percent for those born in 1976. The difference between average percentage-correct scores for whites and blacks declined from about 17 percent correct for the first three assessments to about 12 percent for the most recent.

Findings at Age Thirteen

Reading. Results from the NAEP assessments of reading at age thirteen for school years 1970–1971, 1974–1975, 1979–1980 and 1983–1984 are shown in table A4 (Appendix A) and in figure 2–4. Average reading scores for black students improved from about 45 percent correct for birth year 1957 to about 52 percent correct for birth year 1970. The difference between average reading scores of white and black children declined from 17 percent to 12 percent over that period of time.

Mathematics. Results presented in table A5 (Appendix A) and in figure 2–5 are for mathematics assessments at age thirteen in 1972–1973, 1977–1978, 1981–1982 and 1985–1986. The performance of black thirteen-year-olds improved from an average level of 32 percent for those born in 1959 to 43 percent for those born in 1972. The gap between the average performance of white and black thirteen-year-olds narrowed from about 25 percent to about 12 percent over that period.

Science. NAEP assessed science achievement in 1969–1970, 1972–1973, 1976–1977, 1981–1982 and 1985–1986. Results for white and black thirteen-year-olds appear in table A6 (Appendix A) and in figure 2–6. For blacks, the average percentage correct was about 45 percent for the first assessment; it declined to about 42 percent for the second and then increased in successive assessments to reach 51 percent for the most recent. The difference between average percentage-correct scores for whites and blacks increased from about 18 percent correct for the first assessment to about 20 percent for the second but then declined to about 9 percent for the most recent assessment.

Findings at Age Seventeen

Reading: Evidence from NAEP. In table A7 (Appendix A) and in

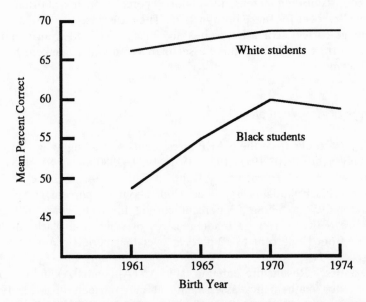

Figure 2–1. NAEP Reading Trends for Black and White Students, Age 9

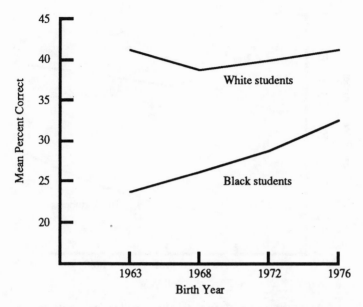

Figure 2-2. NAEP Mathematics Trends for Black and White Students, Age 9

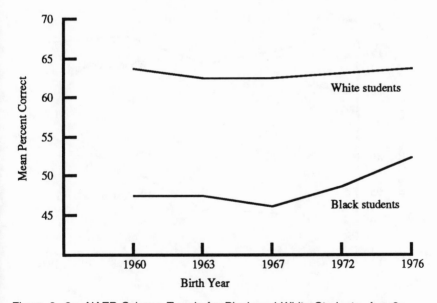

Figure 2-3. NAEP Science Trends for Black and White Students, Age 9

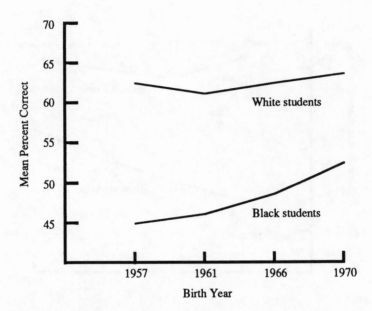

Figure 2—4.   NAEP Reading Trends for Black and White Students, Age 13

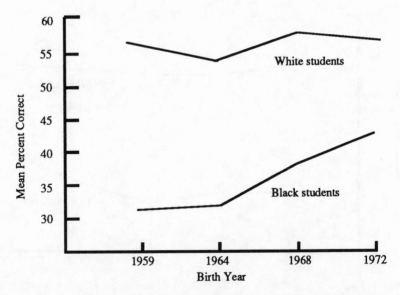

Figure 2—5.   NAEP Mathematics Trends for Black and White Students, Age 13

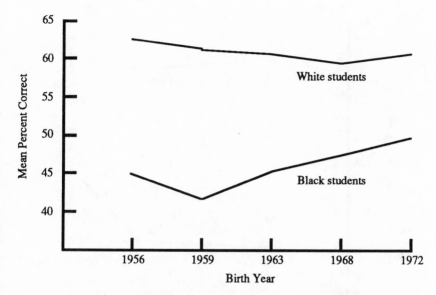

Figure 2–6. NAEP Science Trends for Black and White Students, Age 13

figure 2–7, results appear from the NAEP reading assessments at age seventeen in 1970–1971, 1974–1975, 1979–1980 and 1983–1984, shown separately for black and white students. Average reading scores for black students were stable at about 52 percent correct for black seventeen-year-olds born in 1953–1954, 1957–1958 and 1962–1963, and increased to 60 percent correct for those born in 1966–1967. The difference between average reading scores of white and black children declined from about 19 percent for the first three assessments to about 12 percent for the most recent one.

Reading: Evidence from National Longitudinal Study and High School and Beyond. Reading was assessed for national samples of high school seniors in 1972 (National Longitudinal Study) and again in 1980 (High School and Beyond), and results are shown separately for black and white students in table A8 (Appendix A) by birth year on the assumption that students were eighteen years old at the time of completion of their senior year of high school. The average reading score is 5.6 for black students born in 1962, essentially unchanged from the average score of 5.9 for those born in 1954. This finding is consistent with reading-change results from NAEP (figure 2–7). The white/black difference declined from 4.6, about

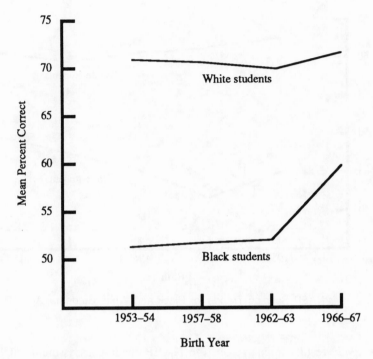

Figure 2–7. NAEP Reading Trends for Black and White Students, Age 17

one within-group standard deviation, to about 4.0, slightly less than one standard deviation.

Reading: Evidence from SAT-V Scores. In table A9 (Appendix A) annual average SAT-Verbal scores appear for black and white SAT test takers from 1976 to 1987, presented by year of birth on the assumption that high school seniors were eighteen years old at the time that they took the test. Results are shown graphically by the lines labeled "V" in figure 2–8. The average SAT-V score for black SAT test takers remained stable at about 330 for cohorts born between 1958 and 1963, increased to about 340 for those born in 1964 or 1965, and increased to about 350 for those in 1969. Average scores for white test takers were more stable, first declining and then increasing, with an overall range from 442 to 451 over the whole period. The average white-black difference declined from 119 points for cohorts born in 1958 to 96 points for those born in 1969.

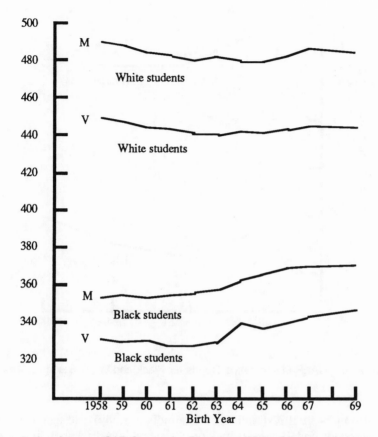

Figure 2-8.   Average SAT Scores for Black and White Students, Age 18

Mathematics: Evidence from NAEP.   Results for age seventeen in table A10 (Appendix A) are for NAEP assessments of 1972–1973, 1977–1978, 1981–1982 and 1985–1986 and are shown graphically in figure 2–9. The performance of black seventeen-year-olds declined from an average level of 34 percent for those born in 1955–1956 to 31 percent for those born in 1960–1961, then rose to an average of 35 percent for those born in 1968–1969. The gap between average performance of white and black seventeen-year-olds narrowed slightly from about 21 percent to about 17 percent over that period.

Mathematics: Evidence from National Longitudinal Study and High School and Beyond.   Mathematics was assessed for national samples of high

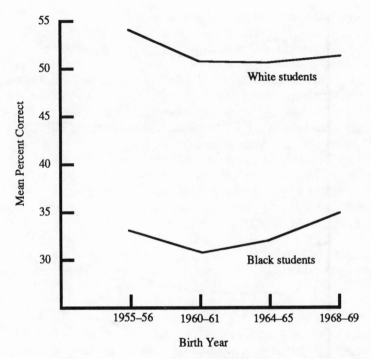

Figure 2-9. NAEP Mathematics Trends for Black and White Students, Age 17

school seniors in 1972 (National Longitudinal Study) and again in 1980 (High School and Beyond), and results in table A8 (Appendix A) are presented by birth year on the assumption that students were eighteen years old at the time of completion of their senior year of high school. The average score of 6.5 for black students born in 1954 is essentially the same as the average score of 6.7 for those born in 1962, a finding consistent with NAEP results for mathematics (figure 2-9). The white/black difference declined from 7.4, slightly larger than one within-group standard deviation, to about 6.3, less than one standard deviation.

Mathematics: Evidence from SAT-M Scores. Table A9 (Appendix A) and figure 2-8 present annual average SAT-Mathematics scores for 1976 to 1985 and for 1987, shown separately for black and white test takers, as reported by the College Entrance Examination Board (1987). Results are shown graphically by the lines labeled "M" in figure 2-8. The average SAT-M score for black SAT test takers increased from 354 for cohorts born in 1958 to 377 for cohorts born in 1969. For the same period, average scores for white test takers declined slightly, leading to a decline in the average white-black difference from 139 points to 112 points.

Science: Evidence from NAEP. Science was assessed at age seventeen by NAEP in 1969–1970, 1972–1973, 1976–1977, 1981–1982 and 1985–1986. Results for achievement trends are shown in table A12 (Appendix A) and in figure 2–10. For black students, the average percentage correct was about 34 percent for the first assessment; it declined to about 27 percent for the third and fourth assessments and was about 32 percent for the most recent assessment. The difference between average scores for whites and blacks changed from about 13 percent correct for the first two assessments to about 15 percent for the third and fourth assessments, and about 12 percent in 1985–1986.

Summary of Findings for U.S. Black Students

Reading. Because NAEP results have been recorded by birth year rather than by assessment year, we consider achievement trends for black and white students by birth-year cohort, regardless of age at the time of assessment. For reading, figure 2–11 displays the average white/black difference in percentage-correct reading scores by birth year (from figures 2–1, 2–4, and 2–7, and tables A1, A4, and A7 of Appendix A). The difference remained in a range of 16 percent to 19 percent for cohorts born between 1954 and 1963, then declined to between 10 percent and 13 percent for cohorts born between 1965 and 1974. Results from figures 2–1, 2–4, and 2–7 show that the decline is largely attributable to improved average reading scores for black students rather than to a drop in average scores for white students.

Black children born in 1965, or later, typically began their schooling after 1969–1970, subsequent to the War on Poverty, the widespread school desegregation efforts of that time, and during a period of increasing concern for improved reading instruction in the nation's schools. The relative improvement in average reading scores for black children may result from these factors, among others. Nonetheless, there remain large disparities in average reading achievement levels between the nation's white and black schoolchildren.

Mathematics. White/black average differences in NAEP mathematics scores approximated 20 percent for cohorts born between 1956 and 1965,

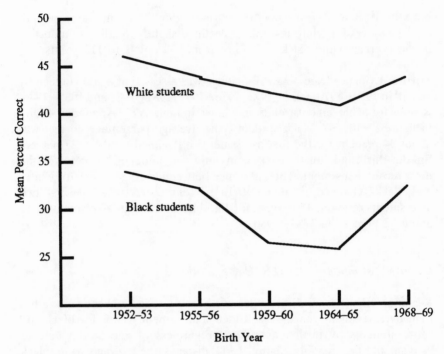

Figure 2-10.   NAEP Science Trends for Black and White Students, Age 17

then declined to 16 percent for students born in 1968, to 11 percent for those born in 1972, and to 9 percent for those born in 1976. Average scores for blacks changed little for cohorts born between 1956 and 1965 but increased about 10 percent for those born after 1968. Average mathematics achievement levels appear to have improved for black students who started school in about 1974 compared with those whose schooling began earlier. Perhaps since the mid-1970s, greater proportions of black students than in earlier years have enrolled in mathematics courses. A strong relation has been found between mathematics test scores and mathematics courses taken; enrollment in those courses for black students is still less than enrollment for white students (Jones, 1987).

Science.   Average white/black differences in NAEP science scores show little systematic change for cohorts of children born between 1953 and 1967. Results from the two most recent science assessments suggest average gains in science achievement for black students born in 1968, or later, of about 5 percent more correct answers than for earlier cohorts.

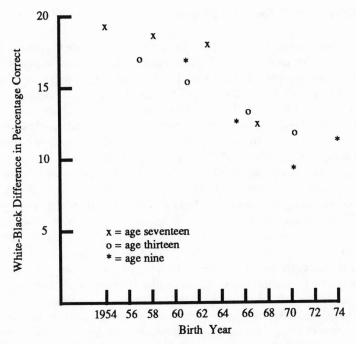

Figure 2–11. Trend in Average White-Black Difference for Reading

Mathematics and Science. While the gap between the average test performance of white and black U.S. students has narrowed in recent years, large differences remain. The lower average achievement of U.S. black students than of U.S. white students is more stark in light of international comparisons that show overall U.S. student performance to fall below the median performance for other developed countries.

For the latest two assessments of mathematics and science, results are available for Hispanic students (National Science Board, 1988, 9–10). Average performance levels for Hispanic students are similar to those for black students. At ages nine and thirteen, it appears that gains have been greater for black than for Hispanic students. This may be due, at least in part, to an increasing proportion of recent immigrants among the Hispanic population and an attendant increase in the proportion of Hispanic students for whom English is a second language.

The Adequacy of Tests Employed

Educational assessment is designed to discover what students have learned in school.[2] The assessment of achievement change between successive groups of student cohorts thus requires the use of test questions that are related to specified educational objectives. In order to accept at face value a conclusion that changes in test scores represent changes in school achievement, those objectives must be clearly defined and should represent important rather than trivial educational goals. Ideally, each test question would have demonstrated validity for an objective. To what extent do the tests that have been employed meet these conditions?

In selecting test items for NAEP and for IEA, a consensus was first established among educators and others concerning the objectives of the school curriculum for a given age level. Test items to measure those objectives were then constructed and subsequently reviewed by panels of reviewers. In the original design for NAEP in the 1960s, it was specified that test exercises should include the use of laboratory apparatus (in science), and that alternatives to the multiple-choice item format should often be employed (in all subjects). However, due to the high costs of developing and scoring other than multiple-choice items, and due to limited project budgets, NAEP has employed the multiple-choice format for all but a small number of mathematics and science exercises.

In a handbook for the development and use of educational indicators, Oakes cites a "critical need for better indicators" of educational achievement. She notes that "we have fairly good paper-and-pencil measures of the most commonly taught basic knowledge and skills. But we lack adequate measures of children's abilities to think critically, to apply their knowledge, or to solve problems" (Oakes, 1986, 34).

In its final report, the National Research Council Committee on Indicators of Precollege Science and Mathematics Education cites the need for improved tests to assess mathematics and science education. The committee recommends "that a greatly accelerated program of research and development be undertaken aimed at the construction of free-response techniques that measure skills not measured by multiple-choice tests" (Murname and Raizen, 1988, 6−7). Recommended techniques include problem-solving tasks, tests of hypothesis formulation, experimental design and productive thinking, hands-on experimental exercises, and simulations of scientific phenomena using microcomputers. The committee recommends "the creation of new science tests for grades K-5...by teams that include personnel from the school districts that have been developing hands-on curricula to ensure that the new tests match the objectives of this type of instruction" (Murname and Raizen, 1988, 7).

The Study Group on the Nation's Report Card recommended that new methods be adopted for the national assessment of mathematics and science to evaluate problem-solving and higher-order skills. "Open-ended and free-response questions...require the student to generate the correct answer, not merely to recognize it. Such assessment items would...allow for more reliable inferences about the thought processes contributing to the answer" (Alexander and James, 1987, 23).

The National Science Board Commission also called for a national assessment that would cover "the ability to write for a purpose, apply higher-level problem-solving skills, and analyze and draw conclusions, rather than minimal basic skills such as the rote memorization of facts" (National Science Board Commission on Precollege Education in Mathematics, Science and Technology, 1983, 12), noting that "it will take time, talent and funds to develop these...tests. These will not be forthcoming, however, unless top priority is given to effecting these changes" (44–45).

Educational assessment instruments typically have been developed based on an expert consensus that test objectives correspond to objectives common to curricula throughout the nation. This procedure has the advantage that test exercises are "fair" to students, regardless of the region of the country or the school district in which they reside. However, the procedure may have resulted in the assessment of more common and rudimentary objectives to the exclusion of higher level but more important ones that are not universally adopted in the nation's schools. The problem may be more severe for science, for which educational objectives may vary considerably from district to district (Burnstein et al., 1985), than for mathematics, for which objectives appear to be less variable. But even for mathematics, assessment exercises focus not on higher-order problem-solving skills, but on "rote calculation and mimicry mathematics" (Steen, 1987).

In the design of national educational assessments, it is important, of course, that test materials be intimately related to appropriate curricula for a given age or grade. It should also be recognized that those tests may influence curricular objectives because they exemplify what is expected to be mastered at a given age or grade. Frederiksen (1984) expresses specific concern that the multiple-choice test format "may influence the cognitive processes involved in dealing with test items and hence the nature of the skills taught and learned" (195). A 1971 review of the effects on students of test format concluded that test format influenced the way in which students prepared for the test. "When students expected an objective test, they studied for details and memorization of material. When studying for an essay test, they focused attention on relationships, trends, organization, and on identifying a few major points around which they could write descriptive or expository paragraphs" (Kirkland, 1971, 315–316). Desired educational objectives more often are in the form of mastery of "relationships, trends, organization" than of "details and memorization." New test design, then, should develop alternatives to the multiple-choice format in order that assessment instruments better serve their purposes.

That there remain significant barriers to new test design cannot be denied. Linn (1986) identifies the relatively high predictive validity co-efficients and the economic viability of existing standardized tests as two towering barriers. For tests of school achievement, however, unlike tests of scholastic aptitude, high predictive validity is seldom of central import-ance. The test is employed to assess current understanding and to serve as an incentive for learning, not to predict future scholastic success. The more pertinent barrier, then, is the economic one. The technology of the multiple-choice test is well developed, and test construction, test adminis-tration, and test scoring and reporting are relatively economical. In contrast, for free-response measures of performance, test theory is as yet poorly articulated, and the cost of item development, scoring, and reporting is relatively high. However, the payoff for better designed tests, in the form of relevance to educational objectives and utility for improving education, is great. Linn writes that "we need to focus on different goals and use different standards for evaluating the effectiveness of the measures if we are to have a significant redesign of testing. At its most general level, the goal I have in mind is the effective use of tests to enhance learning and cognitive development" (Linn, 1986, 72).

The NAEP tests employed in science and mathematics, despite their shortcomings, were constructed to assess performance related to agreed upon curricular objectives. The achievement trends over time, as reflected by those instruments, may overestimate or underestimate trends that would have been detected by more valid instruments. It is unlikely, however, that the direction of trends would change for achievement on the *assessed* objectives, even though their magnitude might change. Assuming no change in objectives assessed, the NAEP test results would be expected to correlate with corresponding test results from more refined instruments because, for mathematics and (to a lesser extent) for science, high correlations are found among a variety of different item types as well as among items that were intended to assess different facets of knowledge or understanding. For different target objectives, however, such as higher level problem solving, improved tests would be required in order better to monitor trends in school achievement.

Some Selected Research Results on Effective Schooling

It is well established that average school achievement levels differ for children with different home environments (for example, Walberg, 1984) and for students of different racial or ethnic origin (Jones, 1984).[3] Many studies have demonstrated that children from impoverished families display lower average achievement scores than children from more affluent families, and a far greater proportion of black students than white students live in poverty: among children in the United States at ages six to fifteen in 1986, 43 percent of black children and 16 percent of white children were classified as living below the poverty line (U.S. Bureau of the Census 1987, tables 16 and 17).

A reduction in poverty rates might have a salutary effect on measured school achievement, but poverty is not subject to direct control by educational policymakers. Yet the influence of poverty on school achievement may be lessened by programs designed to foster conditions in the home that increase support for school achievement. After reviewing nearly three thousand investigations of productive factors in learning, Walberg (1984) concludes that such programs have "an outstanding record of success in promoting achievement."

A clearly successful preschool program has been Head Start, whose goal is to work with the preschool child, the family, and the community to bring about greater social competence for the disadvantaged child (Zigler, 1979, 496). Student achievement is only one component of social competence. Head Start also has a record of success with respect to other components: physical health, social and emotional development, family involvement, and community change (Zigler, 1979, 496–500). In addition, participation of Head Start mothers in the Head Start program has been reported to positively influence the well-being of the mothers; the greater the participation, the greater were feelings of mastery and reports of current life satisfaction and the fewer were psychological symptoms of dissatisfaction at the end of the program year (Parker, Piotrkowski, and Peay, 1987). These influences on some Head Start mothers might exert indirect salutary effects on their Head Start children and on siblings as well.

School achievement is strongly related to the opportunity for students to learn (see, for example, Brophy, 1988; Jones, 1987; Jones, Burton, and Davenport, 1984; Jones et al., 1986; McKnight et al., 1987; Raizen and Jones, 1985; Stevenson et al., 1986; Walberg, 1984; Welch, Anderson, and Harris, 1982). For example, a student who has not enrolled in advanced mathematics courses is unlikely to perform well on exercises that assess what has been learned from such courses and also may have lost the facility to solve mathematics exercises mastered in earlier courses. For students in high school in 1980 to 1982, substantially smaller proportions of black than of white students were enrolled in mathematics courses at the level of Algebra 1 or above, so that, on average, black students had less opportunity than whites to learn mathematics (Jones, 1987). Providing the opportunity to learn is a recurrent theme in recent reports on school reform and is clearly an important responsibility of schools.

The opportunity to learn is a function not only of course offerings and student enrollment in courses but also of hours of instruction, time on task during instructional periods, freedom from distractions, the amount and quality of homework, the appropriateness of course content, and teacher qualifications and teaching effectiveness. A wide body of literature supports the importance of using classroom time more effectively, decreasing transition time between tasks, minimizing distractions to learning, increasing the proportion of class time in which the teacher is actively engaged with students, and assuring that material to be learned is not material already mastered by large numbers of students in a class.

Among major recommendations for educational reform are not only those that pertain to time for instruction but also some that focus on the content of instruction and some that stress the need for effective teaching (and teachers). Underlying many of the recommendations is a recognition of the importance of instituting changes to increase interest and motivation on the part of students, to shift the learning experience from a passive "boring requirement" to an active "exciting adventure."

Based on his synthesis of many studies of productive factors in learning, Walberg (1984) concludes that the introduction of mastery learning or of personalized or adaptive instruction has great salutary effects on student achievement. This conclusion also is strongly supported by Bloom. He and his students have engaged in research aimed at discovering group instructional practices that are as effective as individual tutorial approaches. They report considerable success with mastery learning supplemented by enhanced explanations in instruction, active student participation, and reinforcement of student performance (Bloom, 1984). Smith (1986) set forth some convincing reservations about the adoption of mastery learning. The other ingredients of Bloom's approach seem to have better survived critical scrutiny.

Bloom (1984) also reported beneficial effects from "cooperative learning." Slavin (1987) characterizes cooperative learning procedures as dependent first on instruction by the teacher, then on practice engaged in actively by members of an established student team (of four or five members). Team incentives are provided but depend on the improved individual performance of team members rather than on group performance. Evidence supports the efficacy of this approach to elevate not only achievement but student self-esteem, interpersonal effectiveness, and interracial harmony as well (Slavin et al., 1985). In some ways, cooperative learning resembles "groupwork," as described by Cohen (1986): both approaches entail teams of four or five students, heterogeneous with respect to ability, ethnicity, and gender; both approaches depend on the active, cooperative participation in learning by all team members, a set of conditions especially conducive to achievement gains for black and other students of low socioeconomic status (Brophy, 1988). Group work differs from cooperative learning in its lesser emphasis on the teacher as instructor and its greater dependence on students teaching other students, and in its lesser emphasis on achievement outcomes and its greater emphasis on the elevation of student self-esteem.

Among the most controversial of classroom practices in American schools is the practice of organizing classrooms by groups of students with similar ability levels. Based on a meta-analysis of fifty-two studies of the effects of ability grouping in U.S. secondary schools, Kulik and Kulik (1982) report small salutary effects of ability grouping on student attitudes and student achievement. However, positive effects were consistently found for students who received enriched instruction in honors classes. Perhaps "ability grouping" serves as a surrogate for teacher and student expectations. With an enriched curriculum and high expectations, as is the case for honors classes, benefits appear to accrue; under those conditions, average student benefits might prove to be even greater for heterogeneous than for homogeneous student groups (see Clark, 1972; Cohen, 1986; Goodlad, 1984; Slavin et al., 1985).

Clark (1972) stressed the importance of experiences of academic success to establish higher expectations: "As the child discovers that it is possible to learn, his natural motivation to learn will be enhanced. Conversely, if he experiences failure, he will reduce his motivation for learning as a form of escape from a situation intolerable to his ego." Bock and Moore (1986) also emphasize the importance of establishing higher expectations for achievement in educating black students. In a similar vein, Levin (1986) has initiated elementary school programs of "accelerated learning" for disadvantaged students designed to provide early success experience, to stimulate high expectations, and (with family support) to achieve performance levels at or above the national average by the end of sixth grade.

Some innovations in science and mathematics education have been reported both to be generally effective and to elevate achievement levels for disadvantaged students especially. Bredderman (1982a, 1982b) and Olstad and Haury (1984) report such effects for activity-based science programs in elementary schools. McDermott (1982) presents findings that suggest special benefits in comprehensive laboratory experience as a supplement to lectures and discussion for disadvantaged high school physics students. Burns and Bozeman (1981) report that tutorial computer instruction as a supplement to mathematics course work is particularly effective for disadvantaged students, both at elementary and high school levels. Becker and Gersten (1982), Gersten and Carnine (1984), and Gersten et al. (1984) report similar results for the use in early elementary grades of "direct instruction" and mastery learning, entailing a highly specific curriculum, small-group instruction, and the monitoring of both student and teacher performance (see Becker, 1986). (It should be noted that components of this program have been sharply criticized both by Smith, 1986 and by Weikert, 1987.) Generally, research findings support the efficacy for instruction of introducing mathematical ideas, concepts, and terminology by linking them with concrete objects, pictorial displays, or diagrams (Trafton, 1984). This group of findings suggests that all students are helped, but disadvantaged students especially, by the introduction and use of manipulative materials in the learning of science and mathematics.

An extensive study by Walker and Schaffarzick attests to the need for caution when interpreting results from studies of the effects on achievement of different school curricula. *"Different curricula are associated with different patterns of achievement.* Furthermore, these different patterns of achievement seem generally to follow patterns apparent in the curricula. Students using each curriculum do better than their fellow students on tests which include items not covered at all in the other curriculum or given less emphasis there"* (Walker and Schaffarzick, 1974). This conclusion is totally consistent with findings from studies of planned variations in curricula from Project Follow Through, as reported by Hodges et al. (1980), and with the thesis set forth earlier in this section, that the level of tested student achievement is an intimate function of the opportunity for the student to have learned the skills and knowledge assessed by the particular achievement test employed. It emphasizes the importance of developing and using achievement tests that are high in construct validity for the central objectives of instruction.

Brophy discusses research findings on effective teaching for low-achieving students from backgrounds of low socioeconomic status, a group that includes a disproportionately large number of black students. Brophy concludes that the key to achievement gain by low-achieving students is maximizing the time that they spend being actively instructed or supervised by their teachers. The educational programs likely to be most effective with these students are programs developed on the basis of general principles of good instruction rather than programs designed from the beginning as responses to special needs or learning deficits. (Brophy, 1988, 235)

Brophy cites as a qualification to this conclusion a special need of low-achieving students from backgrounds of low socioeconomic status for "more focused, structured, and redundant teaching, and more personalized and supportive interactions (but within the context of positive expectations and an academic focus)" (260). A review of research findings pertinent to general principles of good instruction may be found in Wittrock (1986). Bonnstetter, Penick, and Yager (1983) present a compelling list of characteristics of effective teachers, inferred from studying effective science programs. Effective teachers are demanding of themselves and their students, are both stimulating and accepting, are models of active inquiry regarding societal issues as well as school topics, are effective communicators, and are flexible rather than rigid with respect to their schedule and curriculum. Based on a review of studies of effective teaching of mathematics, Brophy and Good (1986) stress the importance of teacher and classroom organization, including frequent classroom review of lessons and homework and the regular assignment and monitoring of both seatwork and homework.

Joyce and Clift propose developing "a new culture of teacher education" in which the academic preparation of teachers is increased (with teacher education to become a two-year graduate program of study), clinical training is taught jointly by school and college personnel (to weave theory with practice), and all participants recognize that "most training will occur after employment," thereby relieving pressure on preservice programs to do the impossible and obligating schools and colleges to provide career-long education for teachers (Joyce and Clift, 1984, 13–14). Recognizing the need for in-school education for teachers, Fenstermacher and Berliner (1985) propose a detailed framework for staff development within the school to enhance the worth, merit, and success of the educational process.

Administrative conditions that appear to contribute to effective schooling summarized by Yager (1983b), include a clear vision and plan for excellence that has emerged locally through joint efforts of teachers, local administrators, and citizens of the community, supported and approved by regional administrative officials.

A number of reports have described characteristic features of successful programs already in existence. Yager (1983a, 1983b) characterizes features common to a variety of exemplary science programs. Brannan and Schaaf (1983) describe the implementation of a problem-solving mathematics curriculum for grades four to nine in the Oregon schools. Many reports have been issued that outline instructional procedures adopted by model schools; other reports discuss school reforms adopted by school districts or by states. Comprehensive descriptions of programs of proven success can be helpful to others and should be encouraged.

The National Science Board Commission (1983, 43–44) presents a listing of concrete objectives for mathematics and science education at both elementary and secondary levels and calls for revision of curricula to meet those objectives. A major recommendation of the commission is that "each school district should adopt and carry out programs which will identify and eliminate those barriers to full educational opportunity which discriminate against or otherwise place at a disadvantage elementary and secondary students on the basis of race, gender, ethnic background, language spoken in the home or socioeconomic status" (14). McKnight et al. focus on the need to restructure the mathematics curriculum, "to increase the intensity of content coverage," so that the curriculum is "broadened and enriched"; they urge a reexamination of "the practice of early sorting of students into curricular tracks that lead to vastly different opportunities to learn high school mathematics" (McKnight et al., 1987, xii, xiii, 113). These authors also emphasize the importance of improving mathematics textbooks, of retaining greater proportions of students in high school mathematics programs, and of upgrading the status and rewards of teaching. The Committee on Research in Mathematics, Science, and Technology Education (1987) recommends improvements in curriculum (and achievement testing), teacher education, learning conditions, and school structure. Usiskin (1985) argues that greater instructional use of calculators and computers in mathematics classes could foster a reworking of the curriculum that would shift resources from teaching mechanical skills to teaching the understanding of underlying concepts. "If our present curriculum were a new curriculum that we were testing, we would be forced to pronounce it a failure" (Usiskin, 1985, 19).

The teaching of thinking skills and problem solving is a topic that has received increased attention in recent years (see, for example, Segal, Chipman, and Glaser, 1985). Carpenter and Moser (1984) report success in teaching problem-solving strategies for word problems that involve addition and subtraction concepts to children in early elementary grades, even before the children had been introduced to arithmetic facts. For both elementary and secondary school children, the Feurestein instrumental enrichment program (Feurestein et al., 1980) is designed to help students "learn to learn." The program has been found quite consistently to elevate skills in processing figural or spatial information (Savell, Twohig, and Rachford, 1986). Whimbey and Lockhead (1982) have developed problem-solving materials for use by children of secondary school ages (or by adults). Zhu and Simon (1989) report salutary effects on middle school classes in China of a mathematics curriculum based on "learning by example" as a replacement for traditional lecture methods. All of these developments are consistent with an information-processing conception of human abilities (Newell and Simon, 1972; Simon, 1980; Sternberg, 1984, 1985a, 1985b), and more specifically, with such a conception of mathematical problem-solving abilities (Carpenter, Moser, and Romberg, 1982; Mayer, 1983; Resnick and Ford, 1981); they are rich with implications for improved instructional practice, especially for the education of disadvantaged students.

Rutherford (1985) presents a series of recommendations on science and mathematics education, directed to the school, to institutions that prepare teachers, and to the federal government—all designed to support a national commitment to the improvement of our science education system. Rutherford's central recommendation also included, as a recommendation of the National Science Board Commission, the establishment of an independent body to define national standards in science and mathematics education. Promising steps along these lines have been taken for mathematics by the National Council of Teachers of Mathematics toward developing new curricula that include segments on problem solving, as well as on probability and statistics. Also, the newly established Mathematical Sciences Education Board at the National Research Council is expected to develop curricular goals to serve as guidelines for mathematics education. It would be highly desirable for a comparable body to be established to guide the objectives of science education.

Steen (1987) sets forth an agenda for the improvement of mathematics education:

- Only teachers who like mathematics should teach mathematics.
- Only tests that measure higher order thinking skills should be used to assess mathematics.
- The chief objective of school mathematics should be to instill confidence.
- Good teaching must be rewarded both professionally and financially.
- Mathematics teaching must be based on both contemporary mathematics and modern pedagogy.

• School mathematics should use computers and calculators.
• Mathematics in the schools should be linked to science in the schools. (Steen 1987, 302)

By substituting the words "science" for "mathematics" (and "mathematics" for "science"), Steen's suggestions would apply to science education as well as to mathematics education. Adoption of this agenda in the early elementary years could have conspicuous positive effects on the preparation of disadvantaged minority students. As reported by the National Science Board Commission, "There is a striking relationship between achievement in mathematics, science and technology and the early exposure of students to stimulating teaching and good learning habits in these fields. . . . The skillful and early introduction of mathematics, science and technology in the elementary schools, therefore, is critical" (National Science Board Commission 1983, 13).

Some Policy Implications for the Education of Black Students

The improvement in average achievement test scores for black students has been accompanied by a marked increase in the average level of educational attainment for black citizens and has occurred over two decades during which the social status of U.S. blacks has improved in many ways (Farley, 1984). Noteworthy among federal policies that stimulated such improvements are the initiation of compensatory education programs for poor children and the implementation of public school desegregation, both dating from the War on Poverty in the mid-1960s. Here, after reviewing evidence on the impact of these policies, I will offer some proposals to foster further progress.

As noted by the National Science Board Commission in its discussion of achievement trends of minority students, "Although progress has been made in recent years, unacceptable disparities in achievement, participation and opportunity still exist." After outlining the need for more effective learning conditions in the early grades, the report continues:

These experiences, for societal reasons, are frequently unavailable to many racial minorities, those whose parents do not speak English in the home, and those who are economically disadvantaged. The Commission found, however, that when exposed to a good learning environment, these students perform as well as any. Low achievement norms do not reflect ability; they reflect a lack of preparation and early exposure. . . . [The] artificial disadvantages which handicap the child just entering school must be eliminated so that such a child has an equal opportunity to benefit from good teaching and appropriate curricula. (National Science Board Commission, 1983, 13–14)

The views expressed by the National Science Board Commission are consonant with research findings both for Project Head Start and for compensatory education programs funded under Title I (now Chapter I) of the Elementary and Secondary Education Act. "Head Start children are reportedly found to do better on preschool achievement tests. . .than do poor children who have not had the Head Start Experience" (Zigler, 1979, 498; see also Consortium for Longitudinal Studies, 1983). "Statistical analyses showed significant gains for Title I students, relative to needy students, for the mathematics section of the Comprehensive Tests of Basic Skills. This was true for grades 1 to 6. . . . Significant reading gains were found for grades 1 to 3, but not for grades 4, 5, or 6. . . . The largest relative gains are in the first grade" (Carter, 1984, 6).

Relative to their numbers in the student population, black and Hispanic students are more likely than white students to participate in Head Start and Chapter I programs. Given their effectiveness and their political acceptability, these programs might well be expanded to reach a larger proportion of eligible students; the expansion should be scheduled and controlled to protect program quality.

Since 1969 to 1970, black and white children have attended the same schools in most rural areas to the South, in many small and medium-sized cities of all regions, and in large southern cities where schools are organized on a county-wide basis (Farley, 1984, 198). However, "the public schools in New York, Chicago, Los Angeles, Phildelphia, and Washington were as racially segregated in 1980 as two decades earlier" (206). Based on her review of the literature, Hochschild compiles an impressive list of benefits of successful school desegregation:

Black student achievement increases, sometimes at a faster rate than white student achievement and sometimes to the point that differences in the performance levels of the two races disappear. White student achievement does not decline from desegregation. Race ralations improve, sometimes generating friendships between blacks and whites, more often producing mutual understanding and appreciation of differences, reducing fear and stereotyping, and increasing acceptance of authority figures of the other race. Community morale can improve, particularly if "Let's make it work" campaigns reach bystanders and opponents. Schools become more accessible to parents; patronage systems for hiring teachers and staff are shaken up; black teachers and administrators have more options.

Long-term benefits are as important as short-term ones. Blacks from desegregated schools are more likely than racially isolated blacks to have professional
aspirations, to attend college and do well, to attend desegregated colleges, to
attain a first job soon after high school and to be promoted in it, to be in
desegregated work groups, to hold nontraditional jobs, to live in desegregated
neighborhoods, to have children in desegregated schools, and to have interracial
friendships. Whites are disabused of the ideas that "white is better" and that
"normal" behavior is the behavior usually engaged in by whites. (Hochschild,
1985, 34)

Hochschild (1985) also recommends school procedures designed to
avoid resegregation within desegregated schools:

1) making most classes heterogeneous in race and ability, and training teachers
    to manage this new environment;
2) establishing interacial work groups within and across classrooms;
3) monitoring placement in special education classes and classes for the
    educable mentally retarded to ensure that the benefits of being "pulled
    out" of classrooms outweigh their costs for each participant;
4) developing clear, fair, and consistently enforced discipline codes that focus
    on real violations rather than stylistic differences among students;
5) enhancing counselling programs and designing in-school suspension
    programs for disruptive students;
6) expanding extracurricular activities and making sure that they are
    desegregated;
7) enhancing art and music classes and mingling students of different abilities
    in them; and
8) ensuring that faculty and staff are desegregated and that members of both
    races hold positions of power. (30)

To improve race relations within the school, Hochschild suggests a
number of innovations, which include: ensuring some black superiors and
white subordinates among teachers and administrators; ensuring that
neither race is less than 20 percent of the student body; modifying slogans
and mottos so that neither race is perceived to be invading the other's
culture or society; enabling parents of both races to participate fully and
equally in social activities and in the classroom; encouraging staff and
students to discuss openly racial differences and problems; and ensuring
that textbooks and class discussions incorporate black perspectives.

Hochschild's analysis leaves little doubt about the efficacy of school
desegregation. Continuing progress toward effective school desegregation
should go hand-in-hand with further efforts to improve the quality of
schooling for all children. As promising avenues that lead toward these
joint goals, I propose the following:

1. Increasing the investment in high-quality compensatory education programs designed to aid poor children at preschool and early elementary ages.
2. Expanding the use of manipulative materials in classroom learning, especially in the early grades, and increasing the proportions of class time during which the teacher engages actively and directly with students in the learning process.
3. Seeking more opportunities for cooperative learning by student teams, heterogeneous with respect to race or ethnicity, gender, and ability.
4. Striving to elevate expectations of student success on the part of parents, teachers, and the students themselves.
5. Improving the cirriculum to minimize the repetition of content from year to year and encouraging all students to continue throughout high school to enroll in academically challenging courses.
6. Devising and employing improved achievement tests that are well articulated with instruction and intimately related to the important rather than the trivial goals of learning.
7. Elevating the status of the teaching profession, both to attract better teachers and to improve their morale and thus their effectiveness.

Progress along these lines will require a national commitment and federal funding as well as commitment and additional funding by states. Equally imperative, however, is the maintenance of considerable autonomy at the district, school, and classroom levels to allow teachers to engage actively in establishing goals, designing curricula, and selecting teaching methods.

It is increasingly clear that educational quality and equity are compatible. Public sentiment and the political climate are favorable to changes that are designed both to further equal educational opportunity and to provide American children with the finest education in the world.

Acknowledgments

I am grateful to graduate students Deanna Braddy and Richard Faldowski for assisting in the search of the literature, and Tanja Bekhuis for editorial assistance. I thank Edward Zigler for bringing to my attention several important references. I also thank members of the staff of the National Commission on Testing and Public Policy and commission reviewers James W. Guthrie and Mark Wilson for their constructive suggestions based on their reading of an earlier draft.

Appendix A: Details of the Analysis of Trends for Black and White Students

Findings at Age Nine

Reading. NAEP assessed reading achievement in school years 1970–1971, 1974–1975, 1979–1980, 1983–1984 and 1985–1986; results for reading are not reported for 1986–1986 due to problems encountered in that assessment (Beaton, 1988). On each of the first three of these occasions, a common set of 57 reading exercises was administered to comparable national samples of nine-year-olds. The average percentages of correct answers, shown separately for black and for white nine-year-olds, are presented by NAEP (1981) and appear by birth year in table A1.

For accuracy and consistency throughout, it is desirable that all results be presented as percentage-correct scores on exercises that were identical from one assessment to the next. However, reading results for 1983–1984 are available only in terms of item response theory, or IRT scores, presented on a scale that is considered to be comparable not only from one assessment to another but also from age to age (NAEP, 1985). Based on the relation within age of average IRT scores to average percentage-correct scores for the first three reading assessments, average percentage-correct scores are estimated for 1983–1984 (birth year 1974) and also appear in table A1. The method of adjustment is described in Appendix B. (Comparisons of reading performance trends in IRT-score units for white and black students at ages nine, thirteen, and seventeen are given in NAEP, 1985.)

Mathematics. Mathematics achievement was assessed by NAEP in 1972–1973, 1977–1978, 1981–1982 and 1985–1986. For nine-year-olds,

Table A1. Average Percentage Correct for White and Black 9-Year-Old Students on NAEP Reading Exercises

		Year of Birth		
Ethnicity	1961	1965	1970	1974*
White	66.4	67.0	69.3	69.1
Black	49.7	54.5	59.6	57.4
Difference	16.7	12.5	9.7	11.7

* Percentages estimated from IRT scores (see text and Appendix B).

Table A2. Average Percentage Correct for White and Black 9-Year-Old
Students on NAEP Mathematics Exercises

Year of Birth

Ethnicity	1963	1968	1972*	1976*
White	41.1	39.1	39.8	41.6
Black	23.4	26.3	28.4	32.5
Difference	17.7	12.8	11.4	9.1

* Percentages adjusted to be on the same scale as those for 1963 and 1968 (see text and Appendix C).

results by birth year for white and black students are presented in table A2. The data are from NAEP, 1979; NAEP, 1983; and for the most recent assessment, National Science Board (1988, 174, Appendix table 1.1). Results in table A2 are based on the fifty-five exercises common to the first and second assessment, the 233 exercises common to the second and third assessments, and (for 1985—1986) the exercises that were common to the most recent three assessments. Percentages for the third and fourth assessments have been adjusted to be on the same scale as those for the first and second assessments. The method of adjustment described in Appendix C leaves invariant the difference between average percentages for whites and blacks. (Results for NAEP trends in mathematics scores for black and white students were presented by the Congressional Budget Office, 1986. They are reported to have been adjusted to a common scale of exercise difficulty. However, the adjustment apparently did not leave invariant the difference in average scores between black students and white students; results from that source differ from those presented here.)

Science. Science was assessed by NAEP in 1969—1970, 1972—1973, 1976—1977 and 1981—1982. Results are provided for the first three assessments by NAEP (1978), for 1981—1982 by Hueftle, Rakow, and Welch (1983), and for 1985—1986 by National Science Board (1988, 174, Appendix table 1—2). From Hueftle et al., results for exercises common to the third and fourth assessments measuring Inquiry and Science-Technology-Self (S-T-S) have been combined (after being weighted for different numbers of exercises for Inquiry and S-T-S) to yield for the fourth assessment weighted average percentages of correct response for presentation here. Results are based on 92 exercises common to the first and second assessments, 71 exercises common to the second and third

Table A3. Average Percentage Correct for White and Black 9-Year-Old
Students on NAEP Science Exercises

Year of Birth

Ethnicity	1960	1963	1967*	1972*	1976*
White	64.0	62.8	62.5	63.2	64.7
Black	46.8	46.2	45.9	49.5	52.6
Difference	17.2	16.6	16.6	13.7	12.1

* Percentages adjusted to be on the same scale as those for 1960 and 1963 (see text and
Appendix C).

assessments, and 30 exercises common to the third, fourth, and fifth
assessments. Results for white and black nine-year-olds appear in table
A3; for the third and fourth assessments, results have been adjusted so as
to be on the same scale of average exercise difficulty as exercises common
to the first two assessments (see Appendix C).

Findings at Age Thirteen

Reading. In the NAEP assessments of reading achievement in school
years 1970–1971, 1974–1975, and 1979–1980, a common set of 71 reading
exercises was administered to comparable national samples at age thirteen.
The average percentages of correct answers, separately for black and
white students, are presented by NAEP (1981) and appear here in
table A4.

Results for 1983–1984 are available only in terms of IRT scores (NAEP,
1985). Based on the relation within age of average IRT scores to average
percentage-correct scores for the first three reading assessments, average
percentage-correct scores are estimated by the method of Appendix B for
1983–1984 (birth year 1970) and also appear in table A4.

As with reading at age nine, 1985–1986 results for reading at age
thirteen are not reported due to difficulties attending the administration
of reading exercises in that year.

Mathematics. Results presented in table A5 are based on the 77 exercises
common to the assessments of 1972–1973 and 1977–1978, the 383 exercises
common to the assessments of 1977–1978 and 1981–1982 (NAEP 1979;
NAEP 1983), and the exercises common to all of the most recent three
assessments (National Science Board 1988, 174, Appendix table 1–1).

Table A4. Average Percentage Correct for White and Black 13-Year-Old Students on NAEP Reading Exercises

	Year of Birth			
Ethnicity	*1957*	*1961*	*1966*	*1970**
White	62.6	61.9	62.6	64.4
Black	45.4	46.4	49.6	52.4
Difference	17.2	15.5	13.0	12.0

* Percentages estimated from IRT scores (see text and Appendix B).

Percentages for the third and fourth assessments have been adjusted (see Appendix C) to be on the same scale as those for the first and second assessments.

Science. Exercises common to successive NAEP assessments for age thirteen numbered 60 in 1969−1970 and 1972−1973 and 75 in 1972−1973

Table A5. Average Percentage Correct for White and Black 13-Year-Old Students on NAEP Mathematics Exercises

	Year of Birth			
Ethnicity	*1959*	*1964*	*1968**	*1972**
White	56.6	54.3	57.5	55.8
Black	31.8	32.4	38.9	43.4
Difference	24.8	21.9	18.6	12.4

* Percentages adjusted to be on the same scale as those for 1959 and 1964 (see text and Appendix C).

Table A6. Average Percentage Correct for White and Black 13-Year-Old Students on NAEP Science Exercises

	Year of Birth				
Ethnicity	*1956*	*1959*	*1963**	*1968**	*1972**
White	63.3	61.8	60.4	59.7	60.4
Black	45.0	41.9	46.0	48.5	51.1
Difference	18.3	19.9	14.4	11.2	9.3

* Percentages adjusted to be on the same scale as those for 1956 and 1959 (see text and Appendix C).

and 1976–1977. Of the exercises common to the assessments of 1976–1977 and 1981–1982 (NAEP, 1978; Hueftle, Rakow, and Welch, 1983), the 227 exercises labeled Content, Inquiry, and S-T-S by Hueftle et al. have been used here. Results for 1985–1986 are from National Science Board (1988, 174, Appendix, table 1–2) and are based on science exercises common to the third, fourth, and fifth assessments.

Results for white and black thirteen-year-olds appear in table A6; for the third, fourth, and fifth assessments, results have been adjusted so as to be on the same scale of average exercise difficulty as exercises common to the first two assessments (see Appendix C).

Findings at Age Seventeen

Reading: Evidence from NAEP. In the NAEP reading assessments of 1970–1971, 1974–1975 and 1979–1980, a common set of 71 reading exercises was administered to comparable national samples of seventeen-year-olds. The average percentages of correct answers, separately for black and for white students, are presented by the NAEP (1981) and appear here in table A7.

Results for 1983–1984 are available only in terms of IRT scores (NAEP, 1985). Based on the relation within age of average IRT scores to average percentage-correct scores for the first three reading assessments, average percentage-correct scores are estimated by the method in Appendix B for 1983–1984 (birth year 1966) and also appear in table A7.

Reading: Evidence from National Longitudinal Study and High School and Beyond. Reading was assessed for national samples of high school seniors in 1972 (National Longitudinal Study) and again in 1980 (High School

Table A7. Average Percentage Correct for White and Black 17-Year-Old Students on NAEP Reading Exercises

	Year of Birth			
Ethnicity	1953–54	1957–58	1962–63	1966–67*
White	71.2	71.2	70.6	72.5
Black	51.7	52.1	52.2	60.0
Difference	19.5	19.1	18.4	12.5

* Percentages estimated from IRT scores (see text and Appendix B).

Table A8. Average Reading and Mathematics Scores for White and Black High School Seniors

Year of Birth

Subject	Ethnicity	1954	1962	Standard Deviation
Reading				
	White	10.56	9.60	4.8
	Black	5.94	5.56	
	Difference	4.62	4.04	
Mathematics				
	White	13.95	12.98	6.8
	Black	6.50	6.69	
	Difference	7.45	6.31	

and Beyond). The data have been analyzed by Rock et al. (1984) to estimate separately for black and white seniors changes in average reading scores between 1972 and 1980. Results appear in table A8, presented by birth year on the assumption that students were eighteen years old at the time of completion of their senior year of high school. Entries in the table are estimates of formula-corrected number-right true scores from Rock et al. (1984); the estimated pooled within-group standard deviation also appears in table A8.

Reading: Evidence from SAT-V Scores. In table A9 appear annual average SAT-Verbal scores for black and white test takers from 1976 to 1987, as reported by the College Entrance Examination Board (1987). Results are presented by year of birth on the assumption that high school seniors were eighteen years old at the end of their senior year. (Since SAT results

Table A9. Average SAT-V and SAT-M Scores for White and Black Test Takers

Year of Birth

V/M	Ethnicity	1958	59	60	61	62	63	64	65	66	67	69
V	White	451	448	446	444	442	442	444	443	445	449	447
	Black	332	330	332	330	330	332	341	339	341	346	351
	Difference	119	118	114	114	112	110	103	104	104	103	96
M	White	493	489	485	483	482	483	483	484	486	490	489
	Black	354	357	354	358	360	362	366	369	373	376	377
	Difference	139	132	131	125	122	121	117	115	113	114	112

by ethnic group are not available for 1986, no report is presented for students born in 1968.)

Mathematics: Evidence from NAEP. Results for age seventeen in table A10 are based on the 102 exercises that were common to the assessments of 1972−1973 and 1977−1978, the 383 exercises that were common to the assessments of 1977−1978 and 1981−1982 (NAEP, 1979; NAEP, 1983), and for the 1985−1986 assessment, the exercises common to the second, third, and fourth assessments (National Science Board, 1988, 174, Appendix table 1−1). Percentages for the third and fourth assessments have been adjusted to be on the same scale as those for the first and second assessments (see Appendix C).

Mathematics: Evidence from National Longitudinal Study and High School and Beyond. Mathematics was assessed for national samples of high school seniors in 1972 (National Longitudinal Study) and again in 1980 (High School and Beyond), and results have been analyzed by Rock et al. (1984) to estimate separately for black and white seniors changes in average mathematics scores between 1972 and 1980. Findings from Rock et al. appear in table A8, presented by birth year on the assumption that students were eighteen years old at the time of completion of their senior year of high school. Entries in the table are estimates of formula-corrected number-right true scores; the estimated pooled within-group standard deviations also are reported in table A8.

Mathematics: Evidence from SAT-M Scores. In table A9 appear annual average SAT-Mathematics scores separately for black and white test takers by inferred birth year for SAT years 1976 to 1987 (excluding 1986) as reported by the College Entrance Examination Board (1987).

Table A10. Average Percentage Correct for White and Black 17-Year-Old Students on NAEP Mathematics Exercises

	Year of Birth			
Ethnicity	1955−56	1960−61	1964−65*	1968−69*
White	54.5	51.0	50.9	51.8
Black	33.5	30.9	32.2	35.1
Difference	21.0	20.1	18.7	16.7

* Percentages adjusted to be on the same scale as those for 1955 and 1960 (see text and Appendix C).

Table A11.   Average Percentage Correct for White and Black 17-Year-Old Students on NAEP Science Exercises

Year of Birth

Ethnicity	1852–53	1855–56	1959–60*	1964–65*	1968–69*
White	46.8	44.4	42.8	41.4	44.2
Black	34.1	32.1	27.1	26.9	32.2
Difference	12.7	13.3	15.7	14.5	12.0

* Percentages adjusted to be on the same scale as those for 1952 and 1955 (see text and Appendix C).

Science: Evidence from NAEP.   Science exercises common to successive NAEP assessments for age seventeen numbered 64 in 1969–1970 and 1972–1973 and 70 in 1972–1973 and 1976–1977. Of the exercises common to the assessments of 1976–1977 and 1981–1982 (NAEP, 1978; Hueftle, Rakow and Welch, 1983), the 206 exercises labeled Content, Inquiry, and S-T-S by Hueftle et al. have been used here. Results from the assessment of 1985–1986 (National Science Board, 1988, 174, Appendix table 1–2) are based on the science exercises common to the third, fourth, and fifth assessments.

Results for white and black seventeen-year-olds appear in table A11; for the third, fourth, and fifth assessments, results have been adjusted to the same scale of average exercise difficulty as exercises common to the first two assessments (see Appendix C).

Appendix B: Method of Estimating from Average IRT Scores the Percentage Correct for Reading

For the first three reading assessments, tables A1, A4, and A7 show the average percentages of correct response for black students and for white students on identical sets of exercises that were administered on each assessment: 57 exercises for age nine (table A1); 71 exercises for age thirteen (table A4); and 71 exercises for age seventeen (table A7). NAEP (1985) presents average IRT scores for black students and for white students on reading exercises administered on the fourth reading assessment and also on the first three reading assessments.

At each age, a linear regression equation has been found from the relation of the six average percentage-correct scores (three for black children and three for white children) to the corresponding average IRT scores for the first three assessments. This equation is then used to estimate from the average IRT scores for black and white children in the fourth assessment the corresponding average percentage-correct score. The regression equations and corresponding values of R^2 for the three ages are

$$\text{Age} \quad 9\!: Y' = .37X - 11.8, \ R^2 = .98,$$
$$\text{Age} \quad 13\!: Y' = .45X - 55.0, \ R^2 = .96,$$
$$\text{Age} \quad 17\!: Y' = .40X - 45.8, \ R^2 = 1.00,$$

where Y' is the estimated average percentage-correct score and X is the corresponding average IRT score.

Appendix C: Method of Adjusting Difficulty Levels for Different Sets of Mathematics and Science Exercises

In NAEP assessments of mathematics and science, a set of exercises was common to only two successive assessments; that is, some of the exercises in the first assessment were identical to some of the exercises in the second assessment. Similarly, some of the exercises in the second assessment were identical to some of the exercises in the third assessment. However, the first and third assessments did not necessarily contain any exercises in common. Consequently, the national percentage correct for the exercises common to two successive assessments, for example, the first and second assessments, is expected to be different for the exercises common to the next set of successive assessments, for example, the second and third assessments. For the same reason, the average percentages correct for black students and for white students will also be different. To maintain a comparable scale for average percentage correct across assessments over a span of three years or more, some adjustment is required.

The philosophy of adjustment adopted here is one of capturing cumulative change for successive assessments. Results for percentage-correct scores for black and white students are determined relative to the percentage correct for exercises common to the first two assessments in the following way.

For the first and second assessments, no adjustment is made. The results presented are those for exercises common to those two assessments.

On the second assessment, the average national percentage correct is found separately for exercises common to the first and second assessments and for exercises common to the second and third assessments. A constant is then selected which, when added to the latter, equates it to that for the former to create an adjusted average national percentage-correct score for the second assessment.

On the third assessment, the average national percentage correct is found for exercises common to the second and third assessments. The difference between this figure and the average national percentage correct for the second assessment on the same set of exercises is then added to the adjusted national percentage-correct score for the second assessment to yield an adjusted score for the third assessment.

Average percentage-correct scores for the third assessment are then found separately for black and white children. From each of these, the national average percentage correct for the third assessment is subtracted to provide an average percentage "effect" associated with ethnicity (black or white). Finally, these effects are added to the adjusted average percentage-correct scores for the third assessment to produce the adjusted average percentage-correct scores for black children and white children.

The resultant adjusted values for black and white children are on a scale of exercise difficulty determined by the exercises common to the first two assessments. For the third assessment, resultant differences between average percentages correct for white children and for black children are unchanged from the corresponding unadjusted differences for the exercises common to the second and third assessments.

To generate results for the fourth or fifth assessments, the above adjustment procedures are extended one or two steps further, correcting for differences in average exercise difficulty between exercises common to the third and fourth and fifth assessments in the same way as before, and cumulating additive constants so that all reported percentages correct have reference to the average difficulty of the exercises that were common to the first two assessments. In all instances, the adjustment has no effect on average white/black percentage differences. The sole effect of the adjustment is to maintain the percentage-correct scale of the first two assessment years as the common scale for the average percentage-correct on each subsequent assessment.

Notes

1. I am pleased to acknowledge the excellent history of testing presented by Hilgard (1987, 466–85), which has influenced this presentation.
2. This section is adapted from Jones (1988a).
3. This section is adapted from portions of Jones (1988b).

References

Alexander, L. and H. T. James. (1987) *The nation's report card.* Cambridge: National Academy of Education.

Austin, J. D. (1985) International study of achievement in mathematics—a reanalysis, *School Science and Mathematics,* 8, 635–44.

Bagley, W. C. (1922) Educational determinism: Or democracy and the IQ. *School and Society,* 16, 373–84.

Beaton, A. E. (1988) *The NAEP 1985–86 reading anomaly: A technical report.* Princeton: Educational Testing Service.

Becker, W. C. (1986) *Applied psychology for teaching: A behavioral cognitive approach.* Chicago: Science Research Associates.

Becker, W. C. and R. Gersten. (1982) A follow-up of Follow Through: The later effects of the direct instruction model on children in fifth and sixth grades, *American Educational Research Journal,* 19, 75–92.

Bloom, B. S. (1984) The 2 sigma problem: The search for methods of group instruction as effective as one-to-one tutoring, *Educational Researcher,* 13 (6), 4–16.

Bock, R. D. and E. G. J. Moore. (1986) *Advantage and disadvantage: A profile of American youth,* Hillsdale: Lawrence Erlbaum.

Bonnstetter, R. J., Penick J. E. and R. E. Yager. (1983) *Teachers in exemplary programs: How do they compare?* Washington, DC: National Science Teachers Association.

Brannan, R. and O. Schaaf. (1983) An instructional approach to problem solving. In *The agenda in action: 1983 yearbook,* ed. G. Shufelt and J. R. Smart, 41–59. Reston: National Council of Teachers of Mathematics.

Bredderman, T. (1982a) What research says: Activity science—the evidence shows it matters, *Science and Children,* 20 (1), 39–41.

Bredderman, T. (1982b) The effects of activity-based science in elementary schools. In *Education in the 80's: Science,* ed. M. B. Rowe and W. S. Higuchi, 63–75. Washington, DC: National Education Association.

Brophy, J. (1988) Research linking teacher behavior to student achievement: Potential implications for instruction of Chapter 1 students, *Educational Psychologist,* 23, 235–86.

Brophy, J. and T. L. Good. (1986) Teacher behavior and student achievement. In *Handbook of research on teaching.* 3d ed., ed. M. C. Wittrock. New York: Macmillan.

Burns, P. K. and W. C. Bozeman. (1981) Computer-assisted instruction and mathematics achievement: Is there a relationship? *Educational Leadership,* 21 (10), 32–39.

Burnstein, L., Baker, E. L., Aschbacher, P. and J. W. Keesling. (1985) *Using state test data for national indicators of education quality.* Los Angeles: UCLA Center for the Study of Evaluation.

Burton, N. W. and L. V. Jones. (1982) Recent trends in achievement levels of black and white youth, *Educational Researcher,* 11 (4), 10–14.

Carpenter, T. P. and J. M. Moser. (1984) The acquisition of addition and subtraction concepts in grades one through three, *Journal for Research in Mathematics Education*, 15, 179–202.

Carpenter, T. P., Moser, J. M. and T. A. Romberg, eds. (1982) *Addition and subtraction: A cognitive perspective*. Hillsdale: Lawrence Erlbaum.

Carter, L. F. (1984) The Sustaining Effects Study of compensatory and elementary education, *Educational Researcher*, 13 (8), 4–13.

Clark, K. B. (1972) *A possible reality*. New York: Emerson Hall.

Cohen, E. G. (1986) *Designing groupwork: Strategies for the heterogeneous classroom*. New York: Teachers College Press.

College Entrance Examination Board. (1987) *1987 profile of SAT and achievement test takers: National report*. New York: College Board.

Committee on Research in Mathematics, Science, and Technology Education. (1987) *Interdisciplinary research in mathematics, science, and technology education*. Washington, DC: National Academy Press.

Congressional Budget Office. (1986) *Trends in educational achievement*. Washington, DC: Congress of the U.S.

Consortium for Longitudinal Studies. (1983) *As the twig is bent...lasting effects of preschool programs*. Hillsdale: Lawrence Erlbaum.

Crosswhite, F. J., Dossey, J. A., Swafford, J. O., McKnight, C. C., Cooney T. J. and K. J. Travers. (1985) *Second International Mathematics Study: Summary report for the United States*. Champaign: Stipes Publishing Co.

Doran, R. L. and W. J. Jacobson. (1987) Preliminary results for the U.S.A. participation in the second IEA study—1986. Paper presented at 1987 annual meeting of the American Educational Research Association, Washington, DC.

Farley, R. (1984) *Blacks and whites, narrowing the gap?* Cambridge: Harvard University Press.

Fenstermacher, G. D. and D. C. Berliner. (1985) Determining the value of staff development. Special Issue: Policy implications of effective schools research, *Elementary School Journal*, 85, 281–314.

Feurestein, R., Rand, Y., Hoffman, M. B. and R. Miller. (1980) *Instrumental enrichment: An intervention program for cognitive modifiability*. Baltimore: University Park Press.

Frederiksen, N. (1984) The real test bias: Influences of testing on teaching and learning, *American Psychologist*, 39, 193–202.

Garber, H. L. (1988) *The Milwaukee Project: Preventing mental retardation in children at risk*. Washington, DC: American Association on Mental Retardation.

Gersten, R. M. and D. Carnine. (1984) Direct instruction mathematics: A longitudinal study of low-income elementary school students, *Elementary School Journal*, 84, 395–407.

Gersten, R. M., Becker, M. C., Heiry, T. J. and W. A. White. (1984) Entry IQ and yearly academic growth of children in direct instruction programs: A longitudinal study of low SES children, *Educational Evaluation and Policy Analysis*, 6, 109–21.

Goodenough, F. L. (1940) New evidence on environmental influence on intelligence. In *Intelligence: Its nature and nurture. 39th Yearbook of the National Society for the Study of Education*, Part 1, G. D. Stoddard (Chair). Bloomington: Public School Publishing Co.

Goodlad, J. I. (1984) *A place called school: Prospects for the future*. New York: McGraw-Hill.

Gould, S. J. (1981) *The mismeasure of man*. New York: Norton.

Harnisch, D. L., Walberg, H. J., Tsai, S-L., Sato T. and L. J. Fyans, Jr. (1985) Mathematics productivity in Japan and Illinois, *Evaluation in Education: An International Review Series*, 9, 277–84.

Hilgard, E. R. (1987) *Psychology in America: A historical survey*. Orlando: Harcourt Brace Jovanovich.

Hochschild, J. L. (1985) *Thirty years after Brown*. Washington, DC: Joint Center for Political Studies.

Hodges, W., Branden, A., Feldman, R., Follino, J., Love, J., Sheehan, R., Lumbley, J., Osborn, J., Rentfrow, R. K., Houston, J. and C. Lee. (1980) *Follow Through: Forces for change in the primary schools*. Ypsilanti: High/Scope.

Hueftle, S. J., Rakow, S. J. and W. W. Welch. (1983) *Images of science*. Minnaepolis: Minnesota Research and Evaluation Center.

Humphreys, L. G. (1988) Trends in levels of academic achievement of blacks and other minorities, *Intelligence*, 12, 231–60.

Hunter, J. E., Schmidt, F. L. and J. Rauschenberger. (1984) Methodological, statistical, and ethical issues in the study of bias in psychological tests. In *Perspectives on bias in mental testing*, C. R. Reynolds and R. T. Brown. New York: Plenum. (ed.).

Jacobson, W. J., Doran, R. L. and E. W. Muller. (1985) *Sampling and administration report, Population 1*. New York: Teachers College, Columbia University.

Jacobson, W. J., Takemura, S., Doran, R. L., Kojima, S., Humrich, E. and M. Miyake. (1986) *Analysis and comparisons of science curricula in Japan and the United States*. New York: Teachers College, Columbia University.

Jensen, A. R. (1969) How much can we boost IQ and scholastic achievement, *Harvard Educational Review*, 39, 1–123.

Jensen, A. R. (1980) *Bias in mental testing*. New York: Free Press.

Jones, L. V. (1981) Achievement test scores in mathematics and science, *Science*, 213, 412–16.

Jones, L. V. (1984) White-black achievement differences: The narrowing gap, *American Psychologist*, 39, 1207–13.

Jones, L. V. (1987) The influence on mathematics test scores, by ethnicity and sex, of prior achievement and high school mathematics courses, *Journal of Research in Mathematics Education*, 18, 180–86.

Jones, L. V. (1988a) Educational assessment as a promising area for psychometric research, *Applied Measurement in Education*, 1, 233–41.

Jones, L. V. (1988b) School achievement trends in mathematics and science, and what can be done to improve them. In *Review of Research in Education*, 15, ed. E. Z. Rothkopf. Washington, DC: American Educational Research Association.

Jones, L. V., Burton, N. W. and E. C. Davenport, Jr. (1984) Monitoring the mathematics achievement of black students, *Journal of Research in Mathematics Education*, 15, 154−64.

Jones, L. V., Davenport, Jr., E. C., Bryson, A. Bekhuis T. and R. Zwick. (1986) Mathematics and science test scores as related to courses taken in high school and other factors, *Journal of Educational Measurement*, 23, 197−208.

Joyce, B. and R. Clift. (1984) The Phoenix agenda: Essential reform in teacher education, *Educational Researcher*, 13 (4), 5−18.

Kirkland, M. C. (1971) The effects of tests on students and schools, *Review of Educational Research*, 41, 303−50.

Kulik, C.-L. C. and J. A. Kulik. (1982) Effects of ability grouping on secondary school students: A meta-analysis of evaluation findings, *American Educational Research Journal*, 19, 415−28.

Levin, H. M. (1986) *Educational reform for disadvantaged students: An emerging crisis*. Washington, DC: National Education Association.

Linn, R. L. (1986) Barriers to new test designs. In *The redesign of testing for the 21st century*. Princeton: Educational Testing Service.

Lippmann, W. (1922) The mental age of Americans, etc, *New Republic*, 32, 213; 33, 9.

Loehlin, J. C., Lindzey, G. and J. N. Spuhler. (1975) *Race differences in intelligence*. San Francisco: Freeman.

Matthews, W., Carpenter, T. P., Lindquist, M. M. and E. A. Silver. (1984) The third national assessment: Minorities and mathematics, *Journal for Research in Mathematics Education*, 15, 165−71.

Mayer, R. E. (1983) *Thinking, problem solving, and cognition*. San Francisco: Freeman.

McDermott, L. C. (1982) Problems in understanding physics (kinematics) among beginning college students—with implications for high school courses. In *Education in the 80's: Science*, M. B. Rowe and W. S. Higuchi. (ed.) Washington, DC: National Education Association.

McKnight, C. C., Crosswhite, F. J., Dossey, J. A., Kifer, E., Swafford, J. O., Travers, K. J. and T. J. Cooney. (1987) *The underachieving curriculum: Assessing U.S. school mathematics from an international perspective*. Champaign: Stipes Publishing Co.

McNemar, Q. (1940) A critical examination of the University of Iowa studies of environmental influences upon the IQ, *Psychological Bulletin*, 37, 63−92.

Murname, R. J. and S. A. Raizen, (eds.) (1988) *Improving indicators of the quality of science and mathematics education in grades K-12*. Washington, DC: National Academy Press.

National Assessment of Educational Progress. (1978) *Three national assessments of science: Changes in achievement, 1969−77*. Denver: Education Commission of the States.

National Assessment of Educational Progress. (1979) *Changes in mathematical achievement, 1973−1978*. Denver: Education Commission of the States.

National Assessment of Educational Progress. (1981) *Three national assessments of reading: Changes in performance, 1970−80*. Denver: Education Commission of the States.

National Assessment of Educational Progress. (1983) *The third national mathematics assessment: Results, trends, and issues*. Denver: Education Commission of the States.

National Assessment of Educational Progress. (1985) *The reading report card*. Princeton: Educational Testing Service.

National Science Board. (1988) *Science & engineering indicators−1987*. Washington, DC: National Science Foundation, NSB 87−1.

National Science Board Commission on Precollege Education in Mathematics, Science and Technology. (1983) *Educating Americans for the 21st century*. Washington, DC: National Science Foundation.

Neisser, U. (1986) *The school achievement of minority children*. Hillsdale: Lawrence Erlbaum.

Newell, A. and H. A. Simon. (1972) *Human problem solving*. Englewood Cliffs: Prentice-Hall.

Oakes, J. (1986) *Educational indicators: A guide for policy makers*. Santa Monica: Center for Policy Research in Education, The RAND Corporation.

Olstad, R. G. and D. L. Haury. (1984) A summary of research in science education−1982, *Science Education*, 68, 207−363.

Parker, F. L., Piotrkowski, C. S. and L. Peay. (1987) Head Start as a social support for mothers: The psychological benefits of involvement, *American Journal of Orthopsychiatry*, 57, 220−33.

Raizen, S. A. and L. V. Jones, (eds.) (1985) *Indicators of precollege education in science and mathematics: A preliminary review*. Washington, DC: National Academy Press.

Resnick, L. B. and W. Ford. (1981) *The psychology of mathematics for instruction*. Hillsdale: Lawrence Erlbaum.

Reynolds, C. R. (1982) The problem of bias in psychological assessment. In *The handbook of school psychology*, ed. C. R. Reynolds and T. B. Gutkin. New York: Wiley.

Reynolds, C. R. and R. T. Brown. (1984) *Perspectives on bias in mental testing*. New York: Plenum.

Rock, D. A., Ekstrom, R. B., Goertz, M. E., Hilton, T. L. and J. Pollack. (1984) *Factors associated with decline of test scores of high school seniors, 1972 to 1980, a study of excellence in high school education: Educational policies, school quality, and student outcomes*. Princeton: Educational Testing Service.

Rutherford, F. J. (1985) Lessons from five countries. In *Science education in global perspective: Lessons from five countries*, ed. M. S. Klein and F. J. Rutherford. Boulder: Westview Press.

Samuda, A. J. (1975) *Psychological testing of American minorities: Issues and consequences*. New York: Dodd, Mead.

Savell, J. M., Twohig, P. T. and D. L. Rachford. (1986) Empirical status of Feuerstein's "Instrumental Enrichment" (FIE) technique as a method of teaching thinking skills, *Review of Educational Research*, 56, 381–410.

Scarr, S. (1981) *Race, social class, and individual differences in IQ*. Hillsdale: Lawrence Erlbaum.

Segal, J. W., Chipman, S. F. and R. Glaser, (eds) (1985) *Thinking and learning skills, volume 1: Relating instruction to research*, Hillsdale: Lawrence Erlbaum.

Simon, H. A. (1980) Problem solving and education. In *Problem solving and education: Issues in teaching and research*, D. T. Tuma and F. Reif (eds.). Hillsdale: Lawrence Erlbaum.

Slavin, R. E. (1987) *Cooperative learning: Student teams*. (2d ed) Washington, DC: National Educational Association.

Slavin, R. E., Sharan, S., Kagan, S., Hertz-Lazarowitz, R., Webb, C. and R. Schmuck. (1985) *Learning to cooperate, cooperating to learn*. New York: Plenum.

Smith, F. (1986) *Insult to intelligence*. New York: Arbor House.

Steen, L. A. (1987) Mathematics education: A predictor of scientific competitiveness, *Science*, 237, 251–52, 302.

Sternberg, R. J. (1984) Mechanisms of cognitive development: A componential approach. In *Mechanisms of cognitive development*, ed. R. J. Sternberg. New York: Freeman.

Sternberg, R. J. (1985a) *Beyond IQ: A triarchical theory of intelligence*. Cambridge: Cambridge University Press.

Sternberg, R. J. (ed.) (1985b) *Human abilities: An information-processing approach*. New York: Freeman.

Stevenson, H. W., Lee, S. and J. W. Stigler. (1986) Mathematics achievement of Chinese, Japanese, and American children, *Science*, 231, 693–99.

Stoddard, G. D. (Chr.) (1940) *Intelligence: Its nature and nurture. 39th Yearbook of the National Society for the Study of Education*. Parts 1 and 2. Bloomington: Public School Publishing Co.

Terman, L. M. (1918) The use of intelligence tests in the army, *Psychological Bulletin*, 15, 177–87.

Terman, L. M. (1922a) The psychological determinist, or democracy and the IQ, *Journal of Educational Research*, 6, 57–62.

Terman, L. M. (1922b) The great conspiracy, or the impulse imperious of intelligence testers, psychoanalyzed and exposed by Mr. Lippmann, *New Republic*, 33, 116–20.

Terman, L. M. (Chr.) (1928) *Nature and nurture: Their influence on intelligence. 27th Yearbook of the National Society for the Study of Education*. Parts 1 and 2. Bloomington: Public School Publishing Co.

Thurstone, L. L. (1938) *Primary mental abilities*. Psychometric Monograph No. 1. Chicago, University of Chicago Press.

Trafton, P. R. (1984) Toward more effective, efficient instruction in mathematics, *Elementary School Journal*, 84, 514–28.

Travers, K. J. and C. C. McKnight. (1985) Mathematics achievement in U.S.

schools: Preliminary findings from the Second IEA Mathematics Study, *Phi Delta Kappan*, 66, 407—13.

U.S. Bureau of the Census. 1987 *Current population reports*. Series P-60, No. 157. Washington, DC: U.S. Government Printing Office.

Usiskin, Z. (1985) We need another revolution in secondary school mathematics. In *The secondary school mathematics curriculum: 1985 Yearbook*, ed. C. R. Hirsch and M. J. Zweng. Reston, VA: National Council of Teachers of Mathematics.

Vernon, P. E. (1979) *Intelligence: Hereditary and environment*. San Francisco: Freeman.

Walberg, H. J. (1984) Improving the productivity of America's schools, *Educational Leadership*, 41, 19—30.

Walker, D. and J. Schaffarzick. (1974) Comparing curricula, *Review of Educational Research*, 44, 83—111.

Weikert, D. (1987) Curriculum quality in early education. In *Early schooling: The national debate*, S. L. Kagan and E. F. Zigler (eds.). New Haven: Yale University Press.

Welch, W. W., Anderson, R. E. and L. J. Harris. (1982) The effects of schooling on mathematics achievement, *American Educational Research Journal*, 19, 145—53.

Whimbey, A. and J. Lockhead. (1982) *Problem solving and comprehension*. Philadelphia: Franklin Institute Press.

Wigdor, A. K. and W. R. Garner. (eds.) (1982) *Ability testing: Uses, consequences, and controversies*. Part 1. Washington, DC: National Academy Press.

Williams, R. L., Dotson, W., Dow, P. and W. S. Williams. (1980) The war against testing: A current status report, *Journal of Negro Education*, 49, 263—73.

Wittrock, M. C. (ed.) (1986) *Handbook of research on teaching*. (3d ed) New York: Macmillan.

Wolf, R. M. *Special report on U.S. samples in second science study*. New York: Teachers College, Columbia University.

Wolf, R. M. *U.S. samples in the Second International Science Study*. New York: Teachers College, Columbia University.

Woodworth, R. S. (1941) *Heredity and environment: A critical survey of recently published material on twins and foster children*. Bulletin No. 47. New York: Social Science Research Council.

Yager, R. E. (ed.) (1983a) *Centers of excellence: Portrayals of six districts*. Washington, DC: National Science Teachers Association.

Yager, R. E. (ed.) (1983b) *Exemplary programs in physics, chemistry, biology, and earth science*. Washington, DC: National Science Teachers Association.

Yando, R., Seitz, V. and E. Zigler. (1979) *Intelligence and personality characteristics of children: Social-class and ethnic-group differences*. Hillsdale: Lawrence Erlbaum.

Yerkes, R. M. (1921) *Psychological examining in the United States Army. Memoirs of the National Academy of Sciences.* Vol. XV. Washington, DC: Government Printing Office.

Zhu, X. and H. A. Simon. (1987) Learning mathematics from examples and by doing. *Cognition and instruction, 4,* 137—66.

Zigler, E. (1979) Project Head Start: Success or failure? In *Project Head Start, a legacy of the War on Poverty,* ed. E. Zigler and J. Valentine. New York: Free Press.

Zigler, E. and R. M. Hodapp. (1986) *Understanding mental retardation.* Cambridge: Cambridge University Press.

3 THE STATUS OF RESEARCH ON THE SCHOLASTIC APTITUDE TEST (SAT) AND HISPANIC STUDENTS IN POSTSECONDARY EDUCATION

Maria Pennock-Román

In this chapter, studies evaluating the validity of the Scholastic Aptitude Test (SAT) for use in college admissions of Hispanic students will be reviewed. Other tests for admission to graduate or professional schools are not considered here because small sample sizes and other practical problems limit the number of studies on Hispanic versus white non-Hispanic group differences in validity. Before beginning, it is worthwhile to repeat the cautions in Linn's (1982) preface to his review of group differences in test validity:

> The controversies over testing are neither created by, nor will they be resolved by, the results of investigations of test validity (Cronbach, 1975)....Justification of test use obviously depends upon much more than [how well an ability test predicts academic or professional performance]. Potential benefits and losses for the individual, the institution, and the society at large need to be considered, and the relative importance of the benefits and losses can be expected to vary greatly in the eyes of these various interests. Nonetheless, information about the degree of relationship to test scores to particular criterion measures and about the degree to which the observed relationship is generalizable across situations and from one situation to another is an important component in the evaluation of the use of tests. (335–336).

Also in this chapter, I have taken a broad view of test validity, going beyond considerations of how well tests predict undergraduate grades. Group differences are reviewed in terms of the relationship between test scores and other educational and demographic variables, evaluations of test-item content and format, and the availability of college admissions

75

counseling and guidance information. Discussion of the studies will be organized around the following questions:

1. *Mean Differences.* What factors are associated with ethnic group-mean differences on the SAT? What are the implications of these differences?
2. *Evaluations of Test-Item Content.* Do test items contain material that is differentially more difficult for Hispanic students for reasons that are not relevant to the purpose of the test?
3. *Predictive Validity.* How accurately do selective admissions tests describe the performance of Hispanic students in college? When added to high school grades or other measures of achievement, do tests improve the identification of talented Hispanic students?
4. *Test Preparation.* Do Hispanic students have equal access to the information necessary for long-term and short-term preparation for selective admissions tests?

In evaluating the use of tests for selective admissions to higher education, it is necessary to consider all of these issues because mean differences alone are not sufficient to establish that tests are biased, or that they represent unfair barriers to higher education. We have to carefully determine to what extent tests are giving us accurate information that is relevant to the decisions we have to make. While it is possible that the lower test scores could be due to content or item formats that lead to unintended cultural biases, it is also possible that the lower test scores may reflect real deficits in the quality of preparation that Hispanic students have had for college. If so, then tests are acting as bearers of bad news, and putting the messenger to death will not solve the underlying problem.

One way to approach the issue of test bias is to consider the relative difficulty of individual items for different groups. This procedure, which is called differential item functioning (DIF), can isolate potentially problematic items because these items contribute the most to group differences that are independent of overall ability level. While these methods are very sensitive to group differences on individual items, for reasons to be explained later, they cannot be used to evaluate how much the test as a whole may or may not be biased.

Hence, it is necessary to also examine how well total test scores predict performance in college as the most direct way of evaluating the accuracy of information that the total test score provides. However, as will be explained later, there are many practical problems with validity research that limits its sensitivity to the detection and interpretation of group differences in the accuracy of measurement.

If we find evidence of differential validity, we need to establish why it occurs. It could be related to test content, which leads us again to DIF to determine the sources of these group differences in the items. On the other hand, the problem may be more pervasive and not identifiable with a few isolated items. Alternatively, the source may be an examinee's lack of familiarity with standardized tests, independent of specific content. For this reason we need to examine the resources that Hispanic students have for preparation for tests, both long and short term. However, as with mean differences, to demonstrate greater test naiveté among Hispanic students is not enough to show bias because test naiveté may also affect performance in college where grades are also partly based on test-taking skills. This takes us back to the issue of predictive validity and how accurately tests reflect future college performance. Hence, all of these approaches are pieces of a puzzle that are complementary in the picture they form of group differences in test performance.

In addition to summarizing existing studies and work in progress, desirable directions for new research will be suggested. As you will see, there is simply not enough information at the present time to make definitive conclusions. Much research is still in progress or remains to be initiated. The purpose of this chapter is to outline what we do know and to suggest what questions we should be asking.

Mean Differences Between Hispanic and White Non-Hispanic Students and Variables Associated with Higher Test Scores

Data for this section are taken from the *1987 College Bound Seniors Ethnic/Sex Data* (College Entrance Examination Board [CEEB], 1988) and a College Board press release entitled "National Scores on SAT Show Little Change in 1987; New Data on Student Academic Backgrounds Available" (September 22, 1987). Although these data are representative of college-bound students in states where most institutions require the SAT, they have several limitations. One limitation is that students from central, mountain, some southern, and some western states are not well represented in this data set because the American College Test (ACT) is, more often that the SAT, the required college admission test for institutions in these regions. Also test results in these data are not generalizable to the overall high school student population because of self-selection to take the test and apply to college. The percentage of high school students who take the test varies by state, and the means for states with the largest proportions of examinees tend to be lower because a wider variety of students attempt the test, not just the very best students. While the data set contains extensive information on students' course-taking patterns, it contains no ready measure of the quality of the courses and the high schools attended by the students other than academic versus nonacademic course categories.

For the study of Hispanic students' test performance, it is fortunate that the majority of states with large Hispanic concentrations (California, Texas, Florida, New York, New Jersey, and Pennsylvania) are primarily SAT states, although several states with moderately large Hispanic concentrations (New Mexico, Arizona, Colorado, and Illinois) are primarily ACT states and are, therefore, not well represented in the SAT files.

These data, however, have additional limitations for studying college-bound Hispanic students. The profile of Puerto Rican students is less informative than it could be since it reports residents from both the island (Commonwealth) of Puerto Rico and the continental United States as one category; nevertheless, these groups are quite distinct in language background and language of instruction. From 1981 to 1985, data reported on Puerto Rican examinees in the *Profiles, College Bound Seniors* (CEEB, 1982; Ramist and Arbeiter, 1983, 1984, 1986; Arbeiter, 1985) included only residents of the continental United States and excluded Puerto Ricans residing in the Commonwealth. Regrettably, this distinction was not made in the data analyses for 1987 (L. Ramist, pers. com. January 1988), although the information on residence is available for 1987 and it would have been possible to run the analyses separately for the two groups of Puerto Ricans. Unlike Puerto Rican students residing in the continental United States, Puerto Rican island residents (hereafter called Commonwealth) have usually learned English as a second language and have received much of their schooling in Spanish. The pattern of means for 1985 shows that Commonwealth Puerto Ricans have a lower SAT-Verbal mean (352) than do continental Puerto Ricans (373), although the reverse is true for SAT-Mathematical — 422 versus 405 — for Commonwealth and continental Puerto Ricans respectively (L. Ramist, pers. com. May 1988). Thus it appears that Commonwealth Puerto Ricans have better developed skills in mathematics than do continental Puerto Ricans. Although the lower English proficiency of Commonwealth Puerto Ricans depresses their scores in both subtests, this effect is more evident in the SAT-Verbal.

Another limitation of the SAT data base in that the classification of race/ethnicity is incomplete. In 1987, 5 percent of students did not fill out the optional Student Descriptive Questionnaire that contains the item on self-classification by race/ethnicity, and an additional 1.7 percent left the race/ethnicity question blank. While this response rate is much higher than usually found in social science surveys, studies on race/ethnic groups should be interpreted with caution because 6.7 percent missing values on this question is still a large number of individuals—about seventy-two thousand. Nevertheless, these data provide a comprehensive view of college-bound students in the majority of states in the union. There are several questions of interest that are appropriate here.

1. *How do overall mean SAT scores for Hispanic groups compare with those of the white non-Hispanic group in 1987?*

The means for SAT Verbal and Mathematical scores are shown in table 3—1 by year and by racial/ethnic group, from 1976 through 1987. Results are reported separately for Mexican American, Puerto Rican, and Other Hispanic (also referred to as Latin American) groups. However, separate means for this last group are available only for 1987. In other years, students in this category were included in the "white" or "other" classifications. For 1987, the latest year, we find that in comparison to white non-Hispanic students the Verbal (SAT-V) and Mathematical (SAT-M) means are substantially lower. The largest differences are found for the Puerto Rican group, 87 (SAT-V) and 89 (SAT-M) points, and the smallest differences are found for the Latin American group that scored 60 (SAT-V) and 57 (SAT-M) points lower than white non-Hispanic students. The Mexican American group scored 68 (SAT-V) and 65 (SAT-M) points lower than white non-Hispanic students. The mean differences between black and white non-Hispanic students are larger—96 (SAT-V) and 112 (SAT-M) points—than the above differences for the Hispanic students.

2. *Are there any changes in these differences over time since 1976?*

There are some noticeable changes in means over time, but they must be interpreted with caution because the data are cross-sectional and not longitudinal in nature. That is, changes may represent differences in self-selection trends (who decides to take the test within each group) and not necessarily improvements or decreases in mean-skill levels of groups. For white non-Hispanic students, Verbal scores decreased 9 points between 1976 and 1980, then slowly climbed up 7 points between 1982 and 1985, but in 1987 were still slightly lower than in 1976. A similar pattern is

Table 3–1. SAT Averages by Ethnic Group, 1976 to 1985, 1987

	1976	1977	1978	1979	1980	1981	1982	1983	1984	1985	1986	1987
								SAT-Verbal				
American Indian	388	390	387	386	390	391	388	388	390	392	NA	393
Asian American	414	405	401	396	396	397	398	395	398	404	NA	405
Black	332	330	332	330	330	332	341	339	342	346	NA	351
Mex. American	371	370	370	370	372	373	377	375	376	382	NA	379
Puerto Rican	364	355	349	345	350	353	360	358	358	368	NA	360
Other Hispanic	NA	NA	NA	NA	NA	NA	NA	NA	NA	NA	NA	387
White	451	448	446	444	442	442	444	443	445	449	NA	447
Other	410	402	399	393	394	388	392	386	388	391	NA	405
All Students	431	429	429	427	424	424	426	425	426	431	431	430
All Men	433	431	433	431	428	430	431	430	433	437	437	435
All Women	430	427	425	423	420	418	421	420	420	425	426	425
								SAT-Mathematical				
American Indian	420	421	419	421	426	425	424	425	427	428	NA	432
Asian American	518	514	510	511	509	513	513	514	519	518	NA	521
Black	354	357	354	358	360	362	366	369	373	376	NA	377
Mex. American	410	408	402	410	413	415	416	417	420	426	NA	424
Puerto Rican	401	397	388	388	394	398	403	403	405	409	NA	400
Other Hispanic	NA	NA	NA	NA	NA	NA	NA	NA	NA	NA	NA	432
White	493	489	485	483	482	483	483	484	487	490	NA	489
Other	458	457	450	447	449	447	449	446	450	448	NA	455
All Students	472	470	468	467	466	466	467	468	471	475	475	476
All Men	497	497	494	493	491	492	493	493	495	499	501	500
All Women	446	445	444	443	443	443	443	445	449	452	451	453

Source: This table is reproduced from a press release by the College Entrance Examination Board, "National Scores on SAT Show Little Change in 1987; New Data on Student Academic Backgrounds Available" (9/22/87).

Note: 1976 is the first year for which SAT scores by ethnic group are available. They were not available for 1986 due to changes in the Student Descriptive Questionnaire (SDQ), which students complete when they register for the tests. The SDQ question on ethnic background was changed to found for Mathematical scores for white non-Hispanic students. For black students, SAT-V and SAT-M scores show very little change from 1976 to 1979. Then a steady increase begins in 1979 for SAT-M and in 1981 for SAT-V, and continues through 1987. For black students, the 1987 Verbal and Mathematical means are 19 and 23 points higher, respectively, than in 1976. A similar pattern is found for the Mexican American group, except that the gains are smaller. There is a marked drop in SAT-M scores in 1978, and the 1987 SAT-V and SAT-M means are lower than in 1985. The Verbal and Mathematical means in 1987 and 8 (SAT-V) and 14 (SAT-M) points higher than in 1976 and 9 (SAT-V) and 22 (SAT-M) points higher than in 1978. The Puerto Rican group shows a pattern that is more like the white non-Hispanic trend because there is a steady decline in both SAT-V and SAT-M scores from 1976 to 1978 or 1979, with an upturn beginning in 1980. The highest means are found in 1985, which are 23 (SAT-V) and 21 (SAT-M) points higher than the lowest means in 1979. Hence, the decreases and increases are steeper than for the white non-Hispanic group and the 1987 means are lower than the 1985 means. As a result, there is very little net change between the 1987 and 1976 means. The 1987 SAT-V is only 4 points lower than in 1976, whereas the SAT-M is 1 point higher.

Overall, differences in SAT-V and SAT-M means between white non-Hispanic students and black and Mexican American students have narrowed in the last eleven years. For black students, the differences in 1976 were 119 (SAT-V) and 139 (SAT-M) points; in 1987, they were 96 (SAT-V) and 112 (SAT-M) points. For Mexican American students, the differences in 1976 were 80 and 83 points respectively, and were down to 68 and 65 points in 1987. However, for Puerto Rican students the distance from the white non-Hispanic group has not narrowed appreciably: mean differences were 87 and 92 in 1976, compared with 87 and 89 points in 1987.

Due to recent revisions in the Student Descriptive Questionnaire, we have more information available since 1987 on factors associated with these differences. From the *1987 College Bound Seniors Ethnic/Sex Data* (CEEB 1988), I have selected educational and demographic variables of special interest: high school grades, academic courses taken in high school, language background, and parental education, to be discussed next.

3. *How do group means vary by high school grade point average and number of academic courses taken?*

Table 3–2 shows the mean differences in SAT scores broken down by high school grade point average (GPA) and total years of study in six academic areas. It can be seen that with every increase in category of

Table 3-2. SAT Means and Percent Distribution by High School Grade Point Average (GPA) and Number of Academic Courses

	Mean SAT-V				Mean SAT-M				Percent Breakdown			
	NH White	LA	MA	PR	NH White	LA	MA	PR	NH White	LA	MA	PR
High School GPA												
(1) A+	566	525	501	421	632	587	579	510	4	3	3	3
(2) A	523	468	443	408	581	328	506	474	11	9	9	10
(3) A−	493	439	422	406	547	497	479	459	13	11	12	10
(4) B	434	380	371	356	473	423	413	393	54	57	57	56
(5) C	381	335	336	320	408	370	366	348	17	20	19	21
(6) D or below	370	332	316	306	390	348	348	320	0	1	0	1
Difference in means between (1) and (5)	185	190	165	101	224	217	213	162				
Total years of Study in Six Academic Areas												
(a) 20 or more years	493	434	435	402	539	487	482	453	35	32	32	32
(b) 19 or 19½ years	463	414	411	381	510	460	458	426	13	13	10	12
(c) 18 or 18½ years	447	399	401	366	492	443	449	404	13	14	13	12
(d) 17 or 17½ years	430	377	392	358	472	419	439	394	11	13	15	11
(e) 16 or 16½ years	414	363	369	342	453	402	413	372	9	10	14	10
(f) 15 or 15½ years	401	348	358	328	437	388	401	360	7	7	11	8
(g) Fewer than 15 years	378	318	331	309	411	364	371	340	12	13	20	15
Difference in means between (a) and (g)	115	116	104	93	128	123	111	113				
Overall Mean for Group	447	387	379	360	489	432	424	400				
Overall Number with SAT Scores	788,613	18,895	20,714	10,304	788,613	18,895	20,714	10,304				

Source: This table is derived from data from the *1987 College Bound Seniors Ethnic/Sex Data* (College Entrance Examination Board 1988).

grade point average, there is an increase in test score mean, and this pattern is found for all groups: white non-Hispanic, Latin American, Mexican American and Puerto Rican students. For example, if we subtract the mean for students who had an "A+" average, minus the mean for those who had a "C" or worse, the Verbal and Mathematical differences are 185 and 217 points, respectively, for white non-Hispanic students. For Latin American students these differences are 190 (SAT-V) and 217 (SAT-M); for Mexican American students, 165 (SAT-V) and 213 (SAT-M); for Puerto Rican students, 101 (SAT-V) and 162 (SAT-M) points. (I compared these grade categories because they represented the bulk of students: there were very few students with grades of "D" or below — one percent or less.) These results show that test scores have a high degree of relationship to high school grades for every group.

The same pattern is found for the distribution of total years of study in six academic subjects. With each increase in the number of courses taken in high school, there is a corresponding increase in Verbal and Mathematical test score means for all groups. Overall, the difference between those who took twenty or more course-years versus those who took fewer than fifteen course-years is 115 (SAT-V) and 128 (SAT-M) points for white non-Hispanic students, 116 (SAT-V) and 123 (SAT-M) points for Latin American students, 104 (SAT-V) and 111 (SAT-M) points for Mexican American students, and 93 (SAT-V) and 113 (SAT-M) points for Puerto Rican students.

We must remind ourselves of the often repeated caution that *correlation does not imply causation*. The relationships shown here with course numbers cannot be interpreted causally since associations can be reciprocal. That is, students who have higher achievement levels in school will tend to take more academic courses and will have higher test means. We can also expect that students who take more courses in a given subject area will improve in their achievement in that subject area and in related skills. Nevertheless, the results show the pattern that we would expect to find if the tests were doing their job in terms of measuring academic skills. For every group, the higher achieving students who take more courses tend to receive higher test scores.

Despite this constant pattern within groups, there are mean differences between white non-Hispanic and Hispanic students when we hold constant grades or number of academic courses. The source of these differences deserves further investigation. Perhaps if parental education, language background, course grades, and number of nonremedial academic courses were controlled for jointly (not just one at a time as they are in these tables), these differences would be further reduced. Also, as Richard

Durán shows, there is evidence from data sets such as High School and Beyond and NAEP that Hispanic students are overrepresented in high schools with fewer resources, or in curriculum tracks within high schools that have less demanding courses (Durán 1992). Thus, quality of schooling may be associated with lower test scores for Hispanic students after controlling for grades, number of courses, and background variables. Unfortunately, the data set from the *1987 College Bound Seniors Ethnic/Sex Data* (CEEB 1988) does not contain information on the quality of the high schools, which would enable us to test this hypothesis at this time.

4. Are there ethnic differences in the distribution of the numbers of academic courses taken in high school?

As shown in table 3−2, there are noticeable differences between Mexican American and white non-Hispanic students in the distribution of academic courses. While 35 percent of the white non-Hispanic population takes twenty or more year-long academic courses during high school, only 16 percent of Mexican American students take this many. Twenty percent of Mexican American students take fewer than fifteen course-years of academic subjects, whereas only 12 percent of white non-Hispanic students take this few.

Unlike the distribution for the Mexican American group, the distributions for the other two Hispanic groups resemble the white non-Hispanic pattern very closely, with differences smaller than 3 percent in every category.

5. What is the relationship between type of mathematics courses taken and test means? Are test means higher for students who take more mathematics courses?

The *1987 College Bound Seniors Ethnic/Sex Data* (CEEB, 1988) reported breakdowns in course work for specific subject areas in high school, from which I have selected only the mathematics courses (see table 3−3) because they can be expected to have a more direct and interpretable impact on test means than do other subject areas. As explained earlier, we cannot naively interpret these relationships to mean that taking one more course "raises" means by a specified number of points, because there are two reasons for expecting means to be higher for students who take more challenging math courses — self-selection and honing of skills.

Table 3–3. SAT Means and Percent Distribution by Type and Number of High School Mathematics Courses

	Mean SAT-V				Mean SAT-M				Percent Breakdown			
	NH White	LA	MA	PR	NH White	LA	MA	PR	NH White	LA	MA	PR
Type of Math Course												
(1) Algebra	447	388	380	361	490	434	424	402	97	97	98	96
(2) Geometry	453	395	388	368	498	443	435	412	94	91	90	88
(3) Trigonometry	475	418	414	388	535	479	480	445	57	55	44	51
(4) Precalculus	501	446	438	411	573	520	512	485	28	25	19	24
(5) Calculus	522	463	448	446	608	549	541	534	19	15	12	10
(6) Computer Math	465	409	397	386	523	470	454	435	26	22	19	21
(7) Other Math Courses	423	369	362	343	458	411	402	375	24	26	24	26
Difference in means:												
between (3) and (1)	28	30	34	27	45	45	56	43				
(4) and (1)	54	58	58	50	83	86	88	83				
Years of Study in Mathematics												
(a) More than 4 years	487	418	417	393	568	502	502	465	14	14	11	11
(b) 4 years	457	403	393	374	508	454	447	424	50	47	43	45
(c) 3 or 3½ years	424	368	367	345	444	396	396	373	29	31	35	32
(d) 2 or 2½ years	394	331	337	324	394	346	350	333	7	8	11	11
(e) 1 to 1½ years	363	297	308	300	344	316	323	313	0	1	1	1
(f) Less than 1 year	389	313	301	315	413	337	360	347	0	0	0	0
Difference in means												
between (a) and (d)	93	87	80	69	174	156	179	132				

Source: This table is derived from data from the *1987 College Bound Seniors Ethnic/Sex Data* (College Entrance Examination Board, 1988).
Note: NG White = non-Hispanic white; LA = Latin American other than MA, PR; MA = Mexican American; PR = Puerto Rican.

This is evident in table 3—3, which shows the percentage breakdown and SAT means by type of mathematics courses taken for each ethnic group. Students who took trigonometry, precalcalus and calculus in high school have higher means for *both* SAT-V and SAT-M scores than students who took only algebra. For example, among white non-Hispanic students, a little more than half the population of students take trigonometry, and these score 28 points higher in SAT-V and 45 points higher in SAT-M than students who have had only algebra. For Latin American, Mexican American, and Puerto Rican students, the same pattern is found. Those who took trigonometry had mean SAT-V scores that were 27 to 34 points higher than those who took algebra only and had mean SAT-M scores that were 43 to 56 points higher those those who took algebra only.

Also from table 3—3 we can see the breakdown in means by number of mathematics courses taken. As shown in this table, students who take more years of course work in mathematics get higher scores in both Verbal and Mathematics. For white non-Hispanic students, SAT-V and SAT-M means differ by 73 and 174 points respectively between the group that takes more than four years of math and the group that takes two to two-and-a-half years of math. For Latin American students, these differences are 87 (SAT-V) and 156 (SAT-M); for Mexican American students 80 (SAT-V) and 179 (SAT-M); and for Puerto Rican students, 69 (SAT-V) and 132 (SAT-M) points. (The groups with less than two years of math have very few cases and are not used for comparison purposes here.)

The higher verbal scores among students who took trigonometry and more mathematics courses probably reflect the tendency for higher achieving students to take more challenging courses (self-selection). The increases in mathematics were larger, which may indicate that students become more skilled in applied problem solving as they take higher levels of mathematics. However, we cannot rule out that there is more self-selection for higher mathematics skills than there is self-selection for verbal skills among students who take trigonometry and more mathematics courses. Nevertheless, the results show that the students with the best preparation in mathematics get higher SAT-M means.

In the interest of brevity, I have not included here the breakdowns by numbers of courses in English, social sciences, history, art, music, foreign and classical languages, natural sciences, and computer programming or data processing. However, the patterns generally show an increase in both Verbal and Mathematical means as the number of courses increases. Generally, courses in language arts and social sciences are associated with greater increases in Verbal versus Mathematical means, whereas the natural sciences are associated with greater increases in Mathematical means versus Verbal means. The relationship to SAT-V is less strong for art and music courses than for other courses in the humanities.

Now we shift our focus to the variables that, when held constant, noticeably reduce the size of group differences.

6. *How large are ethnic means differences when we compare Hispanic and white non-Hispanic students of the same (a) language background and (b) parental education?*

As you can see from table 3–4, for each aforementioned variable, there is a breakdown along two dimensions, (a) group membership (columns) and (b) values of a variable (rows). I will first look at row differences, that is, the variation within each group according to different values of the variable. Then I will examine column difference, that is, ethnic group differences within each value of that variable.

Language Background.   Table 3–4 shows the SAT means and percentage breakdown for each category of language background for white non-Hispanic and Hispanic students. Looking at means within each ethnic group, we see that for all groups, students who learned English and another language jointly had SAT-V and SAT-M scores that were lower by 25 to 50 points than those who learned English first. The differences depend on the ethnic group and are largest for the Puerto Rican group. If we compare each ethnic group within each language category, we see a dramatic narrowing of ethnic differences when we consider groups of the same language categories. Among students who learned English as their first language, the means for Latin American students are only 28 (SAT-V) and 34 (SAT-M) points lower than for white non-Hispanic students, as compared to 60 (SAT-V) and 67 (SAT-M) points lower in the total group, ignoring language background. This pattern is also found for Mexican American and Puerto Rican students and at every category of language background.

Hence, there is a very clear relationship here between language background and test performance for all groups, but it cannot be considered a strictly causal one. There are a number of other variables associated with language background, such as socioeconomic status and immigration history, that can also affect test performance.

Nevertheless, a large part of the difference between Hispanic groups

Table 3–4. SAT Means and Group Differences Broken Down by Language Background and Parental Education

	SAT-V Difference in SAT-V Mean Compared to NH White				SAT-M Difference in SAT-M Mean Compared to NH White				Percentage Breakdown			
	NH White	LA	MA	PR	NH White	LA	MA	PR	NH White	LA	MA	PR
Total Subpopulation	447	−60	−68	−87	489	−57	−65	−89	100	100	100	100
Language First Learned												
English First	449	−28	−46	−48	491	−34	−48	−65	94	21	44	23
English and Another	420	−25	−55	−69	460	−30	−53	−80	5	41	40	45
Other Language	396	−36	−46	−53	492	−70	−80	−83	1	38	16	32
Highest Level of Parental Education												
(1) No H.S. Diploma	385	−53	−42	−61	425	−45	−29	−70	2	19	27	18
(2) H.S. Diploma	419	−41	−60	−62	459	−44	−39	−71	37	35	43	40
(3) Associate Degree	428	−35	−36	−74	470	−31	−34	−71	7	6	7	7
(4) Bachelor's Degree	459	−45	−45	−89	503	−41	−49	−78	29	18	13	17
(5) Graduate Degree	486	−56	−54	−88	529	−47	−59	−77	25	22	10	17
Difference in means between (5) and (1)	101	98	89	74	104	102	74	97				

Source: This table is derived from data from the *1987 College Bound Seniors Ethnic/Sex Data* (College Entrance Examination Board 1988).
Note: NH White = non-Hispanic white; LA = Latin American other than MA, PR; MA = Mexican American; PR = Puerto Rican.

and white non-Hispanic students can be explained on the basis of language background and factors associated with language background. There are proportionately many fewer Hispanic students with an English-first background (21 percent to 44 percent depending on the group) in comparison to white non-Hispanic students who are 94 percent English-first background. Thus, language background and associated factors have a much larger net impact on the overall mean for Hispanic students than on the overall mean for white non-Hispanic students, who have mostly learned English as their first language.

Of course there is a large body of research dating back to the classical studies by Sánchez (1932a, 1932b, 1934a, 1934b) about the interpretation of aptitude and intelligence test scores for bilingual students. Obviously, scores on an aptitude test in English are affected not only by the level of aptitude of the individual but also by his or her level of proficiency in the language of the test. This relationship was more explicitly detailed by Alderman (1982) who examined the correlations between SAT scores, English proficiency, and aptitude in examinees' native language for Spanish-speaking students in Puerto Rico. In his study, English proficiency was measured by the Test of English as a Foreign Language and aptitude was measured by a test in Spanish used for college admissions in Puerto Rico. He found that the higher the level of English proficiency, the greater the correlation between the SAT and the aptitude test in Spanish. He partitioned the variability of SAT scores into two components: (1) proficiency in English and (2) aptitude. It was clear that for students with high levels of English proficiency, the SAT variability was mostly due to aptitude and was therefore an appropriate measure of aptitude. For students with very low levels of English proficiency, the SAT was primarily measuring proficiency in English rather than aptitude. Given that the large majority of Hispanic students living in the continental United States are more proficient in English than in Spanish, this research supports the use of an English aptitude test for the majority of Hispanic students. Alderman's findings, however, suggest that even when English proficiency is high, there may be some extraneous variability in the aptitude test scores that is related to language proficiency rather than to underlying aptitude.

At this point we need to ask what implications the effects of language background have in the evaluation to test bias. But first we have to rephrase the question because, as Anastasi (1982) has pointed out, the evaluation of test validity always has to be done in terms of the purpose for which, and the context in which, the test is being used. Hence the rephrased question is, *In the context of college admissions, in which English is the language of instruction, do mean differences in test scores attributable to language background give unambiguous evidence that tests are biased?* The answer is no, because language background may affect college performance in the same way and to the same degree that it affects test performance. If language affects college performance, this would imply that, in a predictive sense, the tests give an accurate reflection of college aptitude when the language of instruction is English.

Some studies of foreign students, for example, show that the Test of English as a Foreign Language (TOEFL) has low to moderate correlations with undergraduate and graduate success in U.S. universities, although quantitative scores on the SAT or GRE usually have higher correlations with college or graduate grades than do the TOEFL scores (reviews of studies, numbers 4, 11, 70, 71, 72, 78: Hale, Stansfield, and Duran, 1984). Thus, there is evidence that for foreign students, proficiency in English does have a modest impact on college performance in the majority of cases.

Of course, these results found with foreign students may not be generalizable to native-born American students with bilingual or multilingual backgrounds, who can be expected to have a much higher level of English proficiency. There are two interesting empirical questions that need to be addressed by examining language background and college performance. Specifically: (1) Do bilingual students perform better in college than one would expect on the basis of their test performance? and (2) Is there more accuracy of prediction (a higher validity coefficient) for students who are monolingual English speakers in comparison with the accuracy for bilinguals? The first of these questions was researched by Pennock-Román (1990); findings are summarized in the section on predictive validity.

Parental Education. Table 3–4 shows the percentage breakdown and SAT means by levels of parental education. For white non-Hispanic and Latin American students, the mean SAT-V and SAT-M scores for the group whose parents did not complete high school are approximately 100 points lower than for those whose parents had graduate degrees. These differences are 89 (SAT-V) and 74 (SAT-M) points for Mexican American students and 74 (SAT-V) and 97 (SAT-M) points for Puerto Rican students. For every group, average test scores increase with parental education level.

Looking within each category of parental education level and comparing ethnic group means, we see a narrowing of ethnic group differences when parental education is the same. Latin Americans differ from white non-Hispanic students of the same parental education by 35 to 56 points for the SAT-V test, and 31 to 47 points for the SAT-M test. These differences are smaller than overall group differences of 60 (SAT-V) and 57 (SAT-M) points when groups are not broken down by parental education level. A similar pattern is found for Mexican American students for whom the differences range from 36 to 60 points for the SAT-V test and 29 to 59 points for the SAT-M test when groups of the same parental education levels are compared. These differences are smaller than the overall group differences of 68 (SAT-V) and 65 (SAT-M) points when parental education level is ignored. For Puerto Rican students, the differences range from 61 to 88 points for the SAT-V test and 70 to 77 points for the SAT-M test. These differences are smaller than the overall group differences of 87 (SAT-V) and 89 (SAT-M) points when collapsing across parental education levels.

Hence, there is evidence here that ethnic group differences are associated in part with parental education level, and these differences are reduced when parental education levels are the same. Again, this finding is not surprising given the extensive body of evidence showing that students with well-educated parents receive a higher quality of education at home and attend better schools. Therefore, they are generally better prepared for college, and this advantage can be expected to be reflected in higher test scores.

Evaluations of Test Item Content

A relatively new methodology for investigating possible test bias at the item level has emerged in the last fifteen years. Typically, members of subpopulation groups (for example, male versus female, black versus white examinees) are contrasted on their performance on individual items, after controlling for overall total test score. Research in this area identifies items that are relatively easier or harder for one group versus another, after taking into account overall score. One way of categorizing this research is to say that it identifies items that are inconsistent with total test score for one subpopulation.

Initially, the area of study was called "item bias" research, but it is now more often referred to as the study of "differential item difficulty" or "differential item functioning," abbreviated DIF. The change in terminology arose from the many instances in which items found to have DIF were not necessarily biased or unfair. The judgment about an item's fairness is usually made on the relevance of the item to the trait being measured, what psychometricians call *content validity*.

An example of an item that had DIF, but was not considered biased, was reported by Breland et al. (1974). They found that an item requiring familiarity with square roots on a mathematics achievement test was relatively more difficult for Hispanic, black, and American Indian students than for white non-Hispanic students. Since the source of the discrepancy reflected a real deficiency in the students' knowledge of the basic concepts necessary for success in mathematics courses, it cannot be considered "unfair" or "biased." However, if a similar discrepancy relating to square roots was found for an item on a *reasoning test*, one could argue that specific knowledge of square roots was independent of reasoning ability and was, therefore, introducing extraneous sources of difficulty in the reasoning test. Hence, an item on a reasoning test involving square roots and demonstrating DIF would be considered biased.

In addition, it is possible that items or aspects of the test format that have references or language that might be stereotypical or objectionable to a subgroup may not necessarily show statistical discrepancies. Nevertheless, the consensus among psychometricians is that such items are unfair and should be eliminated, even if there is no evidence of an increase in performance for members of that group when the item is deleted (Shepard 1982). It is standard procedure that test items at Educational Testing Service (ETS) undergo a sensitivity review by a panel of judges before being included in a test form (see Hunter and Slaughter, 1980). Objectionable items are eliminated or modified before inclusion in a test form.

Items that survive these judgmental reviews are administered to examinees and are later analyzed statistically as part of preliminary item analyses before reporting scores to see if they show DIF for ethnic and gender subgroups. Items that are determined to be statistically discrepant for certain groups (that is, those with large statistical indexes of DIF) are flagged for scrutiny by panels of judges to identify the sources of group differences in performances. If the source of the difficulty is judged to be irrelevant to the test specifications, then the item is not included in computing the score. Also, pretested experimental items that show DIF are usully modified or eliminated from the pool of items to be used in assembling future tests. I know from personal experience in serving on two of these panels that occasionally these statistical methods catch subtle, unexpected content effects that get overlooked by sensitivity reviewers. Thus, the statistical DIF analysis procedures lead to refinements in the test.

Two of the most frequently used statistical methods with college admissions tests are the Mantel-Haenszel and the standardization methods. These procedures subdivide members of the two groups according to intervals of total test score. Then individuals from the two groups at the same score level are compared with respect to their performance on the given item. Although the specific statistical index values for the two methods are on different scales, they are almost perfectly correlated and classify items in the same way.

In the early years of DIF research, judges were not very successful in predicting which items would be discrepant or in finding reasons to explain group differences for those items that turned out to be statistically discrepant for certain groups. Often, items judged to be objectionable or differentially more difficult on an a priori basis did not show any group differences statistically, and judges often disagreed with one another (see review by Pennock-Roman, 1986a, 202–203). Now that we have more accurate statistical methods, the evidence about what content charac- teristics of items tend to produce DIF has been more consistent and interpretable. Often, it is possible to formulate hypotheses about the characteristics of items that lead to DIF, and these predictions are fre- quently confirmed with results from another study.

For example, one of the most consistent findings for Hispanic students, both foreign and American-born, is that vocabulary words that are true Spanish cognates are relatively easier for Hispanic examinees than for white non-Hispanic examinees (Breland et al., 1974; Alderman and Holland, 1981; Chen and Henning, 1985; Schmitt, 1988).

The study by Schmitt (1988) deserves special attention because it is the most extensive analysis to date of item characteristics associated with DIF for Hispanic students. She used the standardization method that compares the percentage of Hispanic versus non-Hispanic white examinees answering the item correctly when controlling for total score. Before discussing her findings, it is important to understand what this index means and what it does not mean.

The cutoff value for the statistical index for the standardization method (D_{STD}) was set of 0.5 for this study. When the value of the index for a particular item exceeds a value of 0.5, it means that on the average, Hispanic examinees answer the item correctly (or incorrectly) 5 percent more often than white non-Hispanic students with comparable scores, which is a very small difference in performance between the two groups. It does not mean that all of the members of one group failed it and that members of the other group answered it correctly. Futhermore, each flagged item is judged independent of examinee performance on other flagged items. An examinee who correctly answers one of the differentially easier items for his or her group will not necessarily answer correctly all of the other items that favor his or her group. Because the effects found by the statistical procedures are subtle and the responses of individual members of a group to the set of flagged items vary, the overall effect on total score produced by flagged items tends to be very small. For example, Shepard, Camilli, and Williams (1984) found that eliminating flagged items on a test changed group means on the test only by a trivial amount. Schmitt examined items that showed DIF in two alternate administrations of the SAT in 1983 and 1984 (which she calls Study One and Study Two) with very large samples. The cutoff set for this study was lower than the usual cutoff to flag items for scrutiny in operational procedures for generating scores or assembling tests.[1] This lower cutoff was set for research purposes in order to cast a wider net and have a larger number of potentially discrepant items that may show group differences. The SAT-M showed few items with DIF in both studies, so Schmitt focused her descriptions on the verbal subtest. From Study One, she identified four characteristics that were apparently associated with DIF on the verbal test. Then she rated the items for the SAT form in Study Two to see how strongly these characteristics were associated with DIF results.

The factors she identified that were associated with higher performance for Hispanic versus white non-Hispanic students in both studies, after controlling for overall test scores, were:

1. True cognates, or words with a common root and common meaning in English and Spanish (for example, pallid and pálido). There were some exceptions, which the author attributed to the presence of other elements of the item that cancelled this effect.
2. Reading comprehension items of special interest to Hispanic students. Specifically, in Study One, a passage on Mexican American women was relatively easier for Mexican American students but not for Puerto Rican students of the same overall score level. In Study Two, a passage on a black mathematician was relatively easier for both Puerto Rican and Mexican American groups in comparison to white non-Hispanic students of the same overall score level.

Factors associated with lower performance for Hispanic versus white non-Hispanic students in both studies after controlling for overall test scores were:

1. False cognates, that is, words that look identical or similar in the two languages but have different meanings in the context of the item (such as "enviable," which in Spanish means capable of being

mailed, or transportable). It should be noted that a given pair of similar words in the two languages can be true cognates for one item and false cognates for another because words have multiple meanings. Some of the meanings match in both language but others do not.

2. Homographs, or words that have more than one meaning (for example, bark of a tree and bark of a dog).

3. Vertical relationships, or word associations extraneous to the analogical relationship. Schmitt and Dorans (1990) found that vertical relationships between the stem and key or the stem and distractors in analogy test items also tended to handicap the performance of Hispanic examinees.

The effects related to language were more strongly evident in the Puerto Rican group in both studies because there is a greater incidence of bilingualism among college-bound Puerto Ricans than among college-bound Mexican American students (see table 3–4 in the section on language background and mean differences). Given that the reading passages provide more context for responses, it is not surprising that the majority of the items that handicapped Hispanic students were found in the antonym and analogy sections of the test.

These findings are highly consistent with research on DIF for black examinees, which has also shown some of the same characteristics as those found by Schmitt. The greater proportion of flagged items has been found among antonym and analogy items (Dorans and Kulick, 1986; Rogers and Kulick, 1987; Schmitt and Bleistein, 1987; Freddle and Kostin, 1990). Complicating the explanation of findings is that black and Hispanic examinees tend to reach fewer items than white non-Hispanic students with the same total score. Researchers found it difficult to disentangle factors that appeared to be associated with DIF because many characteristics were confounded with item position. When this differential-speededness effect was controlled, however, there were still proportionately more analogy items that were flagged as discrepant. Generally, minority examinees performed relatively better on more abstract, more supposedly difficulty antonyms and analogies occurring later in the section, and worse on early, easier items that had homographs. Furthermore, "vertical relationships," or extraneous associations between the stem and distractors, also tended to handicap black and Hispanic examinees. A think-aloud procedure with eleven black and eleven white non-Hispanic students suggested that black students do relatively better with more abstract, difficult analogies than with the easier ones, and this effect was found independently of item position (Freedle, Kostin, and Schwartz, 1987). However, this result is based on just a few cases and needs to be verified in future studies.

It is important to note that, proportionately, very few items showed DIF that handicapped Hispanic students on the SAT-V in these two studies. As shown in table 3−1 from Schmitt's study, out of a total of eighty-five items there were only five discrepant items that handicapped Mexicam Americans and seven for Puerto Ricans in Study One. These items were partially counterbalanced by three other items that favored Mexican Americans and five that favored Puerto Ricans. For Study Two (reported in table 3 of Schmitt's study), out of a total of eighty-five items, there were ten items that handicapped Mexican Americans and nine that handicapped Puerto Ricans. These were partially counterbalanced by four items that favored Mexican Americans and seven that favored Puerto Ricans.

Although Schmitt did not analyze how much the mean difference between Hispanic and white non-Hispanic students could be reduced if the discrepant items were eliminated, it is unlikely that discarding these items would have had much effect on total scores. The items handicapping Hispanic students were relatively few in number and were partially counterbalanced by the items that favored Hispanic students. Furthermore, the statistical discrepancies were small.[2] The index of the D_{STD} had values that equaled or exceeded .11 only once for eighty-five items in Study One and only once for eighty-five items in Study Two, and in both cases the most discrepant item favored Hispanic examinees. This means that the differences between groups in the probability of correctly answering the items were noticeable but not large enough to make an enormous difference in total score. Thus, it is very unlikely that eliminating these items would have substantially reduced ethnic differences on the test.

Another study of Hispanic students that led to interpretable DIF results was with the American College Test (ACT) and was reported by Lloyd (1982). She found that reading passages in the English Usage test had six discrepant items, three favoring white non-Hispanic students and three favoring Hispanic students. Two of the items favoring white non-Hispanic students had interpretable results. She found that these items involved skill in punctuating or adequately placing adjectives and adverbs in a series. These are linguistic features that may have been more difficult for bilingual students. In the Social Sciences Reading test, there were seven discrepant items, three favoring Hispanic students and four favoring white non-Hispanic students. Two out of four of the items favoring white non-Hispanic students required knowledge of the subject matter that was not contained in the reading passage. Thus, the latter finding suggests a deficiency in the educational background of the Hispanic candidates that made these items relatively more difficult. As with the SAT findings, it is unlikely that overall mean difference could be substantially reduced if the flagged items were deleted. There were relatively few flagged items and about half of them favored Hispanic students.

Although the small number of flagged items probably cannot completely account for mean differences between Hispanic and white non-Hispanic students, the results provide important information about the effects of bilingualism and other factors on test performance. It appears that bilingualism has both advantages and disadvantages in test performance, depending on particular linguistic features of the items. In discussing Schmitt's findings at a conference, Shepard (1987) proposed that false cognates and homographs introduce irrelevant sources of difficulty but that true cognates are not necessarily unfair. She recommended that the "proportion of Latin roots [items in the test] [should] mirror what is found, say, in typical freshman reading assignments" (3). However, by the same reasoning, one can argue that false cognates and homographs also occur in college texts and that they too should be proportionately sampled.

Thus, it is evident that procedures detecting discrepant items serve a very important function in revealing test content characteristics that give unexpected results for some groups. They are essential to opening a discussion about what type of content should be specified in a test. Shepard (1987, 5) has pointed out that, ideally, these methods can help us "to search out sources of irrelevant difficulty and to arrive at a better understanding of what a test measures." They can also serve an important diagnostic function because they can point to gaps in minority students' backgrounds. For example, in Breland et al. (1974), the item on square roots in the mathematics test was found to be relatively more difficult for minority students. Thus, it revealed a content deficiency in students' backgrounds that could be used to design curriculum for remedial instruction.

Nevertheless, it is important to keep in mind that this type of methodology is limited because results are always *relative* to other items on the test. Since the statistical methods control for overall test score to identify discrepant items, they cannot tell us if the test score as a whole is artifactually depressed for one group. To test whether the test score as a whole is biased is best achieved by an analysis of the accuracy of prediction of test scores for different groups in identifying who will succeed in college.

Predictive Validity of Admissions Tests for Hispanic Students

As we have seen in the previous sections: (1) Hispanic students score substantially below white non-Hispanic students on selective admissions tests; and (2) there are certain kinds of items that are differentially easier or harder for Hispanic students. In terms of formulating policy, it is important for research to determine whether these differences are reflected in college performance. One of the most direct ways that we can determine the accuracy of the information that tests provide about college aptitude for Hispanic students is to examine how well tests predict college grades. Unfortunately, predictive validity studies are hampered by many practical difficulties.

Methodological Difficulties in Predictive Validity Research

Investigations on predictive validity for Hispanic students have been few in number because there are many practical problems in obtaining large sample sizes in selective colleges. First, the sensitivity (power) of statistical methods to detect differential validity is reduced when sample sizes for Hispanic groups are small. Second, there are also problems in securing adequate identification of which students are truly Hispanic; for example, sometimes a Spanish surname has been used as the only identifier for Hispanicity. Census data indicate that Spanish surname fails to identify as Hispanic about a third of the students who consider themselves Hispanic. Furthermore, about a third of persons with surnames judged to be Spanish do not consider themselves Hispanic because they may be of Italian or Portuguese heritage or have only one very remote Spanish ancestor whose name has been handed down several generations to persons of mostly non-Spanish heritage. When self-reported ethnicity is used, we find that it is sometimes incomplete or inaccurate at many institutions.

Third, validity studies should include several institutions because results at one university may not be generalizable to others. The degree of selectivity of an institution reduces the variance in the predictors, which decreases the values of correlation coefficients and other indexes of prediction. Institutions with high variability among their students generally show higher correlations between college grades and test scores. Even when we control for differences in selectivity, there are variations in grading standards within an institution, and between institutions, that affect how well tests can predict performance at any given university. In sum, evaluations of tests should involve many institutions of different types.

Fourth, college grade point average (GPA) — which is the usual criterion of college success against which tests are evaluated — has many limitations. Grades are internally inconsistent (unreliable) because they vary unsystematically from instructor to instructor and also vary systematically across different fields of study. For example, Strenta and Elliott (1987) have documented that some departments, especially engineering and the physical sciences, have much harsher grading standards than others. The difficulty levels of individual courses are not taken into account, despite the fact that an "A" in a remedial course does not mean the same thing as an "A" in an honors course. If Hispanic students take more remedial courses or more science courses than do white non-Hispanic students, then their college GPAs are not comparable. This presents a serious problem in doing a validity study because artifactual effects will be found. These problems limit the reliability and validity of grades as a measure of college success, thus artifactually lowering correlations between grades and other measures.

A Review of Regression Terms Used to Test Predictive Accuracy in Two Groups

In comparing the accuracy with which tests predict college grades in a majority or reference group versus a minority or focal group, the preferred method is the use of regression equations. This statistical procedure yields several indexes of interest. One is the *multiple R*, which measures the overall accuracy of prediction of the college grades using all of the predictors. (If there is only one predictor, the multiple R and the Pearson correlation coefficient are the same.) When the multiple R is squared, it gives the proportion of variance in the college grades that is explained by the predictor variables. This index is free of the units of college grades. Unfortunately, the multiple R index is subject to some artifactual effects. If the variability of college grades, high school grades, or test scores is restricted in one group and less restricted in another, the multiple R, like a zero-order correlation coefficient, can appear to be lower in the group with restricted variance even when the groups differ little in accuracy of prediction.

Because of the artifactual problems involved in interpreting multiple Rs, there is another index that is preferred for comparing groups — *the standard error of estimate*. The standard error of estimate is the amount of variability of the *residuals*, which are the differences between actual and predicted college grades. It measures the amount of scatter of points away from the regression line and is a function of both the multiple R and the variance in college grades. The larger the multiple R, the smaller the scatter away from the regression line and the smaller the standard error of estimate. However, unlike the multiple R, the standard error of estimate is in the same units as the original college grades. It is less subject to interpretation problems if there is restriction in the variance of college grades because these restrictions in variance are also reflected in the standard error of estimate (see Cohen and Cohen, 1983, 104).

In applying regression analysis to detect group differences, we would expect the multiple R to be smaller (less relationship) and the standard error of estimate to be larger (because there would be more scatter) for Hispanic students if tests were less accurate in predicting college grades for Hispanic students than for white non-Hispanic students.

A third index important in multiple regression is the regression weight for each predictor. In the regression equation, estimates of individuals' college grades are found by weighting their high school grade point averages (HSGPAs) and test scores and summing these weighted values. The more that a variable contributes to prediction independently of the other variables, the higher its regression weight. Thus, these weights depend on the other variables in the equation. For example, when test scores are the only predictors, their regression weights are larger than when HSGPA is included as a predictor together with test scores. If differential validity exists, and tests are relatively better predictors for white non-Hispanic students than they are for Hispanic students, we would expect that the regression weights for white non-Hispanic students' test scores would be larger.

A fourth index of interest is the regression intercept, which represents the point at which the regression line crosses the axis of college grade values (Y) when all of the predictors have zero values. When there are two groups to be compared, with equal regression weights for the predictors, the difference in their intercepts reflects differences in the average value of college grades for any given value of the predictors. That is, if Hispanic students were to get higher grades in college than do white non-Hispanic students with the same test scores, despite having equal weights for the predictors, this means that the Hispanic students' regression line as a whole is higher on the graph than the line for white non-Hispanic students. In other words, the intercept is higher for Hispanic students than it is for white non-Hispanic students. If the intercept were higher for Hispanic students, assuming equal regression weights, one would expect that applying the white non-Hispanic students' regression line to values for Hispanic students would *under*predict Hispanic students' actual college performance. This underprediction can also occur if there are group differences in regression weights such that some portion of the regression line for Hispanic examinees is higher on the graph than the regression line for white non-Hispanic examinees.

In addition, some researchers have also examined how much improvement in the accuracy of prediction is achieved when tests are added to high school grades, in comparison to the accuracy found when high school grades are the sole predictor. (This is called *incremental* validity of tests). It involves taking the difference in two multiple Rs, the multiple R when the equation includes HSGPA plus test scores, minus the multiple R when only HSGPA is used. The difference in multiple Rs measures the improvement in selection of students for admissions (Beaton and Barone, 1981), whereas the difference between the two multiple R^2s measures the amount of additional variance in the college grades that is explained by adding test scores. Hence, if tests count relatively more for white non-Hispanic students, the incremental validity of the tests should be higher for white non-Hispanic students than for Hispanic students.

To summarize, consider what we would expect to find among these indexes if tests were not measuring college aptitude among minority students as well as they do among majority students. First, we might expect that the degree of relationship between scores and college grades would be smaller for Hispanic students, leading to smaller multiple Rs and larger standard errors of estimates for Hispanic students. A second way that tests could be biased is if the verbal or mathematical sections, or both subtest scores, counted less as predictors, leading to lower regression weights for test scores in the regression line for Hispanic students than in the line for white non-Hispanic students. A third possibility is that test scores would systematically underpredict the college performance of Hispanic students — that is, students would receive higher college grades than one would expect on the basis of test scores, which could arise in several ways due to differences in intercept values or regression weights for the two groups. A fourth possibility is that if the tests counted less in the prediction of college grades for Hispanic students, the improvement in prediction when tests are added to grades (difference in multiple Rs as defined above) would be smaller for Hispanic students than for white non-Hispanic students.

Thus, there are several basic questions that are generally asked in comparing regression lines for two groups. One question is how strong is the overall relationship of all predictors (taken jointly) with the criterion (which is measured by the standard error of estimate and the multiple R). A second question is whether there are differences in the degree of relationship between each predictor and college grades (the raw regression weight for each variable). The third question is whether the use of the reference group's regression equation systematically overpredicts or underpredicts grades for most persons in the minority or focal group (which could be the result of differences in regression intercepts and/or regression weights). The fourth question (which is not always asked) is whether the incremental validity of tests beyond the prediction accuracy found with just HSGPA is lower for Hispanic students than for white non-Hispanic students.

Durán's Review (1983) of Predictive Validity Studies

The most complete review of predictive validity studies for Hispanic students was authored by Durán (1983) in which more than fourteen independent analyses were reviewed. The general findings are as follows:

1. Overall, there were no dramatic differences in regression systems between Hispanic and white non-Hispanic students, although some subtle differences were consistently found. In general, Hispanic students tended to perform less well in college than did white non-Hispanic students to a degree that was commensurate with their high school grades or rank and lower test scores.

2. The most consistent subtle difference found was that often there were lower multiple Rs for Hispanic students, for all predictors but especially for test scores. These differences tended to be small and nonsignificant. Rarely did the authors of the validity study discuss whether differences in the multiple Rs and correlations were due to differences in group variances for predictors and college grades. In a footnote, Durán (1983, 139) cautioned that "a more sensitive analysis of differences in prediction should rely on interpretation of standard-error-of-estimate statistics. For the most part, standard-error-of-estimate statistics were not directly available in the predictive validity studies reviewed in this report; in contrast, multiple R or R^2 statistics were readily available for studies."

3. The median zero-order correlations between college grades and predictors showed that the highest correlation found for Hispanic students was for HSGPA, and it differed little from the correlation found for white non-Hispanic students. In contrast, the correlation with quantitative scores was the lowest and had the largest difference between Hispanic and white non-Hispanic students. This correlation was reported separately for only nine studies.

4. Few studies reported explicitly the incremental validity of tests

over the prediction achieved with HSGPA. Goldman and Widawsky (1976) found that it was less than 10 percent for Hispanic students at four campuses of the University of California. They explained this finding by pointing to a larger correlation between test scores and high school grades for Hispanic students than there was for white non-Hispanic students.

5. None of the researchers who tested for ethnic differences in regression intercepts found evidence of underprediction of Hispanic students' grades, and in fact, one study found substantial overprediction (that is, Hispanic students' actual college performance was lower than that predicted by the white non-Hispanic equation). But many researchers did not explicitly test for under- or overprediction.

Hence, there is some subtle evidence of lower accuracy of prediction of tests for Hispanic students in comparison to white non-Hispanic students. Nevertheless, tests have some incremental validity over the prediction based on grades alone for Hispanic students, and this incremental validity varies according to university. For example, it was substantial for students at the University of California at Davis in the Goldman and Widawski (1976) report. These conclusions must be considered tentative because there are many limitations in the studies reviewed thus far. These limitations include the following:

1. Because most of the universities studied were public institutions in the southwest, the research is primarily based on Mexican Americans. With the exception of Astin's (1982) investigation of Puerto Rican college students, there had been no predictive validity on other subgroups at the time of Durán's review. The states and types of institutions sampled were also limited.

2. Often, Hispanic students were only one of several racial/ethnic groups considered, so that results were not reported completely enough to examine all the questions we would want answered. Frequently, important information such as intercorrelations, standard errors of estimate, and degrees of incremental validity was not reported.

3. Although some studies did take gender into account by doing regression analyses separately for males and females, this control was not available in all studies. Controlling for gender can make a difference if there are relatively more females in one group than in another because females consistently get higher college grades than males for the same level of test scores. Furthermore, very few

studies controlled for the effect of different majors on college grades.

4. The effects of language on predictive validity were not addressed by the majority of studies.

Research on Predictive Validity for Hispanic Students Conducted after Durán's Review

In a study recently completed by Pennock-Román (1990)[2] no evidence was found for a lower degree of relationship between the SAT-V and SAT-M tests and college grades for Hispanic than for white non-Hispanic students at six universities. Although some multiple R^2 indexes were lower for Hispanic students, the standard errors of estimate tended to be essentially the same or slightly smaller than those for white non-Hispanic students, which indicated equal accuracy of prediction for Hispanic students. It appears that the lower multiple R^2 indexes were artifactually smaller because of less variability in college grades. Therefore, the results of this research suggest that, at the institutions studied, college achievement for Hispanic students could be predicted from SAT scores and high school grades to the same degree that college achievement for white non-Hispanic students could be predicted using these preadmissions measures.

In regard to other regression parameters in the above study, some small group differences were found in regression weights and in intercept coefficients. However, the differences in regression weights (relative importance of predictors) were not consistent in direction across universities. Specifically, at one university the SAT-M test was of more relative importance in prediction for Hispanic students than for white non-Hispanic students. At another university, the reverse was found, in that the SAT-M was relatively less important in the prediction of college grades for Hispanic than for white non-Hispanic students. No group differences were found in the relative importance of high school grades as a predictor of college grades. On the other hand, at four out of six universities, high-school grades tended to overpredict college achievement for Hispanic students when the white non-Hispanic equation was used because of intercept coefficient differences. This degree of overprediction was related to several factors, including the greater tendency of Hispanic students to major in science fields, which are graded more severely than nonscience fields.

The effect of language background on prediction was also addressed by Pennock-Román (1990). The results showed that students' English proficiency was related to performance on the SAT, but that it added little improvement to the prediction of college grades beyond the accuracy of prediction attained using the SAT and other preadmissions measures. Students' Spanish proficiency and frequency of Spanish use, however, did improve the prediction of college grades, although the results were not consistent across universities. That is, at two universities, students with higher levels of Spanish proficiency and Spanish use tended to receive higher grades than those with lower levels of Spanish proficiency and use, all other things being equal. However, at two other universities, the opposite pattern was found. The findings suggested that the college climate may play a role in the college achievement of bilingual students.

In general, differences in regression systems between white non-Hispanic students within the same university in the study were small in comparison to the large differences among institutions. The importance of tests and high school achievement for the prediction of college grades varied greatly across universities for both groups.

Although the new evidence from the above study has expanded our knowledge about the prediction of Hispanic students' college achievement, the studies are few, sample sizes for Hispanic groups have often been small, and the results have shown much variation across institutions. Thus, definitive conclusions about group differences in prediction would be premature. On the whole, the results from the investigations to date support the use of standardized tests in selective college admissions of Hispanic students. In addition, the findings showed that each university should determine for itself how to weight these factors because the importance of tests versus high-school grades depends in part on the characteristics of the university. At the majority of institutions, however, more weight should be given to high-school achievement as a predictor.

It is important to remember that in selective admissions in higher education there are many other goals besides obtaining students who will receive high grades in college (Linn, 1982). A discussion of frameworks for weighting student characteristics, group membership, and test scores in selective admissions (that is, the so-called fair selection models) is beyond the scope of this chapter, but the interested reader can refer to Pennock-Román (1986b).

Student Awareness of Types of Preparation Needed for College and Admissions Tests

When we focus on ethnic differences in admissions test scores and how lower scores affect access to college for Hispanic students, we tend to overlook what may be the largest problem of access—the fact that so many Hispanic students do not take admissions tests at all. Hispanic students are proportionately overrepresented at two-year colleges that traditionally do not require taking an admissions test and are underrepresented in the population that seeks acceptance to four-year institutions. A study by Lee and Ekstrom (1987) has shed light on some of the complex factors that influence the flow of students in the educational pipeline. In the abstract and discussion, they summarized their findings as follows:

> Using data from the first and second follow-ups of High School and Beyond, including student self-reports, test scores, and high school transcripts, we found that guidance counseling services appear to be unequally available to all public high school students. Students from families of lower socioeconomic status (SES), of minority status, and from small schools in rural areas are less likely to have access to guidance counseling for making...important decisions [about selecting a curriculum track or planning an appropriate course of study] at the beginning of their high school careers. Moreover, students who lack access to guidance counseling are more likely to be placed in nonacademic curricular tracks and to take fewer academic math courses. It appears that students who may need such guidance the most, since they come from home environments where knowledge of the consequences of curricular choices is limited, are least likely to receive it in their schools. (287)

> [Specifically,] less than one-fourth of all high school students select a curriculum with any assistance from a counselor, and only about half of all high school students receive counselor assistance in program planning. Moreover, only slightly more than half of all high school students have access to counseling for their plans after high school....These figures suggest that there is likely to be a group of students who might have either the ambition or the ability to attend college but who have no contact with a counselor until the end of their high school years. As a consequence, such students may not have entered a curriculum track providing preparation for college or, regardless of track placement, may not have taken courses that are either necessary or desirable preparation for college. [306]

Although Lee and Ekstrom (1987) do not explicitly address how counselor access may affect students' preparation for taking college admissions tests, we can certainly expect that these inequities in access to counseling lead to a lack of information about how students should prepare for admissions tests. This lack of guidance probably exacerbates ethnic group differences in test scores because Hispanic students are overrepresented in schools with poor resources.

Fortunately, some states such as California are addressing this problem. As a result of the Tanner initiative, a program has been implemented recently in California to provide minority students in disadvantaged inner-city and rural districts with more college admissions counseling and test-taking guidance. This program reaches out to many students who would normally not attempt to take the SAT and who would most likely not be admitted to four-year colleges.

Concurrently, in a collaboration between the Hispanic Higher Education Coalition, ETS, and the College Board, a kit to help students prepare for the Preliminary Scholastic Aptitude Tests (PSAT) was developed. This kit, *Test Skills: For Teachers of Hispanic students*,[3] was developed primarily by Lorraine Gaire with initial assistance from Charlene Rivera. It was designed to encourage more Hispanic students to register and take the PSAT and to become better prepared for college. It has enough material for a fairly lengthy (one semester or more) orientation program and includes review of basic mathematics courses and many other lesson plans. This kit was piloted at several school districts that have implemented the Tanner Act program.

Don Powers, Monte Perez, and I surveyed student participants (mostly ninth, tenth, and eleventh graders) in several of these programs and obtained their reactions to the kit (Pennock-Román, Powers, and Perez, 1991). The students' reactions to the test-familiarization kit were overwhelmingly positive. It was apparent from their comments that they viewed the course as an opportunity to improve their problem-solving and basic skills, not just to gain test-wiseness. Most of the students wanted the program to be extended and to have more materials. As a result of the program, the number of students intending to take the PSAT or SAT increased from 58 percent to 86 percent.

Thus, it is important to note that the group of students involved in the survey included 42 percent of students who most likely would not have attempted to take the PSAT or SAT tests, and thus, these results give us information on students who are normally not included in our SAT samples. The results of the survey revealed the general neglect these students experience in guidance about the college admissions process and test preparation. One student commented that before participating in the program he was not aware that admissions tests were required for admission to many colleges.

Before viewing the survey results, I expected much of the material in the kit to be new to the students, but I expected perhaps 95 percent to be aware of how to fill in the answer sheet and perhaps 80 percent to be familiar with test directions, test-taking strategies, and the more common types of items such as reading comprehension. But I was wrong. More than 45 percent of the students found that they learned something new from the unit on answer sheets, more than 90 percent learned something new about budgeting their time, understanding the PSAT directions, when and how to guess, and how to approach different kinds of test questions. One student commented that before the program she didn't know how to tell the difference between antonyms and synonyms. This lack of awareness about routine test-taking skills is surprising, given that the use of multiple-choice tests is so widespread. It suggests that in the school districts represented in the survey, multiple-choice tests are administered without adequate preparation of the students and that insufficient time is dedicated to a diagnostic review once test results are received.

In sum, together with Lee and Ekstrom's (1987) findings, our experience suggests that there are many Hispanic students with the ambition and motivation to attend college who lack even the most basic guidance information on how to prepare themselves for college and for admissions tests. This is a population that usually does not appear on tables of results on the SAT. They are the ones who have the most barriers to access to college because they find out too late what steps to take for the college admissions process. The successful implementation of the Tanner Act programs suggests that comprehensive guidance counseling and test-familiarization can make a big difference in these students' lives.

Summary and Conclusions

Let us recapitulate some of the points made in this chapter.

1. Mean differences on the SAT between Hispanic and white non-Hispanic students are relatively large, particularly for Puerto Rican students, and they are associated with differences in language background, parental education, high school grades, and type of academic courses taken. The relationship between test scores and the aforementioned factors is consistent with the view that the tests measure the quality of a students' preparation for college in which the language of instruction is English. However, predictive validity studies are the only way to evaluate whether the mean differences in test scores reveal real deficits in the quality of preparation for college.

2. In studies of differential item functioning, or DIF, the number of items showing differential difficulty levels has constituted only a small percentage of the total test items, and the results have not been linked to differences in predictive validity. Hence, it is not

known if the characteristics leading to unexpected group differences in items represent irrelevant sources of difficulty or if they correspond to real differences in college performance. Some kinds of test item types (specifically, analogies and antonyms) tend to be differentially more difficult for Hispanic students and other minorities. There are some indications that the problems occur primarily with the supposedly easier test items, perhaps because they have more homographs. It is interesting that some results suggest that more abstract kinds of relationships and words are relatively easier for minority students. For Hispanic students, bilingualism is sometimes an asset and sometimes a handicap. Items that contain English words that are true cognates of Spanish words in the stem and answer choices are easier, and those with false cognates are more difficult. Reading passages with content of special interest for minority students are also relatively easier for minority students.

3. A review of pre-1983 studies on predictive validity suggests that tests may be slightly less accurate in predicting Hispanic students' success in college than they are in predicting white non-Hispanic students' success, but more recent investigations show equal accuracy. More research needs to be done on Puerto Rican and Latin American groups. In particular, the effect of language factors and artifactual effects of course difficulty on grading standards need to be investigated. In the majority of studies, there was no evidence that the tests underestimated the college performance of Hispanic students.

4. The largest barrier to access to college for Hispanic students may be inequity in the availability of guidance counseling in junior and senior high school. Since Hispanic students' parents are often not college educated, their family resources cannot compensate for this lack of adequate guidance. Many students with the desire to attend college receive little or no orientation and thus enter nonacademic tracks, or take the wrong courses, and fail to get basic information about college admissions and test preparation. There may be a very large proportion of Hispanic students who inadvertently avoid taking the SAT or the ACT, not realizing their connection to college admissions.

The evidence concerning the adequacy of college admissions tests for Hispanic students is correlational and not experimental in nature and as such has many ambiguities and missing information. Based on the data that are available at this time, I believe that there is room for improvement in current admissions tests, but the major cause of differences in tests scores between Hispanic and white non-Hispanic is inequity in the quality of schooling and guidance counseling. Some subtle effects related to item formats and types of wording have been found by DIF research, but these effects are too small and infrequent to account for the large gaps in means.

On the other hand, there are some large mean differences between students who have had fifteen versus twenty academic course years in high school and specific kinds of courses in mathematics. As pointed out by Messick and Jungeblut (1981), coaching or short-term study for test preparation tends to lead to negligible score gains because underlying skills are not sufficiently altered. However, his analysis suggests that large score gains on the SAT can be achieved with long-term preparation (at least one semester) that develops the overall educational skills and background of the student. Thus, we can expect that the best way to raise the mean scores for Hispanic students is to ensure that they enter academic tracks in school and take as many challenging courses as they can fit into their schedule, beginning in ninth grade, if not sooner.

This step is particularly crucial for Mexican American students. In looking at the course-taking patterns of students who have taken the SAT shown in the first part of this chapter, it appears that Mexican American students, the largest Hispanic group, are not taking adequate numbers of courses for preparation in academic areas. We can expect the situation would be much worse if we were to include all of the other students who do not attempt to take the SAT or ACT.

For many decades, validity research has shown that high-school records are better predictors of college performance than aptitude test scores. However, aptitude test scores give an objective basis for correcting for differences in competitiveness among high schools. A "B" from a magnet school attended by the best students in a school district is not the same as a "B" from a less competitive high school. Thus, the value of adding the SAT or ACT to high school grades for college admissions in the evaluation of Hispanic students depends in part on the university. If a university draws students from a very heterogeneous collection of high schools, test scores can help admissions officers to evaluate student records. The more selective a university is, the more relevant it finds the test score information because the applicants to highly selective institutions are often mostly A-average or B-average students. The test score information helps to identify who received the better quality of preparation and who can keep up with the pace of work at that institution. Although the few studies so far suggest this corrective function served by tests is more successful for white non-Hispanic students, each university has to conduct its own evaluation of the incremental validity of tests for Hispanic students in their own circumstances in order to make the best use of test score information.

Future research should address the following questions: Does the accuracy of prediction of college grades decrease or increase when test items that are differentially harder or easier for minority students are included? Do tests underestimate the college performance of bilingual students? How accurately do test scores predict grades in college for Hispanic students when differences in grading standards by fields and course difficulty are taken into account? How can we improve access to adequate counseling and college preparation for minority students? Furthermore, these questions need to be investigated with a wider variety of tests. Currently we mostly have information on aptitude tests for undergraduate admissions.

Returning to Linn's (1982) caution cited at the beginning of this chapter, we must keep in mind that the psychometric quality of tests is only one component in the evaluation of tests; the benefits and losses that using tests can potentially bring to institutions, individuals, and society as a whole must also be considered.

Acknowledgments

This chapter is a revision of a paper presented on February 26, 1988 in San Antonio, Texas, at a meeting organized by the Intercultural Development Research Association for the National Commission on Testing and Public Policy. It was originally entitled "The Status of Research on Selective Admissions Tests and Hispanic Students in Postsecondary Education." The paper and meeting were sponsored by the Ford Foundation and the University of California at Berkeley. An earlier version of this chapter appeared as an Educational Testing Service Research Report RR-88-36.

The author gratefully acknowledges Leonard Ramist's suggestions for the interpretation of the relationships between academic course-taking and group mean differences in the *1987 College Bound Seniors Ethnic/Sex Data* (College Entrance Examination Board, 1988) and for many other comments. Henry Braun, James Deneen, Alicia Schmitt, Donald Powers, and Carol Slaughter also contributed valuable points in their reviews of this manuscript. Victor Bunderson and Hugh Cline, of Educational Testing Service, provided the funds for the preparation of this manuscript.

Notes

1. In operational item analyses, the cutoff value used to flag items for review is expressed in units of the Mantel-Haenszel delta difference index (abbreviated MH D-Diff). By consensus of psychometricians at ETS and outside consultants, the cutoff value has been set equal to or higher than 1.5, provided that the index is also statistically significantly different from 1.00 (Zieky, 1987). Since the standardization index is used primarily in

research and not in operational item analyses, it has not been necessary to derive the cutoff value for the standardization indexes that is equivalent to the one for MH D-Diff. A general solution to the functional relationship between the standardization index and the Mantel-Haenszel has not been worked out. However, the cutoff for the standardization index that would be equivalent to the 1.5 Mantel-Haenszel cutoff can be estimated through the results of an empirical study by David Wright (1986). This study gives correlations and descriptive statistics that allow us to estimate roughly the regression of the indexes from the standarization method on the Mantel-Haenszel index, and vice-versa, although it is not clear that this relationship generalizes to samples other than the one used by Wright. Using this rough approximation, I found that a cutoff of 1.5 in the MH D-Diff would be approximately equal to a D_{STD} of .11. Thus, the cutoff value that Schmitt used was slightly less than half the size of the estimate for the usual cutoff for operational analyses. Her cutoff would be approximately equal to a MH D-Diff of .68, which flags more items as potentially discrepant than the cutoff of 1.5.

2. The results of this study were not presented at the meeting in San Antonio in February 1988.

3. The kit, *Testskills: For Teachers of Hispanic Students*, is available from ETS, Box 6721, Princeton, NJ 08541−6721.

References

Alderman, D. L. (1982) Language proficiency as a moderator variable in testing academic aptitude, *Journal of Educational Psychology*, 74, 580−87.

Alderman, D. L. and P. W. Holland. (1981) Item performance across native language groups on the Test of English as a Foreign Language. TOEFL Research Report no. 9. Princeton, NJ: Educational Testing Service (ETS).

Anastasi, A. (1982) *Psychological testing*. New York: Macmillan.

Arbeiter, S. (1985) *Profiles, college bound seniors*. New York: College Entrance Examination Board.

Astin, A. W. (1982) *Minorities in American higher education*. San Francisco: Jossey-Bass.

Beaton, A. E. and J. L. Barone. (1981) The usefulness of selection tests in college admissions. ETS Research Report no. RR-81−12. Princeton: Educational Testing Service (ETS).

Breland, H. M. (1979) Population validity and college entrance measures. Research Monograph no. 8. New York: College Entrance Examination Board (CEEB).

Breland, H. M., Stocking, M., Pinchak, B. M. and N. Abrams. (1974) The cross-cultural stability of mental test items: An investigation of response patterns for ten sociocultural groups. ETS Project Report 74−2. Princeton: Educational Testing Service (ETS).

Chen, Z. and G. Henning. (1985) Linguistic and cultural bias in language proficiency tests. *Language Testing*, 2, 155−63.

Cohen, J. and P. Cohen. (1983) *Applied multiple regression/correlation analysis for the behavioral sciences*. (2d ed). Hillsdale: Lawrence Erlbaum.

College Entrance Examination Board. (1982) *Profiles, college bound seniors*. New York: Author.

College Entrance Examination Board. (1987) National scores on SAT show little change in 1987; New data on student academic backgrounds available. Press release, September 22.

College Entrance Examination Board. (1988) *1987 College bound seniors ethnic/ sex data*. Princeton: College Entrance Examination Board.

Cronbach, L. J. (1975) Five decades of public controversy over mental testing, *American Psychologist*, 30, 1–14.

Dorans, N. J. and E. Kulick. (1986) Demonstrating the utility of the standardization approach to assessing unexpected differential item performance on the Scholastic Aptitude Test, *Journal of Educational Measurement*, 23 (4), 355–68.

Durán, R. P. (1983) *Hispanics' education and background: Predictors of college achievement*. New York: College Entrance Examination Board (CEEB).

Durán, R. P. (1988) Testing of Hispanic students: Implications for secondary education. (In this volume)

Durán, R. P., Enright, M. K. and D. A. Rock. (1985) Language factors and Hispanic freshmen's student profile. College Board Report no. 85–3. New York: College Entrance Examination Board (CEEB).

Freedle, R. and I. Kostin. (1990) Item difficulty of four verbal item types and an index of different item functioning for Black and White examinees, *Journal of Educational Measurement*, 27, 329–430.

Freedle, R., Kostin, I. and L. Schwartz. (1987) A comparison of strategies used by black and white students in solving SAT verbal analogies using a thinking aloud method and a matched percentage-correct design. ETS Research Report No. RR-87-48. Princeton: Educational Testing Service (ETS).

Goldman, R. D. and R. Richards. (1974) The SAT prediction of grades for Mexican American versus Anglo-American students of the University of California, Riverside, *Journal of Educational Measurement*, 11 (2), 129–35.

Goldman, R. D. and B. N. Hewitt. (1975) An investigation of test bias for Mexican American college students, *Journal of Educational Measurement*, 12, 187–96.

Goldman, R. D. and B. N. Hewitt. (1976) Predicting the success of black, Chicano, oriental and white college students, *Journal of Educational Measurement*, 13, 107–17.

Goldman, R. D. and M. Widawski. (1976) An analysis of types of errors in the selection of minority college students, *Journal of Educational Measurement*, 13, 185–200.

Hale, G. A., Stansfield, C. W. and R. P. Duran. (1984) Summaries of studies involving the Test of English as a Foreign Language, 1963–1982. TOEFL Research Report no. 16. Princeton: Educational Testing Service (ETS).

Hunter, R. V. and C. D. Slaughter. (1980) *ETS test sensitivity review process*. Princeton: Educational Testing Service (ETS).

Lee, V. E. and R. B. Ekstrom. (1987) Student access to guidance counseling in high school. *American Educational Research Journal*, 24, 287–310.

Linn, R. L. (1982) Ability testing: Individual differences, prediction, and differential prediction. In *Ability testing: Uses, consequences, and controversies*, ed. A. K. Wigdor and W. R. Garner, 335–88. Washington, DC: National Academy Press.

Loyd, B. H. (1982) Analysis of content-related bias for Anglo and Hispanic students. Paper presented at the annual meeting of the American Educational Research Association, March, New York.

Messick, S. (1987) Validity. ETS Research Report no. RR-87-40. Princeton, NJ: Educational Testing Service (ETS).

Messick, S. and A. Jungeblut. (1981) Time and method in coaching for the SAT, *Psychological Bulletin*, 89, 191–216.

Olmedo, E. L. (1977) Psychological testing and the Chicano. In *Chicano psychology*, ed. J. L. Martinez, Jr. New York: Academic Press.

Pennock-Román, M. (1986a) New directions for research on Spanish-language tests and test-item bias. In *Latino college students*, ed. M. A. Olivas, 193–220, chapter 7. New York: Teachers College Press.

Pennock-Román, M. (1986b) Fairness in the use of tests for selective admissions of Hispanics. In *Latino college students*, ed. M. A. Olivas, 246–80, chapter 9. New York: Teachers College Press.

Pennock-Román, M., (1990). *Test validity and language background: A study of Hispanic American students at six universities*. New York: College Entrance Examination Board.

Pennock-Román, M., Powers, D. and M. Perez. (1991) A preliminary evaluation of *Testskills*: A kit to prepare Hispanic students for the PSAT/NMSQT. In *Assessment* and *Access*, eds. G. D. Keller, J. R. Deneen, and R. J. Magallán, 243–264, Chapter 10. Albany, NY: State University of New York Press.

Ramist, L. and S. Arbeiter. (1983) *Profiles, college bound seniors*. New York: College Entrance Examination Board.

Ramist, L. and S. Arbeiter. (1984) *Profiles, college bound seniors*. New York: College Entrance Examination Board.

Ramist, L. and S. Arbeiter. (1986) *Profiles, college bound seniors*. New York: College Entrance Examination Board.

Rogers, H. J. and E. Kulick. (1987) An investigation of unexpected differences in item performance between blacks and whites taking the SAT. 1986 NCME paper in *Differential item functioning on the Scholastic Aptitude Test*, ed. A. P. Schmitt and N. J. Dorans. ETS Research Report No. RM-87-1. Princeton: Educational Testing Service (ETS).

Sánchez, G. I. (1932a) Group differences and Spanish-speaking children: A critical review, *Journal of Applied Psychology*, 16, 549–58.

Sánchez, G. I. (1932b) Scores of Spanish-speaking children on repeated tests, *Journal of General Psychology*, 40, 223–31.

Sánchez, G. I. (1934a) Bilingualism and mental measures: A word of caution, *Journal of Applied Psychology*, 18, 765–72.

Sánchez, G. I. (1934b) The implications of a basal vocabulary for the measurement of the abilities of bilingual children, *Journal of Social Psychology*, 5, 395–402.

Scheuneman, J. D. (1982) A posteriori analyses of biased items. In *Handbook of methods for detecting test bias*, ed. R. A. Berk. Baltimore: Johns Hopkins University Press.

Schmitt, A. P. (1988) Language and cultural characteristics that explain differential item functioning for Hispanic examinees on the Scholastic Aptitude Test, *Journal of Educational Measurement*, 25, 1–13.

Schmitt, A. P. and C. A. Bleistein. (1987) Factors affecting differential item functioning for black examinees on Scholastic Aptitude Test analogy items. ETS Research Report no. RR-87-23. Princeton: Educational Testing Service (ETS).

Schmitt, A. P. and N. J. Dorans. (1990) Differential item functioning for minority examinees on the SAT. *Journal of Education Measurement, 27*, 67–81.

Shepard, L. A. (1982) Definitions of bias. In *The handbook of methods for detecting test bias*, ed. R. A. Berk. Baltimore: Johns Hopkins University Press.

Shepard, L. A. (1987) Discussant comments on the National Council on Measurement in Education (NCME) Symposium. In *Differential item functioning on the Scholastic Aptitude Test*, ed. A. P. Schmitt and N. J. Dorans. ETS Research Report No. RM-87-1. Princeton: Educational Testing Service (ETS).

Shepard, L. A., Camilli, G. and D. M. Williams. (1984) Accounting for statistical artifacts in item bias research, *Journal of Educational Statistics*, 9, 93–128.

Strenta, A. C. and R. Elliot. (1987) Differential grading standards revisited, *Journal of Educational Measurement*, 24, 281–91.

Warren, J. (1976) *Prediction of college achievement among Mexican American students in California*. College Board Research and Development Report. Princeton: Educational Testing Service (ETS).

Wright, D. (1986) An empirical comparison of the Mantel-Haenszel and standardization methods of detecting differential item performance. Paper presented at the annual meeting of the National Council on Measurement in Education, April, San Francisco.

Zieky, M. (1987) Procedures for use of differential item difficulty statistics in test development. Memorandum for ETS test developers, September. Princeton: Educational Testing Service (ETS).

4 PSYCHOMETRIC G AND ACHIEVEMENT

Arthur R. Jensen

Introduction

Education's traditional value of enhancing the quality of life for the individual need not be eclipsed by the growing recognition of its importance to the national welfare. A well-educated population is now deemed crucial in this technological era. The cultivation of excellence in the kinds of achievement that depend on an educated work force is an undisputed goal in all industrial societies. Regardless of differences in coutries' political and economic systems, we see implicit agreement with Adam Smith's dictum that the wealth of nations depends on the abilities of their people. Virtually every head of state appoints a minister of education. The government of Venezuela, in addition, even appointed a "Minister for the Development of Intelligence." Obviously, the modern world perceives the supply of educated intelligence as vitally related to the general welfare.

Our own nation's anxiety about the general level of attainment in our schools was voiced officially in *A Nation at Risk: The Imperative for Educational Reform*, a report of the National Commission on Excellence in Education (1983). The commission noted studies from the past two decades that indicate a general decline in the amount of scholastic learning, with achievement levels below those of many other industrialized countries. It also recognized the continuing inequality between majority and minority racial and cultural groups in the outcomes of schooling. Federal policies and programs to promote equality of educational opportunity, after some thirty years, have not yet massively impacted on the racial disparity in educational outcome or its correlated disparity in the job market.

117

Such formidable and complex problems obviously have too many layers and facets to be grasped from any single viewpoint. There are problems within problems, questions within questions, and each by itself is grist for study. The goal of any research addressed to these problems cannot be like that of the alchemist trying to discover the philosopher's stone, which would all at once answer our questions and remedy the problems highlighted in *A Nation at Risk*.

The extreme diversity and complexity of the problems dictate that the task for any one researcher must necessarily be quite limited. The only feasible tack for the individual researcher is to divide the problem — divide and divide, until some scientifically tractable part is in hand, even if only a small facet of the multifaceted problem. Unfortunately, any single investigator's limited part of the divided effort is dwarfed by the immediate larger problems, and politicians and the general public can get impatient with the plodding and piecemeal scientific approach. Researchers are easily accused of fiddling while Rome burns. But remedies for educational problems seldom arise from global or monolithic notions of their nature. Broad-brush prescriptions scarcely penetrate causal underpinnings.

A realistic goal, I would suggest, is not to create a Grand Solution, but rather to make many small and specific, yet socially consequential, improvements in the particular troubled aspects of schooling. Significant improvement in educational outcomes will most likely only result as the cumulation of many small positive effects of a great many causal factors. Some of these factors lend themselves to educational implementation. But there are also other influences outside the schools' domain that impact on educational outcomes (for example, the "social pathology" in the culture of poverty that blights many urban schools, as vividly depicted by Maeroff (1988). Positive change in this sphere will depend on social reforms and influences far beyond what the educational system can effect alone.

The Special Focus of This Chapter

This chapter, although inevitably related to a larger context, necessarily focuses on a relatively narrow aspect: the relevance of psychometric tests and cognitive psychology for children's scholastic achievement and adults' successful employment.

More exactly, my primary concern is not with the practice of psychometric testing or with questions of test validity, cultural bias, or the fairness of using tests for educational selection and hiring. These topics, although of great importance in their own right, are incidental to my present aim. Nor am I interested in making a case for the routine use of standardized tests in schools or anywhere else.

Psychometrics, however, is an essential tool for studying individual differences and the outcomes of instruction. Lately, psychometrics has been allied with theories and methods of experimental cognitive psychology in the study of information processing, with educational implications for benefiting students ranging widely in aptitude (Snow and Lohman, 1988). Research by personnel psychologists in the armed services indicates that psychometrics and information-processing theory can be brought to bear on selection and training. It has proved particularly important for enlistees who did very poorly in regular school but have benefited from appropriate training programs in the service, permitting them eventually to enter the skilled work force (Sticht et al., 1987).

The main question addressed here is not whether the use per se of psychometric tests is a source of problems, for instance, by limiting opportunity in education and employment. (Whatever the answer, it is not the issue here.) The main question addressed here is: Do mental tests, in fact, measure something that is intrinsic to the larger problems of education previously mentioned? If tests do measure some factors intrinsic to the problems, rather than factors that are merely symptomatic, we then should inquire how we might be able to get around these factors — or, if not get around them, at least take them into account as constructively as possible.

A further limitation: I shall focus here only on those factors that affect achievement in a normally calm, orderly atmosphere for learning and a desire on the part of both learners and teachers to cooperate. Talk of instructional techniques is pointless where discipline is grossly lacking and a defiant attitude toward school prevails. Possible applications of cognitive research are rendered impossible where educational aims are flagrantly obstructed, for example, by the growing social pathology that threatens many inner-city schools — behavior problems, drugs, teen pregnancy, parental indifference, truancy, school dropout, vandalism, gang intimidation, violence, and crime. Such misfortunes spell an altogether different order of school problems from those that stem directly from the inherent difficulty of the material to be learned or the considerable differences in aptitude reflected by psychometric tests. Such adverse conditions for scholastic performance would even block satisfactory achievement by students we would recognize as academically gifted under more favorable circumstances. What is too often lacking in school failures is not ability but the kinds of values and aspirations that inspire achievement.

Although we may be tempted to speculate about possible causal con-

nections between these extrinsic behavioral problems and prior psychological factors, this will be eschewed in the interest of focusing more
intensely on fewer and more closely interrelated issues. This decision
should not be misconstrued as belittling the problem of school discipline.
In certain schools discipline is undoubtedly the first order of business. No
intrinsic educational improvement can possibly take place without it. The
public was recently reminded of this ancient wisdom through the wide
media coverage of Joe Clark, the dynamic New Jersey principal who
ruled his ghetto high school with a bullhorn and baseball bat. (See
the cover story in *Time*, February 1, 1988, 52–58). Clark's "get-tough"
methods, including removal of habitual troublemakers, are hotly debated
by school authorities, but all seem to agree with Clark's insistence that
discipline is the sine qua non for pupils' standing a chance to benefit from
their time in the classroom.

While this chapter pertains mainly to individual differences, it would
be awkward to avoid any mention of racial group differences. The generally
lower scholastic achievement of certain minorities, particularly blacks and
Hispanics, is itself a leading topic in public discussions.

Although some of the psychological factors in average group differences
could probably be discussed entirely at the level of individual differences,
it is important to understand the connections between the phenomena
associated with individual differences and those associated with group
differences. The achievement gap between racial groups, even assuming
the mean difference is analytically indistinguishable from individual differences of similar magnitude, itself generates another whole class of distinc-
tive phenomena—educational, social, and political. These cannot be
properly understood without inquiring whether group differences in school
learning reflect differences in the same psychological processes that characterize individual differences of similar magnitude or whether they reflect
differences in social, cultural, or linguistic factors that are superimposed
on the individual differences within a particular group.

Hence, group differences, as well as individual differences, must be
studied at the same basic level of analysis that experimental cognitive
psychologists are now studying information processes related to scholastic
skills. Investigation of group differences should not be constrained by
thinking exclusively in terms of broad sociological factors that are largely
beyond the school's control, instead of looking at the cognitive processes
directly involved in reading, writing, and arithmetic.

Cognitive psychologists make the reasonable assumption that *all* people
possess the same basic information processes, the very processes involved
in scholastic performance. But people also differ from one another in the
speed, capacity, or efficiency of these processes. Moreover, within any
one person the various processing components differ in efficiency, and

there is now evidence to suggest that differences in the efficiency of certain components are related to chronological age. Much the same thing can be said of conative or motivational factors, as well as of cognitive processes.

What researchers discover about the relation of elementary cognitive processes to manifest achievement by looking only at individual differences, however, may or may not be the same for group differences. It is not known, in fact, whether racial or other group differences in the speed, efficiency, or capacity of such basic processes even exist or are related to the observed group differences in scholastic achievement and psychometric g. But these are empirically researchable questions.

The Organization of This Chapter: An Outline

1. Since the primary concern of the National Commission on Testing and Public Policy is the impact of psychometric tests on opportunity allocation in education and employment, the first question necessarily must be: What do these tests actually measure? Why is whatever they measure educationally, socially, or economically important? What is their impact on minorities?

In virtually all the tests of concern, the chief "active ingredient" (*latent variable* in psychometric terminology) is something called the g factor. It inescapably holds center stage in this inquiry. Any discussion of human mental abilities that fails to recognize the central role of g would be like *Hamlet* without the Prince of Denmark.

2. Next we ask: What do we know about g? Is it measurable? What can we say about the characteristics of its distribution in the population? Then there is the question of the external validity of g: Is it related to real achievement? If so, how much? Can the answer to this question go beyond just a coefficient of correlation? This raises the question, Can we quantify achievement? What can we say about the characteristics of its distribution, and what bearing might this have on the validity of g for predicting achievement?

3. With the stage now set, we can ask: Are there cracks in the psychometric edifice through which lower scoring individuals or groups might to some extent escape the adverse impact of g-loaded tests — that is, without doing away with the use of tests altogether? (Realistically, this isn't going to happen.) Are there valid *psychometric* arguments by which we might to some extent be able to get around the observed correlation between g and achievement? What about the advantages (and disadvantages) of using within-group percentiles to reduce adverse impact where tests are used for selection? Can test coaching be effective?

4. Going beyond purely psychometric considerations, should educators try to raise g itself through psychological means? Why has g been so resistant to such efforts? We occasionally see a dramatic change in a child's IQ without apparent cause. Then, there is the puzzling finding that scores on g-loaded tests have shown a gradual rise in the entire population of the industrialized world over the past forty years, without known cause. Yet the possibility of intentionally raising the level of g in targeted groups, rather than merely training up performance on particular tests, remains in doubt.

5. If differences in g are not presently amenable to intentional change, then are there ways — in school and in occupations — by which we can appreciably reduce the apparent importance of g for success? Can other abilities or traits be substituted for g? I will look at the well-known ideas on this matter, the Level I—Level II notion, as well as aptitude × training interactions (known as ATI) in general, also: mastery learning, programmed instruction, training thinking skills, and directed learning based on hierarchical task analysis. How much does achievement depend on motivation? What in fact is motivation, and can it be intentionally enhanced?

6. Finally, I will try to interrelate psychometric g, learning, and achievement in a general model of information processing. Information-processing concepts afford a closer, more analytic view of the action level at which learning and achievement take place. The information-processing model, unlike factor-analytic models of the structure of abilities, posits a number of specific mechanisms that have different causal relationships to various kinds of learning. The component processes are independently measurable, at least in principle. Hence, besides its explanatory value (which is important from a scientific standpoint) an information-processing model also interfaces closely with instructional methods. Empirical research on information processing is already demonstrating the relevance of such constructs as *working memory* and *controlled and automatic processing* to instruction in reading and math. On the other hand, it is generally conceded that global measures of g (IQ tests, for example) have meager implications for improving instruction.

What Psychometric Tests Measure

Item Performance, Abilities, Factors, and g

A discussion of what our psychometric tests actually measure requires first that we be clear about the definitions of a few technical terms.

Definitions, of course, are not arguably either true or false in any real sense; they are conventions mutually agreed upon for the sake of precise communication, and they can be judged only on that basis.

On that basis, therefore, I must begin by dismissing the term *intelligence*. It will not be used in any of the ensuing discussion, except with quotation marks, and occasionally to warn readers against confusing it with other terms I hope to use with more precision than is possible for intelligence.

As elaborated elsewhere (Jensen, 1987a), I have been forced to the opinion that intelligence is not a scientifically useful term; it has no generally agreed upon meaning, and psychologists seem hopelessly unable to achieve a consensus on what this term should mean (see, for example, Sternberg and Detterman, 1986). Moreover, the word intelligence is fraught with many prejudices and emotional connotations that render it a stumbling block to serious discussion. It should be relegated to popular parlance and literary usage. The problem is only worsened, in my opinion, by talking about *multiple intelligences*. I am not urging that we should try to agree on a proper definition of intelligence, or that it needs to be redefined. That would completely miss the point, for it so happens that the term is simply unnecessary for our purpose, and no other term needs to be substituted for it. I believe that psychology, regarded as a natural science rather than a literary art, not only can get along without "intelligence" in its technical vocabulary, but is much better rid of it.

The few objectively definable key terms that are essential for understanding the subsequent discussion are *item performance*, *ability*, *cognitive factor*, *g*, and *process*. (I urge the reader not to skip over these definitions because some may differ from the meanings these terms have acquired in other contexts.)

Item Performance. Empirical psychometrics must have its basis in objectively observable behavior. But as yet there is no precise standard term for the observable units of behavior upon which the theory and measurement of mental ability must ultimately rest. It must be clearly seen that the superstructure of abstractions, interferences, and theoretical constructs in psychometrics is firmly grounded in objective reality. So to serve this essential purpose, I shall adopt the term *item performance* (IP).

By IP I mean an observable unit of behavior or some objective record of it. An IP is a single, narrowly circumscribed, overt act that occurs at one point in time. It could be a person's response to a single item on a test of any kind; it could be spoken, written, or registered manually, for example, by pressing a button on a reaction-time apparatus. But an IP is not necessarily a part of a test; it is any observable act. An IP is objective only in the sense that there is a high degree of agreement among observers that the IP (or a recorded trace of it) in fact occurred. A person's single act of lifting (or failing to lift) a two-hundred-pound barbell at least two inches above the floor for at least five seconds is one instance of an IP. But for the present exposition, the best example of an IP is a person's response to a single item on an objective test on one occasion.

Now, there are different domains into which IPs may be classified. We are here especially interested in IPs that can be classed in the *ability domain*. An IP is not itself an ability as I shall henceforth use this term. An IP qualifies for classification into the ability domain, however, only if it meets the following two conditions:

1. The IP must be an intentional or voluntary act. This excludes unconditioned and conditioned reflexes, tics, involuntary movements, autonomic emotional reactions, and the like.
2. An IP can be viewed as either a discrete or a continuous variable, or as a simple or complex performance. But to be classed in the ability domain, the IP (or a record of it) must be objectively classifiable or quantifiable in terms of a standard, for example: running the 100-yard dash in x seconds; recalling in correct order seven out of seven presented random digits; pressing a button in x milliseconds at the sound of a tone; correctly dividing two-thirds by one-third; or stating whether the words *generous* and *parsimonious* are synonyms or antonyms. Hence, IPs in the ability domain must in principle be objectively classifiable or measurable. Objective classification or quantification of the IP only means a certain specified high degree of agreement among observers of the IP or their readings of appropriate measuring instruments.

To summarize: An IP in the ability domain is a particular observable act which, in principle, can be referred to some objective standard. It is important to emphasize that an IP is not an abstraction. It is not a hypothetical construct or a latent variable underlying the observed act. The IP is the act itself, or some objective record of it. The number of different possible IPs is theoretically unlimited.

Ability.   An ability is a psychometric abstraction. It is defined in terms of a number of IPs and the relation between them. IPs can represent an ability if they meet both of two criteria: (1) temporal stability (to some specified degree) and (2) generality (to some specified degree). These criteria can be established only on the basis of a number of IPs. To meet the stability criterion, a particular IP must be repeatable over some specified interval of time, which may be anything from minutes to years. Some criterion of stability is required to rule out accidental, adventitious, or chance IPs. On a simple reaction-time (RT) test, for example, the performance on each trial constitutes an IP, and a person may have an RT of 150 milliseconds on a single trial, although the person's median RT based on 100 trials distributed over a twenty minute testing session might be 350 milliseconds. The single trial of 150 milliseconds would scarcely be representative of the person's simple RT. The deviation of the single IP from the average of the IPs over a number of trials constitutes an error in the measurement of the ability that is common to all of the IPs and is best represented by their central tendency (mean, median, or mode).

To meet the generality criterion there must be evidence of some specified degree of consistency or correlation between a number of IPs from a class of highly similar IPs. A person's recalling a set of n digits after one presentation is an IP, but the IP might be idiosyncractic; for example, the digit series might have contained the person's telephone number, thereby making it much easier to recall than some other series of digits of the same length. We cannot known how stable or representative the person's digit span is without observing the person recalling different sets of n digits. Our criterion for saying that the person has the ability to recall a set of n digits may be, say, perfect recall on four out of five trials. Any particular IP may deviate to some extent from the average of some number of IPs of the same type. Such deviations constitute error with respect to the measurement of the ability that is general to this class of IPs.

For conceptual clarity, at this point, the term ability should be reserved for measures obtained from a homogeneous set of IPs (that is, IPs drawn from a quite narrowly specified domain) that meets specified criteria of stability and generality. (Later on, we will see that abilities can be conceptualized in terms of hypothetical factors differing in breadth or generality.)

The stability of a set of IPs is typically quantified by the test-retest reliability coefficient of the set. Generality can be quantified by the average intercorrelation between the IPs in the set or by an index of item homogeneity (which is monotonically related to the average item intercorrelation), such as proposed by Loevinger (1947). Highly homogeneous sets of IPs can be called *testlets*. A testlet, thus, is a measure of an ability having a specified stability (for example, test-retest reliability for a specified test-retest interval) and a specified generality (for example, an index of item homogeneity).

Some psychologists try to make a distinction between *ability* and *skill*, but this distinction is usually connected with notions of "innate" and "acquired" or, more generally, of latent and observed variables. These concepts have a necessary place at another level of analysis, but they should not get mixed up with the basic definitions of the observable IPs and the abilities (or factors) derived from their intercorrelations. Skill may be viewed as a subordinate category of ability in certain contexts, but at this point there is no need to make a distinction between the meanings of skill and ability.

The number of different abilities is theoretically unlimited. Questions pertaining to the origin or history of an ability, whether it is innate or acquired or some interaction of these influences, or whether it is an aptitude or an achievement — these are all separate issues and are wholly irrelevant to the present definition of ability.

Cognitive. In referring to the ability domain, we need some explicit criteria for deciding whether a given ability should be considered a physical ability or a cognitive ability. The question in some cases is not as simple as one might imagine, and there is probably no set of criteria that could unequivocally classify every conceivable ability as either physical or cognitive. Operationally, we can classify abilities in terms of correlations, including only those abilities in a given class that show positive correlations with one another larger than some explicit chosen value. This approach would generally distinguish between most physical and cognitive abilities, but there would surely be a good many ambiguous abilities. The seeming problem is probably best resolved by theorizing that every ability has both physical and cognitive components in varying degrees. The adjective *cognitive*, as in *cognitive ability*, would then mean simply that independent measures of individual differences in simple sensory and motor functions per se do not account for the major part of the population variance in the particular ability.

In psychometric discussions, ability means cognitive ability, unless qualified otherwise. Cognitive and mental ordinarily have the same meaning and are often used interchangeably. But cognitive is the more precise term, having to do specifically with knowledge or the process of knowing, which includes attention, perception, encoding and transforming information, learning, remembering, thinking, and all the other aspects of information processing.

Factor. The context in which *factor* occurs is the clue to whether one of its ordinary dictionary meanings applies, or its strictly statistical meaning (that is, as one of the conditions or classifications of variables in an experimental design or analysis of variance), or its specialized meaning in a variety of closely related multivariate mathematical techniques known as principal components analysis and factor analysis. The term factor is used in this chapter almost exclusively in the last sense.

The explication of factor analysis is beyond the scope of this chapter. Briefly, factors are hypothetical variables underlying observed or measured variables. They are thus latent variables, but no causal relationship between the latent and observed variables is necessarily implied. The relationship between the two is best thought of as a strictly mathematical one, in the nature of a mathematical transformation. The methods of factor analysis are the means for achieving such a transformation. The total variance of an observed variable, for example, can be analytically represented as a linear (additive) composite of a number of independent variances, each one attributable to a different hypothetical factor. Hence, it may be possible to represent most of the variance in a number of observed variables in terms of a considerably smaller number of underlying hypothetical variables, or factors; thus, we can speak in terms of n variables and p factors, when $n > p$. The system of mathematical manipulations involved in factor analysis permits one to determine the coefficients of correlation between (1) each of the n measured variables and (2) each of the p hypothetical variables, or factors "underlying" the n observed variables; such correlation coefficients are termed *factor loadings*.

The essential input for a factor analysis is the total matrix of correlation coefficients among all of the measured variables to be analyzed. The end product is a *factor matrix*, which shows the factor loadings (that is, correlations) of each of the n measured variables on each of the p factors. The part of the total variance of the n variables that is accounted for by the p factors is termed the *common factor variance*, which (since $p < n$) is necessarily less than the total variance of the n variables. The proportion of the total variance of any given one of the n variables that consists only of common factor variance is termed that variable's *communality* (symbolized h^2). (This symbol should never be confused with the identical but conceptually unrelated symbol for heritability used in quantitative genetics.)

Unlike observed variables, factors cannot be directly measured in individuals, but they can be estimated. Such an estimate of an individual's relative standing on a given factor is termed a *factor score*. By estimate is implied some degree of error, that is, a deviance of the estimated value from a hypothetical (hence not directly measurable) true value. The reason that individual factor scores are only estimates is essentially that the p factors account for less than the total variance of the n variables, and so any given variable's total variance is not fully accounted for by the p factors. But an individual's factor score is necessarily derived from a weighted average of the individual's standardized scores on each of the n variables. (The weights are related to the given factor's loadings on each of the n variables.) Hence, there is inevitably less than a perfect correlation between the estimated and the true (but unknown) factor scores. The size of the correlation between estimated and true factor scores is directly related to the average communality of the n variables and to the ratio n/p. When these values fall in the range typically found in factor-analytic studies, the minimum average correlation between estimated and true factor scores will range between about .60 and .90 (Gorsuch, 1983, 258–260). Factor scores are sometimes useful for certain research purposes but are hardly feasible (and are rarely encountered) in the practical uses of mental tests.

Distinction Between Factors and Item Performance. An *item* in a psychometric test is something that calls for a fairly specific response that meets a certain objective standard which some test takers can and some cannot attain. (An item which does not discriminate, that is, one which every test taker passes or every test taker fails, is obviously useless for the measurement of individual differences.) Hence a test item measures an IP, or item performance, as previously defined.

Although each single item on a psychometric test measures an IP, the raw score (the total number of items passed) on a psychometric test composed of a large number of items is at least one step removed from the IPs. The reason for this is not anything that is a logical, mathematical, statistical, psychometric, or methodological necessity per se. It is due purely to a fundamental *empirical* fact, namely, that *all cognitive performances are imperfectly but positively correlated with one another* in the general population. (This empirical generalization may not hold true in a group selected in such a way as to be highly restricted in cognitive abilities; the generalization fails as a direct function of the degree of restriction. Residents of an institution for the mentally retarded, for example, or the membership of the National Academy of Sciences are extremely restricted groups with respect to cognitive ability.)

Thus different test items that measure cognitive IPs show varying degrees of positive correlation with one another. It comes as a surprise to many that the average item intercorrelations in the best tests are very low — generally in the range of +.10 to +.20. Such low correlations indicate that any pair of items picked at random from the same test have very little in common (that is, only about 1 to 4 percent of the variance in one item can be predicted from the other). But the important empirical fact is that the items do measure something in common, however little that something is for any given item.

Hence scores on psychometric tests are measures of abilities of varying degrees of generality, depending on the homogeneity of the items. The higher the inter-item correlations (that is, the higher the homogeneity), the narrower, or less general, is the ability measured by the test score. The score on a psychometric test measures *common factors* plus some unwanted, uninformative "noise" called *measurement error*. This distinction between IPs and factors (or abilities) is an important one, because a good deal of argument and confusion about tests stems from the criticism of tests aimed at the level of single items. It is a common misconception that the IPs per se constitute the ability measured by the test score. In fact, most of the variance (that is, an index of individual differences) on any single item consists of the unwanted noise or error component, which contributes very little to the total variance of any test with high internal consistency reliability.

Psychometricians try to minimize the error component in the test scores. The higher the *internal consistency reliability* of test scores for tests of a given length, the smaller is their *error* (that is, variance contributed by item specificity), the less the test scores reflect any particular IPs, and the more they reflect common factors which define abilities. The total variance in test scores can be divided into two parts: (1) common factor variance among items (or twice the sum of all the item covariances) and (2) variance specific to each item (or the sum of the item variances). For most standard cognitive ability tests, the item-specific variance typically constitutes only about 10 percent of the total variance of the test scores. Increasing the number of test items (drawn from the same item population) reduces the proportion of the total variance in test scores that is attributable to error defined as *item-specific variance* and increases the proportion of what is termed the *true-score variance*. One definition of a test's reliability is the proportion of the total variance in obtained scores that consists of true-score variance. (Reliability and true-score variance are also defined in terms of the stability of obtained test scores between different points in time and are indexed by the test-retest correlation.)

But the main point that must be emphasized here is that the total variance in a distribution of test scores mainly reflects covariance among items rather than item performance per se. Hence, individual differences measured by test scores do not mainly reflect performance on this or that particular item on the test, but rather the total covariance among the items, and this cannot be described strictly in terms of any specific performance. Individual differences are measured not in terms of observed behavior (that is, IPs) but in terms of common factors, which are an abstraction, at least a step removed from the level of any specific performance. But the fact that individual differences in test scores reflect differences in an abstraction (namely, common factors) in no way diminishes their importance or objective reality. No less an abstraction is the force of gravitation, expressed by the g in Galileo's formula $S = \frac{1}{2} gt^2$.

Because common factors have different degrees of generality, they can be conceptualized hierarchically. There is a common factor in just two correlated items. Such a common factor would have relatively little generality and would thus be at the bottom of the hierarchy of generality. The common factor in a very large number of items selected at random from a vast pool of diverse items would have relatively greater generality than the common factor in just a few items selected at random from the same pool.

Here is how we would form a hierarchy of increasing generality. We begin with a large pool of diverse items. These items constitute the base level of the hierarchy. We administer all of the items to a large random sample of the population and obtain the matrix of correlations between every item and every other item. By inspecting the matrix of item intercorrelations we make up groups of items by selecting into any one group only those items that are correlated with one another more than, say, +.20. (An item that correlates less than +.20 with any other items is assigned to the group of items with which it has the highest average correlation.) Each of these groups of items, then, constitutes a testlet. Because the items within any one testlet are more highly intercorrelated than are the items across different testlets, each of these testlets is said to be comparatively more homogeneous than would be any set of less highly intercorrelated items. But whatever is measured by the total score on one of the testlets is something more general than what is measured by any one of the items in it.

Then we can go on and do the same thing with the testlets that we did with items—obtain the matrix of correlations between every testlet and every other testlet, and make up a number of groups of testlets (each such group termed a *test*), such that the testlet intercorrelations within each group of testlets are larger than the correlations across groups of testlets. Each group of such comparatively highly intercorrelated testlets constitutes a test. The test score in this case is simply the sum of the scores on the various testlets it comprises. The true-score variance of the scores on the test consists only of the covariances between all of its component testlets. Such tests are the third level of our hierarchy, and whatever the true-score on one of them measures, it is something more general than what is measured by any one of the various testlets that make it up.

We can go on in the same way to obtain a fourth level of the hierarchy, which we could label *super-tests*. Since there is necessarily a smaller number of groupings at each higher level of the hierarchy, we are finally left with a single group at the apex of the hierarchy; its true-score variance comprises only the covariances among the group of tests immediately below it in the hierarchy. It measures something even more general than tests at any lower level in the hierarchy. Whatever this something is, it seems quite removed from the various items of observable performance that formed the basis (the first level) of the hierarchy.

The pyramid-like hierarchical structure described in the preceding paragraphs serves as a rather easy-to-grasp nontechnical explication of *hierarchical factor analysis*, which is now almost universally considered the most appropriate type of factor analysis for research in the cognitive abilities domain. A technical discussion of it would take us too far off our main course, so readers must be referred elsewhere for more detailed information (Gorsuch, 1983; Gustafsson, 1988; Jensen, 1987b; Schmid and Leiman, 1957; Wherry, 1959). In brief, hierarchical factor analysis is a method for discovering the various latent (or underlying) factors (arranged hierarchically according to their level of generality) that account for the empirically obtained correlations among the multifarious cognitive abilities measured by testlets. The levels of the hierarchy, from the top down, are conventionally labeled as shown in table 4−1. All factors at higher levels than the first-order factors (also termed *primary* or *group* factors) are termed *higher-order* factors; their number depends on both the number and diversity of the variables (testlets or tests) that enter into the factor analysis. In the factor analysis of large batteries of diverse cognitive tests there are virtually never more than two levels of higher-order factors — usually consisting of two to four second-order factors and finally the single general factor, which is conventionally symbolized by an italicized lowercase *g*. In smaller batteries, such as the twelve subtests of the Wechsler Intelligence Scales, *g* comes out as a second-order factor. A hierarchical factor analysis of the Wechsler battery, for example, yields a *g* factor and the three first-order factors labeled verbal, spatial, and

Table 4−1. Levels of a Hierarchical Factor Structure

Level	Descriptive Label
5	General Ability Factor (*g*)
4	Second (or Higher) Order Ability Factors
3	First Order (Group or Primary) Ability Factors
2	Homogeneous Tests (Narrow Abilities)
1	Items (Observed Item Performance)

memory (Jensen and Reynolds, 1982). Primary factors are named in terms of the type of ability represented by the items that compose the tests in which the factors have their largest loadings.

It is important to understand that a general factor is not mathematically inevitable in a hierarchical factor analysis; it cannot emerge from the analysis unless it is actually latent in the set of variables that are factor-analyzed. It is possible to find (or construct) sets of variables that yield no general factor whatsoever when subjected to a hierarchical factor analysis. Hence, *the general factor identified by a hierarchical analysis is not a methodological artifact or mathematical necessity, but an empirical outcome.*

A hierarchical factor analysis is said to be *orthogonalized* when all of the variance that is common between any of the factors at a lower level is removed to the next higher level; this applies at every level throughout the whole hierarchy, going from the primary factors up to *g*. The result is that all of the factors in the hierarchy (both within and between levels) are perfectly orthogonal (that is, uncorrelated with one another). Methods for orthogonalized hierarchical factor analysis have been explicated by Schmid and Leiman (1957) and Wherry (1959).

Hence, the total variance on any one of the tests entered into the factor analysis can be viewed as the sum of a number of linearly independent components of variance attributable to common factors (that is, *g*, possibly other higher-order factors, and primary factors) and uniqueness (specificity + error). A test's specificity is that part of its true-score variance (twice the sum of all its item covariances) that it does not have in common with any of the other tests with which it was factor-analyzed.

The General Factor

The most important factor in the cognitive domain is the general factor, or *g*. This is so for a number of reasons. Probably the most important is the fact that *g* is more highly correlated with various indexes of learning, performance, or achievement outside the set of psychometric tests, from which *g* is derived, than is the case for any other factor or combination of factors (independent of *g*) that can be derived from the factor analysis of the same set of tests. In brief, *g* is the chief active ingredient in the concurrent and predictive validity of most psychometric tests in most of the situations in which tests are used. Also, the *g* factor accounts not only for a larger proportion of the common factor variance of various collections of diverse tests than any other factor, but it often accounts for more of the common factor variance than all of the other factors combined. For example, in a study of eighteen separate factor analyses of test batteries comprising anywhere from six to thirteen tests (averaging 11.1 tests), the g factor accounted on average for 4.3 times as much variance in test scores as all of the other common factors combined (Jensen, 1987c).

But it should also be noted that there is a great deal of uniqueness (specificity + random error) in tests. In the study just mentioned, for example, tests' uniqueness accounts, on average, for nearly one-half of the total variance in test scores. A test's specificity is usually problematic and is often virtually impossible to characterize precisely in psychological terms. Moreover, assuming a particular test was factor-analyzed among a large and diverse battery of other tests, our knowledge of the particular test's specificity would probably have no value for most of the practical purposes for which tests are generally used. For most of the criteria ordinarily predicted by tests, a test's predictive validity would probably be reduced to nil if its general factor and major group factors were partialled out.

The existence of g should not lessen the importance of other substantial group factors (for example, verbal, spatial, memory) and special talents (for example, musical, artistic, mechanical, motoric). But neither does the exisence of these group factors diminish the predominance of g. It is a popular misconception that every person has such large peaks and valleys across the total spectrum of abilities that it is virtually impossible to speak realistically of different persons as being higher or lower in abilities in some average or general sense. But the very existence and size of the general factor absolutely contradicts this notion. It is a logical corollary of g that the average difference between various abilities within individuals is smaller, in general, than the average difference between individuals in their overall average level of ability.

Now we must consider the three most commonly expressed doubts about the g factor. They are hardly compelling.

Different Methods for Extracting g. In the modern psychometric literature g is represented by any one of three methodologically and conceptually rather different methods: (1) as the first principal component (unrotated) in a principal components analysis, (2) as the first principal factor (unrotated) in a common factor analysis (also called *principal factor* or *principal axes* analysis), and (3) as the highest-order factor in an orthogonalized hierarchical factor analysis. It has been found to be true empirically (although it is not necessary mathematically) that the g extracted by any one of these methods is very highly correlated (usually above .95) with the g extracted by either of the other methods in the same set of tests.

The empirical reality of *positive manifold* (that is, the existence of nonzero positive correlations between all cognitive tests) is itself the only fundamental or necessary condition for inferring a general factor, and any correlation matrix displaying positive manifold will yield up a general factor by any method of factor analysis. The only exceptions are those methods, like Thurstone's (1947) multiple factor analysis, which necessarily and intentionally submerge the general factor by scattering all its variance among the (orthogonally rotated) primary factors. I have yet to find a bona fide empirical demonstration of correlations between cognitive ability tests which are negative or zero that are significantly replicable or cannot be explained by some combination of sampling error and restriction of range on g in the subject sample, Guilford's (1964) contention notwithstanding (Jensen, 1980, 224–226).

Although the various methods of factor extraction yield highly similar g factors, a hierarchical factor analysis is preferable for theoretical reasons which I have indicated elsewhere (Jensen, 1987b). Their explication is not essential for the present discussion.

Invariance of g. Although it is not a mathematical necessity, it is an empirical fact that the g factor is quite stable when extracted from different batteries of cognitive tests, provided the tests composing each battery are reasonably numerous and diverse in contents and task demands. In fact, the degree of invariance of g is a direct function of both the number and diversity of the tests. Also, a hierarchical g is generally somewhat more stable than either the first principal component or the first principal factor. I have found, for example, that estimated g factor scores derived from a factor analysis of just the six Verbal subtests of the Wechsler Adult Intelligence Scale (WAIS) are correlated .80 with the estimated g factor scores derived from a factor analysis of just the six nonverbal Performance tests. Yet there is no resemblance between the Verbal and Performance subtests in their information content or specific task demands.

A large-scale investigation of g invariance was conducted by Thorndike (1987). He began with sixty-five highly diverse tests used by the U.S. Air Force. From forty-eight of these tests, six non-overlapping batteries were formed, each composed of eight randomly selected tests. Into each of these six batteries was inserted, one at a time, each of the seventeen remaining "probe" tests. Hence, each of the six batteries was factor-analyzed seventeen times, each time containing a different one of the seventeen probe tests. The six g loadings obtained for each of the seventeen probe tests were then compared with one another. It was found that the six g loadings for any given test were highly similar, although the g loadings varied considerably from one test to another. The average correlation between g loadings across the six batteries was .85. If each battery had contained more tests from the same general test pool, it is a statistical certainty that the average cross-battery correlations between g loadings would be still higher. Thorndike's finding, which is consistent with similar studies, constitutes strong evidence that pretty much the same g emerges from most collections of diverse cognitive tests. This evidence also indicates that the invariance of g across test batteries does not depend on their having identical elements in common, in the sense of elements of test content. Even highly dissimilar tests (vocabulary and block designs, for example) can have comparably high loadings on one and the same g factor.

Just as we can think statistically in terms of the sampling error of a statistic, when we randomly select a limited group of subjects from a population, or of measurement error, when we obtain a limited number of measurements of a particular variable, so too we can think in terms of a *psychometric sampling error*. In making up any collection of cognitive tests, we do not have a perfectly representative sample of the entire population of cognitive tests or of all possible cognitive tests, and so any one limited sample of tests will not yield exactly the same g as another limited sample. The sample values of g are affected by subject sampling error, measurement error, and psychometric sampling error. But the fact that g is very substantially correlated across different test batteries means that the variable values of g can all be interpreted as estimates of some true (but unknown) g, in the same sense that, in classical test theory, an obtained score is viewed as an estimate of a true score.

Is g an Artifact?   This question implies that g may have no significance or substantive meaning other than the mathematical technique used in deriving it. This is a false implication, for three main reasons.

First, a hierarchical general factor is not at all a mathematical necessity, and correlation matrices outside the cognitive realm can be found which yield no general factor. Therefore, the presence (or absence) of a hierarchical g is itself an empirical fact rather than a trivial tautology. It simply reflects the all-positive correlations among tests in the matrix, a condition which is not forced by any methodological machinations.

Second, as Lloyd Humphreys (1968) has argued, a highly replicable mathematical dimension that can be defined under specified conditions is real. It is real in the same sense that other scientific constructs (for example, gravitation, magnetic field, potential energy) are real and measurable, even though they are not directly observable or tangible entities.

Third, g is related to other variables and constructs that lie entirely outside the realm of psychometrics and factor analysis and have no connection whatsoever with these methodologies. For example, the degree to which various psychometric tests are g-loaded is highly related to their degree of correlation with variables such as the *heritability* of individual differences in the test scores, the *spouse correlations* and various *genetic kinship correlations* in the test scores, the *effects of inbreeding* (and its counterpart, *heterosis*) on test performance, *choice reaction time* to visual and auditory stimuli, *inspection time* (or the speed of visual or auditory discrimination), and certain features of the brain's *evoked electrical potentials*. (These studies have been reviewed in Jensen, 1987b.) No other factor that can be extracted from a collection of diverse cognitive tests shows as large or as many correlations with non-psychometric variables as does g. It is clear that g has as much claim to reality as theoretical constructs in other sciences. It is one of the major constructs in psychology, and one of the oldest and most well-established.

Spearman's Hypothesis

The g factor takes on further significance in the subsequent discussion of its central role in educational achievement through its connection with an hypothesis first suggested by Charles Spearman (1927, 379), the English psychologist who invented factor analysis and discovered g. Spearman noted that the average difference (in standardized score units) between representative samples of the black and white populations in the United States differ considerably from one test to another, and he commented that the size of these differences is directly related to the size of the g loadings of the tests on which the differences are found, regardless of the particular type or content of the *tests*.

I have formalized Spearman's notion, calling it *Spearman's hypothesis*, which states that the relative magnitudes of the standardized mean black/ white differences on a wide variety of cognitive tests are related predominantly to the relative magnitudes of the tests' g loadings: the higher the test's g loading, the larger the mean black-white difference. This hypothesis, if true, would seem to have marked relevance for understanding the well-known black/white difference in scholastic performance. More generally, it would mean that understanding the nature of the statistical black/white difference in the cognitive domain depends fundamentally on understanding the nature of g itself.

A proper test of Spearman's hypothesis requires the following conditions:

1. The black and white samples must be fairly representative of their respective populations and should be sufficiently large so that there is small enough sampling error of the correlations among tests to yield stable factors; and the samples should not be selected on any variables, such as educational or occupational level, that would restrict the range-of-talent with respect to *g*.
2. The collection of psychometric tests should be fairly numerous to permit the extraction of a relatively reliable *g* factor.
3. The tests must be fairly diverse in content and task demands, both to ensure a stable *g* and to allow considerable reliable variation in the *g* loadings of the various tests.
4. The tests' reliabilities should be known so that the tests' *g* loadings (and also the standardized mean group differences) can be corrected for attenuation (that is, diminution because of measurement error).
5. The factor analysis must be carried out within either the white or the black sample (or both), but not in the combined samples, so that any differences between the samples cannot possibly enter into the factor analysis.
6. The similarity in the vector of *g* loadings extracted separately from the two groups must be sufficiently high to ensure that the same factor is represented in both groups, as indicated by a coefficient of congruence of .95 or above.

The statistical test of Spearman's hypothesis, then, is the rank-order correlation between the tests' *g* loadings (in either group) and the standardized mean differences between the groups on each of the tests (with loadings and differences corrected for attenuation).

I have investigated Spearman's hypothesis in eleven large data sets that meet these requirements, some more ideally than others (Jensen, 1985a, 1985b; Naglieri and Jensen, 1987). (They were the only published data sets [and hence are accessible to other investigators] that are appropriate for testing Spearman's hypothesis.) The hypothesis was borne out in every study. The larger the number of tests and the greater the dispersion of the tests' *g* loadings, the more strikingly the results accord with Spearman's hypothesis, namely, a large and significant positive correlation between (1) various tests' *g* loadings and (2) the sizes of the tests' standardized mean differences between the white and black samples.

My formalization (or reformulation) of Spearman's hypothesis, it is important to note, states that the variation in the mean black/white differences on various tests is associated predominantly (rather than exclusively) with the tests' g loadings. This weaker version of the hypothesis is dictated by the empirical finding that when we plot the linear regression of black/white differences on tests' g loadings, we find that certain tests consistently show moderate deviations from the regression line. Tests that have an appreciable loading on a *spatial* factor (block designs, object assembly, paper folding, comparison of rotated figures, and the like) consistently show a larger black/white difference than is predicted from the test's g loading. Tests with an appreciable loading on a *short-term memory factor* (digit span, verbal rote learning, digit symbol or coding) show a smaller black/white difference than is predicted by the test's g loadings. So far, these are the only two well-established psychometric factors that have been found to cause rather small but consistent perturbations in demonstrations of Spearman's hypothesis.

Some thirty scholars have published peer reviews of this work in *The Behavioral and Brain Sciences* (1985, vol. 8, 193–262; 1987, vol. 10, 507–537), but no one has refuted the empirical demonstration of my formalized statement of Spearman's hypothesis. Several critics, however, showed a misapprehension that the demonstration of the hypothesis was somehow a mathematical necessity or tautology rather than an empirical discovery, and that confirmation of the hypothesis was an inevitable result of the methodology for testing the hypothesis and thus purely an artifact. This is impossible, for two quite obvious reasons:

1. When Pearson correlation coefficients between tests are calculated, all information about the means and standard deviations of the tests (or their rank-order of magnitudes) is completely lost in the correlations. Consequently, nothing about the tests' means or their rank-order of magnitude can be inferred from the matrix of test intercorrelations. Ipso facto, nothing can be inferred about the rank-order of tests' means from the tests' loadings on g or any other factors extracted from the correlation matrix.
2. The test means of one or the other comparison group (either black or white) are experimentally independent of the data from the group that yielded the test intercorrelations and the g factor extracted from them.

These two self-evident statistical facts necessarily mean that the prescribed method for testing Spearman's hypothesis yields a result that cannot be an artifact or a tautology. If the hypothesis is indeed borne out, it must necessarily have the status of an empirical fact. (The only theoretically possible exception to this assertion would be in the unrealistic hypothetical case whereby the total variance of every test in the battery consisted exclusively of variance in g and variance due to random errors of measurement. In which case, any reliable group difference would necessarily be a difference in g, and variation in the group differences across the various tests would reflect nothing but variation in test reliability.)

Further analyses (Jensen, 1987c) of the data previously used to examine Spearman's hypothesis have revealed additional findings. Into each of eighteen independent correlation matrices, each comprising anywhere from six to thirteen tests (averaging 11.1 tests), with each matrix based exclusively on either a white or a black sample (but never a racially mixed sample), was inserted the point-biserial correlations of each of the tests in the particular matrix with the variable of race treated as a dichotomous variable (quantitized as black $= 0$, white $= 1$). Each matrix was factor-analyzed, with a minimum of three first-order factors extracted from each matrix. The average loading of the dichotomous race variable on the g factor was .55, whereas the average of the corresponding loadings on the three largest first-order factors (uncorrelated with g) was .24. In other words, the black/white variable generally had its major loading on the g factor. A spatial visualization factor is the only non-g factor that rather consistently rivals g in its loadings on the black/white variable (see also Naglieri and Jensen, 1987). Hence, the largest black/white mean difference is seen on those tests that are the most highly loaded on both g and a spatial factor. The smallest black/white mean differences occur on tests that are the least loaded on g and the most highly loaded on a short-term memory factor. Contrary to popular belief, the mean black/white difference on the verbal factor (independent of I) is nil.

Examination of 121 psychometric tests that were factor-analyzed in eleven studies also showed that the g loadings of various tests are distributed as a continuous variable extending over a wide range of values — from about .30 up to nearly .90. On the same set of tests, the black/white mean differences (expressed in standard deviation units) are also distributed as a continuous variable, ranging from close to zero up to about 1.3 standard deviations (SDs). From the linear regression of the mean black/white differences on tests' g loadings, the estimated mean difference on a hypothetically pure measure of g would be approximately 1.2 SDs.

Cognitive Processes

Cognitive *processes*, like factors, are hypothetical constructs. That is, they cannot be observed directly, but must be inferred from behavior. Conceptually, however, processes and factors are altogether different. A factor can arise only from variance and may be thought of as a dimension of individual differences. A process, on the other hand, is one of the operating mechanisms of the mind.

Presumably at some neurophysiological level, processes perform operations on mental representations or transformations of immediate stimulus inputs or the traces of encoded past inputs stored in either short-term or long-term memory. The identification and functional description of processes do not depend on an analysis of individual differences but can be sought through the experimental analysis of the performance of just one person. The usual methodology for this purpose is mental chronometry, or the study of the time course of information-processing in the nervous system (Posner, 1978). There are two main categories of hypothetical processes: elementary cognitive processes and metaprocesses.

Some of the elementary cognitive processes that have been identified are stimulus apprehension (simple awareness of some change in the stimuli impinging on the sensorium), encoding (selecting, recognizing, labeling, or categorizing a given sensory input), discrimination, decision or choice, and retrieval of information from short-term memory or from long-term memory. These elementary processes are inferred and measured chronometrically from a person's performance on a variety of very simple contrived situations known as elementary cognitive tasks (ECTs).

Metaprocesses, on the other hand, are the executive operations that deploy the appropriate elementary processes called for by a particular stimulus situation and govern the planning, sequencing, and execution of processes, as well as their automatization through rehearsal or repetition.

Processes are the operational basis, so to speak, of the cognitive abilities involved in any mental test item. Different items depend upon different processes, or overlapping combinations of processes, for their execution. A reductionist explanation of individual differences in a particular ability, or in the common factors (including g) derived from correlations among abilities, devolves upon an analysis of individual differences at the level of processes. It becomes a question of precisely which processes contribute to the variance in a particular ability or a given factor. Probably the prevailing theory of g is that it results from the existence of individual differences in some quite limited number of distinct elementary cognitive processes that enter into virtualy all cognitive abilities (see, for example, Detterman, 1987; Sternberg and Gardner, 1982). The measurement and analysis of processes and their relation to educational and occupational achievement are more fully explicated later in this chapter.

The External Validity of *g*

Measurement and Population Distribution of g

Discussion of the relationship of *g* to achievement involves questions about the measurement properties of both variables and the characteristics of the population distributions of these measurements.

An individual's standing on the *g* factor of a battery of tests can be measured by means of a factor score but this is seldom done. Conventional IQ tests, however, are always very highly *g*-loaded when factor-analyzed among a collection of diverse cognitive tests, and certain quite complex item-homogeneous tests, such as Raven's Progressive Matrices, are also very highly *g*-loaded. Scores on such tests may serve as a rough proxy for *g* factor scores, although there might be slight contamination by some group factors, most commonly either verbal or spatial

But raw scores (or any transformation or standardization of them) on multi-item tests are just like factor scores in one respect: there is simply no true or natural metric for test scores or factor scores as there may be for certain abilities that can be measured in physical units (for example, a sensory discrimination threshold and reaction time).

By a *true metric* I mean simply a scale with an absolute zero point, additivity of measurement units, ratio properties, and one that retains all these properties and has the same meaning across dissimilar phenomena measured on the same scale. This kind of measurement — only this kind of measurement — permits direct comparisons between dissimilar phenomena (for example, the moon has *x* times greater mass than a pint of water; or, the average distance between the planets Venus and Nepture is *x* times the diameter of a hydrogen atom). Psychometric test scores and factor scores unfortunately do not possess these ratio scale properties. Hence, we are more limited in the kinds of statements and inferences that can be made on the basis of test scores in any form. Many psychologists evince a surprising naiveté on this point. For example, to the best of my knowledge there are no existing tests or psychometric techniques that could render such statements as the following at all meaningful: "A person gains half of his or her adult level of mental ability by the age of five."; "The increase in intelligence (or *g*, or verbal, memory, spatial, and so on) between ages five and ten years is, on average, equal to *x* times the decrease in intelligence (or *g*, and so on) between ages seventy five and eighty."

The plain fact is that test scores (or anything derived from them, such as standardized scores, factor scores, normalized scores, mental age scores, and so on), when the total scores are not based on factor-homogeneous items to which responses are each measured on a single physical scale (for example, response times in milliseconds), can only represent at best an *ordinal* scale. Ordinality means that the only strictly interpretale information in the scores can be expressed only in terms of their rank-order. That is to say, any kind of numerical scores derived from tests do not have the properties of a true metric as in physical scales, and the most that any scores, even from the best-made tests, can actually permit us to do is merely to rank individuals on whatever amalgam of latent variables (that is, factors and uniqueness) are responsible for the total variance in the scores; neither does the test score variance itself have a true metric. So a test score of any kind should be thought of only as a *rank-order correlate* of some latent variable.

Psychometrics is by no means completely stymied by the limitations of ordinal measurement, however. Ordinal information still can be highly useful in scientific inference and for practical prediction. But scores that represent only an ordinal scale are meaningless outside the context of a clearly defined reference group. A particular test score is meaningful or useful only in terms of where it stands in the total distribution of scores in some reference population. Hence, standardized test scores are often referred to as *norm-referenced*. As explained earlier, although the scores in the reference population can have only ordinal (that is, rank-order) meaning, no matter how they have been converted or transformed, they are conventionally expressed most often as percentie ranks or as one or another form of (usually normalized) standardized scores (for example, z scores, T sores, IQ), which have certain known and convenient scale properties and distribution characteristics.

Distribution of Scores on g-Loaded Tests. In light of the foregoing discussion, it should not be surprising that nothing of fundamental empirical or theoretical importance is revealed by the frequency distribution per se of the total scores on any psychometric test composed of items, and this is true regardless of whether we are dealing with raw scores or standardized scores or any otherwise transformed scores. Therefore, it would be trivial and pointless to review the empirical test literature regarding the form of the distribution of test scores of any kind.

In a given population, the form of the distribution of raw scores (that is, number of items passed) is entirely a function of three interrelated item characteristics: (1) the average probability of getting the correct answer purely by chance, or guessing, (2) the average level of difficulty of the items (as indexed by the percentage of the population that fails them), and (3) the average correlation between items. Item difficulty is completely under the test constructor's control. Score increments due to chance guessing are a function of the number and quality of the alternatives in multiple-choice items and the nature of the instructions to subjects regarding the penalty for guessing at the answer instead of omitting response when uncertain (for example, total score based on number of right minus number of wrong answers). The item intercorrelations can be controlled to a considerable degree (but never completely) through item selection. Hence, in constructing a test it is possible, within broad limits, to produce almost any desired form of frequency distribution of the raw scores in a given population.

But if we have no basis for arguing that the obtained scores have true measurement properties, in addition to merely having a rank-order correlation with the latent trait that they measure — and this seems to be typically the case for psychometric test scores — the precise form of the obtained score distribution is essentially arbitrary. The very most that we can say in this case is that (within the limits of measurement error) our test scores have some monotonic relation to whatever the test really "measures." If only we could truly measure whatever latent variable accounts for the variation in the obtained scores on an absolute scale (that is, one having a true zero and additivity of scale intervals), the form of its population distribution could turn out to be quite different from that of the test scores we have actually obtained.

But certain forms of distribution are simply more useful than others, psychometrically and statistically, and it is this consideration that mainly determines the form of the distribution test constructors decide to adopt. The aims of maximizing the statistical discriminability of scores throughout a fairly wide range of talent and of obtaining a fair degree of internal consistency reliability (that is, inter-item correlation) are what largely dictate item selection. The test scores that result under these conditions of item selection typically (and necessarily) have a symmetrical and more or less "bell-shaped" frequency distribution. It is not truly the normal (or Gaussian) curve, although it usually resembles it. By juggling item characteristics, the test constructor can get a distribution that reasonably approximates the normal curve, or the scores can simply be transformed mathematically to approximate a normal distribution. (Such "normalized" scores are gotten by converting the raw scores to ranks, then converting these to percentile ranks, and then, by reference to a table of the areas under the normal curve, converting these to normal deviates, or normalized z scores.) The reason for thus normalizing a score distribution is not mainly theoretical, but statistical. The normal curve has certain uniform mathematical properties that make it extremely useful in statistical analysis and interpretation.

The argument is often made on theoretical grounds, however, that the main latent trait reflected by most complex cognitive tests, namely g, should be normally distributed in the general population. This argument, if accepted, justifies and indeed demands that IQs (or any other type of scores on any highly g-loaded tests) should be purposely scaled so that the form of their population distribution closely approximates the normal distribution. What can be said for this argument? It is rather disappointing. There are three main facets:

First, there is the argument by default: Unless there is some compelling reason to suppose that the form of the distribution of g is something other than normal, we might as well assume that it is normal—convenient statistically, but not very satisfying scientifically.

Second, there is the argument from the *Central-Limit Theorem* in mathematical statistics, which essentially states that the distribution of a composite variable representing the additive effects of a number of independent elements (components, causes, or influences) rapidly approaches the normal distribution as the number of elements increases. This should be the case for g, to the extent that we can argue on various theoretical and empirical grounds that individual differences in g are the result of a great many different additive effects—individual differences in the efficiency of a number of different cognitive processes, each of which is somewhat independently conditioned by polygenic inheritance interacting with a multitude of different environmental influences encountered throughout the course of development since the moment of conception. The population distribution of any variable with such multiple additive determinants, theoretically, should approximate the normal curve.

Third, there is the argument by analogy with human characteristics that actually can be measured on an absolute scale, such as height, brain weight, neural conduction velocity, sensory acuity, choice reaction time, and digit span memory (the number of digits that can be recalled entirely correctly after one presentation on 50 percent of the trials). We may reasonably presume that individual differences in each of these variables has multiple determinants, just as in the case of g. Indeed, we find that in very large samples of the general population the distribution of each of these variables (measured on an absolute scale) approximates the normal curve. Marked deviations from the normal curve usually occur in the regions beyond 2.5 or more standard deviations from the median of the distribution. These deviations can usually be explained in terms of certain rare extraneous genetic or environmental factors that completely override the multiple normal determinants of variation. This line of argument by analogy makes it quite plausible, but cannot prove, that g (or other complexly determined traits) is normally distributed. Also, the argument by analogy is weakened by the fact that not all complexly determined biological variables that can be measured on an absolute scale necessarily conform to the normal distribution. Age at death (beyond 5 years of age), for example, has a very negatively skewed distribution, because the mode is close to 75 years and the highest known limit of human longevity is about 113 years. (Below age 5, the age of death is distributed as a so-called J curve, with the mode immediately after birth.)

So probably the best answer we are able to give at present to questions concerning the distribution of g is that we do not really know the answer and cannot know it by any currently available means. But there is no good reason for not assuming that the distribution of g is approximately normal, at least within the middle range of about five standard deviations. Most psychometricians implicitly work on this assumption, and no argument has come forth that it adversely affects any practical uses of g-loaded tests. The question is mainly of scientific interest, and a satisfactory answer to it cannot come about through improved measurement techniques per se, but will arise only as part of a comprehensive theory of the nature of g. If we have some theoretical conception of what the form of the distribution should be in a population with certain specified characteristics, we can use random samples from such a population to validate the scale we have devised to measure g. The distribution of obtained measurements should conform to the characteristics of the distribution dictated by theoretical considerations.

The g factor as a theoretical construct will never be measured simply and directly as we can measure height with a ruler; but a rigorously testable and empirically substantiated theory of g would itself dictate the form of its population distribution, and our empirical measures of g can then be scaled so as to yield such a distribution. Although we have some notions of the kinds of experimental research and theory development that should advance us toward this scientific goal, a discussion of it here would be an excursive sidetrack. But one of the major features of this development is the use of mental chronometry in psychometric theory and research and the use of *real time* as the fundamental scale for mental measurement.

The Distribution of Achievement. There is no clear-cut or even real distinction between ability and achievement. Both are based on performance. Performances called *ability* and performances called *achievement* both yield a number of latent variables when factor-analyzed. Some of these latent variables, or factors, most notably g, are common to both abilities and achievements and usually constitute a large part of their variance.

A chief difference between the measurement of g and of achievement is that with tests of g our interest is mainly in the latent trait itself and not in the particular class of test items that reflect it and serve merely as vehicles for its measurement. In achievement testing, on the other hand, we are primarily interested in generalizing about the particular class of items in the achievement test. We want to know, for example, whether Johnny or Mary can add mixed fractions or do long division involving decimals. Probably because achievement has more obvious *face validity* (or *content validity*), it is not as problematic from a measurement standpoint as g or other ability factors. The achievement of figuring the unit price of grocery items is much more obviously consequential than solving Raven matrices, which are utterly trivial in themselves, although the g they reflect probably predicts more of the variance in individual differences in a great variety of achievements than any other known latent variable.

Test constructors generally aim for the same desirable psychometric properties in achievement tests that were earlier described for ability tests, with the same consequences in terms of scale properties. Again, the manipulation of item characteristics and standardization and transformation of scores produces the same kind of symmetric, bell-shaped distribution curve in the population for which the test is intended. Except for their narrowly specialized item content, standardized achievement tests are psychometrically indistinguishable from most standardized tests of intelligence or aptitude (tests in which g or other broad latent traits, rather than a particular class of information content or specific skills are uppermost). So the particular scale on which various aspects of scholastic achievement is measured by the standardized tests is no more than some transformation of what is basically just an ordinal scale, and the statistical features of the score distribution in the target population are an arbitrary artifact of the particular type of transformation.

There is reason to believe, however, that achievement should not have a normal distribution. In this respect, achievement might differ profoundly from g or from elementary cognitive processes. Certain aspects of achievement lend themselves to measurement on a cardinal scale, that is, they can be enumerated and the numbers represent a true scale, so the form of their frequency distribution in a given population is a meaningful phenomenon. Objectively countable achievements whose frequency distributions have been subjected to detailed statistical analysis are, for example, number of publications (within a given time interval) by individual research scientists and number of patents by inventors (Shockley, 1957). The distributions of these variables turn out to be very markedly skewed, with a long upper tail. In the total range, the mode is only about 20 percent of the distance above zero, and the median and mean are only slightly higher. The same thing has been found for number of compositions by composers listed in musical encyclopedias. Interestingly, earnings (but not inherited income) show the same kind of distribution in the population.

It is found that these skewed distributions when plotted on a logarithmic scale conform to the normal curve. In other words, the distribution of countable achievements (and of earnings) is long-normal. This result would be expected mathematically if achievement were a function of a number of more elemental variables, each of which is more or less normally distributed and all of which interact with each other in a multiplicative fashion. The product of two or more normally distributed variables necessarily has a skewed distribution, the skewness increasing with the number of variables.

One can only speculate about what these component variables may be (for example, g, energy level and effort, learned technical skills, amount of practice or experience, work habits, persistence, opportunity, and perhaps certain personality traits such as emotional stability, self-confidence, dependability, and the like). When each of these variables acts multiplicatively with all the others, the range of individual differences on each of the component variables need not be very large for their running product to have an extremely wide range of values. A person who is only one standard deviation above the average on each of the components would come out extremely far above the average on their product. From subjective impressions this appears to be the case for achievements. The variance of achievement seems to be much greater than the variance of the basic abilities or of any one of the component traits that seem to influence achievement. But there is presently no way to test this impression rigorously, since we are essentially comparing the coefficient of variation (CV = standard deviation/mean) of some measure of achievement with that of some other variable (for example, g) in a given population, and the coefficient of variation is meaningless unless the variables are measured on a ratio scale. How terribly handicapped psychometrics is by its limitation to ordinal scales! From the standpoint of rigorously testable theoretical development, the lack of ratio scales for the variables of greatest interest in the study of individual differences is probably the single greatest hindrance to scientific progress. One wonders how far the physical sciences could have developed without ratio scales.

But we can measure digit span on a ratio scale and thereby are permitted to illustrate some interesting points. The experimental and correlational analysis of such tractable and adequately measurable phenomena as digit span can possibly give us a better understanding of how individual differences in comparatively elemental abilities are related to achievements involving prolonged practice and application.

In the digit span test, a person sees or hears a series of digits presented at the rate of one digit per second and then immediately recites the digits in the order of presentation. The longest series that can be recalled on 50 percent of the trials is the measure of the person's digit span, and it is a ratio scale. We generally think of digit span as an ability. It is included in some standard IQ tests (Stanford-Binet and Wechsler) and it has a modest g loading (about .40). The range of individual differences in digit span is quite small. In young adults, the distribution of digit span closely approximates the normal curve, and most of the population falls within the narrow range of five to nine digits (hence the phrase well-known to psychologists: the "magic number 7 plus or minus 2"). Now we tend to think of achievements as involving learning and practice. So we can convert, so to speak, the relatively raw ability of digit span into a kind of ahievement by inducing people to engage in short periods of practice on digit series of increasing length, without any specific instruction, every day for several months. Virtually everyone shows a marked increase in digit span, with practice. Also, the variance of individual differences in digit span markedly increases during the course of practice. Some otherwise unexceptional individuals end up after a few months of practice with digit spans of even seventy or more digits! That is well beyond the span displayed by most professional stage performers of mnemonic feats (Ericsson, 1988). (Whether digit span becomes more or less g-loaded after extended practice has not been adequately studied.)

The great increase in the variance of digit span and the far-from-perfect correlation between digit span before and after practice suggests that besides the primary cognitive processes involved in digit span prior to practice, some secondary factor (or factors) comes into play during the course of practice. The great increase in variance is consistent with a multiplier effect of a secondary factor on the primary processes involved in the initial digit span. This secondary factor might be the acquisition of a strategy, such as "chunking" digits or forming meaningful associations to aid recall. Some persons adopt more effective strategies than others. The increase in the variance of individual differences with practice is commonly observed in many tasks that do not have a physiological limit or an intrinsic performance ceiling.

It is especially noteworthy that the great increase in digit span with prolonged practice does not show the slightest transfer to any other task, including memory span for symbols other than digits. The subject's letter span, for example, is not made the least bit longer even after months of practice and dramatic improvement on digit span. This indicates that the elementary cognitive processes involved in span memory have not been affected in the least by practice and that the development of certain metaprocesses or strategies specific to digits must account for the great increase in digit span. Also, the fact that digit span gradually decreases to its original status unless one keeps on practicing suggests that something more than simply knowing a particular strategy is involved (Gates and Taylor, 1925). Its efficiency seems to depend on the degree to which it has become automatized (a gradual process) by practice, and apparently the effects of automatization must be maintained by practice. These concepts are examined in more detail in the final part of this chapter.

Correlation Between g and Achievement

A significant correlation between two variables indicates that they have some factors in common. The fact that highly g-loaded tests show substantial correlations with many criteria of achievement means that these criteria must also be g-loaded to some degree. The most outstanding fact is the diversity of achievement criteria that are g-loaded. No other factors (independent of g) that can be measured with psychometric tests of any kind show as large correlations with as wide a variety of achievement criteria as does g. This is true as an empirical generalization regardless of differing theoretical conceptions of the nature of g.

The evidence on this point is now so vast that detailed documentation of its totality would be quite unfeasible as well as unnecessary. There are countless studies, and most of the main findings have been summarized quite comprehensively elsewhere (Jensen, 1980, ch. 8; Linn, 1982). Quotations from two of the leaders in psychometrics — Lee Cronbach and Robert Thorndike — provide the essential conclusions. Cronbach (with Snow, 1977) has stated that "general abilities are going to correlate with any broad index of later achievement" (500). "Measures of general mental ability or scholastic aptitude or academic achievement do predict learning of new material. The correlation is often in the range of 0.40 to 0.60, about equal to that found when grade averages are the criterion. This is true even in brief learning experiments, where the outcome measures very likely have low task-to-task reliability" (498). And Thorndike (1984) has concluded the following:

Ability tests are of practical significance to us to the extent that they make it possible to predict the events of life outside of and beyond the testing situation. We may well ask, therefore, to what extent this prediction can be made from the common general factor, of which most or all cognitive tests partake, and to what extent it depends upon abilities specific to single tests or limited to groups of similar tests. I have carried out analyses of several extensive data sets in an attempt to answer this question. These analyses have led me to the conclusion that somewhere between 80% and 90% of all the variance in educational or occupational performance that can be predicted by an extended battery of ability tests is accounted for by the common g factor running through all the tests in the set. More limited group or specific factors appear to add not more than another 10% or 20% to the predictable variance when data are accumulated for various school subjects, various training programs, or various jobs. Thus, the notion of general intelligence, or general level of cognitive ability, is significant not only as a theoretical construct but also as the basis of most of the prediction of educational and occupational achievements that tests make possible. (2–3)

Consistent with Thorndike's conclusion is an exceptionally large set of validity data on the U.S. Employment Service's General Aptitude Test Battery (GATB), probably the most widely used test in personnel selection. The GATB consists of eleven quite diverse paper-and-pencil and performance tests. The composite score on the three tests with the largest g loadings (verbal, number, and spatial) provide the G-score of the GATB. My analysis (Jensen, 1984) of the GATB validity data shows that the average of 537 G score validity coefficients for 466 different occupations (with the performance criterion based on supervisor rating or on work samples) was +.27. When the criterion of job performance was predicted by the optimally weighted composite of the GATB tests (including G) that best predict for a given occupation, the average multiple correlation was +.36. This is a remarkably small increment (+.09) in average validity, considering that a multiple correlation mathematically must be non-zero positive and is somewhat spuriously inflated by sampling error, or so-called capitalization on chance. When the multiple correlation is statistically corrected for this bias (that is, the so-called correction for "shrinkage"), the G score, on average, predicts about 80 percent of the total criterion variance predicted by the optimally weighted combination of the various GATB tests, *including* the G composite. It seems a sound conclusion indeed that the predictive validity of tests or test batteries depends overwhelmingly on g. As yet no one has found (or even proposed) any other factor or combination of factors independent of g that could serve as a substitute for g in this respect.

But we also observe that the validity coefficients for highly g-loaded tests reported in the literature vary over an extremely wide range, from about $-.20$ to about $+.80$. There are ten principal causes of this variation which are important to recognize. (For more detail and references on each of these points, see Jensen 1980, ch. 8.)

Sampling Error of Correlation. A validity coefficient is simply a correlation coefficient between a predictor variable (for example, test scores) and a performance criterion (school grades, job supervisor rating), and, like any other statistic, it is subject to sampling error, which is inversely related to the sample size.

Reliability of the Test. Tests vary in reliability, although most published tests have reliability coefficients that are quite high (about .80 to .95), at least in the normative population. Hence, test reliability per se is not a major source of variation in validity coefficients. The square root of a test's reliability sets the upper limit of its possible true correlation with any other variable. (A detailed exposition of reliability can be found in Jensen, 1980, ch. 7.)

Reliability of the Criterion. Criterion reliability is much more problematic, and usually much lower, than test reliability. It depends largely on the type of criterion (see *Type of Criterion* below). Unlike test reliability, criterion reliability is a major source of variability in validity coefficients.

Range of Ability. Restriction of the range of ability lowers the estimated validity of a test. Some samples in which validity coefficients are determined are highly selected on the abilities measured by the test prior to the validity study, either by self-selection for opting to take the test or by imposed requirements that screen those who are finally tested and selected into the situation that yields data for estimation of the test's validity. Applicants to Ivy League colleges, for example, are not a random sample of high school graduates but are already preselected for relatively high academic aptitude, and those who are admitted are even more highly selected.

At every rung of the educational ladder, from elementary school to graduate or professional school, there is some degree of selection and consequent restriction of the range of individual differences in *g* among those who "survive." In my use of highly *g*-loaded tests in studies over the years with some three thousand students of University of California, Berkeley, for example, I find that compared with the distribution of *g* in the general population, the distribution of Berkeley undergraduates falls almost entirely within the upper quartile, and of graduate students, within the upper quintile. These highly select samples, therefore, have less than one-fourth of the variance in g found in the general population. This condition quite severely restricts the size of correlation that can be obtained between a g-loaded test (for example, the SAT) and some criterion measure of academic performance (grade point average, or GPA). It is a general observation that the more selective the institution, the lower the validity coefficients. The highest validity coefficients are seen in colleges with open admissions; the lowest I have seen reported are found in highly selective institutions such as Caltech and MIT. Some years ago I found that the Quantitative score on the Graduate Record Examination (GRE) had near-zero validity for predicting GPA among Berkeley graduate students in mathematics, but the severely restricted variance in test scores was not significantly larger than the test's error variance! Validity coefficients of the GRE for predicting grades in graduate school are typically close to +.30 (Kyllonen, 1986, 4). Tests that are psychometrically no better show much higher validities in less restricted populations. Kyllonen (1986) has reviewed the validities obtained on large samples in as many as fifty-seven different air force training courses over a period of twenty years, in which scores on heavily g-loaded military selection and classification tests were correlated with technical school GPA. The median validities ranged from +.42 to +.82, with a mean of +.61. Yet the air force has the most highly selected inductees of any branch of the armed services.

Selection for lower ability, of course, has the same effect on validity as selection for higher ability. For example, the validity of the Armed Forces Qualification Test (AFQT) for predicting navy enlistees' successful progression from apprenticeship training programs to specialized technical schools was about +.60 for enlistees in all navy classification categories based on the (AFQT), but it was only about +.30 for enlistees in category IV (the tenth to thirtieth percentile on the AFQT) (Cory, Neffson, and Rimland, 1980).

Heterogeneity of Criterion.   It is often the case that the criterion measure is not really the same (although it may be nominally the same) for all members of the sample in which validity is determined. College GPA is a good example of a heterogeneous criterion. It is a composite of non-equivalent components for different students. Various courses and majors clearly differ in their intellectual demands, and students are highly varied in the curricula in which they obtain their grades. It has been found on several campuses of the University of California, for example, that the validity of the SAT is higher for grades *within* courses (that is, a homogeneous criterion, where everyone is graded on the same basis) than for overall GPA, a heterogeneous criterion (Goldman et al., 1974; Goldman and Slaughter, 1976). The heterogeneity of GPA, in combination with the somewhat restricted range of g in most colleges, imposes a ceiling on the validity coefficients of college selection tests, which are typically in the range of .40 to .50.

Initial Selection on Negatively Correlated Criteria. This exacts a heavy toll on validity. It occurs when persons are selected on two or more different criteria which, although they may be positively correlated in the total pool of applicants, are negatively correlated in the finally selected group. While the most prestigious colleges are in a position to select only those high school graduates who have both high GPAs and high SAT scores, many colleges cannot afford to be so choosy. They must select most of their students from among applicants who are high in either GPA or SAT scores while having relatively few applicants who are equally high in both criteria. This selection procedure necessarily "builds in" a negative correlation between the personal traits that make for high GPA despite mediocre ability (largely g) of the kind measured by the SAT, or that make for low GPA despite high ability. The effects of these combinations of traits carry over to students' performance in college and can markedly weaken the validity of SAT scores for predicting college GPA. There have been some extreme cases where graduate students have been selected in this way, with the result that the GRE showed zero or even negative correlations with performance in graduate studies.

Type of Criterion. Various criteria of performance differ not only in reliability but in the degree to which they depend on the cognitive factors measured by psychometric tests. A great deal of evidence supports the following generalizations:

1. In general, education in academic subjects and training in technical courses make greater g demands than most other situations in which g-loaded test validity is estimated. Therefore, it is not surprising that tests show their highest validities for the prediction of scholastic and training criteria. I have elsewhere (Jensen, 1989a) reviewed evidence that the general factor in learning tasks, where the criterion is the rate or amount of acquisition of new knowledge or cognitive skills, is the same general factor g found in psychometric tests. Hence, performance criteria that strongly reflect the acquisition of new knowledge and skills are among the most highly g-loaded and the most predictable by means of psychometric

tests. The highest predictive validities are found between g and scores on achievement tests. This is true even when the predictor test is highly g-loaded but does not contain any information content in common with the achievement test. Tests given prior to a specific course of training, before students have any knowledge whatsoever of the subject matter, can predict the final level of achievement in the course, with correlations as high as .70. The predictive validity is generally highest when all students have had the same instruction and the same amount of study time.

2. Validity is usually much higher when the achievement criterion is scores on an objective achievement test rather than teacher ratings or course grades. But even achievement tests differ in g loading, depending on whether they measure primarily the knowledge content of the course or measure primarily the use of this knowledge in making inferences, interpretations, or solving novel problems. Performance on the latter type of achievement tests is more predictable from g-loaded tests.

The higher predictive validity when the criterion is a paper-and-pencil achievement test is attributable in some part to what is termed *common method variance*. This means that the predictor and the criterion measures are based on highly similar procedures (for example, a multiple-choice format with separate machine-scored answer sheets) which themselves have little or no intrinsic relationship to the abilities or achievements being measured. So persons who are actually equal in achievement may differ in so-called test-wiseness, or familiarity with a particular type of test format. The importance of this source of variance in test scores is less, the more that test takers have been previously exposed to objective tests of various kinds throughout their schooling. For groups that have had such experience in taking tests, the gains resulting from special coaching and further practice in test-taking skills are seldom larger than the test's standard error of measurement (Cole, 1982; Jensen, 1980, 589–596).

Grades generally have lower validity than objective measures of achievement for four main reasons: (1) grades have lower reliability, (2) the grading scale is more coarsely graded than objective measurement scales, (3) grades usually reflect relative standing in a given class, and classes may differ considerably in average level of ability and achievement, and (4) the grades teachers give often reflect their feelings about pupils' personal traits (such as obedience, conscientiousness, effort, forthcomingness, neatness of written work, and the like), which have little or no correlation with either g or achievement. It has long been noted, for example, that girls get higher grades than boys in school—a difference not reflected in scores on objective tests of achievement.

Even when grades are averaged over a number of years, so that different teachers' idiosyncracies in grading are averaged out, the correlation between grades and g is far from perfect. A strong test of the overall relationship between g and grades was made by Gedye (1981), working with the longitudinal data of the Berkeley Growth Study. She extracted a general factor (and individual factor scores) from pupils' teacher-assigned grades in arithmetic, English, and social studies obtained in all grades one through ten. She also extracted a general factor (and factor scores) from the Stanford-Binet IQs obtained on the same pupils on six occasions between grades one and ten; so this is a rather ideal measure of g. The correlation between the general factor score for grades and the Stanford-Binet g is $+.69$. Corrected for attenuation (unreliability), the correlation is $+.75$. The fact that the corrected correlation is not higher indicates that school grades in academic subjects, although highly correlated with g, also reflect consistent sources of variance that are completely independent of g. The difficulty in studying this non-g variance in grades is that it seems to be attributable to a great many small (but relatively stable) sources (personality traits, idiosyncratic traits, study habits, interests, drive, and so on) rather than to just a few large and measurable traits. That is why attempts to improve prediction by including personality measurements along with cognitive tests have not shown much promise. There is no general factor (or even several broad group factors) in the noncognitive realm which, combined with g, would appreciably enhance predictive validity.

3. In personnel selection, g-loaded tests have much higher predictive validity when the criterion is a test of *job knowledge* than when the criterion is *supervisor ratings*. Probably little of this difference in validity coefficients is attributable to common method variance, that is, the fact that both the predictor and the criterion variables are measured by paper-and-pencil tests. Scores on a job-knowledge test obtained after employees have spent several months or more on the job reflect the amount of job-relevant information acquired through intentional and incidental learning while on the job. And the rate of acquisition of *declarative knowledge* is quite highly related to g. That is, persons with higher levels of g generally acquire, per unit of time, more information (especially of the kind that can be verbally articulated) from their experiences than do persons with lower levels of g.

Job knowledge, of course, is important to the extent that it is related to employees' actual proficiency on the job, and jobs differ considerably in the extent to which declarative knowledge plays a part. Specialized knowledge is the sine qua non of some jobs. In others, it is almost superfluous beyond some rather mediocre level. A specialist in some branch of experimental physics who is brought in as a consultant to advise a team of researchers in, say, the Lawrence Berkeley Laboratory, is sought expressly for her or his exceptional fund of specialized knowledge and problem-solving expertise, without which he or she would be of no value as a consultant. However, a gardener working on the Berkeley campus, with its rich variety of flora, might acquire an encyclopedic knowledge of botanical taxonomy and horticultural science, although such knowledge would not be essential for performing the gardening chores.

Not surprisingly, supervisor ratings are more highly correlated with job knowledge than with g. But supervisor ratings are a problematic criterion because they reflect all the factors that influence person perception, and the relevance of these factors varies greatly from one job to another. Factor analyses of a variety of supervisor ratings along with various cognitive tests, including job knowledge, show that ratings contain reliable (and, for some jobs, quite valid) components of variance that are entirely independent of the variance attributable to g and job knowledge (Campbell et al., 1973).

In general, however, job-knowledge tests are more highly correlated with actual proficiency on the job, as measured by objective work samples, than are supervisor ratings. There is no reason to beleive that whatever favorable personal qualities that might enhance effectiveness on the job and are reflected in supervisor ratings would be negatively correlated with either g or job knowledge. What evidence I have found, in fact, indicates a slight positive correlation between noncognitive personal qualities (as rated by supervisors) and job knowledge (Campbell et al., 1973).

Although g is most highly correlated with job knowledge, it is important to note that large-scale meta-analyses of both civilian and military personnel data show that g contributes to variance in actual job performance (as-sessed from work samples) independently of job knowledge. That is, even when workers are statistically equated on job knowledge, g is still signifi-cantly correlated with job performance (Hunter, 1986). As Hunter explains, "Ability [g] predicts performance above and beyond its prediction of job knowledge because it measures the ability to innovate and prioritize in dealing with situations that deviate from those encountered in prior training" (358).

Prediction between versus within Occupations.   Here I will briefly sum-marize points I have fully documented elsewhere (Jensen, 1980, chap. 8). It has often been noted in reviews of test validities in personnel selection that validity coefficients for predicting job performance within specific occupations are rather disconcertingly low, for the most part in the range of .20 to .30. The reason usually given for this is restriction of range of ability within occupations. But this is only one factor in a quite complicated picture and probably a minor one at that. It so happens that predictive validities of g-loaded tests are actually somewhat higher in occupations that have a more restricted range of ability than in occupations with a very wide range of ability. (The reason for this seeming paradox is explained in *Job Complexity and* g *Validity* below.) When we analyze g-loaded test scores from persons in a very large number and extremely wide variety of occupations, we find that approximately one-half of the total variance in scores exists between the means of the various occupations and approximately one-half of the total variance exists within occupations (that is, individual differences among persons within any given occupation). From this empirical observation, it follows statistically that if we rank-order occupations so as to maximize the correlation between their ranks and their mean scores on g-loaded tests, the correlation between individuals' test scores and their occupational ranks would be the square root of one-half, or approximately +.70. In other words, g predicts occupational status with a validity coefficient of +.70. And this degree of correlation is just what is actually found in studies in which many different occupations have been ranked, not on any psychometric criteria, but in terms of their prestige (in the eyes of the subjects who do the ranking), their desirability, and people's subjective judgments of the amount of intelligence they think is required for successful performance in the occupation. (These three criteria, when based on the pooled ranks by a large number of persons, are amazingly consistent with one another and are highly stable throughout the industrialized world and from one decade to another.) It seems impossible to avoid the conclusion that what people ordinarily mean by "occupational status" is quite highly related to psychometric g.

On the other hand, the observed correlations between g and measures of proficiency within given occupations are usually very far below +.70, even though one-half the total g variance exists within occupations. This means that, in general, g is much less able to predict occupational *performance* than occupational *level*. The main reason (aside from the forms of attenuation of the validity coefficient previously mentioned) is that, once employees are up to the minimum level of qualification for performing in a given occupation, a host of other factors independent of g becomes at least as important as g for successful job performance (or the perception of effectiveness by supervisors and co-workers). Most nominal occupational categories accommodate a surprisingly wide range of g above the minimum level, or *threshold*, for a given occupation. This threshold level can be estimated from the mean g-loaded test scores of persons in a given occupation whose scores are at the first percentile of the distribution of scores in that occupation. The g "threshold levels" across a wide variety of occupations vary considerably more than do the mean levels of g across occupations, and the very top levels of g across occupations show surprisingly little variation — only about one-seventh as much (in IQ units) as we see at the threshold level. Some very high-g persons are found in some very low-g occupations, but no very low-g persons are found in high-g occupations. (The evidence is reviewed by Jensen, 1980, 343–45.) This widely recognized threshold property of g, with respect to both education and occupations, is probably responsible in large part for people's anxiety and antipathy concerning tests of mental ability.

Job Complexity and g Validity. If we could factor-analyze a great variety of occupations the way we can factor-analyze tests, we would find that occupations differ in their g loadings, which we could think of as the occupations' g *demands*. Hence the predictive validity of g-loaded tests for all types of job performance criteria improves as a function of the job's g demands. This is mainly characterized by the complexity of the job (Hunter, 1986, 344–45). Job complexity is related to the degree to which successful performance depends on both declarative and procedural knowledge, the making of fine discriminations, decisions, judgments, thinking, problem solving (especially the transfer of already acquired expertise to novel problems), and continual study and learning in order to keep up. Cosmology would seem to be more complex in this sense and to make greater g demands than cosmetology, for example.

Even at the very simplest levels of performance, such as the difference between simple reaction time (that is, RT for response to one signal) and choice RT (a response to only one of two possible signals), psychometric g is slightly but significantly more highly correlated (negatively in the case of RT) with the slightly more complex task. I have discovered this phenomenon within every segment of the total distribution of ability — the mentally retarded, average schoolchildren, super-gifted children attending university at age twelve, unskilled factory workers, navy recruits, vocational college students, university students, and members of Mensa (Jensen, 1982, 1987d).

For many jobs at the very lowest level of g-demands and the least personal responsibility in the whole occupational hierarchy, one finds test validities of zero, or even *negative* validity coefficients as large as −.20 or so. Such validity coefficients (usually based on supervisor ratings) do not reflect actual job proficiency per se so much as they reflect other behaviors that employers consider desirable, such as stable personality, dependability, interest, job satisfaction, low absenteeism, steadiness on the job, good attitude, and duration of employment. Employers have a usually well-founded reluctance to hire persons they regard as over-qualified for a particular job. Among employees in jobs with exceedingly small g-demands and little responsibility in terms of decisions or supervision, there is a slight negative correlation between g and other desirable personal traits. The employee turnover rate in low-g jobs, for example, increases as the employees' ability exceeds the minimum level of ability needed to do the job.

Length of Experience on the Job. The importance of the predictive validity of g for job performance would be fortunately lessened if it were found that the correlation between employees' g-loaded test scores and their quality of job performance steadily diminished with their length of experience on the job. This possibility — that differences in job performance between workers of high general ability and workers of low ability tend to fade the longer they remain on the job and gain more experience — is known as the *convergence hypothesis*. A recent large study that tested this hypothesis failed to detect significant convergence of high- and low-ability groups as a function of time spent on the job. Schmidt (1988) summarized the results as follows:

> We found that for all three measures of job performance — work sample tests, job knowledge tests, and supervisory ratings — the difference in performance between the top and bottom ability halves remained constant out to at least five years on the job. (Beyond that point the data were inadequate to draw conclusions.) Thus our findings disconfirmed convergence theory. It appears that initial ability differences produce job performance differences that are quite lasting. (286)

There is much research evidence to show that tasks with a degree of complexity that requires continual information-processing and on which performance cannot be completely routinized or automatized will continue to correlate with g indefinitely over time (Ackerman, 1987). It is questionable if even the most menial jobs can become so wholly routinized through practice that indexes of performance would cease to reflect individual differences in g.

Psychometric Aspects of Mitigating g Differences

The reality of g, the fact that it can be reliably measured and has useful predictive validity in education and employment, is overwhelmingly substantiated by psychometric research.

Furthermore, it is impossible to ignore the wide range of individual differences in g and the statistical differences between racial groups in the distribution of g. These are facts, regardless of controversy concerning the causes of individual and group differences. Causal questions need not be considered here. The immediate fact, on which there is a general consensus, is that g differences, regardless of their cause, have obviously important consequences for education, for employment, and for the quality of life.

Adverse Impact

Psychometric tests themselves are not responsible for creating the observed differences but are simply a more precise and standardized means of identifying and measuring behavioral differences that have been observed informally throughout human history. But our society's increasing use of tests, especially in educational and employment selection, has highlighted the phenomenon known as *adverse impact*.

Adverse impact refers to the disproportionate selection of applicants from groups that differ statistically in the characteristic measured by the selection test. In the simplest selection procedure, those individuals whose test scores fall above a given *cut-score* are the applicants who are finally chosen, regardless of their group membership.

When the means of two groups with overlapping score distributions differ, selection based on a common cut-shore necessarily results in proportionally fewer persons being chosen from the distribution with the lower mean. The higher the cut-score, the larger is the disparity between the proportions of the two groups that are "favored" by the selection procedure.

An index of adverse impact is the ratio of the proportions selected from the higher and lower groups. A ratio of 1:1 would indicate the complete absence of adverse impact. If the distribution of scores is approximately normal in each group, one can estimate with fair precision the index of adverse impact for any given cut-score from a knowledge of the group means and standard deviations (SDs). For example, if the means of two normal distributions differ by as much as one (within-group) SD and the cut-score is at the mean of the higher group, the index of adverse impact is 3:1. If the cut-score is moved up to one SD above the mean of the higher group, the index is 7:1.

In an applicant pool that includes representative samples of the black and white populations, the degree of adverse impact (for blacks) of any given cut-score depends on the factor composition of the test. In accord with Spearman's hypothesis, the larger the test's g loading, the greater will be the adverse impact. (Also, inclusion of a spatial-mechanical factor increases adverse impact for blacks, on average.) Attempts to reduce adverse impact, either by reducing a test's g loading, or by directly minimizing the group difference by means of item selection techniques expressly aimed at fulfilling this purpose, have been found so greatly to impair the test's validity within either group as to make such a test practically useless (Jensen, 1980, chaps. 11 and 14). Few psychometricians any longer consider this a promising solution.

Given the fact of adverse impact, the next question should be. Are there strictly psychometric and statistical aspects of the phenomenon that, if viewed properly, could permit us to lessen its severity?

Blind Alleys. Before considering the above question in a positive light, I should first explicitly dismiss those commonplace reactions to the problem that, in my judgement, the evidence indicates are conclusively unpromising.

1. The popular claim of *test bias* now carries no weight in the sense that if we could get rid of biased tests and substitute perfectly unbiased tests, the problem of adverse impact would be removed or diminished. It is simply paranoia to believe that psychologists, from the time of Binet to the present, have had a vested interest in producing or using biased tests. In recent years, psychometric researchers, test publishers, and the armed services have worked assiduously at devising methods for detecting and eliminating cultural biases from tests. The expert consensus is that these efforts have largely succeeded. (For an introduction to this now vast literature, see Arvey, 1979; Jensen, 1980; Reynolds and Brown, 1984; Wigdor and Garner, 1982.)

What little bias may exist in some few modern tests is generally so small and inconsistent in direction that its complete elimination would have a negligible effect on adverse impact. More often than not, in fact, the complete elimination of bias would have the effect of increasing the degree of adverse impact on blacks. It is a sound empirical generalization that most tests currently used in education and employment have useful validity in virtually all American-born and American-educated groups in our population. From two articles that contain excellent reviews of the evidence, here are the summarizing statements regarding the research on test bias by Robert Linn, a leading psychometrician, and Frank Schmidt, a leading personnel psychologist:

Whether the criterion to be predicted is freshman GPA in college, first year grades in law school, outcomes of job training, or job performance measures, carefully chosen ability tests have *not* been found to under-predict the actual performance of minority group persons. Contrary to what is often presupposed, the bulk of the evidence shows either that there are essentially no differences in predictions based on majority or minority group data, or that the predictions based on majority group data give some advantage to minority group members. (Linn, 1982, 384)

> We now know not only that cognitive employment tests are equally valid and predictively fair for minorities, but also (1) that they are valid for virtually all jobs, and (2) that failure to use them in selection will typically result in substantial economic loss to individual organizations and the economy as a whole. (Schmidt, 1988, 281)

2. The idea of *banning* the use of tests in the private sector would be completely unrealistic without also contemplating drastic changes in the laws that regulate private enterprise. If employers find that the economic benefit of using tests in employee selection exceeds their cost, it is predictable that they will use tests. The government could exercise its power to ban the use of tests in its own agencies, but it is these very agencies, particularly the civil service and the armed forces, that best appreciate the economics of testing. Tests are used in personnel selection, training assignments, and promotions because the real economic advantages calculated under a wide range of various reasonable assumptions substantially exceed the costs of developing and using appropriate tests. For officials or taxpayers to surrender these advantages, alternatives to testing would be required for selection. So far, no alternative has been suggested that promises to be at least equal to tests in cost-effectiveness or as meritocratic for all classes of applicants.

3. *Depreciation of tests' validity coefficients* by squaring them (thereby making them seem much smaller) is a common but technically improper and misleading way of belittling the value of tests for selection. A validity coefficient, of course, is just a correlation coefficient, and the most predictable conditioned reflex among psychologists (and social scientists generally) is to square every correlation coefficient they see. We all have learned (quite correctly) that the squared correlation coefficient (termed the *coefficient of determination*) indicates the proportion of *variance* in variable *x* that can be "accounted for" (or "explained" or "predicted" or "attributed to") by its linear regression on variable *y*. But this is a quite misleading and scarcely useful interpretation of a validity coefficient.

The proper interpretation of a test's validity, as originally shown in a now classic paper by Brogden (1946), is that the validity coefficient itself is the average proportional gain in the criterion performance that results from the use of the test for selection. For any given selection procedure, and assuming the nature of the criterion is fixed, the selection test's validity coefficient itself is a direct measure of the average improvement in criterion performance (that is, quality of work, worker productivity, and so on) on a ratio scale of 0 to 1, where 0 represents the average performance if the same number of persons had been selected at random from the same pool of applicants, and 1 represents the average performance if the same number of persons had been selected from the same pool of applicants by means of a hypothetically perfect predictor, that is, a test with a validity coefficient = 1. These relationships can be most easily understood in terms of Brogden's formula:

$$r_{xc} = (T - R)/(P - R),$$

where r_{xc} is the tests' validity coefficient (the correlation r between the test scores x and the criterion measures c), T is the average performance of persons selected with the test, R is the average performance of persons selected at random, and P is the average performance of perfectly selected persons, as if $r_{xc} = 1$.

In light of this generally accepted meaning of the validity coefficient, the usefulness of even a quite low validity coefficient (.20 to .30) cannot be regarded as trivial in many situations where efficiency of training (or low failure rates), or competence, quality of work, and productivity are considered especially important, in terms of cost, or safety, or urgency of time, or competition in achieving a goal. However, a test's actual *utility* in any particular situation also depends on other factors besides its validity.

Utility versus Validity

Utility and validity are clearly related, but they are importantly different concepts. In some cases, an argument can be made against the use of a selection test on the grounds of its utility, even when there can be no argument about its validity, which may be commendable. But validity is only one of several elements that determine utility, which is a more complex concept than validity. Although validity is essential for utility, from a practical standpoint, utility is the more crucial.

Utility (a term borrowed from the concept of "marginal utility" in economics) is a function of four independent elements: (1) *validity*, (2) *base rate*, (3) *selection ratio*, and (4) the *cost-effectiveness of alternative methods*. Validity has already been defined above.

The *base rate* is some indicator of the quality of the total applicant pool with respect to the criterion, such as the proportion of all applicants who are capable of satisfactory performance on the criterion, or more precisely, the (hypothetical) mean and SD of all applicants on the criterion. The base rate is determined by whatever conditions "pre-select" those who enter the applicant pool — how potential applicants were informed, requirements of age, education, or experience, and the many personal factors that influence self-selection.

The *selection ratio* is the proportion of the available applicants that are selected. It is determined by the test's cut-score, which is governed by supply and demand or by some required absolute standard of performance.

The higher the base rate and the higher the selection ratio, the lower is the test's utility for any given level of validity. If all applicants were selected, obviously the test's utility would be zero, regardless of its validity. The more severe the selection (that is, the lower the selection ratio), the greater is the utility. For example, given a validity of .50 and a selection ratio of .05, the selectees, on average, can be expected to perform on the criterion 1.04 SD above the mean of applicants selected at random.

How much practical difference 1.04 SD makes with respect to some absolute standard of performance will depend largely on the base rate. If it is quite high, then despite a range of individual differences, nearly all applicants would perform quite satisfactorily, and the practical advantage of using tests for selection might be only a trivial improvement over random selection.

This is where consideration of the time and money cost of testing must be weighed against the performance gain, or benefit. Also, less costly selection procedures with comparable validity may be readily available. Among category IV navy personnel (tenth to thirtieth percentile on the AFQT), for example, it has been found that a few easily obtained items of biographical information (for example, high school graduate versus dropout) actually have higher validity than psychometric tests for predicting job performance (Cory et al., 1980).

Test utility falls drastically when the size of the self-selected applicant pool is very limited, as is the case for many technical jobs. Cronbach and Gleser (1965) claim that if a test is worth using at all, at least twice as many applicants should be tested as will be selected. With a test validity of .50 (which is relatively high) and a selection ratio of .50 (the maximum recommended by Cronbach and Gleser), the selectees would be expected to have an average level of performance on the criterion about 0.4 SD above a randomly selected group. This is not negligible. But many colleges and many employers cannot afford to be as selective as Cronbach and Gleser recommend. Yet, as the selection ratio increases above .50, the utility of testing plunges markedly.

A recent example of the application of utility concepts is an elaborately researched argument for dropping the use of the SAT in the college admissions process (Crouse and Trusheim, 1988). One of the few technically cogent critiques of the SAT, its argument is based entirely on the test's utility. The authors state,

> Unlike many critics, we do not question ETS's claim that the SAT measures important abilities that are related to educational and economic success. Rather, we argue that despite its ability to predict educational success, the SAT is unnecessary. This apparent paradox disappears when one recognizes that even when a test predicts college success fairly accurately, it may not *improve* prediction much when used to supplement information available from high schools about students' coursework and grades. Our argument develops the case against the SAT as a tool in college admissions, not against the test's validity in measuring individual differences important to educational success. (xii–xiii)

Furthermore, their analysis shows that the use of the SAT in college admissions increases adverse impact for blacks over and above what it would be with the use of high school grades alone. But no other broad generalizations on this topic would be feasible here, because the degree of adverse impact due to the SAT as compared to high school grades alone results from the complex interaction of many factors that vary widely across high schools and colleges. Detailed explications are provided by Crouse and Trusheim (1988, ch. 5) and by Gottfredson and Crouse (1986).

The kind of examination from a utility standpoint that Crouse and Trusheim applied to the SAT should be applied to current uses of other tests in other settings.

Nonlinearity of the Test/Criterion Relationship

Imagine this situation: As test scores increase by equal intervals, the criterion measure (grades, job performance, and so on) increases by ever *decreasing* increments; that is, the monotonically positive relation of the criterion to the test scores is a negatively accelerated curve. Hence, for test scores that range below a given cut-score, unit differences between scores would correspond to larger differences in criterion performance than would unit difference between scores that range above the cut-score.

The question then is: Does this type of nonlinear test/criterion function offer the possibility that an optimally placed cut-score would allow strictly *random selection* from the pool of all applicants whose test scores range above the cut-score without sacrificing an acceptable level of utility?

The stated premise makes the question merely rhetorical. The answer has to be *yes*, provided the cut-score is high enough that over the range of scores lying above it the corresponding increments of criterion gain are too small to be of practical consequence. From the standpoint of reducing adverse impact, however, this hypothetical possibility looks extremely unpromising when examined in the light of empirical realities.

The problem has three main aspects: (1) the utility of *random selection* above a given cut-score as compared with *top-down selection* (selecting consecutively from the top score on down in the whole pool of tested applicants until the required number of selectees is obtained); (2) the placement of the cut-score so as to appreciably reduce adverse impact; and (3) the prevalence and consequences of a nonlinear relationship between test scores and criterion.

1. Provided there is a monotonic relationship between the predictor and criterion variables, then for selecting a given number of individuals from among a larger number of applicants, top-down selection has by far the greatest utility of any selection procedure that uses tests. It is always superior to random selection above a given cut-score unless the cut-score is so high that mostly the same individuals are selected by random selection above the cut-score as would be selected by the top-down procedure.

2. The problem with straight top-down selection, however, is that it has the greatest adverse impact of any selection procedure. The argument for random selection is simply the desire to reduce adverse impact. This could be accomplished to a socially significant degree only by setting a very low cut-score. With a very low cut-score, however, the utility of the test is drastically reduced. The typical result is that the random selection model does not select the ablest applicants from either population. Moreover, it has the added disadvantage (as compared with every other selection model) of maximizing the mean group difference among the selectees— an effect that only postpones adverse impact to subsequent decisions about retention and advancement. Also, the fact that there is usually a much higher proportion of majority than of minority persons in the applicant pool means that random selection above a very low cut-score will yield a relatively small number of minority selectees at the expense of getting a large number of substandard majority selectees.

3. Any form of monotonic relationship between predictor and criterion ensures some degree of validity. A linear relationship is not crucial, although it is convenient, because the validity coefficient reflects only the degree of prediction that is made possible by the linear regression of the criterion on the predictor. Nonlinear regression simply lowers the validity coefficient. But this in itself is a trivial problem. In the first place, for

every form of monotonic relationship (linear or nonlinear), top-down selection yields the same result. Moreover, linearity is by far the prevalent condition empirically, especially when criteria of a cognitive nature are regressed on highly *g*-loaded tests. The regression of college GPA on SAT scores is an example of almost perfect linearity, as shown in figure

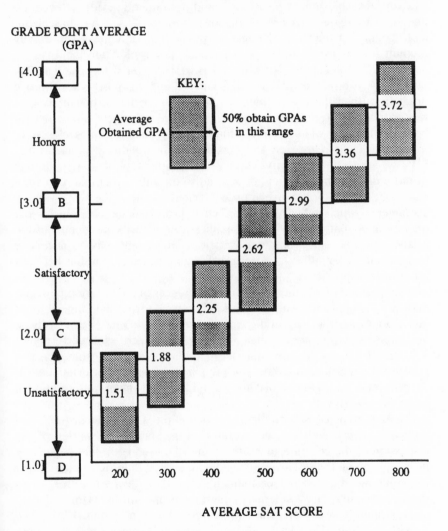

Source: Manning and Jackson 1984.

Figure 4–1. Average College Grades for Students with Different SAT Scores

4-1. Such linearity comes about both "naturally" and by design. When tests are specially designed to have maximum discriminability in the range of ability most relevant to a particular criterion, the regression line is seldom significantly nonlinear. My previous search (Jensen, 1980, chap. 8) for a nonlinear relationship between scores on highly g-loaded tests and various achievement measures found no authentic evidence for nonlinearity. Extreme skewness of the distributions caused by "basement" and "ceiling" artifacts in the test scores or criterion measures usually account for the rare instances of significant deviation from linearity.

Even if nonlinearity exists in a particular case, it can be handled effectively in either of two ways: (1) if the only purpose is to improve prediction, then there is nothing sacrosanct about the particular scale of test scores or criterion measures. We are free to subject either one or both of them to whatever monotonic transformation comes closest to producing linear regression and maximizing the validity coefficient; and (2) if we suspect nonlinearity, we can simply enter each score (x) and one or more of its higher powers $(x^2, x^3,$ and so on) into a multiple regression equation; the multiple correlation coefficient, then, is the test's validity coefficient, which reflects the predictive power made possible by the linear component along with the significant nonlinear components of the relationship between scores and criterion. Hence, there is no necessary loss in validity or utility as a result of a nonlinear relationship between criterion and predictor.

The question of whether individual differences in the criterion performance for all applicants, who are randomly selected from the range above a given cut-score on the selection test, are too trivial to matter can easily be answered by comparing the mean and SD of their criterion performance with that of exactly the same number of applicants selected from the same pool by the top-down method. In any particular situation, evaluation of the difference that is found, of course, would depend on the consideration of other factors as well.

An important consideration in this situation is the *standard error of estimate* (SEest), which is the overall average standard deviation of the dispersion of the criterion measure around the prediction line defined by its regression on the test score. (It should be noted that the standard error in estimating the criterion measurement for an *individual* is not the same as the SEest but may be considerably larger; the proper formulas for each type of error are given in many statistics textbooks and in Jensen, 1980, 379.)

Although the SEest has a perfect inverse relationship to the validity coefficient, it is often the case that the dispersion of the criterion measures does not show the property that statisticians refer to as *homoscedasticity* (that is, uniform dispersion of the criterion measure around the regression line throughout the full range of test scores; for example, going back to figure 4−1, the dispersion of GPA appears fairly homoscedastic). The dispersion of the criterion measure could be much greater in some part of the test score range than is indicated by the SEest, in which case the test would have little practical discriminability in that range.

So if, within the truncated range above some cut-score on the full range of scores, the average criterion difference between individuals in the bottom and in the top 10 percent of the truncated range is not statistically significant (say, at the 10 percent level of confidence), very little of the test's potential utility under top-down selection would be lost by the random selection of applicants ranging above the cut-score. And if the cut-score were not too high, there would be an appreciable reduction of adverse impact.

Temporal Loss of Predictive Validity

In many situations, the predictive validity of test scores diminishes as the length of time between taking the test and measuring the criterion increases. This effect is clearly seen in the prediction of college GPA by the SAT or other high-g tests. Humphreys (1968), for example, obtained a composite score based on several tests given to students on admission to their freshman year at the University of Illinois, and he correlated this composite score with GPA obtained within each of the eight semesters between the freshman and senior years. In one analysis only the sixteen hundred students who had progressed through al eight semesters and graduated were used, so there would be no change in the range of talent over the eight semesters. For this group, the validity coefficients for predicting GPA showed a fairly gradual decline (from +.375 to +.173) between the first and the eighth semester. (Corrected for restriction of range compared to all entering freshmen, the validities over the eight semesters declined from +.47 to +.21.) An almost identical picture is seen when high school GPA was used as the predictor.

The largest part of the observed decline in predictive validity is most likely due to the increasing heterogeneity of the criterion (GPA) as students adjust their course loads, select their courses, shift their majors, and the like, to maintain satisfactory grades. (Not all of the decline in predictive validity is due to the nature of the GPA, however, because test-retest correlations also decline as a function of the interval between test and retest.) But the important point for our present concern is that a stringent selection policy (that is, a high cut-score on the predictor) eliminates some students who initially look unpromising but who would eventually succeed if given the chance. Hence, lenient selection and retention on probationary status for those who fail at an early stage would increase the number that finally succeed academically and are legitimately able to graduate. Humphreys (1968) states, "Senior performance is not predicted well enough from freshman information for one to be at all content with present college admission practices" (378). He recommends, "Perhaps admission tests should be validated primarily against staying in college versus dropping out" (378). Most selection tests are validated only against freshman GPA, but as Humphreys notes, "A good many students who are dropped at the end of first semester would do acceptable work later in college...one simply cannot predict well enough from freshman academic deficiency to senior performance" (378–379).

These conclusions, however, are liable to overly optimistic expectations of the probable consequences of very lenient admission standards. A later study by Humphreys (1973), based on the same data as the previous study (that is, Humphreys, 1968), somewhat dampens the rather common hope that the lowest level of ability (as indicated by the predictor variable) found among those who succeed on the criterion (when there has been no formal prior selection) should determine the level of the cut-score on the predictor variable for screening future applicants. In other words, if we find that there are some self-selected persons who, despite having quite unpromising scores on the predictor, have managed to succeed on the criterion, why should we not recruit and accept applicants at (and above) the same rather mediocre level of ability?

Humphreys (1973) investigated two very large groups of students who had been admitted by standard procedures to the University of Illinois. The "low" group (in terms of academic promise) consisted of students who where below the median (of all students) on both high school rank in class and a composite score on several college aptitude tests; the "high" group was above the median on both. (Humphreys notes that the "low" group is low only relative to university students but is above average in the general population.) What Humphreys found was that the standard entrance measures had considerably higher validity for predicting GPA within the high group than within the low group. But just the opposite was found for predicting dropouts among all students admitted; that is, the admission measures better predict dropout for low-promise than for high-promise students, although even in the high-promise group the predictors are related to dropping out.

Humphreys interprets these results in terms of *unmeasured variables* in the relatively few low-promise students who persisted successfully to graduation. Humphreys (1973) states,

> It is known that close to 100 per cent of students having the characteristics of high rank in high school class and high ACT composite scores attempt college. The rate of college going steadily decreases as the scores on both of these measures decrease. Thus the present low promise group has been selected by family and friends, or self-selected, to a greater extent than the high group on unmeasured variables. As the low group proceeds through college, attrition continues to take its toll and at a much higher rate than in the high group. Those who remain are again highly selected and only in part on the freshman entrance variables.... [I]t is highly probable that the graduates who have the lowest scores on cognitive measures as freshmen have the highest levels on important noncognitive traits.... It is also reasonable to believe that these noncognitive traits are important in later life as well as in college. (390–391)

The problem is that the favorable factors that permitted a small fraction of the low-promise group to persist to graduation are, in all probability, not *negatively* correlated with cognitive ability in the general population, so that when low-promise individuals in general are selected, as would be the case with open admissions or a very low cut-score on the selection test, the noncognitive traits that favor persistence in college are selected for no better than chance. Humphreys (1973) concludes,

> Unless open admissions were coordinated with a drastic change in curriculum content, standards of grading, and standards for degrees, the results would be catastrophic for students entering at levels of freshman predictors below present standards. The present low promise group was low only by relative standards. Their mean high school percentile rank in class was above the median; their ACT scores are undboutedly above the mean of all high school graduates. Yet less than 30 per cent survived to the second semester of the junior year overall and only about 15 percent were still in engineering. (391)

Within-Group Percentile Conversion

There is simply no selection procedure that is both strictly psychometric and "colorblind" that can reduce adverse impact to zero (that is, to the point of proportional parity for minority and majority selectees) without also reducing the utility of the selection procedure to zero. Therefore, if parity is required, strictly meritocratic selection must be forsaken, and individuals' group membership must be taken into account.

The one important question then is, Which procedure will incur the least damaging effect on utility? The unequivocal answer: Select from the top down within each group until the desired proportional parity is attained. This method is by far less damaging to utility than random selection above a low cut-score. For any desired minority/majority ratio of selectees, top-down selection within groups insures maximum utility. The typical percentage loss in utility (compared to top-down selection irrespective of group membership) is reportedly around 10 percent to 15 percent (Hunter, Schmidt, and Rauschenberger, 1984).

Some tests (for example, the GATB) now provide tables of *within-group percentile ranks* normed for various racial and ethnic groups. These permit easy conversion of raw scores to percentiles based on each applicant's group membership. Selection based on a common cut-score on the percentile scale then has virtually no adverse impact. The typically small loss in utility must be weighed against judgments about the long-term social benefits of expanding opportunity at the levels of education and jobs where minorities have been underrepresented. But such judgments, which are absolutely essential for determining policy, depend on considerations that lie outside psychometrics or statistics or science. They can only be discussed in terms of moral, social, and political philosophy. (I have expressed some of my opinions in this sphere in Jensen, 1975.)

Psychological Aspects of Modifying g Differences

This topic can be dealt with quite briefly. Not only is there a high degree of consensus among experts concerning the essential conclusions of the relevant research, but these conclusions encourage us to look in other directions than to changing g itself for dealing constructively with g differences. Two recent books (Detterman and Sternberg, 1982; Spitz, 1986) together afford a comprehensive review of the research and current theoretical viewpoints. In their final summary chapter of the volume edited by Detterman and Sternberg, Brown and Campione (1982) state the implicit gist of perhaps every chapter in the book:

> We now return to the contrast made in the title between training cognitive skills and raising intelligence. We would argue that although the participants may eventually be quite successful at training cognitive skills, their present papers are silent on the issue of intelligence and its modifiability. (226)

My reading of the literature on this subject has not found substantial evidence that the relative differences between individuals in g can be changed by any known psychological or educational techniques. The history of the most intensive attempts by many dedicated workers is well told by Spitz (1986), who arrives at essentially the same conclusion.

The problem is not that scores on specific tests cannot be raised significantly by some form of either direct or disguised "teaching to the test." There have been many such demonstrations. The problem is that the trained individuals show such a surprisingly narrow range of transfer of their training to other cognitive tasks. The fact that training-up performance on one particular type of highly g-loaded task may have no detectable effect on the subject's performance on a different type of highly g-loaded task indicates that g itself has been unaffected by the training. A striking example is digit span memory (which has a modest g loading) on which persons can improve with practice. With several months of daily practice, the average college student can increase her or his memory span from about seven or eight digits up to seventy or eighty! But when the student then is tested on memory span for random letters, it is found to be only about seven or eight letters, which is what it was before all the practice on digits span. Yet letter span also has some g loading. The training or practice on digit span not only had no effect on g, but it had no effect on memory span as a capacity independent of any particular content (Ericsson, 1988). This demonstration epitomizes the many attempts I have seen to "raise intelligence," assuming one accepts g, rather than performance on any particular test, as the sine qua non of intelligence (Jensen, 1989b).

Test coaching, which has become a big business with respect to the SAT, demonstrates much the same phenomenon. The average effect of one hundred hours of professional coaching on the SAT is a rise in the Verbal score of about 0.3 SD and in the Math score of about 0.5 SD. Although these coaching gains may improve some students' chances of admission to a particular college, the gain in actual academic achievement predicted by their trained-up test scores is practically negligible (Messick, 1982). In other words, the increment in test scores produced by coaching is apparently "hollow" with respect to the g factor that normally predicts academic achievement, and consequently the students with such inflated scores, on average, do not live up to them when it comes to actual performance in college.

Psychologists occasionally see a child who shows a quite large change in IQ over an interval of a few years. Does this mean that the level of a child's intelligence, or g, can be considerably altered? In any large cohort of children whose mental development is followed longitudinally, one finds reliable changes in their rank-order on indexes of g, and in some

174 ARTHUR R. JENSEN

cases these changes, either up or down, are quite substantial. Moreover, they are often true differences in g, unlike the narrow contextual effects of special training or test coaching.

The causes of these seemingly spontaneous changes in rank, however, are rarely identified, so they can offer little support for claims that we should be able intentionally to bring about changes of a similar size through some kind of psychological manipulation. There is good evidence that a part of the observed irregularities—the spurts and plateaus—in mental growth rates is genetic, as indicated by the greater similarity between the mental growth curves of monozygotic than of dizygotic twins (Wilson, 1983). Similar effects are seen in the growth curves of other polygenic characteristics, such as height and weight. The effects of different genes that condition a given trait become manifested at different points in time during the course of the individual's development. The fact of spontaneous changes in g, therefore, is not a compelling basis for hopes of intentionally manipulating g by psychological means.

Another striking phenomenon that raises questions about the malleability of g is the apparent gradual secular rise in raw scores on IQ tests, as reported by Flynn (1984). American norms on the Stanford-Binet and Wechsler tests obtained at various times between 1932 and 1978, for example, show an average rate of increase in raw scores equivalent to three-tenths of an IQ point per year, for a total of about 13.8 IQ points. The same phenomenon has been found to varying degrees in Britain, the Netherlands, and Japan. The nature of this increase in test scores, aside from the fact that it seems to be authentic, is not at all understood, either by Flynn or by anyone else. How much of the change, if any, represents a true rise in g and how much is attributable to a general rise in the specific declarative and procedural knowledge content of the tests (as a possible result of the increasing universality and changing content of public education and the general access to radio and television) has not yet been sorted out. A major problem in research on this question is the lack of an absolute scale for the measurement of g.

It seems quite possible, however, that some part of the secular rise in test scores reflects a true change in g. Over the same period of time, in industrialized nations, there has also been a gradual increase in some other variables, such as physical stature, weight, and rate of physical maturation (for example, younger age at puberty and menarche), and this has been accompanied by an increase in birth weight and a decline in infant mortality. All these effects probably reflect improved nutrition and hygiene and the vast increase in inoculations to prevent the many nearly universal childhood diseases of earlier generations. (Each disease could take some slight toll on children's general physical and mental development.) Some such nearly universal causes are also suggested by the fact that the rise in test scores is about the same (in SD units) in all social classes and racial groups in the populations in which such a rise in test scores has been found. It is like a rising tide, which raises all ships equally and leaves their relative heights unchanged.

This constancy of the relative differences makes one question the inference favored by Flynn, that whatever unknown factors are the cause of the secular rise in test scores during the past fifty years or so are the same factors as those causing the social class and racial group differences (which have remained remarkably constant over the same period). There are reasons for suspecting that different causal factors are involved in the two phenomena, but because it would require too great a digression to explicate these here, the reader is referred to the exchanges among Flynn, Nichols, and Jensen in the volume edited by Modgil and Modgil (1987). But this whole matter of a secular rise in scores on all kinds of tests, especially those considered "culture reduced," is at present quite puzzling to everyone. It would be unfortunate to settle on any explanation prematurely; the needed further research on this puzzle might throw new light on the measurement and nature of g. Flynn (1987) has presented the most penetrating analysis of these theoretically troublesome aspects of g.

An explanation of the apparent failure to demonstrate an authentic change in g, by means of training or behavioral manipulation, would have to take into account the fact that, although the g factor is identified by means of psychometric tests, it is enmeshed with other variables completely outside the realm of psychometric tests. Hence, persons who are relatively high or how in g also differ in ways that could not be in the least inferred from examination of the highly g-loaded psychometric tests on which they differ. It is extremely improbable that the kinds of training typically seen in attempts to "raise IQ" would have any effect on many of these correlates of g. The fact that there are nonpsychometric, as well as psychometric correlates of g, could mean that both types of variables reflect some causal substrata that cannot be affected by direct behavioral manipulations, at least not by any kinds that have been tried so far. The "extra-psychometric" aspect of g is evident in findings such as the following:

1. Infants adopted shortly after birth have, as teenagers, IQs that are correlated with the IQs of their biological mothers, with whom they have not had any contact since shortly after they were born (Horn, Loehlin, and Willerman, 1979).
2. Cognitive tests are correlated with evoked electrical potentials of

the brain to the degree that the tests are g-loaded (Haier et al., 1983; Schafer, 1985).

3. Gifted children (IQ > 130) are faster than their average age-mates and their own siblings in reaction times to simple visual or auditory stimuli that have no intellectual content (Cohn, Carlson, and Jensen, 1985; Jensen, Cohn, and Cohn, 1989); they are more myopic than average children or their own lower-IQ siblings (Cohn, Cohn, and Jensen, 1988), and they have more allergies and are more often left-handed (Benbow, 1988).

4. Precise laboratory measurements of the duration of eye fixations on novel stimuli obtained on infants before they are six months old are correlated .5 to .6 with IQ obtained when the children are four to six years of age (Kolata, 1987).

5. Highly g-loaded tests are moderately correlated with "inspection time," or the time (independent of response time) required for making simple visual and auditory discriminations (Brebner and Nettelbeck, 1986).

6. Multivitamin and mineral supplements to the diets of some children increase their IQ (nonverbal IQ more than verbal IQ) by about five points within a few months—a finding consistent with other studies relating optimal neural functioning to adequate levels of thiamine, B vitamins, zinc, and iron (Benton and Roberts, 1988).

In view of such findings, it seems probable that the essential locus of control of individual differences in g will have to be sought primarily at a neurophysiological rather than a behavioral or psychological level. But that is largely unexplored territory and is most unlikely to be helpful at present. So, we are left with the question that educational psychologists necessarily must ask: Are there feasible means within our ken at present that might reduce the untoward effects of g differences in the overall economy of socially valued achievement and self-fulfillment?

Reducing the Effects of g in Education and Training

Before reviewing some of the approaches that my study of the research literature suggests are promising, I should indicate my guiding principles for realistic expectations for all of these approaches.

1. It now seems most unlikely that we will discover some new or previously hidden form of intelligence that will substitute for g and which we can tap into by some innovative instructional methods.

The "pop" psychology notions of developing children's right brains, left brains, creativity, hidden potential, or the like, are not backed by any evidence of promise for meeting the problems we are concerned with here. The hyper-development of a highly specialized ability or talent in the presence of very low g confers exceedingly little benefit, as can be seen most dramatically in the case of so-called idiot savants, who may have extraordinary powers of arithmetical calculation, artistic, or musical ability. Yet, they cannot earn a living by these talents and are never recognized as outstanding mathematicians, artists, or musicians. They have to be taken care of like any other mentally retarded persons.

Thus, the idea of cultivating other intelligences without considering the level of general ability is a blind alley. This opinion is not at all contradicted by the fact that persons we recognize as highly accomplished in any particular pursuit are never outstanding solely by virtue of their general ability, or g. Other exceptional personal assets are invariably a crucial feature in outstanding achievement, while some probabilistic minimum threshold level of g (depending on the type of achievement) is a necessary-but-not-sufficient condition. Consequently, the level of achievement of virtually all truly outstanding achievers is far more exceptional, in a statistical sense, than their level of g.

2. The only known dependable means for substantially reducing variance in overall achievement is by handicapping individuals at the upper end of the ability distribution by inadequate instruction, restricting the opportunity or time available for learning, hindering motivation, setting low standards, and the like. It is much easier to pull down the top of the distribution than to pull up the bottom. But restricting those with higher ability is so obviously unacceptable that it is mentioned here only to be cautioned against as an inadvertent possibility in our effort to make school more rewarding for the less able students.

Unfortunately, the very conditions described above as hindering the possible achievement of high-ability students exist in some schools, particularly schools in which the average achievement level is poor and teachers have become dulled to the special needs of the most able pupils. Then, for these able pupils, achievement may fall shamefully below their actual level of ability to achieve. Just how much wastage of potential achievement occurs for this reason is not known. But it is important that the underachievers be identified by suitable tests and other means for recognizing academic aptitude (or other talents), especially in disadvantaged groups in which academic aptitude is least apt to be recognized by parents, peers, and teachers. This is where appropriate tests and other methods for identifying talent can make a positive contribution. Baldwin

(1985, 1987) has suggested such methods and gives a promising description of their use and results. Much greater efforts along these lines should be encouraged. If the level of ability needed for superior achievement cannot be created by education, it is especially important that schools recognize those individuals who possess superior ability as early as possible and foster their potential.

Such measures, of course, would increase the range of individual differences in achievement. This is almost a basic "law" of individual differences in learning: By improving the conditions of learning, we cannot increase the mean level of performance without also increasing the variance. Experiments with computer-assisted instruction (CAI) for reading in the elementary grades gave striking evidence of this. While the achievement of all pupils receiving CAI showed an improvement over pupils receiving only conventional instruction, the CAI group also showed a much greater spread of individual differences (Atkinson, 1974). I have not seen a demonstration of a group's mean level of achievement being raised without its variance also being increased. (The exceptions involve learning tasks which have a fixed performance ceiling attainable by nearly everyone within the amount of practice time available to everyone.)

A closely related observation has been made by Bereiter (1987), one of the most experienced psychologists in the field of improving instructional methods:

> In my experience any instructional innovation that puts certain skills within the reach of previously failing children also makes it possible for the more successful children to acquire those skills at an earlier age. The resulting acceleration can easily increase the spread of differences. (334)

3. The aim of remedial efforts, therefore, should not be directed at trying to decrease individual differences but rather to increase absolute levels of achievement in essential knowledge and skills sufficiently to allow a larger percentage of the population to become self-sufficient and productive by ordinary societal standards. There will always be large individual differences in the kinds and amounts of knowledge people possess, but certain kinds of knowledge act as an "either/or" threshold for success in a particular society. Basic literacy and numeracy, for example, have become strong predictors of the following dichotomous classification: successful employment versus chronic unemployment. Both *declarative knowledge* (knowing *what* or knowing *that*) and *procedural knowledge* (knowing *how*) are products of learning, and in principle they can be taught. It is only a question of what, how, when, and how much of it to teach.

4. In large-scale evaluation studies (for example, Stebbins et al., 1977) of the variety of compensatory education programs developed in the 1960s and 1970s, the approaches that seemed to show the least promising outcomes emphasized cultural enrichment (that is, the provision of a variety of typically middle-class experiences to economically disadvantaged children), school services, general principles of developmental psychology, and multicultural education. The compensatory programs emphasizing these approaches had an overall slightly negative effect on scholastic achievement, as compared with matched control groups enrolled in schools without compensatory programs.

The one compensatory model that produced the most significant gains in achievement was *direct instruction*, that is, teaching directly the particular knowledge or skills in which the pupil is deficient. Direct instruction has not only proved sounder than other approaches empirically, but it makes more sense in light of what we know about the psychology of learning and cognition. The comparative results of compensatory and "follow-through" programs, however, are subject to controversy, as seen in the methodological critique by House et al. (1978) and the rebuttals to it in the same issue of the *Harvard Educational Review* (1978, no. 2).

Children (and adults) will learn what is directly taught, provided the teaching method elicits pupils' full attention and is not so sketchy or confusing that pupils have to discover for themselves what is being taught, and provided "information overload" is avoided by not trying to teach too much too fast for the pupils' rate of consolidation. Because of large individual differences in rate of consolidating new material, some children learn more than do others per unit of instruction or study time, given equal attention and motivation. For scholastic subjects, these individual differences mainly reflect two factors: g and the degree of mastery of prerequisite material. The second factor, which is subject to direct control in the instructional process, is the essential point of the *mastery learning* model of instruction (see below).

The principle of *direct instruction*, therefore, is uppermost in all of the approaches I will consider, both as a means to remedy existing deficiencies in essential knowledge and skills and to insure adequate mastery of pivotal prerequisites for the learning of new material.

Developmental Readiness

The whole concept of developmental or maturational readiness for particular forms of learning was almost totally eclipsed by the behaviorist-environmentalist influence that pervaded educational psychology in the 1950s. It is amazing how thoroughly the concept of readiness was ignored in the theories and practices of the compensatory education programs that arose in that period. Even the theories of Piaget, looming on the scene at that time, were interpreted in keeping with behaviorist theories. Some educationists expected to accelerate children's scholastic progress by attempting to teach them to perform Piaget's experimental tasks (used by Piaget only to investigate stages in cognitive development) a year or so before the age at which the children would normally be able to do them spontaneously without any instruction.

We now have solid evidence that there are large individual differences in children's readiness for school learning, from kindergarten through high school and beyond. At any given age, these differences are largely *g* differences, and they can make a big difference in the ease with which a child "catches on" to what is typically taught in the primary grades. Early on, these differences between children of the same age look very much like the typical behavioral differences one sees between younger and older children. This is why Binet proposed the idea of "mental age" as a metric for characterizing a child's mental status at a given chronological age. The average first-grader (age six years) has a mental age (MA) of six; just one SD below and above the average MA extends from MA five to MA seven, and two SDs extend from about MA four to MA eight, which embraces about the full range of developmental levels typically seen in the first grade. The range of individual differences in MA increasingly widens in each successive grade.

Psychologists Binet, Gesell, and Piaget have discovered or invented various developmental tasks which the average child finds easy to do at age seven or eight but which the average child of five or six finds either frustratingly difficult or altogether impossible. The very same thing is seen for children with MAs of five or six when compared with those with MAs of seven or eight, regardless of their chronological age. Now, it so happens that these developmental tasks have much in common with the typical learning tasks of the primary grades. Researchers at the Gesell Institute of Child Development at Yale University discovered that children's performance on these developmental tasks are good indicators of their readiness for learning what is typically taught in the primary grades, especially the basic elements of reading, writing, and arithmetic (Ilg and Ames, 1964).

The point is that, because of the wide range of individual differences in school readiness, some children are placed under much greater stress than others and are at risk of failure and lowered self-esteem right from the beginning of the primary grades. The slower child, under pressure to keep up with his or her peers and win the teacher's approval, begins to perceive the school as a punishing experience. School learning then is anything but pleasurable. The strongest reward or reinforcement for learning is the learner's own immediate perception of successful performance following effort to improve. We know from the classic studies by Pavlov and Thorndike that effort and performance not followed by reinforcement lead to extinction and inhibition of both the nonreinforced behavior and the effort that accompanied it. Attempted performance of the complex skills that evidence school learning can take this untoward course of extinction and inhibition when the material to be learned is beyond the child's developmental grasp. Also, when the child's efforts are frustrated by a lack of readiness for the assigned task, the well-known frustration-aggression hypothesis predicts that the child will "act out" with verbal or physical aggression, vandalism of school property, and the like—types of behavior most commonly seen in schools with a high percentage of pupils who are failing to learn.

Since practically nothing has been done with this hypothesis by way of its application to primary education, it would be unwise at this time to recommend more than an experimental approach to delaying instruction in certain skills to accord with a child's assessed level of readiness. Such a radical approach would probably have to be attempted under the auspices of a university laboratory school. The idea runs so counter to the popular push for earlier and earlier introduction of scholastic subjects that many parents predictably would object to having their children take part. The Scandinavian countries, however, have been doing this for over thirty years. Their schools do not even begin reading instruction before age seven. Yet the rates of illiteracy in these countries are among the lowest in the world. Delaying the age of reading instruction to age seven or eight has no adverse effect on the level of reading comprehension attained at later ages, as compared with beginning reading instruction at ages five or six.

The child's level of reading comprehension is highly related to the child's mental age. But MA acts as a readiness threshold for the initial acquisition of basic reading skills in much the same way that it acts as a readiness threshold for the child's ability to perform the developmental tasks of Gesell and Piaget. Many first-graders whose level of reading readiness at age six would cause them to struggle and fail in learning to read in first grade would learn more easily at ages seven or eight, and the obviously disadvantageous effects of frustration and failure in beginning reading would be prevented. The same applies to all other mentally demanding aspects of the primary curriculum.

There is probably no reason to worry about erring on the side of a little more delay than might actually be needed for some children, because the later consequences are nil, and there is still the advantage of minimizing risk of evoking negative attitudes toward school learning by an excess of early difficulties. In my travel in India, I was told by American missionaries, who formerly had been reading specialists in American schools and whose mission in India was to bring literacy to the children in totally illiterate villages, that most of the children introduced to reading for the first time between ages ten and twelve were reading, within a year or so, fully on a par with the average run of American children of the same age, although the latter had been exposed to reading since the first grade (age six). (The missionaries didn't try to teach children under age ten, because, as they put it, they wanted to maximize pupil output for the limited instructional input they could afford in any given village.) Of course, such anecdotal reports cannot qualify as bona fide research and must be weighed accordingly. But I would strongly urge obtaining some hard evidence on this matter. It could quell people's fear of the consequences of experimenting with gearing the curriculum and instruction to individual differences in pupils' readiness.

Aptitude x Treatment Interaction (ATI)

For educational psychologists, ATI has been the ardently sought Holy Grail. The gist of ATI is that the same type of instruction is not optimal for all levels of aptitude (or other learner characteristics) and that different instructional methods work best when they are appropriately matched to students' aptitudes. In terms of the regression of achievement on aptitude, the hoped-for effect of ATI is to reduce the slope of the regression line while not lowering the achievement of the high-aptitude students. Ideally, the optimum method of instruction for low-aptitude students would permit them to achieve at the same level as high-aptitude students, even when those with high aptitude get a different optimum form of instruction to maximize their achievement.

The big problem in ATI is discovering variations in instruction that will dependably produce substantial and desirable effects when the aptitude dimension is general ability, or g. This quest for effective ATIs has spurred a lot of research in the past twenty years. Its results, unfortunately, are confusing and practically impossible to summarize briefly. The final chapter of the most comprehensive book on ATI, by Cronbach and Snow (1977), is still probably the wisest summary. A slightly more recent summary by Snow and Yalow (1982) updates the ATI research but without a material change in conclusions.

First, the bad news. Cronbach and Snow (1977) concluded:

We once hoped that instructional methods might be found whose outcomes correlate very little with general ability. This does not appear to be a viable hope. Outcomes from extended instruction almost always correlate with pre-tested ability, unless a ceiling is artificially imposed. The pervasive correlations of general ability with learning rate or outcomes in education limits the power of ATI findings to reduce individual differences. (500)

Now, the good news. The most general finding of ATI research is that the lower the aptitude, the more the learner will benefit from instruction that reduces the information load per unit of instruction time. Most of the examples of varied instructional methods that yield a beneficial interaction with individual differences in general ability seem to consist of variations on the following general principle: *Modify instruction for low-aptitude students in ways that will relieve them as much as possible of the burden of information-processing.*

The benefits of applying this principle are neither entirely consistent nor very dramatic, but the ATI literature indicates generally positive effects, so it deserves more serious consideration as one of the few promising outcomes of ATI research. The chief value of the approach is not just that it makes it easier for low-aptitude students to achieve what they would have achieved otherwise with a bit more difficulty; it also permits them to acquire essential knowledge and skills that many would not acquire at all if given only the kind of instruction that is most effective for students with higher aptitude. Too much frustration, failure, and the consequent "turn-off" of students' efforts in the early stages of learning a new subject blocks further learning of the given subject. That turn-off can be prevented to a large extent. Since initial performance on complex tasks is generally a poor predictor of final performance, getting all students successfully over the initial "hump" in a new subject is crucial. Instruction can be geared to that purpose for those who would ordinarily have undue difficulty. Many children who are given private music lessons on one of the more difficult musical instruments, for example, soon quit studying, because the first few weeks or months of effort are so unrewarding—the excruciating sound of a beginner's violin or oboe is a far cry from music. Similar frustration is experienced by some children early in their attempts to learn the three Rs, but the personal penalty for quitting is obviously far more serious than not learning to play a musical instrument.

The generalized prescription stated above translates into having highly structured and carefully sequenced instruction: simplifying or breaking down the task; minimizing nonessential elaboration, or maintaining a high degree of "figure-ground" contrast between essential and nonessential content; explicitly pointing out all the intellectual manipulations intrinsic to learning the given task, such as generalizations, logical inferences, deductions, and the like; supplementing verbal explanations with visual or pictorial displays; and substituting concrete or personalized examples for abstractions or generalizations.

These general principles for making learning less dependent on g are well exemplified in the recommended training procedures to facilitate learning and transfer in low-aptitude personnel, termed *functional context training*, derived from research on the training of category IV recruits in the armed services (Sticht et al., 1987). For many academically disinclined or moderately low-g youths, the systematic and conscientious application of these principles in specialized vocational training programs can inculcate certain high-demand occupational skills that permit entrée to productive employment in the economic mainstream.

High-aptitude students can often benefit from a more permissive instructional style that leaves them more to their own ingenuity. For them, inquiry and discovery learning can be challenging rather than defeating. More instruction time can be spent elaborating on the basic content of the lesson and it can often be embedded in a broader or more abstract conceptual context. The highly structured instruction that works well for low-aptitude students risks boring high-aptitude students with what is for them too much explanation and pointing out of the obvious. Well-structured lessons must be appropriately paced for high-aptitude students, who are able to grasp many more of the conceptual connections and inferences without explicit emphasis by the instructor.

ATI research is also full of puzzles and surprises. For example, a review by Clark (1982) of ATI studies that focused only on general ability found that high- and low-ability groups each enjoy a different style of instruction from which, it turns out, surprisingly, they actually benefit least in terms of achievement. High-ability subjects show higher levels of achievement under more permissive types of instruction, yet they generally claim to enjoy and prefer highly structured instruction, which results for them in lower achievement. They enjoy structured instruction more than permissive instruction presumably because they perceive the former as being easier, which it most probably is. Low-aptitude students were found to be just the opposite. They actually achieve more from highly structured instruction, yet they prefer the permissive approach, presumably because the task requirements and standards for performance are less clear-cut and their actual achievement more often escapes being closely monitored, either by themselves or by the instructor. The implication would seem to be that the student's own preference is at best a poor guide to the most appropriate instructional method for enhancing achievement.

Level I and Level II Abilities

The concept of Level I and Level II abilities was introduced about twenty years ago as a way of formulating some empirical generalizations from my research on children's learning (Jensen, 1968). These generalizations can now be recognized as potentially just one more kind of ATI. Because there already exist comprehensive reviews and bibliographies of my own and others' research on the Level I–II formulation (Vernon, 1981, 1987). I will not attempt here to review all the findings but will give only the gist of what seems important for our present purpose — finding ways to mitigate the effects of g differences in education and employment.

Three observations gave rise to Level I-Level II:

1. School-age children from poor socioeconomic (SES) backgrounds (especially low SES black children) with IQs below eighty-five or so and with correspondingly poor scholastic achievement performed very significantly better than middle or upper-middle SES white children (with the same IQs as the low SES children) on a number of experimental learning and memory tasks.
2. The correlation (with or without corrections for attenuation and restriction of range) between performance on the learning tasks and IQ was significantly smaller in low SES groups (especially if they were black) than in middle and upper SES white groups. (Middle SES black children, being scarce in the schools in which we first conducted these studies, were not represented.)
3. The dispersion (SD) of measures on simple learning and memory tasks (for example, forward digit span) in low IQ groups (that is, IQs 70–90) was greater than in higher IQ groups (IQs above 110); that is, the degree of scatter around the line of regression of learning or memory ability on IQ gradually decreased as IQ increased. This form of bivariate distribution suggested the hypothesis that a certain level of learning and memory ability is a necessary-but-not-sufficient condition for the development of a certain level of intelligence (as indexed by IQ). Hence, we see almost the full range of simple learning and memory abilities among persons of low IQ, while very low learning or memory abilities are rarely found in persons of high IQ.

These three observations led to the hypothesis that two separate classes of ability, termed Level I and Level II, were interacting with SES (or with race — black/white) in the performance of different types of tasks.

Level I was conceived as the ability for receiving information and recalling it in very much the same form in which it was presented, with a minimum of elaboration or transformation. The prime example (and test) of Level I ability is forward digit span (FDS), the number of digits that can be recalled entirely correctly in the order of input immediately upon hearing (or seeing) a series of digits presented at the rate of one digit per second. Backward digit span (BDS, the digits have to be recalled in the reverse order) is a less "pure" measure of Level I, because in BDS the subject has to mentally manipulate the input before responding with the output.

Tasks characterize Level I to the extent that a minimum of mental manipulation of the information input is required for correct response output. The nature of a task need not actually preclude a good deal of mental manipulation to be Level I; it is only necessary that it can be (and usually is) performed with a minimum of mental manipulation. One does not think in terms of an absolute zero of mental manipulation on this continuum but in terms of the rank-order of complexity of cognitive operations typically elicited by various kinds of tasks. Other Level I tasks besides FDS used in these studies were serial rote learning, paired-associates learning, and free recall of items during multiple presentations. In all of these learning tasks the information input consisted of simple words, variously colored geometric forms, pictures of familiar objects, or actual familiar objects. The role of knowledge per se was minimized in these tasks, so that individual differences would reflect mainly differences in proficiency of learning in the test situation itself. Generally, low SES/low IQ children performed better on these Level I tasks than did middle SES/low IQ children, and many of the former performed at about the same level as the average run of their white, middle-class age-mates.

Level II ability requires transformation and manipulation of the input information in order to arrive at the appropriate output response. This characterizes most of the items of conventional IQ tests, especially the kinds that are said to measure "fluid" intelligence, that is, problem-solving ability displayed in tasks for which the difficulty level depends much more on the complexity of the mental processing required on the given information than on the recall of specific knowledge acquired outside the test situation. The main measure of Level II in my studies was the Raven Progressive Matrices, a nonverbal test of reasoning based on figural material. It turns out that in numerous factor analyses, the Matrices is the most highly g-loaded of any single test we have found. It soon became apparent that Level II was indistinguishable from Spearman's g; it, therefore, reflected the same magnitudes of SES and race differences typically found with the usual IQ tests. And, of course, it predicts scholastic achievement the same as IQ, regardless of SES and race. In marked contrast, however, Level I tests do not predict scholastic achievement the same as IQ, and they predict differently for low and high SES (and for black and white) populations. Most low SES and black students showed lower scholastic achievement than would be predicted from the regression of achievement on Level I ability in the white, middle-class school population.

The key question then was: is Level I an ability that can be tapped by certain methods of instruction to achieve the basic aims of schooling for children who are below-average in Level II but are average or above in Level I, entirely without respect to SES or race? (Statistically, there is a larger proportion of Low Level II/High Level I individuals in low SES and black populations, so these groups would stand to benefit the most from instruction that capitalizes on Level I ability.)

The answer to this question can really be subsumed under the ATI generalization discussed in the previous section, because Level I can be described in terms of tasks or ways of learning that do not make heavy demands on complex information-processing. To engage pupils' Level I ability, instructional methods would have to be specifically designed to reduce the role of Level II ability, or g, for successful performance.

Because many black and low SES/low IQ children could perform well on Level I experimental learning tasks, and because these tasks were usually forms of "rote learning," the Level I idea became popularly interpreted as the advocacy of teaching by rote, that is, by sheer repetition of stimulus-response associations elicited by the instructor. A more sophisticated notion was that the same ability (Level I) that made it possible for some low IQ children to do well in rote learning tasks could somehow be brought to bear on learning school subjects, but not necessarily by casting them in the form of rote learning. The kinds of instruction besides rote learning that would do the trick were not specified beyond the general ATI principle of structuring lessons in ways that would reduce the burden of information-processing for the learners.

So what has become of these Level I-Level II notions in the last twenty years? In retrospect, it seems they had at least two strikes against them from the beginning: (1) educationists' scorn for anything that hints of rote learning and (2) the unfortunate but unavoidable association of the Level I-Level II theory with *jensenism* — a term coined by the popular media in their sensationalizing of my article "How Much Can We Boost IQ and Scholastic Achievement?" in the *Harvard Educational Review* (Spring, 1969), in which the Levels theory was propounded alongside other controversial topics that made the whole thing anathema to many educators and social scientists.

Although in the following years there were a great many one-shot laboratory studies aimed at testing Level I-Level II strictly as a psychological theory, usually confirming the basic observations that gave rise to the theory (studies reviewed by Vernon, 1981, 1987), I have not found examples of actual long-term classroom instruction explicitly based on Level I abilities and reported in the literature as such.

Yet, over the past twenty years, I have heard comments from teachers in predominantly black schools that their own teaching style has been shaped to a large extent by the particular style of instruction that seemed to work best with their pupils. The teaching style these teachers described is about what one would expect if one wished to promote the learning of scholastic material by pupils whose Level I ability is notably stronger than their Level II ability. The teaching style is shaped in the direction of greater emphasis on rote learning of basic information, frequent rehearsal of immediately past learned material, verbal repetition, and memorization. And the instruction tends to deemphasize intellectualized explanations involving abstractions, generalizations, concepts, and principles—in short, the very cognitive activities that most characterize Level II. These kinds of observations have come from experienced teachers who had never heard of the Levels theory or of Spearman's g. It is also worth noting that children's educational television programs, such as "Sesame Street" and "The Electric Company," include elementary scholastic content (ABCs, simple words and numbers, and so on) presented in the form of brief "lessons" that perfectly exemplify a Level I teaching style.

Obviously there are some problems with this style of teaching. It may work well in the early phase of acquiring simple scholastic knowledge, but success in Level I learning may also reinforce a mental set that encourages pupils to approach all new learning in a rote fashion, which may hinder development of meaningful learning involving conceptual and abstract thinking essential for advanced levels of achievement. As Cronbach and Snow (1977) have cautioned in their discussion of the Level I-Level II theory, "Any attempt to evaluate instruction that is related to memory abilities will have to give as much attention to transfer outcomes (including the growth of Level II abilities) as to the responses directly taught" (485).

One answer to this criticism of instruction that caters to Level I abilities is that there are some children low in Level II who would likely fail at the more advanced levels of conceptual academic learning in any case, and it is better to teach them the things that they can learn with the abilities they possess than to try to teach them these things in ways that virtually guarantee failure. There are many useful and necessary kinds of knowledge and skills that can be successfully learned by those with average Level I ability despite their being well below-average in Level II ability. But for such students, a Level II approach hinders or prevents the learning of these things.

It is a matter of degree as to how much of the conceptual underpinning of knowledge and skills one must acquire for them to be useful for the individual's particular purpose. Russell and Whitehead in their *Principia Mathematica*, for example, take some one hundred pages to establish an understanding of the logical basis for the concept of the number one, without which presumably no other number can be truly understood. Yet most of us have been using numbers in arithmetic and mathematics in our work and daily lives without the least idea of what Russell and Whitehead expounded. Rote learning has indeed been very underrated in education circles, even though it in fact plays a big part in everyone's life, regardless of one's status on Level II. I am here typing away on a computer key pad. Yet, I have almost zero knowledge of how my computer works, knowing only how to make it do what I want (most of the time) by hitting various keys, which I had to learn completely by rote (or Level I processes), since there is no intrinsic logic to the labels and locations of the keys. True, one cannot understand something like theoretical chemistry in Level I terms. But even if a Linus Pauling wanted to tend bar, he would have to learn how to make all the popular mixed drinks by rote memorization. One can easily think of countless other examples of the essential role in one's life and work played by Level I types of learning.

So, I still believe that the main idea of the Levels theory may have promising applications in schooling and in specialized forms of job training, although there is scant evidence that it has yet been systematically tried and evaluated. In their review of the Levels theory, Cronbach and Snow (1977) present what seems to me a wise evaluation:

> Some educational objectives could perhaps be better-attained, for the student averaging high in Level I and low in Level II, by making more use of rote methods in the classroom. No evidence regarding the relevance of memory tests to school learning under alternative procedures is now available, however. (485)

> This suggestion [that basic skills be taught by rote or drill to those who are comparatively weak in reasoning] is not to be rejected out of hand merely because the word "rote" is distasteful. Better that primary pupils attain literacy and numeracy by whatever means than that they should fail; perhaps a similar case can be made at later grades. But...if beginners are not shown meaningful connections, they will not learn from logically coherent instruction. Hence, purely rote learning leaves them permanently unfit for meaningful instruction. Assuming that the ATI for rote vs. meaningful instruction does become solidly established in some subject at some grade level, it would then be defensible to

make rote the main vehicle for teaching that subject to certain students. But alongside this teaching there must be an effort to promote skill in the kind of learning at which these students are deficient. A coordinated attack could capitalize on strengths while repairing weaknesses. [521]

At about the time of the Cronbach and Snow review, the U.S. Navy took cognizance of the Level I-Level II idea in connection with their research on the success of category IV recruits (those between the tenth and thirtieth population percentiles on the AFQT, a general ability test) in apprenticeship and technical training programs. The navy researchers included a Level I test, auditory "Memory for Numbers," in their battery of prediction tests. In studies (Cory et al., 1980) based on very large samples, it is interesting that although this relatively pure Level I test showed nearly zero validity for predicting overall grades in navy schools, it had significant validity (+.18; corrected for attenuation, +.30) for category IV trainees — a slightly (but not significantly) higher validity than the AFQT. The validity of the Level I test (Memory for Numbers) was even higher (+.25; corrected for attenuation, +.44) in predicting *advancement* of category IV recruits into technical jobs; and again, it had better validity than ten other psychometric tests, including the highly g-loaded AFQT. This supports the hypothesis that success in the training of persons who are relatively low in g depends in part on their status on Level I abilities. The low-g category IV recruits who were highest in Level I were the most successful in terms of advancement from apprentice positions to technical training and subsequent technical jobs and in terms of global performance marks.

Hence, the Level I-Level II notion should not be abandoned but should be afforded a true experimental test on a large enough scale to inspire confidence in the conclusions concerning its practical efficacy. What is really needed is a clear-cut ATI design which would yield a statistical assessment of training outcomes in terms of the main effects and interactions of all combinations of both high-/low-ability groups on both Level I/Level II abilities, under both rote/meaningful instruction treatments (that is, a three-way analysis of variance).

To determine if some of the educational psychologists who are knowledgeable in the field of instructional psychology knew of any informal or unpublished studies that might throw more light on the potential merits or demerits of Level I-Level II, I wrote and spoke to a number of key researchers. Although they could point to no ideal studies, they all expressed positive but qualified opinions of the potential value of Level I types of instruction, much like the previously quoted views of Cronbach and Snow (1977). One prominent correspondent (who wishes not to be quoted by name) added the following observation to his comments on Level I-Level II:

I believe your earlier [Level I-Level II] idea still has merit, but when it comes to achievement, the black underclass has huge deficits which are not at all mandated by their lower Level II, but by their behaviors in other ways not nearly so evident in majority youth of equivalent ability, and behaviors that are indeed susceptible to molding, channeling, and reinforcement. This leads me to a belief that the place to concentrate is on family life, and the re-design of welfare and other policies to encourage fathers to stick—not discourage them as we do now; and to encourage fiscal independence, not pauperism or the rackets. My own research lead me to believe in the social benefit from the dogmas and activities of religion—these variables appear to be about zero correlated with IQ, but indeed are correlated with achievement. (Anon., March 1, 1988)

The Carnegie Corporation is presently sponsoring several large-scale projects in inner-city schools based on these very ideas, in which churches in the black community have organized programs for parents and children expressly to promote the kinds of morale, social attitudes, and personal lifestyle that favor scholastic endeavor (*Carnegie Quarterly*, 1987−88).

The Demise of Level I-Level II as a Theory. This has no bearing on the possible educational applications of the Level I-Level II concept, but I never viewed this formulation as a theory so much as merely a set of fairly well-established empirical generalizations. Some ten years ago, I quit using the terminology of Level I-Level II and also gave up all thoughts of trying to develop it as a theory. I abandoned Level I-Level II as a potential theory for three reasons:

1. There were futile arguments among researchers as to whether certain tasks should be classified as Level I or Level II, and there were no objective means for resolving these arguments. Many of the purported disproofs of the "theory" were based on flagrant misconceptions of the meaning of the two levels and hence a lack of agreement among different investigators in the classification of experimental tests as Level I or II. I have little use for theories that cannot be empirically falsified or cannot compel agreement among reasonable persons on the basis of empirical evidence. The ambiguities of definition that foiled the rigorous testing of the theory undermined its attractiveness from a scientific viewpoint.

2. The application of factor analysis to the correlations among a number of different Level I tests and Level II tests revealed that (a) Level II is indistinguishable from Spearman's g and (b) Level I is not a unitary factor. Various Level I tests (memory span, serial learning, paired-associates

learning, and free recall) largely part company in a factor analysis, and the relatively small general factor among Level I tests is nothing other than g. Hence, it was necessary to speak of Level I abilities in the plural, as being whatever different *non-g* factors were involved in tasks that could be classified together as either requiring rote learning or short-term memory. Since such tasks did not necessarily cluster in a factor analysis, there was no objective means for settling arguments as to which particular tasks could be legitimately classified as valid measures of Level I. In fact, just about any task with a very low g loading and a large specificity would behave with respect to race and SES differences much like the best Level I tasks, although they would not necessarily be memory or learning tasks. In other words, Level I had a big problem with construct validity. And since Level I measures behaved just like any other non-g (or very low g) ability measures, it also lacked divergent validity. In essence, Level I and Level II abilities boiled down to g and non-g factors.

3. Hence the most compelling reason for abandoning the Level I-Level II "theory" is that it turns out to be unnecessary. The Law of Parsimony requires that it be dropped. I came to realize that the Level I-Level II theory was essentially a special case of what I have termed *Spearman's hypothesis* (that is, the magnitude of the mean black/white differences on various tests is a function of their g loadings).

Also, the fact that the Level I-Level II generalizations held up much better when tested in terms of black and white groups than when tested in terms of high and low SES white groups reinforced the belief that they were actually a demonstration of Spearman's hypothesis. In the course of my empirical investigations of Spearman's hypothesis, however, I substantiated a subsidiary hypothesis (unknown to Spearman) that is an important supplement to Spearman's hypothesis for fully comprehending the observations that gave rise to Level I-Level II. The subsidiary hypothesis is this: When representative black and white groups are matched on g (or g is statistically controlled), blacks, on average, outscore whites (and, it turns out, Asians and Hispanics as well) on a memory factor (mainly loaded on digit span). Hence all the descriptive aspects of black/white differences on various kinds of psychometric tests can be comprehended strictly within a completely objective factor-analytic framework in terms of Spearman's hypothesis plus the subsidiary hypothesis that blacks, on average, outperform whites on tests of memory independent of g. Unlike the Level I-Level II theory, the modified Spearman's hypothesis can be (and already has been) put to completely objective and statistically rigorous tests and is strongly borne out (Jensen, 1985a, 1985b, 1987c; Jensen and Reynolds, 1982; Naglieri and Jensen, 1987).

Mastery Learning

Individual differences in g (or IQ) are highly correlated with the time to learn a new lesson up to a given criterion of mastery (Gettinger 1984). In typical classrooms, the slowest pupils take 500 to 600 percent more time than the fastest pupils to learn a given amount of material to the same level of mastery. Conversely, given a uniform amount of time, the fastest pupils should be able to learn five to six times more than the slowest. The pacing of instruction in typical heterogeneous classes usually does not allow either of these extremes. Slow learners attain low levels of mastery in the knowledge or skill content of a given lesson before having to move on to the next, while fast learners often attain a high level of mastery and are ready to move ahead well before they are presented the next lesson.

The idea of *mastery learning* is to keep pupils working at a given lesson, with the teacher's help, until they reach a uniformly high level of mastery, as indicated by a test of the lesson's content. All pupils are required to attain the same high level of mastery (say, 90 percent correct on a test designed to sample the lesson's contents), even if there is a wide range of individual differences in the total time needed to reach the required degree of mastery. This procedure obviously demands frequent and specific monitoring of pupil performance and hence can be administered more effectively with individual than with group instruction, where teachers may get bogged down in testing and record keeping. Also, it has been found that in group instruction teachers tend to allow the average pace to be set by the slower pupils (generally those in the tenth to twenty-fifth percentile of learning rates), thereby limiting the achievement of the faster learners — a condition that educators have termed the "Robin Hood effect." Obviously, computer-assisted instruction, which permits individuals to learn at their own pace, is a decided boon to mastery learning.

Contrary to some of the exaggerated claims made about the benefits of mastery learning, there is no getting around the fact that it amounts to a trade-off between the level of mastery achieved and the amount of material covered. If we decrease the range of individual differences in level of mastery attained on any unit of instruction by providing all pupils sufficient time to attain the same level, we correspondingly increase the range of individual differences in the number of units that can be covered in a school term, assuming that the pacing of instruction is not drastically slowed down for the faster learners. Mastery learning appears to decrease the range of individual differences in achievement only when the outcomes are assessed by means of specially designed achievement tests that test only for the information that was directly taught. Hence, under mastery learning of a limited and clearly specified content of information which is exclusively the basis of the outcome measure, a performance ceiling is imposed, which theoretically should reduce individual differences in performance to near zero.

In practice, however, comparisons of mastery learning classes with control classes show achievement gains in the range of one-half to one SD, but only on tests of explicitly taught material. The effect size is small indeed when achievement is measured by conventional standardized tests. Besides assessing performance on what was directly taught, standardized achievement tests also assess related incidental learning, inferences drawn from the explicitly taught material and generally a broader range of information in the given domain of subject matter than is tapped by the tests specifically designed to assess mastery learning outcomes. These broader aspects of achievement, which reflect general transfer of training, tend to be highly g-loaded. Consequently, mastery learning only slightly reduces the range of individual differences in scores on standard achievement tests.

Much of the research on mastery learning outcomes and their problems is impressively reviewed by Slavin (1987a), along with a number of critical commentaries (Anderson and Burns, 1987; Guskey, 1987; Bloom, 1987). Slavin (1987b) concluded, "To value the results of mastery learning research, it helps to hold a philosophy that reducing the variance in student performance is more important than increasing the mean for all students" (234).

There is no reason in theory, however, that mastery learning should necessarily have this undesirable effect. Properly applied, with sufficient attention given to individual differences in learning rates, it should be able to increase the level of achievement for all students without reducing variance in performance. One of the main problems with the mastery learning approach is the trade-off between level of mastery and breadth of coverage of subject matter. It is necessarily a trade-off, because children can spend only a limited amount of time in school. (At a conference I attended some years ago, a mastery learning enthusiast suggested it should be theoretically possible, if given a sufficient amount of time, to bring a retarded child up to the level of Bertrand Russell in mathematics. Asked "How *much* time?" his answer was "Perhaps two hundred years.") Obviously, there have to be choices of precisely which scholastic material everyone should be required to master to a high criterion and which subjects we can allow to have a much wider range of variation in degree of mastery. Reading text and reading music are contrasting examples.

A limited use of mastery learning for just those elements in the curriculum that constitute the most basic declarative and procedural knowledge that are essential tools for further scholastic progress is feasible and theoretically should raise the achievement levels of many pupils who ordinarily would "top out" at a socially unacceptable level. Failure to attain a high level of mastery of the essential prerequisites for learning a given subject increasingly hinders further learning and imposes a low ceiling on the student's eventual level of ahievement in that subject area. Some students, for example, are unable to learn the kinds of arithmetic normally taught in the fifth and sixth grades because they have not sufficiently mastered the more elementary arithmetic taught in the third and fourth grades. Some elements must be mastered, or overlearned, to the point of being "automatized," if they are to benefit students when they are confronted with more advanced material. The reasons for this are understandable in terms of recently researched models of information-processing, which are discussed in the final section of this chapter. The potential efficacy of mastery learning can best be understood in the context of information-processing theories.

Teaching Thinking Skills

The mental activity of thinking is certainly not the same thing as g. Thinking is actually a form of behavior, and so, like any other behavior, is subject to the principles of learning. Hence it can be taught, reinforced, shaped, and honed, much as any other skill. Thinking is essentially talking to oneself, overtly or covertly, in ways that interrelate and organize certain items of knowledge or experience to construct a coherent and consistent model of some phenomenon. It is also a way of asking questions of one's experience, recognizing problems, and discovering what is needed to solve them. Thinking skills are fairly generalizable processes or strategies, such as simple classification and hierarchical classification, sequential ordering of things along some dimension, reasoning by analogy, breaking down complex concepts into simpler components, reducing a complex problem to its essential elements, and the like. Study skills are really just the application of the appropriate thinking skills to the learning of a given subject matter.

Everyone agrees that a primary goal of education is to teach students how to think. Yet, in recent years, the schools have been accused of falling short in this endeavor. In an era of rapidly developing and changing information-intensive occupations, it is thought that learning and thinking skills are more called for than a fund of specific subject knowledge per se, beyond the basic tools for educational advancement—the three Rs. But these skills are best acquired in the context of some real, relevant, and culturally recognized subject matter. Education critics, and many educators themselves, have argued that more explicit teaching of thinking skills must be infused into this subject matter context. Some even advocate separate courses for the teaching of thinking skills.

This is one of the presently debated issues in this field—whether thinking skills can be taught separately or whether they must be an adjunct to some conventional content area, such as science, social studies, or literature. Thinking obviously requires content—it does not take place in a vacuum. It has long been argued that thinking skills, although they are transferable to a wider context than that in which they were specifically taught, show drastically diminished transfer to other domains that have few elements in common with the training context. But I doubt that any broad generalization is warranted on this issue. The extent of transfer of training of thinking skills depends on so many variables that there are virtually no principles that will reliably predict the transfer outcome of any given training procedure, and so arguments about the effects of any given program of training must be answered empirically (Nisbett et al., 1987). One argument made for teaching thinking skills in separate courses rather than exclusively in the context of a specialized subject domain is that the instruction does not have to contend with the usual wide range of individual differences in the knowledge of a particular subject.

In recent years, we have seen an explosion of programs for training thinking skills. It has become a growth industry in education. Some of the better known programs are Instrumental Enrichment, Philosophy for Children, Structure of Intellect (SOI), Problem Solving and Comprehension: A Short Course in Analytical Reasoning, and Odyssey. They are all diverse in their methods and the types of students for which they are intended. The research that I have seen on most of these programs is methodologically so far below the normal standards of referred psychological and educational journals as to afford little basis for appraisals or comparisons of their efficacy.

The most notable exception is the Odyssey program, which was developed and tried out in connection with Venezuela's Ministry for the Development of Intelligence. The study by Herrnstein et al. (1986), based on the Odyssey program, could well serve as a model for research in this field. It is one of the few large-scale studies that uses proper control groups and assesses transfer outcomes with a variety of criterion measures that do not overlap the specific training tasks, and the results are encouraging. Some four hundred Venezuelan seventh-grade students were given, during one school year, one hundred lessons of about forty-five minutes each in various thinking skills involving language, reasoning, problem solving, decision making, and inventive thinking. Training outcomes were measured with a target based on the instructed material and three standard tests of general abilities (Otis-Lennon, Cattell, and GAT) that had been designed without reference to the instructional program. The gains over an untrained control group were of the order of 0.3 SD to 0.4 SD on the standard tests and about twice that amount on the target tests. These well-substantiated effects seem especially remarkable considering the brevity of the training. There is not yet evidence of the degree of persistence of these training effects or of their transfer to subsequent scholastic achievement, but the initial effects certainly warrant further studies of the Odyssey program in American schools.

The training of thinking skills thus appears to be one of the most promising avenues for improving students' competence, especially in ways that should be beneficial beyond their formal education. But few of the thinking skills programs are specifically designed for the kinds of students who have the greatest difficulty in school. We will need more demonstrations of the effectiveness of such training for this group. It is likely that we will need to develop special programs to be optimal for different levels of general ability. It is most encouraging, in this respect, to note that there were very similar *percentage* gains for students across the entire spectrum of general ability in the study by Herrnstein et al. (1986).

But there are so many complex theoretical and empirical issues in this field, and so many different approaches and empirical findings around which the current debates revolve, that it would be quite impossible to do them justice in this brief introduction. Fortunately, there are now some superbly thoughtful and critical reviews of the main currents in this field (Adams, 1989; Nickerson, 1988; Sternberg and Bhana, 1986) — essential reading for those who would venture into this field.

An Information-processing Model of Psychometric *g*

The phenomenon of psychometric *g* was discovered eighty-five years ago (Spearman, 1904), and it has been a classic "black box" in psychology ever since. Psychologists are still trying to discover the nature of the mechanisms or processes that can explain *g* and its relation to other phenomena. The experimental psychologist's endeavor is not unlike the physicist's effort to fathom the basis of matter. Various behavioral (and a very few physiological) correlates of psychometric *g* are measured under specially devised laboratory conditions, and the data are used as probes to develop and test hypotheses or models of what goes on in the black box. The cutting edge of this research today is allied with recent work in experimental cognitive psychology. It has largely adopted the terminology, concepts, and metaphors of the information-processing models that originated with the development of computers and work on artificial intelligence (Newell and Simon, 1972).

Rather than explicating any specific model that has been the focus of theoretical investigation to any particular school of thought in this field, I will try to indicate some of the main research aims in terms of a simple generic model that incorporates the essential features of many other models. To begin, a few definitions will help.

An *elementary cognitive process* (ECP) is a hypothetical construct that plays a crucial role in information-processing. A specific mental content (that is, sensation, percept, image, memory) is acted upon (discriminated, encoded, repeated or rehearsed, transformed, stored, retrieved) in some singular way by a particular ECP. The information-processing system has some limited (but as yet undetermined) number of ECPs. It is assumed (and empirically demonstrated in some ECPs) that there are individual differences in ECPs, but it is not yet settled how independent (uncorrelated) the ECPs are. My present surmise from the available evidence is that various ECPs are correlated, but far from perfectly. There is probably a common factor (most likely at the neural level) in all ECPs, but this common factor in ECPs constitutes only some fraction (probably less than one-fourth) of the total variance of psychometric g. Hence, the ECPs would have considerable independence, and a great many different patterns of individual differences would exist that could not be explained by any single factor common to all of the ECPs. It seems most likely that variance in psychometric g comprises both the common factor variance of all the ECPs and the specific variance of each of them. Getting a solid answer to this conjecture is one of the major aims of investigation.

An *elementary cognitive task* (ECT) is (usually) a laboratory contrivance for measuring an ECP in terms of response time, which affords an absolute scale. Most ECTs unavoidably measure two or more ECPs, but the separate ECPs can often be measured indirectly by comparing measurements derived from two or more different ECTs that are hypothesized to reflect different ECPs. For example, one ECT measure reflects the operations of ECPs $a + b$, while another ECT measure reflects the operations of $a + b + c$. By subtraction we can obtain a measure of c. (There are also other more complex methods than simple subtraction that we need not go into here [see Jensen, 1985c].) ECTs measure elementary processes such as stimulus apprehension, encoding of sensations, discrimination, choice or decision, and retrieval of information short-term or long-term memory.

Because ECTs are necessarily exceedingly simple tasks, individual differences cannot be measured in terms of number of correct or incorrect answers, as in conventional psychometric tests. It is usually an essential requirement of the experiment that all subjects be able to perform the ECT with a very high level of accuracy. Error rates are usually kept so low that individual differences in errors are almost random and hence have low reliability. Reliable measurement of individual differences, therefore, depends on the use of chronometric techniques (Jensen, 1985c). The main measures of interest, then, are (1) speed of response, or the median reaction time (RT) over n trials, and (2) the consistency of response speed from trial to trial, measured as the SD of the RTs over the n trials.

Every component of information-processing occurs in time and the amounts of time for various components can be measured with great precision. The fact that time is measured on a true ratio scale with internationally standardized units is one of the great scientific advantages that experimental research and theoretical development based on mental chronometry has over conventional psychometry.

In normal young adults, the total time required for the performance of most ECTs is very short, usually less than one second between stimulus and response, and many ECTs are in the range of two hundred to six hundred milliseconds. Some part of this time (something between one hundred and two hundred milliseconds) consists of sensory lag plus afferent and efferent neural conduction time. The rest is central processing time. Now, it is an important empirical fact, quite apart from any theoretical interpretation, that virtually every ECT in which individual differences have been tested chronometrically has shown a significant correlation with psychometric g. Individual differences in median RT and in trial-to-trial consistency (that is, intra-individual variability) of RT are both correlated with g, each somewhat independently of the other. The correlations vary, depending on the particular ECT — its degree of complexity, or the number and types of different ECPs it is hypothesized to reflect. The correlations are generally in the .2 to .4 range but are seldom higher than .5 or .6, even after corrections for attenuation and restriction of the range of talent.

Multiple correlations based on a number of different ECTs, however, can be considerably higher. This suggests that psychometric g reflects the operations of a number of at least partially independent cognitive processes, no single one of which can account for more than about 10 percent to 15 percent of the true variance in g. But there is reason to believe that some processes probably contribute more than others to the variance in g. The simplest or most elemental process we have yet found to be significantly correlated with g (recently demonstrated in my lab in collaboration with Professor T. E. Reed) is the time for a visual stimulus to arrive at the visual cortex. It is less than about one-fourth of the time required for conscious recognition of the stimulus. So this represents just the pre-conscious phase of stimulus apprehension, reflected by the brain-evoked potential, occurring on average about one hundred milliseconds following onset of the visual stimulus. Yet, amazingly, it is very significantly correlated with nonverbal IQ in a restricted range of college students. I mention these surprising findings to emphasize that even the most basic and elemental information processes contribute some part of the variance in g. Many examples of correlations between ECTs and g have been re-viewed by Snow and Lohman (1988) and in a recent book edited by Vernon (1987).

The term *metaprocess* in this domain refers to executive processes, or processes which govern the deployment and organization of ECPs for problem-solving routines, planning a course of action, and monitoring performance. Its metaphoric overtones of a homunculus acting somewhere in the brain like a traffic cop or orchestra conductor makes it seem a rather unappealing construct. It is acceptable, however, if metaprocess is used generically to mean any kind of learned strategy, complex routine, or integrated set of covert or overt responses that play a part in pur-posive behavior. Some metaprocesses, by becoming "automatic," theoretically explain marked variation in the efficiency of complex information-processing.

A simple schematic representation of the hypothetical information-processing system is shown in figure 4–2. No special virtue is claimed for this particular schema, but it includes the main elements of many other proposed models. Research in mental chronometry shows that each of these processing stations (represented as rectangles) takes some amount of time, as does the transfer of information between them (represented as arrows). The total processing time between stimulus input and response output will depend on:

1. the complexity of the input,
2. how many processing elements are involved,
3. how many paths are traversed,
4. how many transformations are made, and

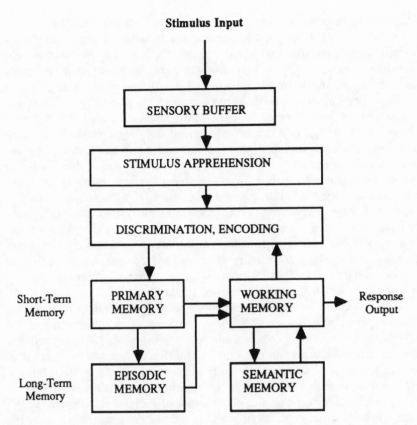

Figure 4−2. Hypothetical Schema of Information-Processing Components, with Arrows Indicating the Direction of Information Flow

5. how efficiently all these processes occur, both separately and as an integrated system.

All of these variables seem to be positively correlated to different degrees with *g*.

The largest source of *g* variance is the short-term memory (STM) system. A theoretical interpretation of the research findings in this system makes it necessary to posit two distinct aspects of STM, termed *primary memory* and *working memory*. Primary memory is a passive, limited-capacity, short-term storage system. It is passive in the sense that it does not perform transformations or other manipulations on the information contained in it. It has limited capacity in the sense that it can "hold" only a limited amount of information at one time; further input beyond that limited amount interferes with and "erases" the previous information held in primary memory. And it is short-term in the sense that the most recently input information is rapidly lost as a function of time.

Working memory can be thought of as the focal point of g in the whole system. It has been referred to as the mind's scratch pad, but it is better likened to a computer's central processing unit. The working memory transforms and manipulates information received from primary memory or retrieved from semantic memory. In most learning and problem solving, the working memory retrieves from long-term semantic memory whatever information is needed to interpret the recently input information in primary memory. Like primary memory, the working memory has a limited capacity and the information it operates on is also subject to rapid loss over time. The working memory can transform information received from primary memory and return it to primary memory for later use, or it can further encode and rehearse the information to get it into long-term memory (LTM) from which it can be retrieved for later use.

Two properties of working memory are hypothesized to account for what experimental evidence leads us to surmise about its functions: (1) the *speed* or efficiency of performing its operations and (2) its *capacity*, or the amount of information or number of different operations it can deal with at one time. These two attributes seem to be closely related, but the exact nature of the relationship is still obscure. Yet both seem necessary for understanding some of the phenomena of individual differences. We know that when the capacity of working memory is strained by requiring the subject to perform a dual task (some mental manipulation on one task while holding immediately previous input information in STM), the RT on the target task is increased over what it would have been if the same task had been presented as a single task. (Intra-individual variability in RT is also increased in the dual task condition.) And the g loadings of both variables are larger in the dual than in the single task condition. If there were individual differences in only one underlying process (either speed or capacity), single tasks and dual tasks should correlate equally with g when corrected for attenuation. There are also more complicated findings (which would require too much explication for inclusion here) that cannot be explained if we hypothesize a single basic individual-differences parameter in working memory rather than at least two. I hypothesize a model in which an individual's RT to a given ECT is a function of the total time (T_0) in seconds taken by all the processing of the input and output that occurs outside the working memory, the processing speed (S) of working memory (in bits per second), the *capacity* (C) of working memory (in bits), and the *number* (N) of bits of information that have to be processed. Thus RT = f(T_0, N, S, C). But the exact form of the equation has not yet been worked out.

If $N > C$, either processing must occur in stages, if possible, or there is a "breakdown" in performance. The variable of capacity (C) can be measured indirectly and expressed in real time units by the size of its effect on RT. When a given amount of information x is being processed in working memory and then is increased by the addition of information y to the STM system, the RT to x is increased, and the amount of increase in RT is inversely related to the capacity of the individual's working memory.

Studies of memory span for digits probably illustrate the capacity hypothesis most simply. For example, I have found that Berkeley students have a memory span of about eight digits on average, but only if they are presented no more than eight digits. If as many as twelve digits are presented, students typically can recall only the first three. But individuals who are perfectly matched on a digit span of, say, eight will show significantly different amounts of interference loss as a result of having to pay attention to the additional four digits in the twelve-item digit series (Jensen, 1965). It seems impossible to account for this phenomenon in terms of a single underlying process. An even more striking example is the difference between forward and backward digit span (FDS and BDS). The fact that FDS and BDS are not highly correlated even when corrected for attenuation indicates that at least two different processes are involved. The sheer storage requirements of the FDS and BDS tasks are identical. But because in BDS the set of digits has to be perfectly reversed between input and output, BDS makes a considerably greater processing demand on working memory than does FDS. BDS is always smaller and has a longer latency of response than FDS. Hence, both the capacity and speed of working memory are better measured by BDS than by FDS, and one index of the overall efficiency of working memory is the difference between BDS and FDS. As should be expected from our theory of the central role of working memory in information-processing, the g loading of BDS has been found to be about double that of FDS (Jensen and Figueroa, 1975).

The importance of processing speed in the operation of working memory stems directly from the capacity limitation and the rapid decay of information in STM. The limited capacity of the working memory severely restricts the number of operations that can be performed at any one time on the information that enters the system from external stimuli or from retrieval of information stored in primary memory or in LTM. Quickness of mental operations is advantageous because more operations per unit of time can be executed without overloading the system. Also, because there is rapid decay of stimulus traces in the sensory buffers and of information in primary memory, there is an advantage to speediness of any operations that must be executed on the information while it is still available. To compensate for limited capacity and rapid decay of incoming information, the individual resorts to rehearsal and storage of information into LTM, which has a relatively unlimited capacity. But the process of storing information in LTM itself uses up channel space, so there is a "trade-off" between the storage and the processing of incoming information. The more complex the information and the more operations on it that are required, the more time that is necessary, and consequently the greater is the advantage of speediness in all the elementary processes involved. Loss of information due to overload interference and decay of information that was inadequately encoded or rehearsed for storage and retrieval from LTM results in a failure to grasp all the essential relationships among the elements of a complex problem needed for its solution. Speediness of information-processing, therefore, should be increasingly related to success in dealing with cognitive tasks to the extent that their information load strains the individual's limited capacity.

The most discriminating test items are those that "threaten" the information-processing system at the threshold of overload or "breakdown" — the point that most fully reflects both the speed of operations and the capacity of working memory. In a series of items of graded complexity, this breakdown would occur at different points for various individuals. Processing time and probability of breakdown are closely related. For example, we (Jensen, Larson, and Paul, 1988) have found that in a set of extremely easy test items suitable for third-graders whose average failure rate on the items under an untimed testing condition is only about 17 percent, the different failure rates (that is, breakdown) on the various items are almost perfectly correlated with the response latencies on the same items obtained from young adults who were given each item as a reaction-time test. (The adults' error rates were almost nil.) Also, the adults' RTs on this test were significantly correlated with psychometric g.

Measurements of individual differences in the speed of elemental components can be obtained on tasks that are so simple as to make breakdown failure very unlikely, as in the various ECTs based on chronometric techniques in which RT is found to be correlated with scores on complex psychometric tests, such as the Wechsler Scales and the Raven Matrices. A faster rate of information-processing permits more information to be processed per unit of time, and since all knowledge and skills acquisition depends on information-processing, persons who process information faster acquire more knowledge and skill from a given amount of experience. One of the best researched ECTs measures an individual's speed of mentally scanning very recently input information in STM (Sternberg, 1966). These speeds are very fast, averaging in young adults about seventy-five milliseconds per each digit scanned, and these speeds are substantially correlated with g (Jensen, 1987d). Although individual differences in the extremely short RTs to ECTs seem very slight, often amounting to no more than a few milliseconds, they become of considerable consequence when multiplied over an extended period of time. For example, the seemingly slight but reliable differences in RTs to very simple ECTs between average and gifted children (even when the average and gifted are full siblings reared together) are correlated (at about age twelve) with quite large differences in amounts of general knowledge, vocabulary, and academic skills (Cohn, Carlson, and Jensen, 1985; Jensen, Cohn, and Cohn, 1989). These findings are consistent with the well-substantiated fact that the time required to learn scholastic subjects to a uniform criterion of mastery is highly correlated with IQ, that is, mainly with g.

Semantic memory (returning to figure 4–2) has practically unlimited capacity and is a reservoir of verbally or otherwise symbolically encoded information, including past-learned meanings, relationships, rules, and strategies for operating on certain classes of information (such as words, syntax, numbers and arithmetic operations, musical notation, chess combinations, and the like). Specific contents of semantic memory may be crucial for solving certain problems. The amount of information in semantic memory is a function of experience, interest, motivation, and learning opportunities, but mostly it is a function of the efficiency of working memory, which is the agency through which information becomes stored in semantic memory. Its usefulness to the individual, aside from the amount of information stored, depends on its accessibility to working memory. The speed of access to information in LTM is a joint function of the processing speed of working memory, the manner in which information is encoded and organized in semantic LTM, and the amount and recency of practice in retrieving the information. A number of ECTs, all variations on the well-known "Posner paradigm" (Posner, Boies, Eichelman, and Taylor, 1969), have been used to measure the speed with which individuals can access various kinds of information in semantic LTM. The speed of access even to extremely simple and highly over-learned verbal codes in LTM, such as the letters of the alphabet, is correlated with g and with verbal ability (independently of g) in university students (Hunt, 1976).

In any learning situation, working memory brings the products of past learning from LTM into conjunction with novel inputs to arrive at problem solutions or to encode and rehearse the perceived relationships of the "new" information to the "old" information in preparation for storing it in semantic LTM. Hence, the information content of LTM is cumulative, but the degree and system of organization of the stored information is an important determinant of its later accessibility and usability. This is obviously an aspect of the information-processing system in which instructional methods could play an important role.

Episodic LTM is of lesser interest in the present context. It is a store of non-semantically encoded spatial-temporal experiences. "Recognition memory" of faces and places and memories of sensory and emotional experiences and specific events and their contexts are classed as episodic memory. Some episodic memories can be tagged, encoded, or transformed by the working memory for storage in the semantic LTM.

The efficiency of the operations performed in a given individual's working memory is not a constant but can vary markedly according to the processing strategies adopted and the amount of practice the individual has had in processing a particular kind of information. Single bits of information can be organized or "chunked" into larger units, which can then be dealt with as single bits by the working memory. The net effect is equivalent to increasing the capacity of the individual's working memory. But this strategy seems to be less general in enhancing the total economy of information-processing than the phenomenon termed *automatic processing*, or *automatization*.

Cognitive theorists have made the important distinction between *controlled* and *automatic* processing, which some theorists regard not just as quantitatively different aspects of processing (for example, slow versus fast and hard versus easy), but as qualitatively different kinds of processing (Shiffrin and Schneider, 1977). The development of automatic processing through learning and practice, however, is necessarily always preceded by controlled processing (Shiffrin and Dumais, 1981).

Because automatic processing is mainly a function of learning and practice, it probably has greater implications for education than any other single aspect of cognitive theory.

Controlled Processing. Controlled processing of information demands the individual's focused attention, requires conscious mental effort, is relatively slow, and deals with information input sequentially, being able to deal with only very limited amounts of information at one time and being unable to execute different operations simultaneously. These of course are all recognized as the characteristics associated with working memory. In some circumstances the input demand on controlled processing may crowd the full capacity of working memory; any faster rate of input overloads the system and results in "breakdown" or "turn-off." Solving novel problems, learning new knowledge or skills, and consciously monitoring an unpredictably changing situation that calls for varied responses all involve controlled processing. If everything we did mentally had to depend entirely on controlled processing, life would be intolerably burdensome indeed, and our efficiency would be greatly impaired. Fortunately, the evolution of the human brain has provided it with the means for escape from such a fate, namely, the development of automatic processing.

Automatic Processing. Practice, if sufficiently long-term, can automatize certain information-processing routines, which frees working memory for the controlled processing of other information. In contrast to controlled processing, automatic processing does not demand one's entire attention; it is relatively effortless and can deal with large amounts of information and perform different operations on it simultaneously.

The degree to which task performance can become automatized depends on how consistent, predictable, or routine the information-processing demands of the task are. Automatization is easier the more consistent the required sequence of operations between input and output. In learning to send Morse code, for example, there is an invariant relationship between letters of the alphabet and their corresponding dot-and-dash codes. The act of sending and receiving messages becomes completely automatized for expert telegraphers.

Most skills, however, involve both controlled and automatic processing. Driving a car is a good example. In the early stage of learning to drive, controlled processing predominates. To minimize external distractions, the learner must practice in a quiet street. The learner's full and undivided attention is required to execute smoothly the simultaneous operations of the clutch, the gear shift, the gas pedal, the steering wheel, and the brake, and also to remember to make the appropriate hand signals at the right times. While doing all this the learner finds it impossible to converse, listen to the radio, or think about other things, without risk of grinding gears, killing the engine, running off the road, or worse.

With more practice, driving skill becomes increasingly automatic. The seasoned driver performs all these operations without having to think about them at all. Controlled processing is still necessary, however, to deal with constantly changing traffic conditions. We have to relinquish conversation or other attention-demanding activity momentarily when traffic conditions change suddenly or look complicated and unpredictable. The working memory is briefly occupied to full capacity. That is controlled processing. If all of the driver's operational skills were not fully automatic, they would encroach on the capacity of working memory and thereby impair the efficiency of the controlled processing needed to get through the traffic crisis without a mishap.

A perfect example of the combined roles of controlled and automatic processing is sight-reading an unfamiliar piece of music — an essential requirement of professional orchestra players. The controlled processing aspect of this feat occupies a considerable part of the capacity of working memory, especially if the performer must play up-to-tempo and at the same time be highly responsive to the conductor's expressive signals. Yet it would be utterly impossible for controlled processing to accomplish this kind of performance were it not for the fact that in professional musicians both the reading of musical notation and its execution on their instruments are about 99 percent automatized. Scarcely any thought at all need be given to those aspects of the musical notation per se that normally demand so much of the novice's attention, or to the incredibly complex combinations of perfectly coordinated muscular movements required to produce the correct sequences of notes on a musical instrument.

Indeed, many complex skills can never be mastered at all without a high degree of automatization of many of its components, because just the absolutely irreducible demand on controlled processing alone takes up the full capacity of the working memory, making it necessary that other components of the skill occur automatically. A high degree of automatic processing is not just a greatly speeded-up form of controlled processing. It is most characterized by simultaneity of different processes and "pattern thinking." Duffers at chess, for example, think only one move ahead at most. Excellent chess players often think several moves ahead. But world-class chess masters work quite differently. Research on the nature of their skill in chess has discovered that they seldom think ahead at all. They instantly perceive a whole pattern on the chessboard, and the properties of the pattern largely dictate the optimal move in light of the player's particular strategy. Chess masters easily memorize entire chess games in terms of such patterns, much as we can recall a sentence we have just read, without any conscious attention to the sequence of all the individual letters it contains. Yet studies have shown that chess masters do not have an exceptional memory in general. Given various memory tests unrelated to chess, they perform on a par with most college students. The difference is that the chess master's LTM is extraordinarily well-stocked with chess rules, strategies, positions, combinations, and the like, which are automatically accessed the moment the chess master looks at a particular configuration of pieces on the chessboard. The phenomenon is akin to literacy in one's native language.

Although the speed of controlled processing and the capacity of working memory are of great importance because of their heavy contribution to variance in g, recent research on persons who show truly exceptional performance in any field indicates that the critical difference between them and the average run is not raw g, but depends essentially on a much greater than ordinary amount of automatization of certain knowledge and skills in the person's field of achievement (Ericsson and Crutcher, in press).

The road to automatization—apparently the only road—is practice, and plenty of it, accompanied by conscious effort to improve performance. Few people realize the exceeding amount and consistency of practice that recent studies have revealed to be the indispensable precursors of surpassing skill or expertise in any field. Paderewski, who routinely practiced the piano ten hours a day in his youth, when later acclaimed a genius, remarked, "Yes, and before I was a genius I was a drudge." (See references to this research literature in Ericsson and Crutcher, 1990.)

Automatization and g. Individual differences in the development of automatization are also probably related to g, or at least to that part of its variance associated with the processing speed and capacity of working memory. However, the most thorough discussions of the research on this topic I have found in the literature (Ackerman, 1986, 1987; Ackerman and Schneider, 1985) give no definitive evidence that automatization is related to g. But it seems to me almost inevitable that the development of automatization would be related to the efficiency of controlled processing in working memory, because that would govern the amount of information that could be processed per unit of practice time. It is common knowledge among music teachers, for example, that high IQ children acquire skill on a musical instrument faster than low IQ children. The nominally same amount of practice generally results in greater improvement in the brighter children, quite apart from a musical talent factor. So when future research eventually answers this question, it would be most surprising if no correlation were found between individual differences in automatization and psychometric g. But this in no way rules out the potential value of increasing automatization in some people who, for whatever reason, have not adequately automatized certain essential skills.

Motivation and Automatization. The development of automatic processing in a particular area is strongly related to how motivated the person is in that area. Attempting to improve students' motivation is always problematic, but it is especially so in connection with low ability. The reason is that the behavioral characteristics we recognize as indicating a high level of motivation for learning and practice in a particular subject are really just the predictable result of positive reinforcement. And one of the most fundamental "laws" in psychology is that positive reinforcement increases both the strength and the frequency of the reinforced behavior.

Generally, the most effective reinforcements in human learning result from the learner's immediate perception of the successes and failures in the learner's own performance, as the learner assesses it, in terms of its external consequences or by comparison with the performance of others or by subjective comparison with an internalized standard. One of the most important functions of a teacher is to set the standard or model of performance for the student to internalize. Both the student's performance and the effort that accompanies it are positively reinforced every time the student perceives he or she has made a closer approximation to the internalized standard. A fairly optimal schedule of such reinforcements results in the characteristics we recognize as a motivated student. The ablest individuals in any domain usually get a more optimal schedule of reinforcement and therefore become more motivated in the successful activity. It is a positive feedback loop. Just the opposite occurs for the least able learners. If one's attempts to learn something are insufficiently reinforced, with the consequent decrease in motivation, the person usually drops the learning activity with impunity, unless it involves an educationally or economically critical skill.

There are also individual differences in energy level. It is a general factor probably with a strong biological basis. Energy level interacts with motivation. But motivation itself is not a general factor, it is acquired in a particular context and remains connected with specific activities. Highly motivated performance sustains the most practice and therefore is more subject to automatization of those aspects for which controlled processing is not essential. Such automatization, like motivation, also creates a positive feedback in the person's further progress in the practiced domain. Thus, we see the magnifying effect of experience on individual differences in every kind of achievement that does not impose a low ceiling on performance.

Assessment of Automatization. Before explaining the importance of automatization in school learning, something must be said about the assessment aspects of it. Automatization is difficult to study experimentally because it develops only over extended periods of practice. For practical educational and diagnostic purposes, however, it is feasible to study the automatization of certain scholastic skills in which students are known to have received a given number of months or semesters of instruction. Little is known about individual differences in automatization tendency when practice conditions are held constant. But we do know that amount of experience, or practice, is a major determinant of automatization. So when we assess individual differences in the automatization of material learned in natural settings, such as school learning, we are probably measuring an amalgam of both intrinsic differences in tendency to automatization of learned material and differences in the amount of practice that has been devoted to it, whatever the cause of these differences may be.

As already explained, the automatization of knowledge and skill has mainly two results: (1) it greatly speeds up access to the needed information in LTM and (2) it frees some of the capacity of working memory. The assessment of automatization, therefore, must reflect both of these aspects. To make the discussion realistic, say we are concerned with the automatization of the simple "number facts" in arithmetic, for example, the multiplication of all the single digits one through nine with each other. (The importance of automatizing such simple skills is discussed in the following section.)

Automatization is meaningless unless some content to be automatized already exists. The first thing we must do, then, is to determine if the student actually knows the times tables, which can be revealed by a non-speeded paper-and-pencil test. Assuming we find that the student knows all the times tables, we then have to determine to what extent this knowledge has been automatized. Like much of medical diagnosis, the task involves interpreting a number of different clues. Chronometric techniques are essential for doing this. A baseline measurement is the student's median RT and intra-individual variability (SD of RT over trials) for the student's binary responses (True/False) to number discriminations that involve approximately the same amount of visual information as the multiplication facts, for example, $5 = 5 = 5$ (T) or $3 = 5 = 3$ (F). The very same RT variables are then obtained on the multiplication facts, for example, $3 \times 5 = 15$ (T) or $3 \times 5 = 18$ (F).

We have determined in our laboratory that median RTs on these kinds of tasks can be obtained with reliability coefficients above .90 in about twenty minutes of testing. In a group of age-matched students, there will be a moderate correlation between the median RTs on the two tasks just described. The regression of RT for multiplication on RT for simple number discrimination, then, affords one index of automatization. Students who place significantly above the regression line are suspected of not having automatized access to the multiplication facts as well as those who fall below the regression line. The slope of the regression line should decrease as a function of age and increasing skill in arithmetic, and a person's RTs can be viewed in relation to the regression line in various normative age and ability groups. The possibility that simple number recognition itself has not been well automatized can be investigated in the same way, from the regression of (1) the median RT in the simple number discrimination task on (2) the median RT in a binary choice RT task using visual stimuli that have no scholastic content, such as red versus green lights.

Intra-individual variability can be analyzed in the same way. Some students are very uneven in the degree of automatization of number facts, and this shows up in their much greater variability in RTs across different items.

The degree to which automatization of one skill frees the capacity of working memory for dealing with some other input can be assessed by means of a *dual task* procedure, which also depends on the measurement of RTs. It requires one task that inescapably demands controlled processing and occupies the working memory. A good example of such a task is the Semantic Verification Test (SVT). In the SVT a simple statement of the following type appears on the screen:

A before B

(The negative counterpart, A not before B, appears on half of the trials; also A after B, and A not after B are used.) After two seconds, the statement goes off, and after a one-second blank interval, the two letters appear side-by-side, A B (or B A), and the subject responds either True or False (by pressing buttons labeled T of F), indicating whether the order of the paired letters agrees or disagrees with the stem statement. There are considerable individual differences in the median RT. University students were found to have a 0.67 SD faster RT than age-matched navy recruits on a three-letter SVT for which median RT was correlated $-.45$ with the highly g-loaded Raven Matrices scores in university students (Jensen, Larson, and Paul, 1988). The SVT obviously makes a considerable demand on the working memory. The target task, say, is multiplication facts, for example, $5 \times 4 = 20$ (T). Median RTs (and SD of RT) are obtained on both the SVT and the target task, each administered separately. But then the two tasks are also combined as a dual task, in which the sequence of presentation is as follows:

A before B   (two seconds)
$5 \times 4 = 20$ (T)   (RT in milliseconds)
B A (F)   (RT in milliseconds)

Interposing the target task between the stem and the reaction stimulus of the SVT has the effect of increasing the RT on both tasks, as compared to the RT when the tasks are given separately in the single-task conditions. The measured increment in the RTs is inversely related to the degree to which the retrieval of the information called for by the interposed task has been automatized.

These kinds of procedures and variations of them can be used to study individual differences in the elemental components of controlled and automatic processing of the kinds of information that constitute the basic knowledge and skills on which scholastic achievement beyond the elementary grades critically depends.

Controlled and Automatic Processing in Scholastic Skills

Proficiency in the three Rs depends on a high degree of automatization of numerous subskills, as does the learning of most other school subjects. At every step in learning complex subject matter, the consistent or routine aspects of the task must become automatic in order to free the working memory to cope with the novel aspects of the task, or to process new information coming from the teacher or the text. Much that is learned without becoming automatic turns out to be functionally inadequate when the learned material must serve as a prerequisite for more advanced learning. The failure to automatize certain subskills at one stage of learning can prove a severe handicap when the learner reaches a more advanced level. In some cases, more advanced learning is even impossible, because the task demands on controlled processing greatly exceed the capacity of working memory. Hence, progress is possible only if most of the task demands have already been automatized, leaving the working memory free to deal with only those novel aspects that can never become automatic. Experts differ from novices in (1) the extent of their task-relevant knowledge in LTM, (2) the way it is encoded and organized in LTM, and (3) the speed of its retrieval and use through automatic processing. It is mainly these three factors that account for experts' superior problem-solving skill and their ability to learn something new in their field of expertise much easier and faster than is possible for novices, regardless of their IQ.

Reading Comprehension. A prime example of these concepts of information-processing and automatization is reading comprehension. The act of reading is an incredibly complex process that depends on virtually every element in the entire information-processing system as well as the automatization of many subskills. Reading, in fact, is so complex and its information-processing demands are so great that it would be impossible if so much of it were not automatized. In good readers, the decoding (that is, letter and word recognition) processes are completely automatic. If decoding depended on controlled processing and usurped the reader's working memory, reading *comprehension* would be virtually impossible.

Most people fail to realize the degree of complexity involved in reading, such as the fact that a number of specific subskills have to be coordinated, because these subskills have become so automatized that good readers have lost all awareness of them—letter recognition, name retrieval, word decoding, and semantic access (that is, the automatic search and elicitation of meanings stored in LTM). In recent years, research on reading has become highly sophisticated. Information-processing conceptions and the use of chronometric techniques make it possible to observe and measure the different components of reading skill at an extremely fine-grained level (see, Carpenter and Just, 1981; Jackson and McClelland, 1979; LaBerge and Samuels, 1974; Lesgold and Perfetti, 1981; Perfetti, 1983; Waldron, 1987). Automatic processing, which is unconscious, is found to be much faster than controlled processing, and even automatic processes in reading that occur within 1/100th of a second can be specifically identified.

Some of these automatic processes can be isolated from the context of actual reading, to be subjected to analytical study of their general properties in the experimental laboratory. It is a telling fact that when a number of the subskills of reading are measured separately, the correlations between them are higher in a group of good readers (that is, high scorers on standardized reading tests) than in a group of poor readers. This suggests that the good readers have mastered each of the subskills at the automatic level, whereas the poor readers have automatized some of the subskills but not others. Chronometric methods have also revealed many other ways that good and poor readers differ. Poor readers show a slower speed of retrieving well-learned letter or name codes from LTM, and they are slower in semantic matching, that is, responding either same or different to a pair of familiar words depending on whether they are synonyms or antonyms—a test that reflects speed of access to the meanings of words and phrases stored in LTM. Poor readers also show a slower speed of initiating the pronouncing of pseudo-words; individual differences in this simple task were found to be correlated .68 with scores on a standard test of reading comprehension (Fredericksen, 1980).

Word-span is the number of unrelated words that can be perfectly recalled *in toto* immediately following a single presentation of a set of words at a given rate. Word-span shows only low to moderate correlations with reading comprehension scores on standard tests. The correlations are not higher evidently because passive memory span requires little controlled processing and involves the primary STM more than the working memory.

This conjecture led Daneman (1982) to invent an exceedingly simple but clever test, known as the *Reading Span Test*. The subject has to read aloud sets of two to five unrelated sentences, with the instruction that the last word in each sentence would have to be recalled after the set of sentences had been completed. The task is surprisingly difficult. Scores among university students range from two to five final words recallled, with a mean of about three. Obviously the controlled processing demands of reading these sentences with comprehension takes up much of the capacity of working memory, unlike the passive word-span test. But the most striking finding is that scores on the Reading Span Test are typically correlated about .7 with scores on standardized tests of reading comprehension. This indicates that even when the decoding process is highly automatized, reading comprehension depends heavily on the efficiency of working memory, which helps explain why tests of reading comprehension are just about as highly *g*-loaded as either verbal or nonverbal IQ tests in groups that have no trouble with the decoding aspect of reading.

Not surprisingly, the Reading Span Test is correlated almost as highly with tests of listening comprehension, because verbal comprehension makes much the same processing demands on working memory, regardless of whether the subject actively reads or simply listens to the material. Individual differences in either reading comprehension or listening comprehension arise largely from individual differences in the efficiency of working memory.

All these points (and others) are well illustrated in some excellent research in the armed sevices that separately measures the decoding and comprehension aspects of reading (Sticht, Hooke, and Caylor, 1981). But this research also reveals some important points that would be almost impossible to demonstrate in studies of reading based exclusively on university students. In 1976, some 50 percent of enlistees at an army base had reading levels at the fifth grade and below. In such groups with borderline literacy, measures of decoding skills measured independently of comprehension account for even more of the variance in scores on standard reading comprehension tests that does the efficiency of working memory. Thus, considerable improvement in the absolute level of reading comprehension could be achieved by training aimed at the automatization of decoding skills in such groups of poor readers. Persons who are poor readers because they have not fully automatized all of the decoding processes can be identified by means of a clever test of word decoding used by Sticht et al. (1981) and also by their showing significantly better listening comprehension than reading comprehension. Poor readers who show good listening comprehension are the most apt to benefit from training in decoding.

Arithmetic and Mathematics. These subjects have as yet received much less empirical study from an information-processing perspective than reading. Yet, they are nearly as important in the school curriculum, and they lend themselves ideally to conceptualization in information-processing terms and to analysis by chronometric techniques. (A good overview of current thinking in this area is provided by Briars [1983].) The learning of arithmetic and mathematics is hierarchical, that is, ease of learning at each higher level of complexity depends on prior mastery of more elementary skills. Such mastery depends heavily on the development of automatic processing if it is to promote more advanced learning.

Many pupils begin to experience unusual difficulty in learning arithmetic when they are in fourth to sixth grade, even when they have not evinced any real difficulty in earlier grades. Usually they can obtain perfect scores on non-speeded paper-and-pencil tests of elementary arithmetic requiring knowledge of simple number facts, such as addition, subtraction, and multiplication of single-digit numbers. Then, quite suddenly, in grades four to six, when more complex arithmetic operations and applications are introduced, such as short and long division, fractions, decimals, percentages, powers and roots, and words problems requiring these operations, some pupils experience inordinate difficulty. As a result, many are completely "turned off" to math and swell the ranks of adult innumerates. Such problems can be studied most fruitfully in the context of information-processing by means of chronometric techniques.

An obvious hypothesis from an information-processing standpoint is that the elementary skills may have been learned sufficiently to pass the ordinary tests of these skills, but they have not been sufficiently "over-learned" to be automatized. They, therefore, require too much controlled processing and usurp too much of the capacity of working memory whenever these elementary skills are needed to deal with more complex kinds of problems that make heavy demands on controlled processing. Without automatization of basic skills, the presentation of more advanced material that depends on them simply overloads the student's processing capacity, causing a breakdown in learning.

This probably holds true at every level of learning mathematics. The importance of rule automation for learning and transfer in algebra transformations and word problems is shown in a series of studies by Cooper and Sweller (1987). Their findings suggested training techniques that facilitated the development of automation (as they call it). Most interesting is their finding that the strongest effect of automation is its facilitation of *transfer* of the learning of one type of problem to different types of problems. Breadth of transfer is a well-known correlate of *g*. Individuals with low IQ show little transfer of specific skills they have learned to novel conditions. But automation of a skill is a relatively slow and prolonged affair compared to just learning the skill. What seems to have happened in the study by Cooper and Sweller is that as students automatized certain aspects of algebra, it freed their working memory and, in effect, conserved their *g*, which made for greater transfer. Transfer of training depends on the subject's analysis of the relatively novel transfer problem to find familiar features, and that requires controlled processing. This analytic process is hindered if the algebraic subskills relevant to the familiar features in the transfer problem have not been automatized.

Aims of Future Research

A disturbing feature of the contemporary research scene in educational psychology has been its conspicuous retreat from large-scale programmatic research on the cognitive aspects of children who are "at risk" for unacceptably low levels of achievement.

The tidal wave of studies of the educationally disadvantaged in the 1950s and 1960s was based mainly on sociological and behaviorist theories. The prevailing thoughts about educational deficit and compensatory education during that period largely ignored the body of knowledge and methods of differential psychology. Since the 1940s, this field had become a stagnant backwater in psychology. Its methodological legacy from such past luminaries as Galton, Spearman, Thorndike, and Thurstone became submerged in the more thriving field of psychometrics. With education's burgeoning research on the disadvantaged, fostered by abundant funding in the Kennedy-Johnson era, psychometrics unfortunately became a disfavored discipline and assumed a defensive and apologetic posture.

Information-processing theory and the revival of mental chronometry were scarcely more than mere seedlings at that time, so they could hardly have made an impact on educational research. At about the same time that these newer approaches to the study of cognitive abilities came fully into their own, in the 1970s and 1980s, there was a striking revival of resarch on most of the traditional problems of differential psychology. New journals and scientific societies sprung up devoted entirely to research on intelligence and behavioral genetics. These fields acquired a new look — more distanced from psychometrics and education and increasingly allied with experimental cognitive psychology, information-processing concepts, the methods of mental chronometry, and the neurosciences. It is hardly an exaggeration to say that there has been greater scientific ferment and progress in theory and research on the nature of human abilities in just the past decade than in all of the preceding half-century. And progress continues apace.

A peculiar thing has happened along the way, however — the earlier intense interest in the educationally disadvantaged rapidly dwindled and all but vanished. It was not taken up — or perhaps it was intentionally avoided — by the new school of cognitive researchers. Their studies are based largely on college students, scholastically mainstream students, and the gifted. Children with specific learning disabilities and the clinically retarded have also figured in some of this research. With the exception of studies of low-ability personnel in the armed services, however, present-day cognitive researchers have largely shunned the educationally "high-risk" schoolchildren who were the focus of so much research in the 1960s and 1970s. There are some scientifically legitimate reasons for this seeming avoidance, such as the need for experimental studies of cognitive processes per se, unencumbered by the social complications and controversy involved in studying population differences in scholastic performance.

The popular sociological and anthropological theories of educational disparity are too indirect and overarching to explain precisely the nature of children's achieving or failing to achieve in school. A quite different order of research and analysis are required to discover the mechanisms through which cultural and social factors, to whatever extent they may be involved, actually exert their effects on scholastic performance. The broadbrush concepts of sociology and anthropology seem unsuited for the level of analysis required.

If we are concerned with the fine grain of such questions, psychologists can probably best contribute by bringing the concepts and methods of information-processing research to bear on the study of children who sooner or later fail to benefit from schooling as we know it today.

Such research would not be just more of the same, which has been so discouraging in the past. Achievement is a complex product of different cognitive processes, each of which makes its contribution. A failure to learn what has been taught, or inordinate difficulty with some subject, or poor retention, or poor conceptual grasp — any of these deficits may be traced to one or more specific deficiencies in the information-processing system. For example, although studies have shown that the efficiency of the working-memory component accounts for most of the variance in reading comprehension among young adults, cognitive processing research on persons who were born deaf indicates that their mediocre verbal IQ and poor reading comprehension are not at all connected with the efficiency or capacity of their STM or working memory, but with a deficit of semantic codes in LTM — a remediable condition. Thus deficits in cognitive performance have to be understood at the process level in order to discover precisely what we can or cannot feasibly do about them.

Making such discoveries is probably possible with presently available methods. But if it is to be accomplished in the foreseeable future, it will require a concerted research effort by a great many of the most experienced investigators in this field, with financial support on a par with that of other major scientific missions, like discovering a cure for AIDS or deciphering the human genome.

The three classes of phenomena we still need to know much more about if we are to attempt educational innovation with good chances of success are the following:

1. Since psychometric g accounts for such a large part of the variance in scholastic performance, we need to know specifically which processing components are involved in g and the relative contributions each of these processes makes to the total variance in g. Going beyond mere correlation coefficients, we need to know how psychometric g is causally related to various kinds of achievement. Also, the design of research in this area must take account of the distinct possibility that the answers may not prove to be the same for different age brackets, for culturally different populations, or between the sexes. Scientifically compelling answers are not yet in our grasp.

2. We also need to develop a science and technology of cognitive process analysis for different types of achievement (for example, academic learning and vocational skills). This is an extension of traditional task analysis, which focuses on overt skills, to the underlying mental processes. The application of such analytical techniques to the study of reading, as indicated earlier, is a model for the study of many other elements of the curriculum at every level of education.

3. Finally, the presently most neglected subject of research: Focusing the process analysis of g and achievement directly on those segments of the school population that are now most predictably "at risk" for scholastic failure — mainly blacks and Hispanics in our inner-city schools. To coordinate such research with innovative educational experiments, it may be

necessary to bring a number of such "high-risk" schools under the auspices of university research departments organized for this purpose.

The cognitive process analysis of g and achievement, with their seemingly intractable variance in the school population, would yield knowledge that, if scientifically valid, could only turn out to be good news for education.

References

Ackerman, P. L. (1986) Individual differences in information processing: An investigation of intellectual abilities and task performance during practice, *Intelligence*, 10, 101–39.

Ackerman, P. L. (1987) Individual differences in skill learning: An integration of psychometric and information processing perspectives, *Psychological Bulletin*, 102, 3–27.

Ackerman, P. L. and W. Schneider. (1985) Individual differences in automatic and controlled information processing. In *Individual differences in cognition*, Vol. 2, ed. R. F. Dillon. New York: Academic Press.

Adams, M. J. (1989) Thinking skills curricula: Their promise and progress, *Educational Psychologist*, 24, 25–77.

Anderson, L. W. and R. B. Burns. (1987) Values, evidence, and mastery learning, *Review of Educational Research*, 57, 215–23.

Arvey, R. D. (1979) *Fairness in selecting employees*. Reading, MA: Addison-Wesley.

Atkinson, R. C. (1974) Teaching children to read using a computer, *American Psychologist*, 29, 169–78.

Baldwin, A. Y. (1985) Programs for the gifted and talented: Issues concerning minority populations. In *The gifted and talented: Developmental perspectives*, ed. F. D. Horowitz and M. O'Brien. Washington, DC: American Psychological Association.

Baldwin, A. Y. (1987) I'm black but look at me, I am also gifted, *Gifted Child Quarterly*, 31, 180–85.

Benbow, C. P. (1988) Neuropsychological perspectives on mathematical talent. In *The exceptional brain*, ed. L. K. Obler and D. Fein. New York: Guilford Press.

Benton, D. and G. Roberts. (1988) Effect of vitamin and mineral supplementation on intelligence of a sample of school children. *Lancet* No. 8578:140–43.

Bereiter, C. (1987) Jensen and educational differences. In *Arthur Jensen: Consensus and controversy*, ed. S. Modgil and C. Modgil. New York: The Falmer Press.

Bloom, B. S. (1987) A response to Slavin's mastery learning reconsidered, *Review of Educational Research*, 57, 507–8.

Brebner, J. and T. Nettelbeck. (1986) Intelligence and inspection time. Special issue, *Personality and Individual Differences*, 7, 603–729.

Briars, D. J. (1983) An information processing analysis of mathematical ability. In *Individual differences in cognition*, Vol. 1, ed. R. F. Dillon and R. R. Schmech. New York: Academic Press.

Brogden, H. E. (1946) On the interpretation of the correlation coefficient as a measure of predictive efficiency, *Journal of Educational Psychology*, 37, 65−76.

Brown, A. L. and J. C. Campione. (1982) Modifying intelligence or modifying cognitive skills: More than a semantic quibble? In *How and how much can intelligence be increased?*, ed. D. K. Detterman and R. J. Sternberg. Norwood: Ablex.

Campbell, J. T., Crooks, L. A., Mahoney, M. H. and D. A. Rock. (1973) *An investigation of sources of bias in the prediction of job performance, a six-year study*. Final Project Report PR-73−37. Princeton: Educational Testing Service.

Carnegie-Quarterly, (1987−1988) Black churches: Can they strengthen the black family? *CQ*, 33 (1), 1−9.

Carpenter, P. A. and M. A. Just. (1981) Cognitive processes in reading: Models based on readers' eye fixations. In *Interactive processes in reading*, ed. A. M. Lesgold and C. A. Perfetti. Hillsdale: Erlbaum.

Clark, R. E. (1982) Antagonism between achievement and enjoyment in ATI studies, *Educational Psychologist*, 13, 19−101.

Cohn, S. J., Carlson, J. S. and A. R. Jensen. (1985) Speed of information processing in academically gifted youths, *Personality and Individual Differences*, 6, 621−29.

Cohn, S. J., Cohn, C. M. G. and A. R. Jensen. (1988) Myopia and intelligence: A pleiotropic relationship? *Human Genetics*, 80, 53−58.

Cole, N. (1982) The implications of coaching for ability testing. In *Ability testing: Uses, consequences, controversies*, Part II, ed. A. K. Wigdor and W. R. Garner. Washington, DC: National Academy Press.

Cooper, G. and J. Sweller. (1987) Effects of schema acquisition and rule automation on mathematical problem-solving transfer, *Journal of Educational Psychology*, 79, 347−62.

Cory, C. H., Neffson, N. E. and B. Rimland. (1980) *Validity of a battery of experimental tests in predicting performance of Navy Project 100,000 personnel*. San Diego: Navy Personnel Research and Development Center.

Cronbach, L. J. and G. C. Gleser. (1965) *Psychological tests and personnel decisions*. Urbana: University of Illinois Press.

Cronbach, L. J. and R. E. Snow. (1977) *Aptitudes and instructional methods: A handbook for research on interactions*. New York: Irvington.

Crouse, J. and D. Trusheim. (1988) *The case against the SAT*. Chicago: University of Chicago Press.

Daneman, M. (1982) The measurement of reading comprehension: How not to trade construct validity for predictive power, *Intelligence*, 6, 331−45.

Detterman, D. K. (1987) What does reaction time tell us about intelligence? In *Speed of information-processing and intelligence*, ed. P. A. Vernon. Norwood:

Ablex.

Detterman, D. K. and R. J. Sternberg, (eds.) (1982) *How and how much can intelligence be increased.* Norwood: Ablex.

Ericsson, K. A. (1988) Analysis of memory performance in terms of memory skills. In *Advances in the psychology of human intelligence*, Vol. 4, ed. R. J. Sternberg. Hillsdale: Erlbaum.

Ericsson, K. A. and R. J. Crutcher. (1990) The nature of exceptional performance. In *Life-span development and behavior*, Vol. 10, ed. P. B. Baltes, D. L. Featherman, and R. M. Learner. Hillsdale, NJ: Lawrence Erlbaum.

Flynn, J. R. (1984) The mean IQ of Americans: Massive gains 1932 to 1978, *Psychological Bulletin*, 95, 29–51.

Flynn, J. R. (1987) The ontology of intelligence. In *Measurement, realism and objectivity*, ed. J. Forge. New York: Reidel.

Frederiksen, J. R. (1980) Component skills in reading: Measurement of individual differences through chronometric analysis. In *Aptitude, learning, and instruction*, ed. R. E. Snow, P. Federico, and W. Montagu. Hillsdale: Erlbaum.

Gates, A. I. and G. A. Taylor. (1925) An experimental study of the nature of improvement resulting from practice in mental function, *Journal of Educational Psychology*, 16, 583–93.

Gedye, C. A. (1981) *Longitudinal study (grades 1 through 10) of school achievement, self-confidence, and selected parental characteristics.* Doctoral dissertation, Dept. of Education University of California, Berkeley.

Gettinger, M. (1984) Individual differences in time needed for learning: A review of literature, *Educational Psychologist*, 19, 15–29.

Goldman, R. D. and R. E. Slaughter. (1976) Why college grade point average is difficult to predict, *Journal of Educational Psychology*, 68, 9–14.

Goldman, R. D., Schmidt, D. E., Hewitt, B. N. and R. Fisher. (1974) Grading practices in different major fields, *American Educational Research Journal*, 11, 343–57.

Gorsuch, R. L. (1983) *Factor analysis.* (2d ed). Hillsdale: NJ: Erlbaum.

Gottfredson, L. S. and J. Crouse. (1986) Validity versus utility of mental tests: Example of the SAT, *Journal of Vocational Behavior*, 29, 363–78.

Guilford, J. P. (1964) Zero correlations among tests of intellectual abilities, *Psychological Bulletin*, 61, 401–4.

Guskey, T. R. (1987) Rethinking mastery learning reconsidered, *Review of Educational Research*, 57, 225–29.

Gustafsson, J.-E. (1988) Hierarchical models of individual differences in cognitive abilities. In *Advances in the psychology of human intelligence*, Vol. 4, ed. R. J. Sternberg. Hillsdale: Erlbaum.

Haier, R. J., Robinson, D. L., Braden, W. and D. Williams. (1983) Electrical potentials of the cerebral cortex and psychometric intelligence, *Personality and Individual Differences*, 4, 591–99.

Hernstein, R. J., Nickerson, R. S., deSanchez, M. and J. A. Swets. (1986) Teaching thinking skills, *American Psychologist*, 41, 1279–89.

Horn, J. M., Loehlin, J. C. and L. Willerman. (1979) Intellectual resemblance among adoptive and biological relatives: The Texas Adoption Project, *Behavior Genetics*, 9, 177–207.

House, E. R., Glass, G. V., McLean, L. D. and D. F. Walker (1978) No single answer: Critique of the follow-through evaluation, *Harvard Educational Review*, 48, 128–60.

Humphreys, L. G. (1968) The fleeting nature of the prediction of college academic success, *Journal of Educational Psychology*, 59, 375–80.

Humphreys, L. G. (1973) Predictability of academic grades for students of high and low academic promise, *Educational and Psychological Measurement*, 33, 385–92.

Hunt, E. (1976) Varieties of cognitive power. In *The nature of intelligence*, ed. L. B. Resnick. Hillsdale: Erlbaum.

Hunter, J. E. (1986) Cognitive ability, cognitive aptitudes, job knowledge, and job performance, *Journal of Vocational Behavior*, 29, 340–62.

Hunter, J. E., Schmidt, F. L. and J. Rauschenberger. (1984) Methodological, statistical, and ethical issues in the study of bias in psychological tests. In *Perspectives on bias in mental testing*. C. R. Reynolds and R. T. Brown (eds.). New York: Plenum.

Ilg, F.L. and L. B. Ames. (1964) *School readiness*. New York: Harper and Row.

Jackson, M. D. and J. L. McClelland. (1979) Processing determinants of reading speed, *Journal of Experimental Psychology: General*, 108, 151–81.

Jensen, A. R. (1965) *Individual differences in learning: Interference factor*. Cooperative Research Project No. 1867. Washington, DC: U.S. Office of Education.

——. (1968) Patterns of mental ability and socioeconomic status, *Proceedings of the National Academy of Sciences*, 60, 1330–37.

——. (1975) The price of inequality, *Oxford Review of Education*, 1, 59–71.

——. (1980) *Bias in mental testing*. New York: Free Press.

——. (1982) Reaction time and psychometric g. In *A model for intelligence*, ed. H. J. Eysenck. Heidelberg: Springer-Verlag.

——. (1984) Test validity: g versus the specificity doctrine, *Journal of Social and Biological Structures*, 7, 93–118.

——. (1985a) The nature of the black-white difference on various psychometric tests: Spearman's hypothesis, *Behavioral and Brain Sciences*, 8, 193–219.

——. (1985b) The black-white difference in g: A phenomenon in search of a theory, *Behavioral and Brain Sciences*, 8, 246–63.

——. (1985c) Methodological and statistical techniques for the chronometric study of mental abilities. In *Methodological and statistical advances in the study of individual differences*, ed. C. R. Reynolds and V. L. Willson. New York: Plenum.

——. (1986) g: Artifact or reality?, *Journal of Vocational Behavior*, 29, 301–31.

——. (1987a) Psychometric g as a focus of concerted research effort, *Intelligence*, 11, 193–98.

——. (1987b) The g beyond factor analysis. In *The influence of cognitive psychology on testing and measurement*, ed. J. C. Conoley, J. A. Glover, and R.

R. Ronning. Hillsdale: Erlbaum.

——. (1987c) Further evidence for Spearman's hypothesis concerning black-white differences on psychometric tests, *Behavioral and Brain Sciences*, 10, 512−19.

——. (1987d) Individual differences in the Hick reaction time paradigm. In *Speed of information-processing and intelligence*, ed. P. A. Vernon. Norwood: Ablex.

——. (1987e) Process differences and individual differences in some cognitive tasks, *Intelligence*, 11, 107−36.

——. (1989a) The relationship between learning and intelligence, *Learning and Individual Differences*, 1, 37−62.

——. (1989b) Raising IQ without increasing *g*? A review of "The Milwaukee Project: Preventing mental retardation in children at risk," *Developmental Review*, 9 (3), 234−58.

Jensen, A. R. and R. A. Figueroa. (1975) Forward and backward digit-span interaction with race and IQ: Predictions from Jensen's theory, *Journal of Educational Psychology*, 67, 882−93.

Jensen, A. R. and C. R. Reynolds. (1982) Race, social class, and ability patterns on the WISC-R, *Personality and Individual Differences*, 3, 423−38.

Jensen, A. R., Cohn, S. J. and C. M. G. Cohn. (1988) Speed of information processing in academically gifted youths and their siblings, *Personality and Individual Differences*, 10, 29−34.

Jensen, A. R., Larson, G. E. and S. Paul. (1988) Psychometric *g* and mental processing speed on a semantic verification test, *Personality and Individual Differences*, 9, 243−55.

Kolata, G. (1987) Early signs of school age IQ, *Science*, 236, 774−75.

Kyllonen, P. C. (1986) *Theory-based cognitive assessment*. AFH Technical Paper 85−30. San Antonio: Manpower and Personnel Division, Brooks Air Force Base.

LaBerge, D. and S. J. Samuels. (1974) Toward a theory of automatic information processing in reading, *Cognitive Psychology*, 6, 293−323.

Lesgold, A. M. and C. A. Perfetti, (eds.) (1981) *Interactive processes in reading*. Hillsdale: Erlbaum.

Linn, R. (1982) Ability testing: Individual differences, prediction, and differential prediction. In *Ability testing: Uses, consequences, and controversies*, Part II, ed. A. K. Wigdor and W. R. Garner. Washington, DC: National Academy Press.

Loevinger, J. (1947) A systematic approach to the construction and evaluation of tests of ability, *Psychological Monographs*, 61, 1−49.

Maeroff, G. E. (1988) Withered hopes, stillborn dreams: The dismal panorama of urban school, *Phi Delta Kappan*, 69, 633−38.

Manning, W. H. and R. Jackson. (1984) College entrance examinations: Objective selection or gatekeeping for the economically priviledged. In *Perspectives on bias in mental testing*, ed. C. R. Reynolds and R. T. Brown. New York: Plenum.

Messick, S. (1982) Issues of effectiveness and equity in the coaching controversy:

Implications for educational and testing practice, *Educational Psychologist*, 17, 67–91.

Modgil, S. and C. Modgil. (1987) *Arthur Jensen: Consensus and controversy*. New York: The Falmer Press.

Naglieri, J. A. and A. R. Jensen. (1987) Comparison of black-white differences on the WISC-R and the K-ABC: Spearman's hypothesis, *Intelligence*, 11, 21–43.

National Commission on Excellence in Education. (1983) *A nation at risk: The imperative for educational reform*. Washington, DC: U.S. Government Printing Office.

Newell, A. and H. A. Simon. (1972) *Human problem solving*. Englewood Cliffs: Prentice-Hall.

Nickerson, R. S. (1988) On improving thinking through instruction, *Review of Research in Education*, 15, 3–57.

Nisbett, R. E., Fong, G. T., Lehman D. R. and P. W. Cheng. (1987) Teaching reasoning, *Science*, 238, 625–31.

Perfetti, C. A. (1983) Individual differences in verbal processes. In *Individual differences in cognition*, Vol. 1, R. F. Dillon and R. R. Schmeck (eds.). New York: Academic Press.

Posner, M. I. (1978) *Chronometric explorations of mind*. Hillsdale: Erlbaum.

Posner, M. I., Boies, S., Eichelman, W. and R. Taylor. (1969) Retention of visual and name codes of single letters. *Journal of Experimental Psychology*, 81, 10–15.

Reynolds, C. R. and R. T. Brown. (eds.) (1984) *Perspectives on bias in mental testing*. New York: Plenum.

Schafer, E. W. P. (1985) Neural adaptability: A biological determinant of *g* factor intelligence, *Behavioral and Brain Sciences*, 8, 240–41.

Schmid, J. and J. M. Leiman. (1957) The development of hierarchical factor solutions, *Psychometrika*, 22, 53–61.

Schmidt, F. (1988) The problem of group differences in ability test scores in employment selection, *Journal of Vocational Behavior*, 33, 272–92.

Shiffrin, R. M. and S. T. Dumais. (1981) The development of automatism. In *Cognitive skills and their acquisition*, ed. J. R. Anderson. Hillsdale: Erlbaum.

Shiffrin, R. M. and W. Schneider. (1977) Controlled and automatic human information processing: II. Perceptual learning, automatic attending, and a general theory, *Psychological Review*, 84, 127–90.

Shockley, W. (1957) On the statistics of individual variations of productivity in research laboratories, *Proceedings of the IRE*, 45, 279–90.

Slavin, R. E. (1987a) Mastery learning reconsidered, *Review of Educational Research*, 57, 175–213.

Slavin, R. E. (1987b) Taking the mystery out of mastery: A response to Guskey, Anderson, and Burns, *Review of Educational Research*, 57, 231–35.

Snow, R. E. and D. F. Lohman. (1988) Implications of cognitive psychology for educational measurement. In *Education measurement*. 3d ed., ed. R. L. Linn.

New York: Macmillan.

Snow, R. E. and E. Yalow. (1982) Education and intelligence. In *Handbook of human intelligence*, ed. R. J. Sternberg. Cambridge: Cambridge University Press.

Spearman, C. E. (1904) "General intelligence" objectively determined and measured, *American Journal of Psychology*, 15, 201–93.

Spearman, C. E. (1927) *The abilities of man: Their nature and measurement*. London: Macmillan.

Spitz, H. H. (1986) *The raising of intelligence: A selected history of attempts to raise retarded intelligence*. Hillsdale: Erlbaum.

Stebbins, L. B., St. Pierre, R. G., Proper, E. C., Anderson, R. B. and T. R. Cervo. (1977) *A planned variation model. Vol. IV-A: Effects of follow through models*. Washington, DC: U.S. Office of Information.

Sternberg, S. (1966) High speed scanning in human memory, *Science*, 153, 652–54.

Sternberg, R. J. and K. Bhana. (1986) Synthesis of research on the effectiveness of intellectual skills programs: Snake-oil remedies or miracle cures?, *Educational Leadership*, 44, 60–67.

Sternberg, R. J. and D. K. Detterman. (eds.) (1986) *What is intelligence?* Norwood: Ablex.

Sternberg, R. J. and M. K. Gardner. (1982) A componential interpretation of the general factor in human intelligence. In *A model for intelligence*, ed. H. J. Eysenck. Heidelberg: Springer-Verlag.

Sticht, T. G., Hooke, L. R. and J. S. Caylor. (1981) *Literacy, oracy, and vocational aptitude as predictors of attrition and promotion in the armed services*. HumRRO.FR-ETSD-81–11. Alexandria: Human Resources Research Organization.

Sticht, T. G., Armstrong, W. B., Hickey, D. T. and J. S. Caylor. (1987) *Cast-off youth: Policy and training methods from the military experience*. New York: Praeger.

Thorndike, R. L. (1984) *Intelligence as information processing: The mind and the computer*. Bloomington: Center on Evaluation, Development and Research.

Thorndike, R. L. (1987) Stability of factor loadings, *Personality and Individual Differences*, 8, 585–86.

Thurstone, L. L. (1947) *Multiple factor analysis*. Chicago: University of Chicago Press.

Vernon, P. A. (1981) Level I and Level II: A review, *Educational Psychologist*, 16, 45–64.

Vernon, P. A. (ed.) (1987) *Speed of information-processing and intelligence*. Norwood: Ablex.

Waldrop, M. M. (1987) The workings of working memory, *Science*, 237, 1564–67.

Wherry, R. J. (1959) Hierarchical factor solutions without rotations, *Psychometrika*, 24, 45–51.

Wigdor, A. K. and W. R. Garner. (eds.) (1982) *Ability testing: Uses, consequences, and controversies. Part 1: Report of the committee; Part 2: Documentation section.* Washington, DC: National Academy Press.

Wilson, R. S. (1983) The Louisville Twin Study: Developmental synchronies in behavior, *Child Development*, 54, 298–316.

5 EENY, MEENY, MINY, MOE: TESTING POLICY AND PRACTICE IN EARLY CHILDHOOD

Anne E. Cunningham

Introduction

Early childhood education (ECE) is probably more vulnerable than any other educational sector to the winds of economic, political, and social change. This is largely due to the lack of a stable and universally agreed upon curriculum core, and because the inputs to the system, namely young children themselves, typically have not received formalized education, which would firmly anchor the ECE curriculum and provide "inertia" to the system. Nonetheless, certain practices *are* influencing the quality of early childhood education. The practice of testing young children is becoming more and more common, with significant social consequences, yet very little analysis has been carried out to ascertain the value, if any, of such a policy. It is therefore critical that we begin examining the consequences of standardized testing for young children. In this chapter, the practices and policies surrounding ECE and testing will be reviewed and conclusions drawn regarding their current effectiveness.

Early childhood education has been a separate field of study because of the nature of young children. The more important qualities of young children in this respect are: (1) the enormous variability of the rate of development both within individuals and within populations; (2) the fact that children entering school have not yet been exposed to the behavioral norms and social structures prevalent within a school; and (3) the fact that the children are only marginally familiar with one medium of instruction-spoken language, and are usually ignorant of the other—the printed

229

word. These qualities also mean that the testing of children to assess ability is fraught with difficulties and results are not easy to interpret. At the same time, the educational decisions made at this point in a child's life can have enormous consequences.

Before plunging into the maelstrom of technical issues surrounding testing, let us pause to discuss what it is that early childhood education should be achieving and how that mission has been impacted by recent socioeconomic trends in the United States.

Although programs in ECE vary considerably in their theoretical underpinnings and their areas of emphasis, the underlying objectives and goals across programs tend to be quite similar. Sigel (1987) describes the goal of ECE programs as providing an "expanding horizon" for young children. "Preschool as an educational experience is based on the hypothesis that children [at the preschool age] are ready to profit from extended educational experiences, that the home cannot maximize such opportunities, and finally that development is cumulative where early experiences facilitate children's realization of their capabilities" (131). Therefore, a central purpose of ECE programs is to meet the needs of young children to develop their intellectual, social, emotional, and physical skills in an environment that is both challenging and appropriately tied to their current individual status.

The specific demands made of ECE have expanded significantly in recent decades. It may seem that somehow the nature of children has changed over the past fifty years or so; the forces of media, industry, and education tell us that children are more competent now. For example, four- and five-year-old children can lift weights, run mini-marathons, and program computers, all things that even their parents themselves may find difficult to do. But is this for real? Are children now capable of comprehending and performing activities that were once the preserve of older children and adults (see Elkind, 1981, 1987 for a review)? Surely not. Even the wackiest theories of evolution do not allow for significant change in one or two generations. Children are, by and large, the same as they were fifty or five thousand years ago, as far as their innate capabilities are concerned. To be sure, they eat Wheaties now, but this has not been shown to raise IQ significantly. In discussing the changing role of the child within our educational system, it is important to remember that our notions of children and their development stem not from children themselves, but from our own perceptions and theories of their development. Social forces, then, are the major instrument of change in ECE.

One of the most striking social trends over the last fifty years has been the integration of women into the work force. Fully 54 percent of women with children under six now work, as opposed to only 38 percent as recently as 1975 (Grubb, 1987, citing U.S. Bureau of Labor Statistics, 1986). Combined with the increase in single-parent families, this means that more than half of our young children live without parents for most of the day. These trends have resulted in an enormously increased demand for daycare, preschool, and kindergarten services. Every state now provides public kindergarten education as an option, and there is currently strong pressure for state provision of preschool programs.

In addition to the increase in the sheer numbers of children involved, there has been a significant change in the composition of the population in preschools and kindergartens. Before the 1960s, with the exception of some charity-run schools, kindergartens were the preserve of white upper- and middle-class children (Grubb, 1987), who suffered not at all from, for example, dietary deficiencies or a home environment of illiteracy. As a result of desegregation, the drive toward social equality, and the need for both parents in many families to work, the nature of the kindergarten population has changed dramatically, and the early childhood education system is still struggling to catch up. With the wide variations in home environments, we can no longer assume that the low-achieving child must have some inherent disability. Furthermore, we can no longer tolerate a school system that is content to relegate the poor and minorities to a second-class status rather than address their real needs. Both testing and teaching practices must change to meet these challenges. Fortunately, progress in education, psychology, and medicine has enabled us to better identify and treat children suffering from physical or mental handicaps. Testing has played a significant role in this improvement. On the other hand, progress in understanding other causes of failure has been less impressive, and the ill-informed use of testing has often served to aggravate the effects of this lack of understanding.

Another issue that has had an indirect yet profound influence on early childhood education has been the national concern, whipped up perennially (or biennially or quadrennially) by politicians, about the supposed low quality of our educational system, particularly in comparison to the educational systems of our foreign industrial competitors. This is compounded by the desire to get more value for the money spent on education in an era of decreasing resource allocations. Naturally, both these concerns cause us to focus on quantifiable performance measures. The resulting shift in emphasis back to drilled academic basics has filtered down, even into preschools and kindergartens, to such an extent that many parents are now reluctant to expose their children to the rigors of the early educational system until their sixth or seventh year.

The next section of this chapter discusses in more depth the movement toward more formal instruction in early childhood education, the nature of the early childhood curriculum, and the factors influencing it. Section three discusses the technical aspects of evaluating young children and the factors influencing their performance on tests; it also describes the uses of testing in this age group. Section four examines the content of standardized tests and the specific functions and uses of these tests. The research concerning our practice of testing and sorting of children on the basis of age and ability are discussed as well. Section five presents the conclusions and recommendations for research and policy studies.

Movement Toward More Formalized Instruction

To understand the role and impact of testing in ECE, it is necessary to examine the changing nature of the system. This section briefly discusses theoretical models of development upon which ECE programs are based and the educational practices that have grown up around those theories. Two conflicting influences are examined: the federal Head Start program, which emphasized the development of the whole child, and the recent trend toward academic emphasis at lower and lower levels in our schools.

The Nature of the ECE Curriculum

It is fair to say that the preschool and kindergarten curriculum *does* differ from the elementary curriculum in many ways. This is due primarily to the manner in which preschool and kindergarten programs have evolved; early childhood programs have, by and large, been based upon theoretical models of child development and have had relatively unrestricted opportunities to experiment and implement the resulting curricula.

Preschool Curriculum. The focus of preschool and its curriculum has changed over time as various theoreticians such as Froebel, Freud, G. Stanley Hall, Gesell, Piaget, and Bruner have made an impact. The content and form of most preschool programs are derived from these theoretical bases. Evans (1982) has termed this the *models* approach: practice is derived from theory and research. Several theoretical traditions have influenced early childhood education practices and policies today. Kohlberg (1968) described these theoretical positions as "maturationist-socialization," "cultural transmission" or behaviorist, and "cognitive developmental" (see also Kohlberg and Mayer, 1972). These categories, however imprecise, suggest the theoretical influences that have shaped programs of education for preschool and kindergarten age children. Early childhood programs today are in many ways operational definitions of these theoretical positions.

The *maturationist-socialization* view has its philosophical roots in the work of Rousseau and its psychological roots in the theories of Gesell. According to this view, development is seen as the natural unfolding of a preformed biological structure that is minimally influenced by chronological age and environmental stimulation or intervention. The function of education is to provide positive social and emotional experiences that allow young children to reach their inherent potential, which is determined by their own "internal clocks." One of the controversies to be discussed in later sections regarding children's readiness for school experiences centers around this philosophy.

The *cultural transmission* view has its philosophical roots in the work of John Locke and the behaviorist psychological theories of Thorndike and Skinner. The role of education is to prepare children for later educational experiences and to socialize children into their future role as responsible citizens. Education should provide a structured and carefully sequenced series of activities that will aid children in their learning of the knowledge, skills, values, and social rules of society. The end product of education is defined in terms of behavior, which is determined primarily by a child's experiences. Many Head Start programs are modeled on this conception.

The *cognitive developmental* approach is rooted in the theories of Piaget and Bruner. Development is viewed as the result of children interacting with their physical and social environment. Children's adaptation is dependent upon their maturational level and the nature of their experience of the surrounding environment. Learning takes place as an interaction among an organic, maturing structure, an acquired cognitive organization, and immediate inputs. Therefore, the role of education is to foster this interaction by setting up meaningful and appropriate challenging experiences for the young child.

Most early childhood education programs (including kindergartens) are modeled on one of these three theories (Fein and Schwartz, 1982). Nevertheless, they represent only approximations of these theoretical positions and display wide variability in their interpretations and subsequent applications. While the majority of educators realize that there is no definitive perspective on children's development or ability to learn, most can identify the theoretical perspective they favor (Evans, 1982).

Kindergarten Curriculum. The first kindergarten was developed in Germany in the mid-nineteenth century by Friedrich Froebel. This approach was a child-centered one in which children were essentially taught about philosophical idealism (Spodek, 1986). The kindergarten movement represents our first preschool program and was brought to the United States in 1856 (Spodek, 1988). Over time, kindergartens evolved into programs that prepared children for the transition between home and elementary school. It was here that children learned about their future role as students — the importance of academic skills, readiness skills, and socialization factors. In many ways, kindergarten programs were representative of the cultural transmission theory.

So what is going on in kindergarten classes today? What is taught in modern kindergarten programs? How does the kindergarten curriculum differ from a preschool or a first-grade curriculum? Finally, what form does this instruction take? Needless to say, there are no simple answers to these questions. Over the past thirty years, the form and content of kindergartens have changed (Spodek, 1972, 1983) and consequently there is greater variability among kindergarten classes in this country. Crude distinctions can be made. We can describe these programs along a continuum according to degree of emphasis on child-centered versus teacher-centered approaches (Beller, 1973). Some kindergarten programs continue to employ a model that is more child-centered, emphasizing free play and choice of manipulatives mixed in with more structured group activities. Other kindergarten programs tend to be more teacher-centered; they resemble first-grade classrooms in which the teacher directs the whole class and relies less on "centers" as avenues for learning and more on pencil and paper.

The distinction between child-centered and teacher-centered programs of education has become a point of contention within the field (Sigel, 1987). The goals of educators and policymakers are often in conflict because of their differing theoretical points of view regarding young children's learning. As a result of the existing difference in ECE and early elementary programs, some (Sigel, 1987; California State Department of Education, 1988) have argued that the transition from preschool to kindergarten to first grade needs to be smoother, with formal lines of cooperation between the systems firmly established. The differing methods and practices found in early childhood programs, such as strong parent involvement, meeting the needs of the child's social, emotional, and physical development, and a child-centered approach are often abandoned in the elementary school curriculum.

Head Start

Compensatory programs of education in preschool represent a special category of early childhood education. These programs were developed in the 1960s with the explicit goal of meeting the needs of disadvantaged children—those unlikely to attend preschool. The major intervention in this area has been the federal program Project Head Start, although some states do have preschool programs. The states of California and New York, for example, have well-articulated and well-developed policies and programs for ECE. As Campbell (1987) remarks, the New York State Experimental Prekindergarten Program is in the twenty-second year of what was to have been a five-year program. So successful has this program been that annual extensions have been made. The prekindergarten program was intended to address two questions: (1) whether a publicly administered program was feasible and (2) what impact such a program would have on children's subsequent development in elementary school (Campbell, 1987). The policy developed in ECE programs in New York states that "all learning has its roots in sound social and emotional development with the intellect an integral part of the whole child, and the involvement of parents is an essential factor in the education of children" (Campbell, 1987, 67). Although the program does not serve all eligible children, it apparently represents a model program from which to develop other programs.

More states have developed or are formulating policies on ECE. The concern for quality programs of education at the preschool and kindergarten level has grown dramatically over the past twenty years. Clearly, the curriculum of ECE is not as well developed as early elementary curricula, but the lack of clearly defined curriculum may be a blessing in disguise. Federally funded ECE programs, however, originated with Project Head Start, and ECE curriculum continues to be influenced by the practices developed by Head Start.

Rationale and History. At present, a national policy in ECE does not exist. Project Head Start represents the largest and primary source of federal funds for ECE, although Head Start currently serves only 24 percent of the three- and four-year-olds living in poverty (Schweinhart and Koschel, 1986). Initiated in the mid-1960s as part of a massive community-action program designed to eliminate poverty, Head Start represents a systematic attempt to meet young children's health, social, and educational needs (Laosa, 1984; Zigler and Valentine, 1979). Head

Start is a *multidisciplinary* program that emphasizes children's emotional and social development by encouraging self-confidence, curiosity, and self-discipline. The importance of dignity and self-worth for both the child and family is stressed, as well as the development of a responsible attitude toward society. The development of children's intellectual capabilities is part of the program but not the central component. A climate of high optimism for children's academic success exists and is reinforced by direct attention to children's developing conceptual and verbal skills. Children's nutritional health and physical abilities are attended to as well. In short, Head Start has attempted to represent the very best of current child-development theories, practice, and public policies.

Social Competence. As with any federally funded project, a method of program evaluation needed to be developed for Head Start. The method of evaluation could have focused on the criterion that many schooling enterprises employ to measure student progress: intellectual achievement. Indeed, Head Start initially emphasized this aspect of a child's development. Later, an alternative measure of program success, and therefore of individual success, was developed. Over the past twenty years, Edward Zigler has eloquently and rationally addressed the issue of individual differences in development and its implications for education and public policy. As one of the designers and the original director of Head Start, Zigler (1973a) developed the concept of social competence as a criterion for evaluating the effectiveness of Head Start and other preschool programs.

Social competence is loosely comprised of four domains of competency: physical health, cognition, achievement, and social and emotional skills (Zigler, 1970, 1973a; Zigler and Trickett, 1978). Each aspect of social competence is given equal importance: physical health includes nutritional status, appropriate height and weight, and inoculation history; cognition is defined as children's level of intellectual ability as measured by IQ and Piagetian tasks; achievement is defined as knowledge children have gained as a result of specific educational programs and is measured by standard achievement tests; and finally the last component of Zigler's model of social competence consists of children's level of motivation and social and emotional skills. These include their attitudes about school and achievement, responsiveness to adults and their peers, self-esteem and confidence.

Although the construct of social competence has yet to be defined or fully articulated in terms of outcome measures, it has served to direct our thinking and planning of early childhood education (see Zigler and Trickett, 1978 for a more complete description of social competence). The development of social competence as a goal for young children is singularly different from the development of children's intellectual capabilities, a distinction that will be important for our discussion of children's readiness for primary school.

Academic Versus Social Skills. The balancing of academic development with social, emotional, and physical development continues to be a controversial issue in early childhood education. The model of schools as places where students develop only academic skills is considered shortsighted by many researchers, practitioners, and policymakers. They argue that a degree of social competence should result from schooling. Furthermore, the development of academic skills does not equal or necessarily result in a high level of social competence. We do not, for example, view a child who has a high level of academic achievement as necessarily being socially competent, nor do we view a child who has a low level of academic achievement as necessarily being socially incompetent. Academic achievement, therefore, constitutes one aspect of the development of social competence. As an example, we can all sympathize with the child who, although quite brilliant, bursts into the classroom and disrupts the lesson with a tale about information learned in the library. Does this brilliant child exhibit a sophisticated level of social competence? Would the child benefit from experience or instruction in other areas or domains of life? Again it all comes down to a matter of degree; we can appreciate the importance of academic achievement and at the same time allocate attention to other aspects of a child's development that may be of equal importance in determining the type of individual he or she will become (Zigler, 1970, 1987).

The Inclusion of the Family. Head Start was the first comprehensive program for preschoolers. Its goal was to reach the whole child and the family. This goal was based on the theory that the family, as opposed to the school, was the ultimate source of a child's behavior and values (Laosa, 1984). It was felt that schools play a minor role in a child's development unless a parent-school partnership is formed (Zigler, 1973a, 1973b). Research supported that initial policy decision by demonstrating that the effects of early childhood intervention are more powerful when parents play an active role (Bronfenbrenner, 1974; Slaughter, 1983). Ancillary programs to Head Start, such as Home Start (a program for mothers and infants) and Follow Through (a program for elementary age children), were subsequently developed to provide a continuous level of support for families and children.

Effectiveness. How effective was this unique program in meeting its goals of developing social competence in young children? A number of evaluative studies were conducted on the effects of Head Start on children's competencies. Initially, the answer for many lay exclusively within the cognitive domain. The question became: Did Head Start make disadvantaged children smarter? It was easy to try to evaluate the educational benefit of this intervention program with IQ tests. Direct benefit was indeed observed: children enrolled in Head Start displayed significantly higher IQ scores, but the effects were not lasting (Gray, Ramsey, and Klaus, 1982; Lazar et al., 1982; Westinghouse Learning Corporation, 1969). Yet follow-up reports demonstrated that children who had attended Head Start programs were less likely than control children to fail a grade or be placed in special classes (for example, Lazar et al., 1982). Because the Head Start program did not seem to effect permanent changes in IQ, the superior achievement of these children had to be attributable to factors other than intelligence. Indeed, many years later, benefits such as improved self-esteem, positive attitude toward school and achievement, higher high school graduation rates, and higher incidence of full-time jobs were shown to be a positive outcome of enrollment in Head Start (Deutsch, 1985; Lazar et al., 1982). Thus, it has been argued that the positive effects are due both to changes in parents' and children's attitudes toward school and to the emphasis placed on children's own social and emotional development. As set forth by Zigler (1970, 1973a, 1973b) and Zigler and Trickett (1978), the initial hypothesis that factors other than intellectual stimulation in the early years significantly contribute to success in school (and success in life) appears to have been borne out in the research.

The role that socialization factors play in early childhood education clearly merits further examination as we move toward an educational system that relies most heavily upon intellectual factors in predicting future school (and life) success. Although there has been a recent surge of interest in examining the contribution of social and emotional skills to the learning process (Ames and Ames, 1984, 1985; Covington, 1984; Covington and Omelich, 1979; Hallahan and Kauffman, 1986), the picture remains far from clear.

Academic Trickle Down

The move toward greater accountability in school performance and the need for children to become more independent at an earlier point in development have influenced the curricula of current preschool and primary education. Traditionally, elementary grades have emphasized academics and allocated proportionately less time toward children's social, emotional, and physical development; group instruction and lecture format are standard. In contrast, as discussed earlier, the traditional early childhood curriculum has allocated proportionately more time to social, emotional, and school-readiness factors (for example, listening skills, following directions, interacting with peers, expressing feelings, holding a pencil). Moreover, the academic content included in early childhood education is often qualitatively different in form from that of primary education. Traditionally, the academic curriculum of preschool through kindergarten has focused upon exploration, observation, and conceptualization at a broader level of understanding than that typically found in elementary grades. Emphasis is placed upon concrete problems as opposed to symbolic and quantitative (and therefore more abstract) representation. Lecture format is rarely employed and much less emphasis has been placed on memorization of information. The process of children's learning is emphasized over the product of learning.

The differences between preschool and early elementary programs are no longer as great as they once were. Both researchers and practitioners have noted the change, arguing that the elementary model of educating children is being extended downward to the primary curriculum, particularly kindergarten (for example, California State Department of Education, 1988; Elkind, 1987; Gredler, 1980; May and Welch, 1984a, 1985; Roberts, 1986; Sigel, 1987; Smith and Shepard, 1987). This "academic trickle down" may have harmful effects on the young child (Katz, 1985, 1987; Winn, 1983). As with most large social changes, the process has been gradual. Furthermore, it is a multifaceted issue in which the roots of change are often hard to discern and document. Nonetheless, we can begin to identify and address some of the causes that underlie the blurring of these distinct programs of education.

A primary influence has been the trend toward more quantitative assessment of academic skills for children of all ages. The importance of this issue has waxed and waned over the history of education. In the 1980s, teachers, schools, and school systems have been held more and more accountable for the development of children's measured skills. The pressure has come from public policymakers, parents, and administrators and has resulted in greater emphasis being placed on academic performance in the later elementary grades (National Commission on Excellence in Education, 1983). A second major cause is the growing desire on the part of society to get more for our money in educating children. Despite media attention highlighting the value of education and endless debate regarding increased funding for education, the actual per capita allocation of resources toward education has decreased dramatically in the past decade.

As a result of decreased funding and a general distrust on the part of policymakers regarding local educators' abilities to provide quality education to students, policymakers have attempted to standardize the curriculum directly through state-adopted curricular guides and textbooks and indirectly through state-mandated tests. As a response to these policies of standardization, practitioners have sought to group children by ability to create a more efficient system. A more efficient system results from the creation of a more homogeneous curriculum and, by necessity, a more homogeneous population within each grade. The same underlying "economy of scale" argument is used here as has been applied to the production of consumer goods. The end result for early childhood education is that kindergarten teachers have become gatekeepers of the system, since homogeneous populations need to be created at this juncture in the educational process.

The pressure to achieve, which is experienced by older elementary-age children (Darling-Hammond and Wise, 1985), has recently "trickled down" to the primary grades and created an "accountability culture" (Shepard and Smith, 1988) within even the kindergarten and first-grade classrooms. The trickle-down process seems to happen in the following way. As third-grade teachers experience pressure for their children to perform well on standardized tests, they in turn put pressure on the second- and first-grade teachers to prepare their children for the demands of the third-grade curriculum. The pressure to promote only children who can read fluently and who know their math facts influences primary teachers' curricular decisions. As a result, the emphasis of their curriculum turns toward activities that will prepare children to perform well on the criterion measure: standardized tests of reading and math. This is in fact a tall order for most first-grade and kindergarten teachers and children because there is a great deal of information to digest in learning how to read and compute numbers, and children display various levels of readiness for these skills. In order to accomplish the task, instructional time must be allocated to direct instruction and application of many of the prerequisite skills. Of necessity, instruction in the various areas of children's social, emotional, and physical development must take a back seat to the accomplishment of these goals. Within this system, performance is assessed in the realm of quantifiable skills (math and reading) and not in the realm of social turn-taking or ability to express and articulate feelings. Moreover, within the field of cognition and instruction, we may be sacrificing more comprehensive and deeper levels of understanding of a cognitive domain by focusing on skill and drill methods of instruction (see Cunningham, 1990).

Teaching children abstract skills, such as learning to read and compute numbers, requires that children be able to learn these skills. Therefore, first- and second-grade teachers want children who are ready to learn information of this type, that is, ready to learn at a level that is relatively unconnected to the child's everyday, physical world. Children who cannot attend to such lessons prove to be an unacceptable handicap to the teacher. As a result, we have begun to see a grouping or screening process taking place between kindergarten and first grade, and even more recently between preschool and kindergarten, that essentially attempts to control the product that is being forwarded to the elementary schools.

The effect of academic trickle down to kindergarten and first grade, therefore, has consequences that extend beyond the cognitive domain. The process of screening and the associated stigma of official failure at such an early age can have a significant impact upon children's social and emotional development (Bell, 1972; Elkind, 1987; Katz, 1987; Sigel, 1987).

In this move toward screening children for entrance into the primary grades, tests are often employed to aid in the decision-making process. In fact, tests are often the principal method by which we sort children into groups. Properly developed tests can be of enormous value as they provide objective and standardized information about the child to aid in the decision-making process. In the following section, the definition of tests and the technical considerations regarding test use will be presented. The issues surrounding their use and the factors that may influence young children's test performance will be discussed as well.

Evaluating the Performance of Young Children: Technical Considerations in Testing

Standardized tests have been used in assessing older children's academic performance for over a half-century. The practice of testing in elementary, intermediate, and high school education is considerably more common than in early childhood education. Our educational system has both benefited and suffered from the use of standardized tests. Many lessons have been learned by educators, policymakers, and testmakers in devising and implementing these instruments.

Over the past twenty years, we have observed a trend that has resulted in an increase in standardized evaluation of school-age children, as well as an increase in the level of teacher accountability for student performance (Sarason, 1987). Furthermore, the increase in testing has had an impact on the curriculum. Darling-Hammond and Wise (1985), for example, reported in one of their studies that 60 percent of the teachers sampled reported that the increased emphasis on standardized testing had affected their own teaching, and they were confident that 90 percent of other teachers' curricula had been affected by this change in emphasis. Their findings have been borne out by other studies examining teacher perceptions of curricula and the effect testing has had on their development (Shepard and Smith, 1985).

This change in emphasis has, of course, both positive and negative outcomes. Many teachers in Darling-Hammond and Wise's study reported that the pressure to cover specific topics proved to be a benefit to their curriculum by forcing the inclusion of additional courses. Furthermore, there is evidence that basic reading and mathematics scores have increased over the past decade (NAEP, 1979, 1981). This increase has been attributed in part to the increase in standardized testing.

However, with the increase in basic reading and math scores, we have observed a corresponding decrease in science, writing, problem solving, and analytical reading scores (NAEP, 1979, 1981; National Research Council, 1979). These findings have lent support to the criticisms that the increased emphasis on standardized testing serves to alter the curriculum. Teachers may be "teaching to the test," a test that only taps into basic reading and mathematical abilities. Thus, the argument is that the focus of instruction turns away from areas not covered on the tests (for example, science and higher order thinking such as analytical problem solving) and turns toward only test-related content. Many argue that this is a qualitatively different type of instruction. Indeed, Darling-Hammond and Wise (1985) argue that the emphasis on standardized testing results in "distortions introduced into the curriculum" (320).

Not only is the content of instruction changed but the depth of instruction may be altered as well. Focusing on more superficial knowledge enables students to perform well on the test, yet current research is demonstrating that these same students do not always possess a conceptual understanding of the problem (see, for example, Schoenfeld, 1985). This research supports and parallels Elkind's (1988) argument that we may, in fact, be teaching our children a series of "tricks" that enable them to perform well on our measures of basic reading and mathematics, yet leaves them markedly deficient in their level of understanding. Children are often being called upon to manipulate symbols without an understanding of the concrete reality to which the symbols refer.

Therefore, drawbacks of standardized testing may be that (1) it does not assess a subject completely, and (2) it alters the curriculum in ways that discourage comprehensive treatment of the subject matter. Indeed, many teachers in Darling-Hammond and Wise's (1985) study reported that they felt "the path from establishing standards in standardized testing to standardized curriculum and standardized teaching to be short" (33). It is clear that well-developed standardized tests are neither good nor bad in and of themselves; the issue is how they are used and the direct or indirect effects they may have on the educational system.

In this section, the issues surrounding the testing of young children have been discussed. The reasons behind the need to test and the influence testing has or may have on the curriculum have been introduced. But now it is time to become more specific: what do we mean by test, what makes for a good test, and what are some of the factors that influence children's performance on tests?

Definition and Goals of Testing

What Is a Test?   By sampling the behavior and products of young children, we can begin to make generalizations about their abilities and achievements. Tests are a systematic way of collecting samples of information about children. The administration of tests allows the same behavior to be sampled in many children and comparisons to be made across the group tested. The terms *test*, *assessment*, and *evaluation* are often used interchangeably, but there are subtle distinctions between them. Test is considered to be the narrowest of the three terms. A test is a specific instrument composed of selected items that results in a numerical value of performance. The term assessment connotes a broader process: we can measure performance through observation, rating scales, and other devices that allow us to gather information in quantitative form, without necessarily observing behavior specifically induced for the purpose of measurement. Evaluation is typically used to describe the comparison of specific educational goals with the performance (using multiple measures) of an individual. Evaluation connotes more comprehensive assessment of students and instructional programs.

There are different purposes for measuring behavior. We are often interested in how a child performs relative to children of her or his chronological age group (*norm-referencing*). For example, Susie did better than 93 percent of the students in her cohort on a test of addition and subtraction. Or we can interpret a child's performance by comparing it to some specified behavioral criterion of proficiency (*criterion-referencing*).

When interested in whether a child has achieved a certain set of objectives, a criterion-referenced test is appropriate. In this case, we want to compare a child's score against a criterion, for example, 70 percent of the addition problems were solved. The role tests play in early childhood education will be discussed in relation to the evaluation of individual children and programs.

Standardized Tests. The role standardized testing plays in early childhood education will be examined in this section. Clearly, nonstandardized measures (for example, checklists, systematic observation) are used successfully in the field, but standardized measures have the greatest impact for setting agendas for educational policy. A standardized test is designed to provide a systematic sample of individual performance. It is composed of empirically selected items which are administered according to prescribed directions, scored in accordance with predetermined rules, and interpreted in reference to certain normative data (Mehrens and Lehmann, 1984). Furthermore, a report on the test's reliability and validity must be available for consideration.

Why Do We Need or Want to Test Young Children? One of the issues involved in testing and early childhood education is the functional utility of testing this population. The ultimate purpose of any test is to help in making educational decisions. If test results do not enable practitioners to make decisions better than those made without a test, then one must question the usefulness of the test. Collecting information on a child is of little value unless the data are collected as an aid to a particular decision. Therefore, the need for a decision must be established before assessment begins.

This leads us back to the original question: Why test young children? What educational decisions do we need to be making that require the use of formalized tests? One decision concerns children's need for special assistance as a result of impairment in visual, motor, auditory, or cognitive abilities. Recent research has demonstrated that when handicapped children receive assistance prior to formal schooling, their associated problems are often reduced or alleviated (Consortium for Longitudinal Studies, 1979; Meisels and Margolis, 1988). On the other hand, one problem with wholesale screening intended to uncover hidden learning disorders has been the overidentification of learning disabilities and other mild handicaps. Thus, there must be good evidence of a need for testing prior to its administration.

A second decision may concern placement of children in appropriate educational programs. In reality, there are not that many different functional placement categories for young children. In preschool and kindergarten there are two options available to children: they are placed either in the regular classroom or in a special education program. Recently an additional category of placement has developed, the transitional or readiness grade, which occurs before first grade. In all, placement decisions for end-of-the-year preschoolers and kindergartners involve (1) promotion to a regular kindergarten or first-grade classroom, (2) promotion to a special education kindergarten or first-grade classroom, or (3) retention in a preprimary program for another school year (this placement can take the form of retention in a kindergarten program or a special transition or developmental first-grade classroom).

Determining which children are at-risk for future educational problems and placement of these children in appropriate programs of education are decisions of enormous consequence for the lives of the children and their families. These decisions involve the judgment of parents, professionals, and society-at-large. Decisions of such importance must be based on sound research and multiple determinants, such as systematic observation by professionals, observations and anecdotes of parents and family, samples of individual children's work, and finally appropriate and valid tests of readiness. Appropriate tests provide valuable information in the decision-making process, but as the National Association for the Education of Young Children (NAEYC) has aptly pointed out in its position paper on the testing of young children, decisions of such importance "should never be based on a single test score" (NAEYC, 1988). It must also be remembered that no decision-making process, however complete, can compensate for invalid treatment of a problem. This is particularly true in the case of extra-year programs. As we will discuss in later sections of this chapter, there appears to be little data to support the treatment of providing children with an "extra year to grow."

However, in the case of identifying children with special needs and/or placing children in special education programs, tests can prove to be of enormous value. Properly developed tests can provide invaluable pieces of additional information to aid in the decision-making process. What properties of standardized tests are important? More specifically, what properties are important in the testing of your children? These questions require discussion both of the properties of tests and of the specific testing factors that may affect the performance of young children.

Psychometric Properties of Tests

Test Validity. Validity is the single most important concept in testing. Validity refers to the extent to which useful inferences can be drawn from a test. The process of gathering information about the appropriateness of a test's inferences is called validation. Knowledge of test validity is important because it allows one to evaluate how well a test accomplishes its stated purpose. A test's validity can be assessed in three ways: by determining content validity, criterion-related validity, and construct validity.

Content validity measures how well a test samples the domain about which the inferences are being drawn. Content validity is determined by examining the test items for the appropriateness of the types of items included, the completeness of the item sample, and the manner in which the items assess the content. Thus, one must consider whether a test question is appropriate and whether the item really measures the domain. For example, in many prereading tests one of the controversies is whether items such as sequencing and visual discrimination accurately represent the reading process. Content validity is clearly an important component of test validation.

Criterion-related validity refers to the extent to which an individual's performance on criterion tasks can be estimated from scores. This is inferred by the relationship (correlation) between the test and the criterion. Many psychometricians make a distinction between concurrent validity and predictive validity. The distinction between these two validities relates to the time the criterion data were gathered.

Concurrent validity refers to how accurately an individual's current test score can estimate current performance on the criterion.

Predictive validity refers to how accurately an individual's current test score predicts future performance on the criterion. This distinction is often forgotten by those who use testing in early childhood. Achievement tests are a good example of such a mismatch. By and large, achievement tests have a good concurrent criterion-related validity but poor predictive validity for kindergarten-age children. Many educators have ignored this fact and employed achievement tests as a method to predict future performance on criterion. A second aspect of predictive validity that has particular importance in the field of early childhood education is the level of a test's true positive and true negative hit rate. These are important indexes of a test's predictive validity in developmental screening tests. Such classificational analysis, often used within the field of medicine, computes a test's "hit or miss rate." The proportion of at-risk test takers who are correctly identified (true positive) and the proportion of those not at-risk who are correctly identified and who, therefore, do not receive further testing (true negative) are properties of a test that need to be examined. "If the purposes of developmental screening are not to be obscured, it is essential that screening test validity data indicate the proportions of over- and underinclusions, and that they demonstrate high sensitivity and specificity" (Meisels, 1988, 531).

Construct validity refers to the degree to which a test measures a theoretical trait. An example in early childhood is the use of the Gesell test to measure the construct of developmental age. Validation of the test of this construct involves experiments to disconfirm, in effect, that this test is a valid measure of developmental age. Only through accumulating evidence can we begin to know with some certainty that a test possesses good construct validity. Factor analytic studies of the Gesell test, for example, have shown that its factor structure is highly similar to the factor structure of intelligence tests (Kaufman, 1985b). Therefore, in this instance, we would question the construct validity of the Gesell to measure developmental age. One could also argue that the Gesell lacks discriminant validity from IQ because it correlates as highly with IQ as with Piagetian measures of development (Kaufman, 1985b).

Other factors affect or "threaten" the validity of a test. In fact, "Any factor that results in measuring 'something else' affects a test's validity" (Salvia and Ysseldyke, 1985, 138). Some of those factors include unsystematic error (or unreliability) and systematic bias.

Test Reliability.   Reliability is a necessary but not sufficient condition for validity. Reliability refers to the consistency of scores that are obtained by the same person when he or she is tested (with the same test or an equivalent form) on different occasions (Anastasi, 1988). Thus, test reliability represents the extent to which individual differences in test scores are attributable to true differences in the behavior under consideration versus the extent to which they are attributable to chance errors, or error variance. Error variance is essentially any condition one would consider irrelevant to the purpose of the test. In group testing of young children, time limits and practice booklets are attempts to reduce error variance, thus making the tests more reliable measures.

Three different measures of test reliability are commonly employed: test-retest reliability, alternate-form reliability, and split-half reliability. *Test-retest reliability* is simply repeating the identical test on a second occasion. Retest reliability demonstrates the extent to which scores on a test can be generalized across testing sessions: the higher the reliability coefficient, the lower the chance fluctuations of testing conditions. Other factors make retesting less desirable than the other methods of computing reliability; there is a practice effect when taking the same test, as well as the opportunity to remember specific items. *Alternate form reliability* is retesting with an equivalent form of the same test. This method is more desirable because it gets around the problem of using the same test again and it provides a useful measure for evaluating the test. Thus, both content sampling of the test and temporal stability can be assessed. When one is confronted with only a single administration of a test, *split-half reliability* provides a measure of reliability by dividing the test into two equivalent halves. This procedure provides a measure of consistency with regard to content sampling, whereas temporal stability of the test is not considered because only one measure is administered.

Systematic bias can affect the validity of a test as well. The method of measuring a trait may affect test performance. In early childhood, factors such as group versus individualized testing may introduce systematic bias. Some children may perform poorly in group-administered tests but perform significantly better if that same test is individually administered. Conclusions are also drawn regarding children's incoming behaviors. For many children, particularly in California, English is a second language. Nonetheless, tests are often administered to these children in English, a decided disadvantage that results in systematic bias against them. Item selection can also be a problem that results in systematic bias. For example, test-makers presume that all test takers have had the same exposure to the skills or concepts measured by the test. If, however, the teacher has not taught the content being tested or the childen have not even been enrolled in school, the results of the achievement test are invalid. When decisions are made about a child's abilities on the basis of a test for which that child has not received instruction, systematic bias is introduced.

Factors Influencing Young Children's Performance on Tests

By and large, individually administered tests present fewer problems for young children than group-administered tests. The examiner can take the time to establish a rapport with the student and to interpret and probe the answers the child provides. On the other hand, the scores are open to greater examiner bias and the tests are expensive to administer. In group testing, the examiner has less opportunity to establish rapport with and maintain the interest of the examinees. There is some evidence, for example, that individuals who are unaccustomed to testing are more handicapped on group tests than individual test (Anastasi, 1988) and that emotionally disturbed children perform better on individual than group tests (Willis, 1970).

Group-administered tests have their own set of problems that are only exacerbated when young children form the test pool. First, preschool and kindergarten-age children have not been socialized to sit for extended periods of time in a large group and to attend to one individual giving oral directions about marking pieces of paper. The practice of following directions in a large group generally begins in kindergarten (although there is great variability in kindergarten curricula across the country). Kindergarten is not, however, mandatory in this country, and therefore assumptions regarding children's comprehension of and experience with such an activity should not be made. Furthermore, making judgments about a child's capabilities or readiness for school when the child may not understand the task or have sufficient practice in this area is unwarranted. Thus, we must seriously consider the validity of such a practice: are we really gathering useful information regarding children's abilities?

In the event that this practice must continue there are several steps that can be taken to facilitate accurate assessment of a child's performance on group-administered tests. First, several adults or cross-age peers are helpful in administering tests. This permits teachers to read the directions out loud calmly and at a consistent pace. In the meantime, the other adults can walk around the room and help children to stay on task, find their places in the test booklet, and provide individualized help to those students in particular need (but only helping with the task demands and not coaching on the content). The utilization of the practice tests provided with standardized tests is essential. Abbreviated practice tests provide children with the conceptual understanding of "testing," which involves listening to the teacher pronounce various sounds or concepts out loud, searching for the correct row on the piece of paper, scanning the row for the correct match between what the teacher said and the options provided on this piece of paper, and finally indicating the answer with the correct marking. We know from research in developmental psychology that when children do not understand the nature of the task demands, performance is affected, and conclusions drawn regarding ability are often erroneous (for example, Gelman, 1969, 1978; Gelman and Gallistel, 1978).

In addition to the test-taking skills that a child is being asked to learn, the child is being asked to conceptualize the content of the teacher's directions and abstract the meaning of, for example, segmenting the first sound of a word and marking the letter that represents that sound. This process requires rather abstract reasoning for a four- or five-year-old to perform in relatively new surroundings. Consequently, for any representative behavior to be elicited from the child, special emphasis needs to be placed on the acquisition of test-taking skills prior to any true evaluation of a young child's abilities.

In this section, we have discussed the properties of tests that make them appropriate or inappropriate for use in sorting and in making other policy decisions. The properties include validity, reliability, and stability. Particular attention needs to be paid to the validity of group testing of young children and the special difficulties that exist in assessing young children who often need to receive training in test-taking skills. In the following section, we will discuss the categories and types of tests that are most commonly employed to diagnose problems and to group or sort children and the issues surrounding their use in early childhood education.

Purposes and Uses of Tests in Early Childhood Education

Types of Tests: What Is an Appropriate Test?

What constitutes an appropriate test of a child's abilities? Again, this depends upon the goal behind the testing. When testing to screen for any indication of developmental disabilities, then *developmental screening tests* should be employed. Once a disability has been suggested through the use of a screening test, more intensive testing is required in the form of *diagnostic tests*, such as intelligence tests. Finally, when making decisions regarding specific curricula for young children, *achievement tests* can be employed. In the following section, these three categories of tests will be discussed. The first category evaluates a broad range of children's abilities, including intellectual, motor, and social-emotional capabilities, while the next two categories tap children's cognitive abilities.

Developmental Screening Tests. Developmental screening tests are administered by schools, primarily to provide a brief examination of whether students are in need of any special or further attention. Screening tests are the first step in an evaluation and intervention process whose goal is to identify children who may display a particular problem, disorder, or disability (Lichtenstein and Ireton, 1984; Meisels, 1984). Developmental screening also satisfies school districts' obligation to comply with Public Law 94-142 to identify and serve handicapped children. At present, more than twenty-five states mandate developmental screening for three- to six-year-olds (Meisels, 1986).

Screening tests serve as means to prevent later problems for children and to reduce the need to remediate problems in the future. Recent research has demonstrated that early intervention can alter a child's developmental potential (for example, Consortium for Longitudinal Studies, 1983; Meisels and Anastasiow, 1982). Consequently, the practice of screening children before their problems are further compounded within the educational system has increased over the past decade.

Essentially, screening tests are comprised of a wide range of items that evaluate children's speech, receptive language ability, cognition, perception, gross and fine motor skills, and social and emotional development. These tests measure a child's ability or potential to learn school-related skills. Nonetheless, they have limited ability to predict school performance for more than one or two years into the future (Meisels, 1985).

Several developmental screening instruments have been developed and meet the American Psychological Association's testing requirements. These tests are norm-referenced and have high reliability and predictive validity. When choosing a screening test, Meisels (1988) has discussed the importance of considering a test's sensitivity (the proportion of at-risk children who are correctly identified) and test specificity (the proportion of children at-risk who are correctly excluded from further assessment) as a means of evaluating a test's accuracy.

Listed in the appendix are several of the most common screening instruments that adhere to strict psychometric standards. These tests identify children who may be at-risk, examine a wide range of developmental (as opposed to achievement-related) skills, and report data on the reliability and validity of the tests.

Individual Intelligence Tests. Intelligence testing has always generated much controversy and debate. Numerous definitions have been proposed and several theories have been advanced to describe and explain intelligence and its development. The definition of intelligence is obviously a central issue in any analysis and measurement of this construct. This issue, however, is rarely raised in discussions about intelligence and intelligence testing. Kail and Pellegrino (1985), for example, argue that "psychologists and lay persons alike seem too quick to accept the cliché that intelligence is what intelligence tests measure." IQ is really an expression of an individual's ability level at a given point in time, in relation to current age norms (see Anastasi, 1983, 1986; Sternberg and Detterman, 1986).

The assessment of intellectual ability is generally used to aid in educational assessment and placement. Intelligence tests are designed to help educators match programs of instruction to children's abilities. By and large, intelligence tests are employed when a child has been targeted as deviating from the norm and in need of special attention. These categories of special consideration have typically been reserved for children considered to be intellectually gifted, retarded, or learning disabled (a gross disparity between intelligence and achievement). The mental tests available are numerous (see, for example, Anastasi, 1988; Mitchell, 1985). Tests directly pertaining to intellectual ability in early childhood will be described in this section.

Traditionally, formal intelligence testing of preschoolers and kindergarten-age children has been avoided except under unusual circumstances. Such cautionary action has been due primarily to the poor validity and reliability of these tests in younger children. The stability of intelligence test scores is typically low in young children. The causes of error include fluctuation in test takers' attentiveness, motivation to perform, and emotional state. The low correlations observed between earlier and later samplings of intelligence are also a result of the instability of the construct of intelligence from early childhood to adulthood. Moreover, the constructs of intelligence measured in early childhood and adulthood may prove to be quite different.

Intelligence and aptitude batteries were also developed to predict future academic achievement. It is important to examine each test's predictive validity, the ability to predict differences among individuals. Many of the measures used to assess intelligence among preschool-age children have been shown to have relatively poor predictive validity. That is, assessing children at three and four years of age does not reliably predict how they will perform on aptitude, intelligence, or achievement tests in the future, or how successful they will be in a broader sense.

Much research has demonstrated the poor stability of IQ testing in young children. For example, Bayley (1949) observed no relationship between intelligence measured at age one and at age seventeen. With increased age, the stability of intelligence test performance increases. By the time children are four years of age, however, correlations of .71 have been observed between mental age at four and seventeen years (Bayley, 1949). Most psychometricians argue that intelligence (in the sense of general intelligence, but see Sternberg, 1977; 1985 and Gardner, 1983; 1987 for alternative positions) is a fairly stable construct after the age of five (Anastasi, 1988; Cronbach, 1970; Jensen, 1981). The relationship strengthens considerably as children enter elementary school age: correlations in the .70–.75 range are observed between mental age at eight and seventeen years.

In summary, within the early chilhood age range, we find that intelligence tests do not provide sufficiently accurate assessments to predict future development and therefore their use must be justified on the basis of measuring present developmental status alone.

Group Intelligence Tests. Group intelligence tests are employed primarily to assess the specific abilities which have been shown to predict children's future academic achievement. The composition of these omnibus tests reflects psychometric theory in that they have a high loading on g, or a general ability factor. These tests yield a single overall score which reflects this general ability factor, as well as the specific factors of verbal and quantitative abilities. Group intelligence tests are administered as screening devices to identify children who may need further assessment. For example, in screening for gifted populations, some school districts employ group intelligence tests in conjunction with an achievement test to assess the relationship between these abilities. Group intelligence tests are quick to administer but, like any group-administered battery, depend upon a child's ability to sit for extended periods of time, use a pencil, and follow oral directions. Multiple-choice items are employed instead of open-ended items. The tests are divided into subtests that are separately timed. Brief descriptions of three commonly employed intelligence tests, the WPPSE, McCarthy, and Otis-Lennon, are provided in the Appendix.

Achievement Tests. In the early 1900s numerous studies began documenting the unreliability of teachers' grading (Starch and Elliott, 1912, as cited in Mehrens and Lehmann, 1984). As a result, more objective batteries were developed to measure children's academic achievement. These batteries measured a variety of skills, such as reading, mathematics, and problem solving, in contrast to the previously employed single-subject tests. Achievement tests are designed to assess a child's knowledge and skills in a particular content area at a particular point in time, sampling the products of past formal and informal educational experiences. They typically cover content areas such as reading comprehension, spelling, number operations, computation, science, and social studies. In early childhood education, achievement tests have primarily assessed dimensions of children's reading knowledge. The educational purpose of achievement tests is to ascertain whether a child possesses the skills and knowledge requisite to begin receiving instruction within a particular domain. Achievement tests differ from readiness tests, however, because the children have not all been exposed to a common curriculum.

Achievement tests estimate a child's current level of functioning and compare that information to the level of children of the same age, whereas diagnostic achievement tests provide much finer-grained analyses of a child's specific strengths and weaknesses. The Metropolitan Readiness Test (MRT), Boehm, and CIRCUS tests described in the Appendix are good examples of group achievement tests, whereas the Woodcock-Johnson is an excellent diagnostic achievement test. Diagnostic tests are given individually to students by highly trained professionals. The goal of a diagnostic test is to identify the specific problems a student is having, for example, in the area of reading. A diagnostic test would tell us if the student was having difficulty discriminating the sounds of language, representing those sounds with their corresponding letter symbols, or automatizing the whole word.

When using the tests to measure current functioning and attainment, particular care must be paid to a test's content validity. The utility of any achievement test depends upon an appropriate match between a particular test and a school district's primary curriculum. It is therefore critical when selecting an achievement test to match the content of what is being tested with what has been taught.

We discussed the three major types of standardized tests with regard to their content and intended use. In the next section, the policy and practice of evaluating and testing young children will be examined. A case study of standardized testing in kindergarten to determine first-grade readiness will be discussed, as well as the issues surrounding the practice of using these tests.

Uses of Tests in Early Childhood Education

Behind all the statistics employed to measure the significance and validity of tests are issues related to values and ethics. Who is to be tested? What do we mean by intelligence and achievement, and do our values agree with those implied by the tests we use to measure these constructs? What are the pros and cons of grouping children for instruction by measures such as age, achievement, and ability? What are the consequences of testing children? What are the consequences of testing children who come from varied home and cultural experiences? These are critical issues and ones that must be addressed *before* we can properly utilize tests.

Within the field of early childhood education, the use of tests has by and large been more limited than in the later educational years for a variety of reasons discussed in section III. Over the past decade, however, the demand for standardized evaluation of young children's performance has increased, and many educators and policymakers have suggested that the use of standardized tests within ECE will become even more prevalent. It has been suggested that the state of Georgia's recent mandate may only represent the beginning of a national trend.

The Practice of Formal Testing in Early Childhood Education: Georgia, a Case in Point. The passage of a Georgia state law requiring children to be tested before they can enter public school institutionalizes a process that heretofore had only been an informal trend in other parts of this country. The Quality Basic Education (QBE) Act required all students seeking to enter a public first-grade class in the fall of 1988 to have "achieved the State Board of Education's established criteria on the first grade readiness assessment" (Georgia Department of Education, February, 1988). The QBE Act was a response by the legislature to the issue of minimum competency for Georgia's early elementary-age students. The goal of the QBE Act was to "preserve and/or establish quality education programs" by guiding the instructional decisions practitioners must make regarding children's promotion into the following grade or retention in the same grade.

The readiness assessment is a combination of a standardized test and the teacher's evaluation of the student's achievement of state curriculum objectives. Formal evaluation of all kindergarten-age children is therefore mandatory in the state of Georgia. A kindergarten student cannot enter first grade without (1) taking a ninety-minute exam and (2) receiving a passing score on this measure *and* the teacher evaluation.

The Achievement Test: The standardized test is an achievement test developed in collaboration with McGraw-Hill, publishers of the California Achievement Test (CAT). The test is called the California Achievement Test, Georgia Edition. Subtests were chosen from the CAT (1982, Form E, Level 10) that "best discriminated between the children who were considered to be ready or not ready" for entrance into first grade (Georgia Department of Education, February, 1988). The subtests chosen represent a narrow sampling of abilities: visual recognition, sound recognition, and mathematics concepts and applications. Thus, the test does not sample many other critical dimensions of a child's abilities, such as motor development, attention, motivation, and so on. Furthermore, the Georgia CAT includes only 44 percent of the items from the complete Level 10 test. A composite score is calculated for each individual. The minimal performance level (passing score) was determined by state-wide pilot testing of kindergarten children in the spring of 1986 and in 1987, research by McGraw-Hill, and consultation with early childhood educators. Despite the claim by the state of Georgia and McGraw-Hill that this test is a valid predictor of future success in first grade, to date this contention remains totally unsubstantiated.

The Teacher Evaluation: The teacher evaluation was added later "to address the concerns of early childhood educators that had been voiced over the past year" (Georgia Department of Education, March 1, 1988). The evaluation of student behavior and potential is unstandardized; no criteria for teacher evaluation have been provided by the state. In the event that the Georgia CAT and teacher evaluation do not agree, the superintendent of schools has indicated that "an additional assessment" be used in deciding a child's appropriate placement. Unfortunately, no guidance has been provided by the state superintendent as to what the appropriate assessment should be. Thus, it is not at all clear what would happen if a child failed the Georgia CAT but received a favorable teacher evaluation.

The Policy Implications: It is apparent from Georgia's policy that achievement tests are believed to be good predictors of children's academic performance in first grade. When policymakers use phrases such as "these subtests were found to be the best predictors in a statewide research study involving 90,000 kindergarten children" (Georgia Department of Education, February, 1988), it is clear that assumptions regarding children's ability to learn or benefit from instruction are being made. Indeed, The tests are touted as being highly predictive of future success, particularly in the area of reading (Georgia Department of Education, pers. com., March 17, 1988). In other instances, however, the state of Georgia is utilizing achievement tests strictly for instructional purposes within the classroom. The student who has already been retained in kindergarten once must take the CAT for instructional diagnostic information, *but the student's future placement is not to be decided on the basis of this score.* In this situation, the achievement test provides information to the first-grade teacher on the incoming student. Individualized or small group curricula can be designed ahead of time for these students. The achievement test is used as an aid for instructional programming, not to predict how well the child will perform in the upcoming year. The distinction between using achievement tests for instructional diagnosis and predicting future performance is a critical distinction and will be discussed in greater detail below.

The Result of Achievement Testing: In the Georgia field testing of the CAT, 8 percent of the Georgia kindergartners did not achieve the criterion score. The failure ratio ranged from 1 percent in some districts to as high as 26 percent in others (Georgia Department of Education, pers. com., March 17, 1988). It has not been determined whether disadvantaged or minority groups are overrepresented in the populations of children who did not pass the test. Nonetheless, the social and political ramifications of excluding as much as 26 percent of the population from entering a regular first-grade classroom through the practice of grouping at-risk children in transitional rooms need to be examined carefully. This is particularly important in light of the fact that research on the benefits of transitional rooms has not shown that such placements contribute to children's future success (Abidin, Golladay, and Howerton, 1971; Bell, 1972; Gredler, 1984; May and Welch, 1984a; Shepard and Smith, 1985; Smith and

Shepard, 1987). Furthermore, some studies have demonstrated that children from disadvantaged backgrounds may be systematically excluded from first grade as a result of such a policy (Featherman, 1980; Abidin et al., 1971).

What Does This Case Study Suggest? The policy set forth by the state of Georgia formalizes a trend that has been occurring over the past twenty years in the field of early childhood education. Kindergarten teachers are being called upon to predict who will succeed in the primary grades and who will not. Their role as gatekeepers in a system emphasizing academic excellence has never been more clear. Futhermore, the decision-making process as to who is ready to learn has been clearly delineated for early childhood educators by policymakers. This decision is based primarily upon the achievement of academic skills: the standardized achievement test (which is completely academic) and the teacher evaluation, which "includes measures of readiness (academic/preacademics) and/or language development or conceptual development" (Georgia Department of Education, February, 1988). Furthermore, no criteria have been provided for the teacher evaluations of children's abilities. Early childhood educators may add other developmentally appropriate assessments in order to produce a more complete picture of the child. However, such measures of motor coordination and social/emotional development are not a part of the minimum state decision placement model (Georgia Department of Education, February, 1988).

The decision to perform mass screening of kindergarten children's present level of academic skills was made to help both children and teachers in meeting the educational requirements established by the Georgia Department of Education (see Georgia Quality Basic Education Act for a review of the state curriculum objectives and competency testing requirements for students in kindergarten, third grade, and high school). Nonetheless, this practice may represent a restriction of the opportunity for a fair and equitable education. This possibility should be seriously considered by teachers and policymakers. For, as we will discuss below, tracking children by placing them in readiness rooms or transitional rooms may be premature and of questionable value.

Stratification of Children for Instruction. Historically, most modern, Western educational systems have organized children into groups for the purpose of instruction in school. Considerable variation exists in how these groups are formed; nonetheless, some type of grouping takes place, and only the criteria for grouping differ crossculturally and historically. Over the past fifty years, the two principal methods of sorting children in the United States have been by age and ability (Leinhardt, 1980; Shepard and Smith, 1986, 1988). Sorting children by chronological age is a criterion that has engendered relatively little controversy due to its supposedly objective status. Recently, however, children's school entrance age has become a controversial issue within the field of early childhood education. The entrance age for school is being moved back further and further, requiring children to be considerably older in order to be permitted to receive public education. Clearly, the consequences of excluding children from public education at earlier ages must be seriously considered by parents, teachers, and policymakers.

Considerably more controversy has surrounded the second principal method of sorting children: the practice of grouping by ability. Historically, the composition of ability groups has been determined by physical handicaps, mental handicaps, learning disabilities, giftedness, special mathematical talents, and achievement groupings within and between classrooms. The issues are complex; the criteria for determining ability are (1) subjective, (2) socially determined, and (3) politically determined. Compounding the problem, the empirical work conducted in this area has been spotty and often contains a (sometimes poorly) hidden political agenda. Discussions regarding grouping practices have been largely polemical. As Katz (1977) aptly pointed out,"it is a general principle that any field characterized by a weak data base has a vacuum which is filled by ideology."

The small body of research that has investigated the various dimensions of grouping by age and ability has produced mixed results. For example, grouping children by ability proves occasionally to be effective for children who are older and more skilled (Cartwright and McIntosh, 1972; Dahllof, 1971; Eschel and Klein, 1978; Hart, 1967; Jackson, 1975; Olson, 1967) but is generally not effective for the less-skilled students (Goodlad, 1960; Oakes, 1981, 1985). Despite the lack of research documenting the positive effects of homogeneous grouping and a fairly substantial body of research outlining its educational and social costs (Hadermann, 1976; Holmes and Matthews, 1984; Kirp, 1974; Lefkowitz, 1972; Milofsky, 1974; Oakes, 1981, 1985), we have in fact observed a trend toward more homogeneous grouping of children in the primary grades (Shepard and Smith, 1986; Smith and Shepard, 1987).

The movement toward grouping by ability arises, as we have said, partly from the escalating academic emphasis placed on the primary curriculum. Teachers feel increasing pressure to produce children who are "up to snuff" (Smith and Shepard, 1987) and often feel at an unfair disadvantage in accomplishing their goals when they do not have the appropriate student population. Many teachers believe that homogeneous grouping may aid them in their delivery of the required product. The argument is a simple one: the teachers do not have to provide multiple curricula to children of varying ability and as a result, can more efficiently direct instruction to the group as a whole with less need for individual attention. If a child is placed in an appropriate ability group then the need for much special or remedial education is lessened (Ilg and Ames, 1965). Despite the widespread belief in this position, there is, in fact, no evidence to support it.

Therefore, these two practices of sorting children by age and ability continue to be areas of concern and clearly need to be scrutinized more closely by researchers, policymakers, and practitioners alike. Early child-hood educators have (often unwittingly) become the gatekeepers of a system of escalating academic demand within primary and elementary education. Our choice of "appropriate" age and ability levels has a profound influence on individual children, their families, and our educational system.

Grouping by Age: As our needs for standardization of educational curriculum have become greater over the years, there has been a corresponding increase in grouping children by age for purposes of instruction. This is best illustrated by examining this issue historically. At one point in our history, one-room schoolhouses were the norm in many parts of this country (Osborn, 1975; Zelizer, 1985). Within that room, children of multiple ages and abilities were taught the necessary social and academic skills. In the nineteenth century our educational resources and needs changed. As a result, we began dividing children into smaller, more homogeneous groups. This was first accomplished by separating children on the basis of chronological age. The categories were essentially groupings of children within a twelve-month age span. These cuts began when children were six years of age with their entry into a category called first grade. Soon another category called kindergarten was developed to prepare children for the educational process that was to begin when they were six years of age. The decision as to when formal education should commence was quite specific and measurable. In the system, the school year began in September and children had to be at least 4.9 years of age to enter school. All children were to be legally enrolled in the first grade by the age of six, and the majority of states provided kindergarten as an additional option.

Over the past thirty years, there has been a trend to raise the age at which children are legally entitled to enter kindergarten. Children have become progressively older when they enter public school in the United

States. Shepard and Smith (1986, 1988; Smith and Shepard, 1987) have examined this issue in great depth, and along with Gredler (1978, 1980, 1984), have provided much of the seminal work in this area. In 1958, for example, four-year-old children whose birthdates were after December 1 were not allowed to enter kindergarten. In the 1970s, the cutoff date in most districts was moved back to October 1: children had to be five years old by this date to receive education. In the 1980s, the trend was toward an earlier cutoff date of June 1 in some areas of the country (Shepard and Smith, 1986). There has also been a corresponding move toward retaining children in kindergarten in lieu of first grade. In California, for example, the kindergarten retention rate has almost doubled from 2.4 percent in 1976–1977 to 4.6 percent in 1983–1984 (California State Department of Education, 1988). As a result, we as a nation are requiring kindergarten and first-grade children to be older and presumably more mature in order to fit into our educational system. We are therefore postponing entry into our public educational system for a significant portion of our population. Had these laws been in effect thirty years ago, many readers would have started formal schooling a year later. The educational consequences of this shift in entrance age are unclear, but some other effects are obvious.

Raising the school entrance age has been considered an easy way to increase test scores (Davis, Trimble, and Vincent, 1980). This temptation arose when researchers and practitioners demonstrated that younger children do not perform as well as the older children in their class. The research is sparse in this area, but a trend has appeared. Younger children, for example, are more likely to repeat a grade (Langer, Kalk, and Searls, 1984) and to be considered at-risk for "maladjustment" (Weinstein, 1968–1969). They are also more likely to be labeled as learning disabled (Diamond, 1983; Maddux, 1980). Furthermore, within-grade age effects are observed for children in the first grade, demonstrating that younger children do perform more poorly than their older peers (Beattie, 1970; Davis et al., 1980; Hall, 1963; Shepard and Smith, 1986). The inference is drawn that these children may not be ready to learn.

But is this age difference surprising? "The 'age effect' literature verifies that children who are youngest in their first grade class are at a slight disadvantage...hardly surprising since an 11-month period of growth and development is a significant portion of a lifetime for a six-year-old" (Shepard and Smith, 1986, 83). It would in fact be odd if older children did not perform better on tests of academic achievement than children one year younger (Green and Simmons, 1962).

The arguments for removing these younger children from the educational process are undoubtedly fallacious. Excluding the youngest children from a group becomes a never-ending process. For as Shepard and Smith (1986) have pointed out, age is relative within a classroom. There will *always* be younger children within a group. The mean age of the group may change, but someone has to be younger. This cannot be avoided without creating a new entering class for every day of the year. Therefore, although the practice of continually raising the age requirement may appear to provide a temporary solution to the problem of primary school readiness (and thereby giving elementary school teachers their desired level of "player"), raising the entrance age "merely creates a new youngest group" (Shepard and Smith, 1986, 82). Contrary to many practitioners' beliefs, the underlying goal of creating a more homogeneous grouping is not achieved by cutting off the bottom sector of younger children. The distribution of students within a classroom has merely shifted upward, so that the mean age of the group will be older than prior to the age cut (Shepard and Smith, 1986). The apparent increase in test scores arises simply because the new scores belong to a different category of student: the younger students have not become smarter, they have just become uneducated and unmeasured. The other "free lunch" from raising the entrance age, namely, the temporarily smaller class size, is equally illusory, since future restoration of educational coverage will result in a temporary overpopulation of the same dimensions.

Being young and therefore not ready for school (for example, Weinstein, 1968–1969) is not a fixed state of affairs but is relative to the group one is being compared to (Miller and Norris, 1967; Shepard and Smith, 1986; Smith and Shepard, 1987). The age effect is not absolute: children are not magically transformed at six years of age into competent school learners. Readiness for school is dependent upon the context in which children exist (Cole and Scribner, 1974; Rogoff, 1982) and upon the norms and values of the culture. At the present time, our culture tends to be more product-oriented in regard to children's achievement.

Nowhere is the effect of context more clearly illustrated than by examining the crosscultural variation in school entrance age requirements. In England, children begin public school when they are four years old, while in Sweden and the Soviet Union, children begin formal schooling at seven years of age (Austin et al., 1975; Baranova and Rozyeva, 1985). Gredler (1975, 1978, 1980) provides a survey of school entrance age in other countries. Despite the fact that England, Sweden, and the United States have different entrance ages, the incidence of academic failure in reading, for example, is similar across countries (Gredler, 1978). Learning to read is of course a complex process of which age is only one factor among multiple determinants of reading ability (Perfetti, 1985). Nevertheless,

Gredler (1980) has pointed out that all Western societies bemoan the problem of younger children performing more poorly than their older peers; he and DiPasquale et al. (1980) label this problem the "birthdate effect." Gredler cites a study by Jinks (1964) illustrating that teachers in England consistently praised the learning abilities of their older students, students who, in the United States, would be the youngest and most maligned population. He concludes that it "seems school personnel complain in every society about how poorly young children perform. The only problem with the examples used is that the children are all of different ages — 7, 6, and 5" (Gredler, 1980, 12).

The important questions are: how real and lasting are these initial academic differences between younger and older kindergarten-age children within the same class, and does the younger child end up better or worse off than the older child at the same age? In fact, these age differences, while statistically significant, are practically quite small. For example, Shepard and Smith (1985) compared the reading and math scores of children who were in the youngest three-month block in the class with children in the oldest three-month block. On average, the younger children scored at the 62d percentile in reading and the oldest group at the 71st percentile. This represents a difference of nine percentage points in reading scores. The difference was smaller for math — six percentage points. When Davis et al. (1980) examined children's performance on an achievement battery, they found that children who were five years old when they entered first grade were nine percentage points behind children who were six years old when they entered first grade.

Moreover, Shepard and Smith (1986) have pointed out that the disadvantage younger children are experiencing relative to their older peers is really a combination of both age and ability. For example, when Shepard and Smith examined their data by children's ability, there was no difference in achievement between the youngest and oldest age groups for children who were above the 75th or 50th percentile points of their respective age intervals. On the other hand, somewhat larger differences were observed in children who scored below the 25th percentile, leading these researchers to conclude that ability may be contributing to the "age effect." It is not only chronological age that determines performance on tests of achievement and school performance but also incoming knowledge or ability to learn. Even so, these initially small ability differences between the youngest and the oldest within a class diminish over time (Langer et al., 1984; Miller and Norris, 1967; Shepard and Smith, 1985). In summary, whereas the differences in performance between the youngest sector of the classroom and the oldest are genuine, they appear to be a combination of age, ability, and teacher biases (see Shepard and Smith, 1986, and Gredler, 1984, for a more complete discussion of teacher effects).

Oddly enough, limiting school entrance by selecting for older children accomplishes exactly the opposite of the intended goal — creating a homogeneous population of learners and reducing the academic escalation within the classroom. "Raising the entrance age might contribute to the problem of increasing academic demand, if teachers then adjust their teaching to the capabilities of five-and-a-half- and six-year-olds" (Shepard and Smith, 1989). Inadvertently, the policy of excluding younger children creates an older body of students, which may only feed the trend toward more academics in the primary curriculum and less curricular time allocated to children's social, emotional, and physical development. Additionally the longer children remain outside the public school system, the greater is the differentiating effect of the wide variation in home circumstances.

In summary, the argument that entrance age is a determining factor in academic achievement has not been substantiated. Clearly, further studies are needed to address this important issue and policymakers need to reconsider current regulations and trends in light of the above arguments.

Grouping by ability: Children can also be placed in groups on the basis of their perceived ability or achievement. Depending upon the curriculum, children are grouped by their overall level of skill or their specific level of skill within a content area (for example, mathematics, sports, reading). These types of ability groupings are largely determined by standardized and informal tests and by teacher and parent observations. The tests can be measures of intelligence, achievement, or more recently, developmental age. The tests themselves are described in the fourth section above and in the Appendix. In this present section, the issues raised as a result of their use for grouping will be discussed.

Within early childhood education, grouping by ability occurs when (1) providing individual programs of education for children with special needs (for example, physically or mentally handicapped); (2) when making curriculum decisions in teaching specific skills in a content area (for example, reading); and (3) when screening children for entry into kindergarten or first grade. Each of these groupings has the potential to help children and teachers achieve an optimal program of instruction. When properly executed, they are legitimate reasons for examining and grouping young children. Physically or mentally handicapped children often need additional educational programs and separate ones in some cases, although even this ability grouping has had its share of controversy (Madden and Slavin, 1983; Semmel, Gottlieb, and Robinson, 1979). Grouping by achievement within a classroom serves the needs of various children and attends to the individual differences that exist within any group. The practice of screening children by ability for entrance into either kindergarten or first grade has, however, become a particularly controversial issue of late. The controversy rests particularly on the issue of readiness for school learning: Is the child ready to benefit from formal instruction as provided by the public school system? Ability grouping of this type is clearly based on the philosophy that there are absolute levels of readiness for primary school.

Two methods of sorting children for entrance into first grade have gained popularity over the past twenty years. The first method has required children to be of a certain developmental age as determined by developmental instruments (Gesell Institute of Human Development, 1978, 1979), and the second method requires children to be at a certain level of academic achievement as determined by achievement tests. That is, children who are not considered to be of an appropriate developmental age or level of achievement would not be admitted to first grade.

Developmental age is a relatively new criterion for sorting children. It is considered to be independent of chronological age and is a concept underlying many primary educational practices. The idea is that children should be taught at the same developmental level, and therefore that classrooms should be comprised of children who are functioning at approximately the same level of development. The construct of developmental age and methods for its assessment will be discussed below.

Grouping children by their level of academic achievement, on the other hand, measures a child's specific level of knowledge within a content area. In the past fifty years, assessment batteries have been developed for many different content areas. Important areas of achievement for kindergarten children, generally, are: the ability to recognize the letters of the alphabet and their corresponding sounds, to recognize and use numbers from zero to twenty, to understand left-to-right sequence, to recognize shapes, and so on. Proponents of achievement testing for entrance to first grade, therefore, believe that children should enter first grade with a minimum level of competency in all these areas.

The issue of grouping is hotly debated between those reseachers and practitioners in favor of placement by *developmental age* (DiPasquale et al., 1980; Donofrio, 1977; Donofrio and O'Hare, 1969; Ames and Ilg, 1964; Wood, Powell, and Knight, 1984) and those that question the validity of the construct of developmental age (Bear and Modlin, 1987; May, 1986; May and Welch, 1984a, 1984b; Meisels, 1987, 1988; Niklason,

1984; Shepard and Smith, 1988). Sorting children by *achievement* for entrance into first grade has become an enforced practice in some areas of the country (for example, Georgia Department of Education, March 1, 1988), yet it is also a practice that is variable even within school districts. Smith and Shepard (1987), for example, found that "in some schools, no kindergartners were retained; whereas in others, as many as one-third completed two years in kindergarten before entering first grade" (131). The topic of readiness for formal education has been discussed in educational circles (Bredekamp, 1987; NAEYC, 1988) and in the media (Henig, 1988; Putka, 1988a, 1988b; Seligman and Murr, 1988). More recently, researchers have begun reviewing (Meisels, 1986, 1987; Shepard and Smith, 1986, 1988; Smith and Shepard, 1987) and investigating the validity of using measures of developmental age and achievement to screen children's entrance into the public schools (Barnes, 1982; Lichtenstein, 1980; May and Welch, 1984a, 1984b, 1985, 1986; Meisels, 1985; Shepard and Smith, 1986). In the following paragraphs, we discuss the practices of screening and retention, the tests used to make these decisions, and the research evidence bearing on the validity of both.

Retention by Any Other Name: The primary reason for sorting and testing young children is often to determine their readiness for first grade. When we sort children by ability, either achievement or developmental age, for the purpose of screening them from kindergarten or first grade, we are really talking about *retention*. Retention should be contemplated only when a student is considered to be at-risk for future learning and/or has already had an unsuccessful school experience. Retention in ECE is essentially the practice of having a child "stay back" a year, either at home, in preschool, kindergarten, or a readiness class (for a review, see Plummer et al., 1986). *Social promotion* is the practice of allowing the child to enter the next grade (usually first grade or kindergarten in this case) despite doubts concerning the child's present capabilities. The popularity of retention has undergone wild gyrations over the past century. This complex issue is determined by multiple factors. There are arguments for and against the practices of retention and social promotion. The following arguments favor retention:

- A child who is not ready to meet the academic demands of the first grade classroom will fall to the bottom of the class and be forced to participate in academic (and other) activities that are beyond his or her capabilities.
- As a result, the child will experience frustration, poor self-esteem, apathy, and consequently have discipline problems.

- Retaining children allows them to master skills that are at their ability level and provides them with time to mature and develop the necessary prerequisite abilities to succeed in school-related tasks.
- Moreover, retaining children who are not ready for first grade allows for more homogeneous grouping and makes instruction easier to manage for the children and the teacher (Carstens, 1985).

The arguments in favor of promoting children to kindergarten and first grade despite varying abilities are as follows:

- When children are "held back" they are usually stigmatized as failures by themselves, their families, peers, and teacher (we do not know the consequences of retention for a child's social and emotional development, but the limited research appears to substantiate the fears that it lowers motivation and self-esteem).
- Being placed within a homogeneous group of "not ready" children is an understimulating environment, and repeating the kindergarten curriculum will not address the specific needs of the child.
- This is simply too young an age to predict if an individual child will fail or succeed in his or her school career.
- Retention is costly for both financial and social reasons: poor and minority children are overrepresented in the ranks of retainees (Carstens, 1985; Featherman, 1980). Retaining children adds another year to the thirteen-year system and is an unnecessary expense.

Decisions regarding retention need to be based on our best available information. Researchers, policymakers, and teachers all agree that such an important decision deserves to be based upon carefully conceived and executed studies that examine the effects of promotion and retention in early childhood education. This information will facilitate thoughtful and intelligent decisions about state or district policy and individual children. Decisions based upon intuition or what makes sense to the practitioners are often misguided. Current psychological research (Kahneman, Slovic, and Tversky, 1982) has shown that normal adults are extremely poor at making decisions when the outcome is uncertain, particularly when the information about children provided by tests contains significant inaccuracies. It is possible that the application of straightforward techniques from formal decision analysis might result in considerable clarification of testing policy. A common failing in research on retention, for example, has been the tendency to compare the subsequent performance of those who failed a test and were retained with the performance of those who passed and were not retained. Clearly, if the retention test is in question, this kind of study is not ideal.

Certainly the most impressive general review of retention and promotion policies throughout the educational system appears in the often cited study by Jackson (1975). Jackson surveyed over one hundred studies and analyzed forty-four studies that were original research. The great majority of the studies suffered from one or more of the following four weaknesses: (1) they failed to sample from varied populations of students (thereby limiting their generalizability); (2) they failed to define the treatments children received as a result of being retained or promoted; (3) they were of a short-term nature and not longitudinal (thereby limiting our ability to discuss the long-term effects of retention practices); or (4) they failed to examine the complex interactions between the treatment and student characteristics. Jackson concluded that "educators who retain pupils in a grade do so without valid research evidence to indicate that such treatment will provide greater benefits to students with academic or adjustment difficulties than will promotion to the next grade" (627).

Although retention practices are considered to be of dubious value for older children, the sentiment of some researchers and practitioners is that they may be of greater value for younger children (Cooke and Stammer, 1985; Plummer et al., 1986). This is, however, an empirical question, and one we can begin to investigate; we are not left to our own intuition of what seems appropriate. We will be able to establish sound policy on this issue only through the accumulation of multiple studies, appropriately designed and executed to examine the following question: over the course of a child's school career, to what degree does it help or hinder the child's social, emotional, physical, and intellectual development to provide him or her with another year to mature before entering the academic climate of first grade?

The research examining the two methods of sorting children by ability (achievement or developmental age) is sparse and inconclusive. The object of the studies is to ascertain the possible benefits, if any, of retention, as opposed to direct entry into first grade for children who score below a threshold level on a standardized achievement test or development test. One methodological difficulty with any such study is that in most cases retention is not mandatory, so there is the additional factor of parental selection to be taken into account. The effects on such a study of parents with high aspirations for their child, for example, are hard to measure.

Gredler (1984) has reviewed several studies that examined the outcome of retention policies based on achievement tests. The studies are discussed in the following paragraphs. Bell (1972) studied children whose achievement test scores were low and who were recommended by their teachers for retention. Some of the children were retained, with the concurrence of their parents, but some went into first grade directly. Bell concluded that the latter group made greater achievement gains than those placed in the readiness room. In addition, contrary to the opinions of many proponents of retention, the self-esteem, as measured by standard self-concept tests, of the children who were retained was significantly damaged relative to those who went directly into first grade.

Talmadge (1981) studied a retention system in which the decision was made on the basis of a low score on the Metropolitan Readiness Test (MRT), an achievement test, combined with a teacher's recommendation. Importantly, this basis is very similar to that used in the current Georgia program of mandatory retention. It was found that, despite claims that readiness rooms provide a superior foundation of pre-reading skills (Gredler, 1984), the reading performance of retained children by the end of first grade was no better than that of children who had gone on to first grade without retention. Similarly, Rose et al. (1983) and Holmes and Matthews (1984) observed in their studies that when retained children who were equally low achievers were compared with socially promoted children, the children who had been promoted scored higher on both achievement tests and indexes of social-emotional health.

Raygor (1972) found that there was a slight improvement in achievement skills for kindergarten-retained and readiness-room-retained children, compared to children also found to be at-risk but who nonetheless went on to first grade. This improvement largely disappeared, however, by the end of third grade, with the exception of reading ability.

Perhaps the most significant finding of the Raygor study was that, by the end of fourth grade, there were virtually no significant differences in achievement between children recommended for retention and those recommended for entry when both went directly into first grade. This suggests that placement by achievement testing is inappropriate, presumably because of the large number of exogenous factors affecting achievement. Clearly, more research is needed on other, less drastic methods to overcome low achievement in five-year-olds.

Leinhardt (1980) undertook just this kind of study. Using a population of predominantly black students, Leinhardt examined three groups: retention-eligible children who nonetheless went into first grade and received group instruction using the normal basal-reader; a similar group that received individualized attention; and a third group that received the same individualized attention but in a readiness room. The results showed that the children receiving individualized attention within the first-grade classroom significantly outperformed both of the other groups. Leinhardt also noted that the amount of reading content in the first-grade curriculum was almost twice that in the readiness room, and cited this as a main cause of the findings. The teacher-pupil ratio in the readiness room was three times higher, but this seemed not to help.

Overall, there seems little evidence that academic performance is improved by retention in readiness rooms on the basis of achievement. Given that retention is expensive and seems to harm the self-esteem of children, it seems more reasonable to investigate the use of resources for additional, individualized attention within the normal, first-grade setting for children who are thought to be at-risk.

As mentioned above, the Gesell Preschool Readiness Test (Haines, Ames, and Gillespie, 1980) is intended to measure the developmental age of a subject, that is, the degree to which a child's mind has matured. Based on the research of Gesell (1954), the Gesell Institute has propounded the view that a "mentally immature" child will not benefit from certain types of instruction and, therefore, should not be educated until reaching the appropriate level of maturity. The Gesell test has become more and more popular in recent years; the institute estimates that as many as 18 percent of young children in the United States are screened for kindergarten and first-grade entry using the test, or close to half a million a year. Research has been carried out both on the properties of the Gesell test itself and on its use in screening.

The Gesell tests contain items designed to measure motor, cognitive, language, and personal-social development. For example, a large portion of the test consists of items such as asking the child to identify the left ring finger and to place it on the right eyebrow. The tests also include many items taken directly from IQ tests such as the Stanford-Binet, despite the Gesell Institute's claims that "the assessments measure primarily maturity and not intelligence or experience." Indeed, Kaufman, (1985b) demonstrated that the factor structure of the Gesell School Readiness test was similar to that of IQ tests. Furthermore, Shepard and Smith (1985) and Kaufman (1985b) have found that the test lacks discriminate validity from IQ tests. In a recent study, Bear and Modlin (1987) showed that the Gesell test possessed no additional diagnosticity for future performance beyond that provided by math and reading achievement scores. Finally, the Gesell tests appear to have extremely poor psychometric properties. "The major difference between the Gesell and current intelligence tests appears to be the lack of emphasis on psychometric properties of the scale (for example, no standardization sample, no factor-analytic results or reliability coefficients)" (Naglieri, 1985b, 608).

Practices regarding a child's readiness for school on the basis of developmental age, as measured by the Gesell test, are based mainly on the recommendations of the Gesell Institute. J. Haines, the institute's director of training, stated in a personal communication to Samuel Meisels (Meisels, 1987) that "the validity of the work has been through years of experience in application. A validity study has not been completed at this time." The Gesell Institute (1987), in a response to Meisels's article, cites a study by Ames and Ilg (1964) as evidence of the tests' capability to predict sixth-grade performance, although this study provides only correlational information, with no accuracy information for classification decisions. A study by Wood, Powell, and Knight (1984) is cited as evidence of predictive validity, but analysis of the same data by Shepard and Smith (1986) showed that *for every potential failure accurately identified, a successful child was falsely identified.*

What Does All This Mean? As described in the earlier section, information from achievement tests has two major uses in our current early-childhood system: (1) to help subsequent teachers help individual children and (2) to make placement decisions, particularly with respect to retention.

Standardized achievement tests, as opposed to district- or teacher-developed instruments, are not as sensitive to the regional curriculum but do provide teachers with some indication of a child's present level of knowledge. This is only helpful, of course, if a teacher compares a child's performance on each of the various subtests. The total score will not prove to be as diagnostic and will not provide a profile of an individual child's strengths and weaknesses. Employing a standardized achievement test for purposes other than diagnosis of present skills has questionable value for children as young as four and five years of age. The individual differences in exposure to academics are enormous at this age due to familial and developmental factors. Therefore, it is not always clear what the children should have learned by the time they enter kindergarten and first grade and how important nationally (or state-) normed information is for their subsequent instruction.

Samuel Meisels at the University of Michigan has been particularly concerned with the misuse of achievement tests for placement decisions (Meisels, 1984, 1985, 1986, 1987, 1988). Achievement tests, often under the possibly misleading title of readiness tests (for example, the Metropolitan Readiness Test, or MRT), have been used to deny children entry to first grade. Sometimes this use has been contrary to the intentions of the test formulators. Placement in special programs should only be the result of testing using developmental screening instruments, which have high predictive validity for failure in normal education programs. Readiness tests do not have sufficient reliability or validity to support retention decisions. As many as one-third of children classified as unready by even such a psychometrically respectable instrument as the MRT are in fact being misdiagnosed.

Evidence on the nature and use of the Gesell Preschool and School Readiness tests is even more damning. As discussed above, the tests seem to measure IQ more than anything else, despite the claimed intent to measure developmental age. As Shepard and Smith (1986) have noted,

Changing the name of what the test measures has profound policy implications. Many decision makers would be willing to hold out of school or place in a two-year track children who are "developmentally young." It is much less defensible to hold out of school children who are below average in IQ, especially since a disproportionate share of these children will come from low socioeconomic backgrounds. (83)

Summary

There is no doubt, of course, that the vast majority of the proponents of achievement testing in Georgia, and of the proponents and users of the Gesell tests, are well intentioned. However, it is all too easy to feel comfortable with decisions made about a child's life as long as those decisions are made with the child's best interests at heart. We must remember that this is *not* the same as making decisions that are in the child's best interest — this can only be established by rigorous studies on the scientific underpinnings and educational effects of the decisions. One cannot but agree with the position adopted by the National Association for the Education of Young Children (1988):

It is the professional responsibility of administrators and teachers to critically evaluate, carefully select, and use standardized tests only for the purposes for which they are intended and for which data exists demonstrating the test's validity (the degree to which the test accurately measures what it purports to measure. (44)

Even with the use of well-studied tests, no sorting practice for retention in kindergarten or readiness rooms has shown reliable, lasting, or reproducible benefits for the children involved. The widespread popularity of testing and retention, then, may have been encouraged by the perception of efficiency benefits from homogeneous classrooms and the perception that screening makes it easier for school system or teacher to raise test scores, especially in the current environment. We would argue that achievement testing and the resulting screening in early childhood can be expensive, are educationally ineffective, and deny opportunity to individual children who would otherwise benefit from integration into the public education system with their peers. Clearly, more attention must be given to other means of assisting young children who enter the school system with a lower level of acquired skills and academic knowledge. In particular, flexible curricula and individualized instruction within the normal classroom are promising in this regard.

Conclusions and Recommendations

Having surveyed the nature and role of testing in early childhood education, some conclusions can be drawn as to the validity of the policies associated with testing. Clearly, there are definite and quantifiable benefits to be derived from certain types of tests when carried out under the right circumstances. But it must be concluded that the indiscriminate use of testing, particularly of achievement and developmental-age testing, has serious consequences for the quality of education of young children. Further research is warranted on several aspects of testing and remediation, and recommendations will be given for the improvement of early childhood curricula to help overcome the problems that both cause and result from the current emphasis on quantifiable performance measures.

Benefits of Standardized Testing

Screening Tests. The most important kinds of variation an individual child can exhibit (excluding more serious impairments such as mental retardation and physical handicaps) are the various physical and mental disabilities, such as deafness, severe myopia, or attentional deficit, that require specific medical or psychological intervention. There is evidence (Lichtenstein and Ireton, 1984; Meisels, 1985; Meisels and Wiske, 1983) that developmental screening tests, the ESI, for example (see the fourth section), provide good early indication that a child may be at-risk. The benefits to the child so identified can be enormous. Despite the enactment of several federal laws to encourage screening, not all states have screening programs, and efforts to identify handicapped children are often poorly coordinated (Meisels, 1984). In addition, of the 150 or so tests purporting to provide indication of potential handicaps, only 3 appear to have been validated successfully (Meisels, in press).

Information for Subsequent Teacher. As has been emphasized throughout the chapter, the principal issue here is what one does with the results of tests. A standardized achievement test, with its results properly interpreted through statistical studies and broken down into the various sub-areas of intellectual competence, can provide a first-grade teacher with valuable information on each child in the incoming class. It should be emphasized that the scores can only be interpreted as indicating a deficit or surplus of knowledge in a subject area and not of ability. Particularly in an area of mobile or heterogeneous population, the existence and quality of a child's prior formal and informal education can vary widely. Test scores should thus be used to help the teacher in designing individual programs of instruction to make up for previous deficits or to provide additional stimulation.

Enforcement of Minimum Curriculum Standards. There is a natural tendency toward wide variation in the curricula provided by schools, especially at the kindergarten level, where many different educational theories have been promulgated. A possible benefit of standardized testing is that it may impose a crude kind of quality control on the more experimentally oriented members of the teaching profession (Darling-Hammond and Wise, 1985). The merits of this conjecture have been seriously questioned (Kagan, 1987).

Negative Consequences of Testing in ECE. Tests are often a blunt instrument in the hands of the uninformed or misguided. Misperceptions about the nature of the tests themselves, or about the benefits of the decisions being made using the tests' results, can have catastrophic consequences for the children involved. Some of the most common misperceptions and their negative effects are discussed below.

Testing and Classroom Homogeneity. As discussed above, there is a widespread and growing tendency for schools and teachers at elementary, junior, and senior high school levels to be judged on the basis of the students' performance on standardized achievement tests. When combined with the economic pressures resulting from decreased resource allocations for education, this results in many administrators and teachers demanding minimum achievement levels from incoming students in order to provide a more homogeneous (and purportedly more efficient) classroom and to ease the task of ensuring good scores at the end of the year. Teachers and administrators know the easiest way to ensure an 800 average at year's end is to insist that students entering already score 750. This mentality, when extended downwards to the kindergarten and first-grade levels, simply results in an ever-increasing average age of entry into any given grade as more children are held back (Gredler, 1978, 1980; May and Welch, 1986; Shepard and Smith, 1986, 1988; Smith and Shepard, 1987).

Another serious consequence of a policy of classroom homogeneity is that it de-emphasizes individual attention in favor of programmed instruction. Individuality in children is both desirable and inescapable — the only truly homogeneous classroom is a single-student classroom. The use of standardized achievement tests to limit entry into a grade does not eliminate variation, it simply ignores it. It is argued below that we must face up to the task of providing more individualized instruction.

Biasing the Curriculum.   Perhaps the most insidious effect of standardized testing is that it biases the early-childhood curriculum toward academic content, namely pencil-and-paper symbolic tasks, replacing the actual concrete experience that the symbols are intended to reflect. It is a crucial misconception to believe that, for example, mathematical skills reside in the ability to carry out formal manipulations of numbers and variables. Those who have studied the psychology of mathematical discovery (Polya, 1957) emphasize that mathematical ability is greatly facilitated by direct apprehension of the concrete models for which mathematical symbols are an abstraction. Suppose we want to teach the concept of commutativity of addition. We can drill students on dozens of examples: $1 + 2 = 3, 2 + 1 = 3, 4 + 3 = 7; 3 + 4 = 7; 2 + 6 = 8, 6 + 2 = 6$, and so on. Or we can have them join sticks together and observe that the order of joining does not affect the aggregate length. There is a good deal of evidence (for example, Genesereth, 1980) that concrete models of formal systems are a principal tool of cognition and greatly improve ability to solve complex problems over simple symbol manipulation methods. Mathematics and language itself were developed to aid in our ability to deal with reality and are not ends in themselves. Training to a test in formal symbolic skills while neglecting children's basic conceptual understanding may result in serious difficulties in connecting formal problems to real problems and in comprehending and using more advanced material in later life. Unfortunately, it is difficult to put reality into a standardized test.

Misuse of the Developmental-Age Construct.   Gesell and subsequent adherents of this theoretical position (Ames, 1980; Diamond, 1983; DiPasquale et al., 1980; Donofrio, 1977; Gesell Institute of Human Development, 1980; Ilg and Ames, 1965; Ilg et al., 1978) have proposed the use of developmental age, as measured by the Gesell School Readiness test, as a criterion of readiness for education at a given level. A widespread and increasingly common practice (up 67 percent since 1984) resulting from this doctrine is the retention of children in various kinds of readiness programs until they reach the right "developmental age." The Gesell Institute has argued that up to 50 percent of our school problems could be remediated or prevented by placing children within the appropriate grade for their developmental age (Ilg et al., 1978). However, several studies (Bear and Modlin, 1987; Shepard and Smith, 1985; Smith and Shepard, 1987) suggests that the Gesell test actually measures something very close to IQ. If this is in fact the case, we would be alarmed to discover that, by most estimates, over five hundred thousand children a year (Putka, 1988b) are being sorted and possibly held back on the basis of something they can do nothing about. Until we have specified what is meant by developmental age and validated the most common instrument used to measure it, allocating precious funds and retaining children on the basis of this theory and test, is an irresponsible practice.

To Retain or Not to Retain?   The inappropriate use of achievement testing to try to create homogeneous classrooms has already been pointed out. What of the more well-intended application—to identify the child in need of additional preparation? Retention of children in kindergarten or in a readiness room until they are able to achieve a minimum score is becoming a standard practice in many areas and is mandatory in the state of Georgia.* There appears, however, to be little evidence that retention has any benefit for the young child (Bocks, 1977; Carstens, 1985; Niklason, 1984), just as retention is known to be valueless for older students (Holmes and Matthews, 1984; Oakes, 1981, 1985). A possible reason for the failure of retention to achieve its intended goals is that the achievement test may identify the child that has problems in achieving (that is, scoring high on the test), but a child may get a low score for any number of reasons, only one of which is a lack of ability to learn. Poor home environment, behavioral difficulties, and poor test-taking skills are other common reasons for low scores, and none of these will be addressed by putting the child in a stigmatizing program for children who are "not up to snuff" or by putting the child back into the same kindergarten program with a group of younger children. Furthermore, standardized testing puts the stamp of approval—"doctors recommend..."—on a practice that

---

* The state of Georgia has since amended their policy requiring all Kindergarten age children to reach a certain criteria on their standardized test.

only defers and compounds, rather than alleviates a child's difficulties. The creation of readiness rooms, effectively an additional grade, to accommodate from 9 percent to 20 percent of young children is expensive, costing perhaps as much as $1 billion per year nationwide. This is a roundabout way to rename grades.

What Is to Be Done?

The most obvious policy recommendations to emerge from the above analysis are the following:

1. The practice of using achievement testing for screening entry into first grade should be discouraged. Achievement tests have poor predictive validity for young children and continual pressure to increase test scores has an upward ratcheting effect on entry age for all grades, even leading to the creation of additional grades at the low end.
2. Standardized testing for young children has effectively distorted the curriculum away from conceptual fundamentals; we need to reverse this trend.
3. Retention of children in kindergarten or readiness rooms cannot be justified on current research evidence and should be reconsidered as a policy.
4. The use of the Gesell test to dictate the pace of education of individual children should be ended, pending further research into its theoretical basis as an indicator of maturation. Its poor psychometric qualities suggest that its use cannot be upheld.
5. Given that retention seems unsuccessful in most cases, research on and experimentation with curriculum alternatives are indicated. These include the following:
   a. A formalized association between home and school whereby parents participate in the social, motivational, and academic aspects of their children's education; this association is similar to that envisaged in the Head Start program but covers the entire period from preschool to elementary school;
   b. Intensive individualized/small-group instruction (without the remedial label), based on specific learner characteristics and needs;
   c. Individual tutoring, or content-specific instruction occurring outside school;
   d. Kindergarten through third grade ungraded classrooms.

Thus, it seems that a priority for researchers should be the cost-benefit assessment of retention and other interventions as methods for assisting young children who achieve poorly on standard curricular tests. The first need is for more wide-spectrum, longitudinal studies to examine the long-term effects of retention in kindergarten. However, as with many studies of young children, it is likely that this research will reveal great variability in its final outcome because of the unstable characteristics of the population and because of the wide variation in subsequent education. In addition to empirical studies, then, we need to get a better idea of what causes a child not to do well. What are the cognitive, maturational, and educational factors that determine performance? The success of intervention programs such as Head Start suggests that intrinsic ability may be only a small factor. Until we have better cognitive models of children to help us understand learning, and until we can accurately diagnose the specific reasons for a child's poor performance, our blind efforts to help may be both damaging and expensive.

To give one example: until recently, it was thought that children having trouble with subtraction were either lazy or simply incapable of correct application of the skills they had been taught: they were not good learners. The treatment was to prescribe large numbers of repetitive exercises until the children "got it right." But research in psychology and artificial intelligence (Sleeman and Smith, 1981; VanLehn, 1983) has shown that the vast majority of children are absolutely reliable and accurate in applying their subtraction skills — but they have the wrong algorithm. This has one of several causes: the major one is lack of understanding of the semantic basis for subtraction — what it is supposed to achieve and what real-world processes it abstracts. Another reason is the use of poorly designed examples in texts, from which children generalize incorrectly. In-depth understanding of learning processes enables in-depth, and successful, remediation. More generally, it is important not to blame children's *supposed* lack of ability for failure to perform, a tendency that reliance on, and teaching to, standardized achievement tests unfortunately encourages.

The issues and policies surrounding testing of young children also highlight the need for more work on curricular design. Instead of pushing underachievers under the carpet and hoping they will go away, we need to find ways to address their various needs within the mainstream.

Standardized tests, by their nature, can only examine a small portion of a child's capabilities, particularly her or his skills in recognizing and manipulating symbolic material. Teaching to such tests neglects social, physical, and conceptual skills that are crucial to a child's success and are

often particularly hard for disadvantaged children to acquire outside
school. Since it is clear that testing drives curriculum changes, Zigler
(1970, 1973a, 1973b) has advocated educating and testing the "whole
child." Therefore, a realistic solution to meeting the needs of the whole
child is to develop less one-sided instruments.

The concern that academic material has filtered down into the kindergarten curriculum, partly as a result of testing, has been expressed in this
chapter. The position taken here is not that this material is entirely
inappropriate, but that the methods of teaching have been distorted along
with the content. It is essential to provide children with concrete experiences
of the concepts and skills being taught. Some educators, however, alarmed
at the overemphasis on academics, have examined this issue and concluded that we need to abandon the teaching of academic skills and
instead let children "bloom" or "blossom" through unguided experiences
(see, for example, Charlesworth, 1985). This position is considered to be
equally irresponsible. Young children are ready to absorb material concerning written language and mathematics, provided it is taught in the
right way, with concrete models and appropriate metacognitive direction
and not to the exclusion of other domains, such as the child's social,
emotional, and physical development. Indeed, the way the world is itself
developing, it will become more and more important for children to build
a sound base for the ultimate achievement of a high level of academic
competence. A proficiency akin to that of parrots does not constitute such
a base.

Acknowledgments

I would like to thank Stuart Russell, Catherine O'Connor, Keith Stanovich,
and Mark Wilson for their helpful comments on sections of the manuscript.
I am also most appreciative of the scholarly reviews that Lorrie Shepard,
Howard Gardner, Samuel Meisels, Valora Washington, and Sandra Fox
provided. Thanks to Robin Hencke for her assistance with various details
of this manuscript. I wish to thank Bernard Gifford, commissioner for the
Ford Foundation National Commission on Testing and Public Policy, for
providing the opportunity to think and write about issues of testing in
ECE. This work was written and supported in 1988 by a grant from the
Hewlitt Foundation.

Appendix: Tests in Common Use

Developmental Screening Tests

The McCarthy Screening Test (MST). The MST (McCarthy 1978) is an individually administered test for children ages four to six years, five months. The MST is comprised of six subtests taken directly from the McCarthy Scales of Children's Abilities. These subtests include right-left coordination, verbal memory, draw-a-design, numerical memory, conceptual grouping, and leg coordination. The inclusion of right-left orientation and leg coordination are considered to be questionable because they are unreliable measures and have low predictive validity for future school success (Kaufman 1985a; Naglieri 1985a). The MST may not be sampling a wide range of skills but instead may be simply measuring one construct in varying degrees. Nonetheless, the test is viewed as a promising and "highly valuable contribution to the assessment field" (Kaufman 1985a, 929). But it must be used with caution, especially regarding its predictive validity (Meisels 1985).

Early Screening Inventory (ESI). The ESI (Meisels and Wiske 1983) is an individually administered test for children ages four to six years. The ESI is comprised of thirty items within three subtests measuring visual-motor adaptive functioning, language and cognition, and gross-motor body awareness. The ESI "samples the domain of developmental tasks that all children of normal abilities should be able to perform, rather than the domain of specific learned accomplishments that indicate academic readiness" (Meisels, Wiske, and Tivan 1984, 26). The test has moderate to high sensitivity (Meisels, Wiske, and Tivan 1984), and therefore any error will result in overselection of students considered to be at-risk. Similar to other screening instruments, the ESI has limited predictive validity (Meisels 1984) and should be only used for screening decisions for a year before being readministered. The ESI is considered to be an excellent test and an important contribution to the field of developmental screening tests.

Minneapolis Preschool Screening Instrument (MPSI). The MPSI (Lichtenstein 1980) is an individually administered screening test for children ages three years, seven months to five years, four months. The test is comprised of fifty items and eleven subtests that assess building, copying and matching shapes, naming colors, counting, providing information, completing and repeating sentences, gross motor skills, and identifying body parts. The MPSI is considered to be a comprehensive and very efficient measure about one that has limited predictive validity for future school success.

Denver Developmental Screening Test-Revised (DDST-R). The DDST-R (Frankenburg and Dodds 1981) is an individually administered test for children ages two weeks to six years. The DDST-R is a comprehensive test which has four basic subtests: personal/social, fine motor adaptive, language, and gross motor, with a total of 105 items. A basal and ceiling are established within each category, making it necessary to administer only a portion of the test. The DDST-R can be administered several times over the course of a child's development. One of the problems associated with the DDST-R is its relatively poor standardization and predictive sensitivity, resulting in an unacceptable rate of children at-risk who may be overlooked if caution is not taken in interpreting the results (Meisels 1984).

Intelligence Tests

Wechsler Preschool and Primary Scale of Intelligence (WPPSI). The WPPSI (Wechsler 1967) is designed for children from ages four to six and a half years. The WPPSI consists of eleven subtests, eight of which are downward extensions of the Wechsler Intelligence Scales for Children-Revised (WISC-R) subtests. The subtests are divided into two major groups, representing verbal and nonverbal scales. The verbal subtests include information, vocabulary, arithmetic, similarities, and comprehension, and the performance subtests include animal house, picture completion, mazes, geometric design, and block design. An overall IQ score as well as the verbal and performance IQs are reported.

The WPPSI was developed as a replacement for the WISC, which is believed to be too difficult for testing disadvantaged and mentally retarded children. Yet the WPPSI itself has been criticized as being too difficult for the lower-performing four-year-olds and too long for young children generally (Sattler 1982). Furthermore the WPPSI has been criticized as being unappealing to young children. Nonetheless, the WPPSI is considered to be an instrument that has excellent psychometric properties (Freeman 1985) and is currently being revised and renormed.

McCarthy Scales of Children's Abilities. The McCarthy Scales of Children's Abilities (MSCA) (McCarthy 1972) is a comprehensive battery that evaluates the general intellectual level of children from two-and-a-half to eight-and-a-half years of age. The test is comprised of a General Cognitive Index which includes a verbal scale, perceptual-performance scale, memory scale, and quantitative scale. A separate motor scale exists that is independent of the General Cognitive Index as well.

The tasks in the MSCA are considered to be highly interesting and enjoyable to young children and should therefore hold their attention. Furthermore, the MSCA yields a variety of useful information about a given child. Some (Sattler 1982) have argued that the MSCA has greater potential for providing information about individual children, particularly exceptional children, than the Binet or Wechsler Scales. This claim has yet to be substantiated because exceptional children were not included in the standardization and there is no evidence for the validity of the scale with specific groups (Salvia and Ysseldyke 1985). Overall, the MSCA is considered to be an excellent test with strong psychometric properties.

Group-Administered Intelligence Test

The Otis-Lennon School Ability Test (OLSAT). The purpose of the OLSAT is to "provide an accurate and efficient measure of abilities needed to acquire the desired cognitive outcomes of formal education" (Otis and Lennon 1979). The OLSAT is viewed as a measure of children's ability to learn school-related tasks and is quickly becoming one of the most frequently used group intelligence tests in the United States. The Primary I level is used for children in grade one, but some school districts have administered the OLSAT to kindergarten-age children as well. The test consists of subscales of pictorial and geometric classifications and analogies, quantitative problems and verbal comprehension, and following directions. The Primary I level is verbally administered in two different sessions.

One criticism of the lower level tests is that children's performance is vulnerable to wide variations in the speech tempo and fluency of the examiners who administer the test (Dyer 1978). For purposes of a group-administered aptitude test, the Otis-Lennon is considered to be an adequate measure of school-related abilities (Oakland 1985).

Achievement Tests

Metropolitan Readiness Test (MRT). The MRT (Nurss and McGauvran

1976) is a group-administered, multiple-skill battery designed to assess skills deemed necessary for school success. The MRT consists of two levels. Level I is designed for children in the beginning to the middle of kindergarten, while Level II is designed for children at the end of kindergarten or the beginning of first grade. The Level I test is comprised of six subtests: auditory memory, rhyming, letter recognition, visual matching, school language and listening, and quantitative language. The Level II test is comprised of eight subtests: beginning consonants, sound-letter correspondence, visual matching, finding patterns, school language, listening, quantitative concepts, and quantitative operations.

The test items are presented orally by the teacher and the child is to mark his or her answer directly in the booklet. The test requires approximately eighty to ninety minutes to be completed in several different sessions. In Level I, a total pre-reading score is provided as well as composite scores for visual and language areas. In Level II, composite scores for auditory, visual, and language areas are derived. Once again, the total raw score is considered to be a pre-reading composite score. level II begins to tap into children's quantitative knowledge and provides a composite quantitative score.

The designers of the MRT employed a systematic, curriculum-based analysis to guide their selection of items. One strength of the MRT is that it allows the child to work with typical primary classroom material. The test requires children to sit for extended periods of time, stay on task, and follow directions. There is, therefore, a good match between the required activities of a typical first-grade classroom and the test.

Boehm Test of Basic Concepts (BTBC). The BTBC (Boehm 1971) is a group-administered test that measures abstract concepts commonly found in preschool and primary curricula. There are fifty concepts dealing with fundamental properties and relationships (for example, next to, after, first). The concepts can be categorized into four groups: space, quantity, time, and miscellaneous.

The BTBC is considered to be a general estimate of cognitive development and receptive language abilities. The underlying components tapped by the BTBC appear to be mature conceptual understanding, partial conceptual understanding, lexical knowledge, facility with complex syntactic constructions, auditory receptive and association skills, ability to quantify, compare, and order, and reversible thinking (Smith 1986). A problem with the test may be its underlying assumption that a point of convergence between children's cognitive and linguistic abilities exists and, furthermore, that this test can tap those abilities. Concept attainment is not, in reality, a unitary construct, unrelated to particular domains of knowledge representable by a single score.

Circus. The CIRCUS (1979) is a group-administered achievement test battery designed for four grade levels from preschool through grade three. The test is comprised of three categories: Basic Assessment Measures (listening comprehension, mathematics computation, pre-reading and reading vocabulary), Other Measures (phonics, general knowledge, problem solving, perceptual-motor coordination, visual memory, visual discrimination, letter and numeral recognition, receptive vocabulary, auditory discrimination, functional language, discrimination of real world sounds), and Measures for Special Purposes (cognitive and affective variables). The CIRCUS scores are not combined into a composite score, and therefore any section of the test may be employed for specific needs. Furthermore, the test is both criterion- and norm-referenced. The test is viewed as excessively long and sometimes tedious for young children (Aiken 1985; Ligon 1985). Nonetheless, the CIRCUS is viewed as an important contribution to the field of early childhood education and provides a tool for the assessment of a wide range of skills among preschool and kindergarten children.

Woodcock-Johnson Psycho-Education Battery (W-J). The Woodcock-Johnson is an individually administered measure of cognitive ability, academic achievement, and scholastic interest. The achievement portion of the test is designed to assess reading, mathematics, written language, science, social science, and humanities. The preschool section of the battery consists of six subtests: letter-word identification, applied problems, dictation, science, social studies, and humanities. The kindergarten and early elementary-age section includes reading, mathematics, written language, and knowledge. The W-J is considered to have excellent psychometric qualities, particularly in terms of its reliability and concurrent validity.

A major criticism of the W-J is that the materials are not child-oriented enough for three- to six-year-olds (Kaufman 1985a). The materials are not interesting or attractive and require no manipulation on the part of the child. The reliabilities for the preschool clusters are markedly lower than for primary grades but are respectable "in view of the difficulties usually associated with reliability in a preschool population" (Cummings 1982). Although the W-J appears to be an excellent psychometric instrument for elementary-age children, at this point it appears less desirable for kindergarten and preschool-age children.

References

Abidin, R., W. Golladay and A. Howerton. (1971) Elementary school retention: An unjustifiable discriminatory and noxious educational policy, *Journal of School Psychology*, 9, 410–17.

Aiken, L. R. (1985) Review of the CIRCUS. In *The ninth mental measurements yearbook, volume 1*, ed. J. V. Mitchell, 326–28. Lincoln: The University of Nebraska Press.

Ames, C. and R. Ames. (1984) Goal structures and motivation, *Elementary School Journal*, 85, 40–51.

Ames, C. and R. Ames, (eds.) (1985) *Research on motivation in education. Vol. 2: The classroom milieu*. Orlando: Academic Press.

Ames, L. B. (1980) Retention: A step forward, *Early Years*, 10, 11.

Ames, L. B. and F. L. Ilg. (1964) Gesell behavior tests as predictive of later grade placement. *Perceptual and Motor Skills*, 19, 719–22.

Anastasi, A. (1983) What do intelligence tests measure? In *On educational testing*, ed. S. B. Anderson and J. S. Helmick, 5–28. San Francisco: Jossey-Bass.

Anastasi, A. (1986) Intelligence as a quality of behavior. In *What is intelligence? Contemporary viewpoints on its nature and definitions*, ed. R. J. Sternberg and D. K. Detterman, 19–21. Norwood: Ablex.

Anastasi, A. (1988) *Psychological testing*. New York: Macmillan.

Austin, G., De Vries A., Thirion, A. and K. Stukat. (1975) Early childhood education in three countries, *International Journal of Early Childhood*, 7, 157–65.

Baranova, T. I. and N. S. Rozyeva. (1985) From the history of the experimental teaching of six-year-old children in the USSR, *Soviet Education*, 27 (5), 22–38.

Barnes, K. E. (1982) *Preschool screening: The measurement and prediction of children at-risk*. Springfield: Charles C. Thomas.

Bayley, N. (1949) Consistency and variability in the growth of intelligence from birth to 18 years, *Journal of Genetic Psychology*, 75, 165–96.

Bear, G. G. and P. D. Modlin. (1987) Gesell's developmental testing: What purpose does it serve?, *Psychology in the Schools*, 24, 40–44.

Beattie, C. (1970) Entrance age to kindergarten and first grade: Its effect on cognitive and affective development of students. ERIC/ED 133 050.

Bell, M. (1972) A study of the readiness room in a small school district in suburban Detroit, Michigan. Ph.D. diss., Dept of Psychology, Wayne State University.

Beller, E. K. (1973) Research on organized programs of early education. In *Second handbook of research on teaching*, ed. R. Travers, 530–600. Chicago: Rand McNally.

Bocks, W. M. (1977) Nonpromotion: A year to grow?, *Educational Leadership*, 34 (5), 179–82.

Boehm, D. (1971) *Boehm test of basic concepts*. Cleveland: The Psychological

Corporation.

Bredekamp, S. (1987) *Developmentally appropriate practice in early childhood programs serving children from birth through age 8*. Washington, DC: National Association for the Education of Young Children.

Bronfenbrenner, U. (1974) *Is early intervention effective? A report on longitudinal evaluations of preschool programs*. Washington, DC: Office of Child Development, Department of Health, Education, and Welfare.

Buros, O. K., (ed.) (1978) *The eighth mental measurements yearbook*. Highland Park: Gryphon Press.

California State Department of Education. (1988) *Here they come, ready or not!: Report of the School Readiness Task Force*. Sacramento: California State Department of Education.

Campbell, B. D. (1987) From national debate to national responsibility. In *Early schooling: The national debate*, ed. S. L. Kagan and E. F. Zigler, 65–82. New Haven: Yale University Press.

Carstens, A. (1985) Retention and social promotion for the exceptional child, *School Psychology Review*, 14, 48–63.

Cartwright, G. P. and D. K. McIntosh. (1972) Three approaches to grouping procedures for the education of disadvantaged primary school children, *Journal of Educational Research*, 65, 425–29.

Charlesworth, R. (1985) Readiness: Should we make them ready or let them bloom? *Day Care and Early Education*, 12, 3, 25–27.

CIRCUS. (1979) Monterey: CTB/McGraw-Hill.

Cole, M. and S. Scribner. (1974) *Culture and thought: A psychological introduction*. New York: Wiley.

Consortium for Longitudinal Studies. (1979) *Lasting effects after preschool, summary report*. Washington, DC: U.S. Department of Health and Human Services, Administration for Children, Youth and Families.

Consortium for Longitudinal Studies. (1983) *As the twig is bent... Lasting effects of preschool programs*. Hillsdale: Lawrence Erlbaum Associates.

Cooke, G. and J. Stammer. (1985) Grade retention and social promotion practices, *Childhood Education*, 4, 302–10.

Covington, M. V. (1984) The self-worth theory of achievement: Findings and implications, *Elementary School Journal*, 8, 5–20.

Covington, M. V. and C. Omelich. (1979) Effort: The double-edged sword in school achievement, *Journal of Educational Psychology*, 71, 169–82.

Cronbach, L. (1970) *Essentials of psychological testing*. New York: Harper and Row.

Cummings, J. A. (1982) Interpreting functioning levels: Woodcock-Johnson Psycho-Educational Battery, *Psychological Reports*, 50, 1167–71.

Cunningham, A. E. (1990) Explicit versus implicit instruction in phonemic awareness. *Journal of Experimental Child Psychology*, 50, 429–444.

Dahllof, U. S. (1971) *Ability grouping, content validity, and curriculum process analysis*. New York: Teachers College Press.

Darling-Hammond, L. and A. E. Wise. (1985) Beyond standardization: State standards and school improvement, *The Elementary School Journal*, 85, 315–36.

Davis, B., Trimble, C. and D. Vincent. (1980) Does age of entrance affect school achievement? *The Elementary School Journal*, 3, 133–43.

Deutsch, M. (1985) New vitality in follow-ups of Head Start youngsters, *The Brown University Human Development Newsletter*, 1 (June), 6.

Diamond, G. H. (1983) The birthdate effect—A maturational effect? *Journal of Learning Disabilities*, 16, 161–64.

DiPasquale, G., Moule, A. and R. Flewelling. (1980) The birthdate effect, *Journal of Learning Disabilities*, 13, 4–8.

Donofrio, A. F. (1977) Grade repetition: Therapy of choice, *Journal of Learning Disabilities*, 10, 28–30.

Donofrio, A. F. and M. O'Hare. (1969) Childhood misdiagnosis: The bias for psychogenicity, *Psychology in the Schools*, 6, 369–70.

Dyer, C. O. (1978) Review of the Otis-Lennon. In *The eighth mental measurements yearbook*, 1107–11 (See Buros, 1978.)

Elkind, D. (1981) *The hurried child: Growing up too fast too soon*. Reading: Addison-Wesley.

——. (1987) *Miseducation: Preschoolers at risk*. New York: Alfred A. Knopf.

——. (1988) The "miseducation" of young children, *Education Week*, 7 (19), 24.

Eschel, Y. and A. Klein. (1978) The effects of integration and open education on mathematics achievement in the early grades in Israel, *American Educational Research Journal*, 15, 319–23.

Evans, J. (1982) Curriculum models and early childhood education. In *Handbook of research in early childhood education*, ed. B. Spodek. New York: The Free Press.

Featherman, D. (1980) Schooling and occupational careers: Constancy and change in worldly success. In *Constancy and change in human development*, ed. O. Brim and J. Kagan. Cambridge: Harvard University Press.

Fein, G. and P. Schwartz. (1982) Developmental theories in early education. In *Handbook of research in early childhood education*, ed. B. Spodek. New York: The Free Press.

Frankenburg, W. K. and J. B. Dodds. (1981) Denver Developmental Screening Test-Revised. Denver: LADOCA Publishing Foundation.

Freeman, B. J. (1985) Review of Wechsler Preschool and Primary Scale of Intelligence. In *The ninth mental measurements yearbook, volume 2*, ed. J. V. Mitchell, 1725–26. Lincoln: The University of Nebraska Press.

Gardner, H. (1983) *Frames of mind*. New York: Basic Books.

Gardner, H. (1987) Developing the spectrum of human intelligence, *Harvard Education Review*, 57, 187–93.

Gelman, R. (1969) Conservation acquisition: A problem of learning to attend to relevant attributes, *Journal of Experimental Child Psychology*, 7, 167–87.

Gelman, R. (1978) Cognitive development, *Annual Review of Psychology*, 29, 297–332.

Gelman, R. and C. Gallistel. (1978) *The child's understanding of number*. Cambridge: Harvard University Press.

Genesereth, M. R. (1980) Metaphors and models. In *Proceedings of the 1st National Conference on Artificial Intelligence, Stanford, CA*, 208–11. American Association for Artificial Intelligence.

Georgia Department of Education. (1988) February, *Promotion and Retention*. Atlanta, Georgia.

Georgia Department of Education. (1988) March. Memorandum to system superintendents. Atlanta, Georgia.

Gesell, A. (1954) The ontogenesis of infant behavior. In *Manual of child psychology*, L. Carmichael (ed.), 335–73. New York: Wiley.

Gesell Institute of Human Development. (1978) *Gesell Readiness Screening Test*. Lumberville: Programs for Education.

——. (1979) *Gesell Preschool Test*. Lumberville, PA: Programs for Education.

——. (1980) *A gift of time...A developmental point of view*. New Haven: Gesell Institute of Human Development.

——. (1987) The Gesell Institute responds, *Young Children*, 43 (2), 7–8.

Goodlad, J. I. (1960) Classroom organizations. In *Encyclopedia of educational research* 3d ed., ed. C. Harris, 221–26. New York: Macmillan.

Gray, S. W., Ramsey, B. K. and R. A. Klaus. (1982) *From 3 to 20: The early training project*. Baltimore: University Park Press.

Gredler, G. R. (1975) Readiness for school: A look at some critical issues. In *Reading and related skills*, ed. M. Clark and A. Milne, 37–45. London: Wood Lock Education.

Gredler, G. R. (1978) A look at some important factors in assessing readiness for school, *Journal of Learning Disabilities*, 1, 25–31.

Gredler, G. R. (1980) The birthdate effect: Fact or artifact? *Journal of Learning Disabilities*, 13, 239–42.

Gredler, G. R. (1984) Transition classes: A viable alternative for the at-risk child? *Psychology in the Schools*, 21, 463–76.

Green, D. R. and S. V. Simmons. (1962) Chronological age and school entrance, *Elementary School Journal*, 63, 41–47.

Grubb, W. N. (1987) May. *Young children face the states: Issues and options for early childhood programs*. Washington, DC: Center for Policy Research in Education.

Hadermann, K. F. (1976) Ability grouping—Its effect on learners, *National Association of Secondary School Principals Bulletin*, 60, 85–89.

Haines, J., Ames, L. B. and C. Gillespie. (1980) *The Gesell Preschool Test manual*. Lumberville: Modern Learning Press.

Hall, V. (1963) Does entrance age affect achievement? *The Elementary School Journal*, (April), 391–96.

Hallahan, D. P. and J. Kauffman. (1986) *Exceptional children*. 3d ed. Englewood Cliffs: Prentice Hall.

Hart, R. H. (1967) The effectiveness of an approach to the problem of varying abilities in teaching reading. In *School organization: Theory and practice*, ed.

M. P. Franklin, 443–48. Chicago: Rand McNally.

Henig, R. M. (1988) Should baby read? *New York Times Magazine*, (22 May), 37–38.

Holmes, C. and K. Matthews. (1984) The effects of nonpromotion of elementary and junior high school pupils: A meta-analysis, *Review of Educational Research*, 54, 225–36.

Ilg, F. L. and L. B. Ames. (1965) *School readiness*. New York: Harper and Row.

Ilg, F. L., Ames, L. B., Haines, J. and C. Gillespie. (1978) *School readiness: Behavior tests used at the Gesell Institute*. New York: Harper and Row.

Jackson, G. B. (1975) The research evidence on the effects of grade retention, *Review of Educational Research*, 45, 613–35.

Jensen, A. R. (1981) *Straight talk about mental tests*. New York: The Free Press.

Jinks, P. C. (1964) An investigation into the effect of date of birth on subsequent school performance, *Educational Research*, 6, 220–25.

Kagan, S. L. (1987) Early schooling: On what grounds? In *Early schooling: The national debate*, ed. S. L. Kagan and E. F. Zigler, 129–50. New Haven: Yale University Press.

Kahneman, D., Slovic, P. and A. Tversky. (1982) *Judgement under uncertainty: Heuristics and biases*. Cambridge: Harvard University Press.

Kail, R. and J. W. Pellegrino. (1985) *Human intelligence: Perspectives and prospects*. New York: W. H. Freeman and Company.

Katz, L. G. (1977) Early childhood programs and ideological disputes. In *Talks with teachers*, ed. L. G. Katz. Washington, DC: National Association for the Education of Young Children.

Katz, L. G. (1985) Dispositions in early childhood education, *ERIC/EECE Bulletin*, 18, 2.

Katz, L. G. (1987) Early education: What should young children be doing? In *Early schooling: The national debate*, S. L. Kagan and E. F. Zigler, 151–67. New Haven: Yale University Press.

Kaufman, N. L. (1985a) Review of the McCarthy Screening Test. In *The ninth mental measurements yearbook, volume 1*, ed. J. V. Mitchell, 928–30. Lincoln: The University of Nebraska Press.

Kaufman, N. L. (1985b) Review of Gesell preschool test. In *The ninth mental measurements yearbook, volume 1*, ed. J. V. Mitchell, 607–8. Lincoln: The University of Nebraska Press.

Kirp, D. L. (1974) Student classification, public policy, and the courts, *Harvard Educational Review*, 44, 7–52.

Kohlberg, L. (1968) Early education: A cognitive-developmental view, *Child Development*, 39, 1013–62.

Kohlberg, L. and R. Mayer. (1972) Development as an aim of education, *Harvard Educational Review*, 42, 449–96.

Langer, P., Kalk, J. M. and D. T. Searls. (1984) Age of admission and trends in achievement: A comparison of blacks and caucasians, *American Educational Research Journal*, 21, 61–78.

Laosa, L. M. (1984) Social policies toward children of diverse ethnic, racial, and language groups in the United State. In *Child development research and social policy*, ed. H. W. Stevenson and A. E. Siegel. Chicago: University of Chicago Press.

Lazar, I., Darlington, R. B., Murray, H. W. and A. S. Snipper. (1982) Lasting effects of early education: A report from the Consortium for Longitudinal Studies, *Monograph of Society for Research in Child Development*, 47 (195, Serial No. 2–3)

Lefkowitz, L. J. (1972) Ability grouping: Defacto segregation in the classroom, *Clearing House*, 46, 293–97.

Leinhardt, G. (1980) Transition rooms: Promoting maturation or reducing education? *Journal of Educational Psychology*, 72, 55–61.

Lichtenstein, R. (1980) *The Minneapolis Preschool Screening Inventory*. Minneapolis: Minneapolis Public Schools.

Lichtenstein, R. and H. Ireton. (1984) *Preschool screening: Identifying young children with developmental and educational problems*. Orlando: Grune and Stratton.

Ligon, G. (1985) Review of the CIRCUS. In *The ninth mental measurements yearbook, volume 1*. J. V. Mitchell (ed.) 328–29. Lincoln: The University of Nebraska Press.

McCarthy, D. (1972) *McCarthy Scales of Children's Abilities*. New York: Psychological Corporation.

McCarthy, D. (1978) *McCarthy Screening Test*. New York: Psychological Corporation.

Madden, N. A. and R. E. Slavin. (1983) Mainstreaming students with mild handicaps: Academic and social outcomes, *Review of Educational Research*, 55, 519–59.

Maddux, C. (1980) First-grade entry age in a sample of children labeled learning disabled, *Learning Disability Quarterly*, 3, 79–83.

May, D. (1986) Relationships between the Gesell Readiness Test and standardized achievement and intelligence measures, *Educational and Psychological Measurement*, 46, 1051–59.

May, D. and E. Welch. (1984a) Developmental placement: Does it prevent future learning problems? *Journal of Learning Disabilities*, 17, 338–41.

May, D. and E. Welch. (1984b) The effects of developmental placement and early retention on children's later scores on standardized tests, *Psychology in the Schools*, 21, 381–85.

May, D. & E. Welch. (1985) The effects of developmental placement on young children's cognitive and social-emotional development, *Early Child Development and Care*, 22, 195–209.

May, D. and E. Welch. (1986) Screening for school readiness: The influence of birthdate and sex, *Psychology in the Schools*, 23, 100–105.

Mehrens, W. A. and I. J. Lehmann. (1984) *Measurement and evaluation in education and psychology*. (3rd ed.) New York: Holt, Rinehart and Winston,

Inc.

Meisels, S. (1984) Prediction, prevention, and developmental screening in the EPSDT program. In *Child development research and social policy*, ed. H. W. Stevenson and A. E. Siegel. Chicago: University of Chicago Press.

——. (1985) *Developmental screening in early childhood: A guide*. Washington, DC: NAEYC.

——. (1986) Testing four- and five-year-olds: Response to Salzar and to Shepard and Smith, *Education Leadership*, 44, 90–92.

——. (1987) Uses and abuses of developmental screening and school readiness testing, *Young Children*, 42 (2), 4–6.

——. (1988) Developmental screening in early childhood: The interaction of research and social policy, *Annual Review of Public Health*, 9, 527–50.

——. (1989) Can developmental screening tests identify children who are developmentally at-risk? *Pediatrics*, 83, 4, 578–585.

——. and N. J. Anastasiow. (1982) The risks of prediction: Relationships between etiology, handicapping conditions, and developmental outcomes. Vol. 3 of *The young child: Reviews of research*, ed. S. Moore and C. Cooper. Washington, DC: NAEYC.

Meisels, S. and M. S. Wiske. (1983) *The Early Screening Inventory*. New York: Teachers College Press.

Meisels, S. and L. Margolis. (1988) Is the early and periodic screening, diagnosis, and treatment program effective with developmentally disabled children? *Pediatrics*, 81, 262–71.

Meisels, S., Wiske, M. and T. Tivan. (1984) Predicting school performance with the Early Screening Inventory, *Psychology in the Schools*, 21, 25–33.

Miller, W. and R. Norris. (1967) Entrance age and school success, *Journal of School Psychology*, 6, 47–59.

Milofsky, C. D. (1974) Why special education isn't special, *Harvard Educational Review*, 44, 437–58.

Mitchell, J. V., (ed.) (1985) *The ninth mental measurements yearbook*. Lincoln: The University of Nebraska Press.

Naglieri, J. A. (1985a) Review of the McCarthy Screening Test. In *The ninth mental measurements yearbook, volume 1*, ed. J. V. Mitchell, 930–32. Lincoln: The University of Nebraska Press.

Naglieri, J. A. (1985b) Review of Gesell Preschool Test. In *The ninth mental measurements yearbook, volume 1*, ed. J. V. Mitchell, 608–09. Lincoln: The University of Nebraska Press.

National Assessment of Educational Progress. (1979) *Changes in mathematical achievement, 1973–78*. Denver: NAEP.

National Assessment of Educational Progress. (1981) *Reading, thinking and writing: results from the 1979–80 National Assessment of Reading and Literature*. Denver: NAEP.

National Association for the Education of Young Children. (1986) NAEYC position statement on developmentally appropriate practice in early childhood programs serving children from birth through age 8, *Young Children*, 41 (6), 3–19.

National Association for the Education of Young Children. (1988) NAEYC position statement on developmentally appropriate practice in the primary grades, serving 5- through 8-year-olds, *Young Children*, 43 (2), 64–84.

National Commission on Excellence in Education. (1983) *A nation at risk: The imperative for educational reform*. Washington, DC: U.S. Department of Education.

National Research Council. (1979) *The state of school science*. Washington, DC: Commission on Human Resources.

Niklason, L. B. (1984) Nonpromotion: A pseudoscientific solution, *Psychology in the Schools*, 21, 485–99.

Nurss, J. R. and M. E. McGauvran. (1976) *Metropolitan Readiness Tests*. New York: Harcourt Brace Jovanovich.

Oakes, J. (1981) A question of access: tracking and curriculum differentiation in a national sample of English and mathematics classes. *A study of schooling: Technical report, No. 24*. Los Angeles: University of California.

Oakes, J. (1985) *Keeping track*. New Haven: Yale University Press.

Oakland, T. (1985) Review of the Otis-Lennon. In *The ninth mental measurements yearbook, volume 1*, ed. J. V. Mitchell, 1111–12. Lincoln: The University of Nebraska Press.

Olson, W. C. (1967) Ability grouping: Pros and cons. In *School organization: Theory and practice*, ed. M. P. Franklin, 449–54. Chicago: Rand McNally.

Osborn, K. D. (1975) *Early childhood education in historical perspective*. Athens, GA: Education Associates.

Otis, A. and R. Lennon. (1979) *Otis-Lennon Mental Ability Test*. New York: Harcourt, Brace and World.

Perfetti, C. A. (1985) *Reading Ability*. Boston: Oxford University Press.

Plummer, D. L., Lineberger, M. H. and W. G. Graziano. (1986) The academic and social consequences of grade retention: A convergent analysis. In *Current topics in early childhood education: Volume 6*, L. G. Katz (ed.), 224–52. Norwood: Ablex.

Polya, G. (1957) *How to solve it*. 2d ed. New York: Doubleday.

Putka, G. (1988a) Schools start flunking many more students in drive on mediocrity, *Wall Street Journal*, November 30, 1, 10.

Putka, G. (1988b) Tense tots: Some schools press fast-track children so hard that they become stressed and fearful. *Wall Street Journal*, July 6, 1, 12.

Raygor, B. (1972) *A five year followup study comparing the school achievement and school adjustment of children retained in kindergarten and children placed in a transition class*. Ph.D. diss., Dept of Psychology, University of Minnesota.

Roberts, C. M. (1986) Whatever happened to kindergarten? *Educational Leadership*, 44, 34.

Rogoff, B. (1982) Integrating context and cognitive development. In *Advances in developmental psychology: Vol. 2*, ed. M. E. Lamb and A. L. Brown, 125–70.

Hillsdale: Lawrence Erlbaum Associates.

Rose, J., Medway, F., Cantrell, V. and S. Marcus. (1983) A fresh look at the retention-promotion controversy, *Journal of School Psychology*, 21, 201–11.

Salvia, J. and J. E. Ysseldyke. (1985) *Assessment in special and remedial education.* 3d ed. Boston: Houghton Mifflin.

Sarason, S. B. (1987) Policy, implentation, and the problem of change. In *Early schooling: The national debate*, S. L. Kagan and E. F. Zigler (eds.), 116–28. New Haven: Yale University Press.

Sattler, J. M. (1982) *Assessment of children's intelligence and special abilities.* 2d ed. Boston: Allyn and Bacon.

Schoenfeld, A. H. (1985) Metacognitive and epistemological issues in mathematical understanding. In *Teaching and learning mathematical problem solving: Multiple research perspectives*, E. A. Silver (ed.), 361–79. Hillsdale: Lawrence Erlbaum Associates.

Schweinhart, L. S. and J. Koschel. (1986) *Policy options for preschool programs.* Ypsilanti: High/Scope Early Childhood Policy Papers.

Seligmann, J. and A. Murr. (1988) Making the (first) grade: Georgia puts kinder-garten skills to the test, *Newsweek*, (April 25), 58.

Semmel, M. I., Gottlieb, J. and N. M. Robinson. (1979) Mainstreaming: Per-spective on educating handicapped children in the public school. In *Review of research in education: Vol. 7*, D. C. Berliner (ed.), 223–79. Washington, DC: American Educational Research Association.

Shepard, L. A. and M. L. Smith. (1985) March. *Boulder Valley kindergarten study: Retention practices and retention effects.* Boulder: Boulder Valley Public Schools.

——. (1986) Synthesis of research on school readiness and kindergarten retention, *Educational Leadership*, 44, 78–86.

——. (1988) Escalating academic demand in kindergarten: Counterproductive policies, *Elementary School Journal*, 89, 135–45.

——. (1980) Effects of kindergarten retention at the end of first grade, *Psychology in the School*, 24, 4, 346–357.

Sigel, I. E. (1987) Early childhood education: Developmental enhancement or developmental acceleration? In *Early schooling: The national debate*, ed. S. L. Kagan and E. F. Zigler, 129–50. New Haven: Yale University Press.

Slaughter, D. T. (1983) Early intervention and its effects on maternal and child development, *Monograph of the Society for Research in Child Development*, 48 (4, Serial No. 202)

Sleeman, D. H. and M. J. Smith. (1981) Modeling structural problem solving, *Artificial Intelligence*, 16 (2), 171–87.

Smith, E. F. (1986) The validity of the Boehm Test of Basic Concepts, *British Journal of Educational Psychology*, 56, 332–44.

Smith, M. L. and L. A. Shepard. (1987) What doesn't work: Explaining policies of retention in the early grades, *Phi Delta Kappan*, 69, 129–34.

Spodek, B. (1972) *Teaching in the early years.* Englewood Cliffs: Prentice-Hall,

Inc.

———. (1983) Early childhood education and evaluation: An overview, *Studies in Educational Evaluation*, 8, 203–7.

———. (1986) Development, values and knowledge in the kindergarten curriculum. In *Today's kindergarten: Exploring its knowledge base, extending its curriculum*, ed. B. Spodek, 32–47. New York: Teachers College Press.

———. *(1988) Conceptualizing today's kindergarten curriculum, Elementary School Journal*, 89, 203–11.

Starch, D. and E. C. Elliott. (1912) Reliability of grading high school work in English, School Review, 20, 442–57.

Sternberg, R. (1977) *Intelligence, information processing, and analogical reasoning*. Hillsdale: Lawrence Erlbaum Associates.

Sternberg, R. (1985) *Beyond IQ*. New York: Cambridge University Press.

Sternberg, R. J. and D. K. Detterman. (1986) *What is intelligence? Contemporary viewpoints on its nature and definitions*. Norwood: Ablex.

Talmadge, S. J. (1981) *Descriptive and predictive relationships among family environments, cognitive characteristics, behavioral ratings, transition room placement, and early reading achievement*. Ph.D. diss., University of Oregon.

U.S. Bureau of Labor Statistics. (1986) August. Half of mothers with children under 3 now in labor force. Washington, DC: USDL 86–345.

VanLehn, K. (1983) Human processing skill acquisition: Theory, model, and psychological validation. *Proceedings of the 3rd National Conference on Artificial Intelligence*, 420–23. Washington, DC: American Association for Artificial Intelligence.

Wechsler, D. (1967) *Manual for the Wechsler Preschool and Primary Scale of Intelligence*. New York: The Psychological Corporation.

Weinstein, L. (1968–1969) School entrance age and adjustment, *Journal of School Psychology*, 7, 209–28.

Westinghouse Learning Corporation. (1969) *The impact of Head Start: An evaluation of the effects of Head Start on children's cognitive and affective development: Vols. I-II*. Athens: Ohio University.

Willis, J. (1970) Group versus individual intelligence tests in one sample of emotionally disturbed children. *Psychological Reports*, 27, 819–22.

Winn, M. (1983) *Children without childhood*. New York: Penguin.

Wood, C., Powell, S. and R. C. Knight. (1984) Predicting school readiness: The validity of developmental age, *Journal of Learning Disabilities*, 17, 8–11.

Woodcock, R. and B. Johnson. (1977) *Woodcock-Johnson Psycho-Educational Battery*. Hingham: Teaching Resources Corporation.

Zelizer, V. A. (1985) *Pricing the priceless child: The changing value of the child*. New York: Basic Books, Inc.

Zigler, E. (1970) The environmental mystique: Training the intellect versus development of the child, *Childhood Education*, 46, 402–12.

Zigler, E. (1973a) Project Head Start: Success or failure? *Children Today*, 2, 2–8.

Zigler, E. (1973b) Myths and facts: A guide for policymakers, *Compact*, 7, 18-21.
Zigler, E. (1987) Formal Schooling for Four-Year-Olds? No, *American Psychologist*, 42, 254-60.
Zigler, E. and P. Trickett. (1978) IQ, social competence, and evaluation of early childhood intervention programs, *American Psychologist*, 33, 789-98.
Zigler, E. and J. Valentine. (1979) *Project Head Start: A legacy of the war on poverty*. New York: Free Press.

6 CHANGING STATEWIDE READING ASSESSMENT: A CASE STUDY OF MICHIGAN AND ILLINOIS

Charles W. Peters, Karen K. Wixson, Sheila W. Valencia and P. David Pearson

Introduction

The importance of large-scale testing has increased steadily in American schools during the past fifteen years. Testing influences policies affecting individuals, teachers, schools, districts, states, and our nation as a whole. The proliferation of testing at the state and national levels prompted Gregory R. Anrig, president of the Educational Testing Service, to remark, "There is an old army saying, 'If it moves, salute it.' Today some educational reformers believe, 'If it moves, test it.'" (Fiske, 1988, 16).

Anrig is not the only prominent testing expert to make this observation. Archie Lapointe, Executive Director of the National Assessment of Educational Progress, believes that there is more testing going on now than at any other time in our history (Lapointe, 1988). In fact, the National Center for Fair Testing estimates that primary and high school students as a group take more than one hundred million standardized tests a year. Approximately fifty-six million are locally mandated standardized achievement, minimum competency, and basic skills tests (Fiske, 1988). At least thirty-nine states have some form of statewide testing (Berk, 1986).

Discontent with the American educational system has contributed to

---

* This paper was prepared for the National Commission on Testing and Public Policy. However, the views expressed are those of the authors alone.

the increased use of tests. As legislators and policymakers at the state and national level have become increasingly frustrated by what they perceive as intransigence on the part of local districts to change, they have looked to testing as a means of controlling and improving education. Tests are being used both to identify and to solve today's educational problems (Madaus, 1985).

As test scores have become the index of a quality education, local districts have felt more and more pressure to align their curriculum with the content of tests. The irony of this situation is that what is on the test becomes more important than what is learned in the classroom, thus making tests the hidden curriculum (Darling-Hammond and Wise, 1983). Because people teach to tests, tests must shoulder some new responsibilities. In particular, it is essential that the content of tests reflects current knowledge about theory and practice. A mismatch between current knowledge and test content often leads to unproductive curricula and instruction. People strive for higher test scores rather than increased learning (Haney, 1984).

Reading is one curricular area in which there is a serious mismatch between current theory and research and the content of most existing tests. The lesson of the last fifteen years of research is that reading is a holistic, interactive process. It is not, as once thought, an aggregation of isolated subskills. Tests that rely on a set of subtests that, added together, yield a "reading" score fail to reflect this holistic perspective, nor can the essence of reading be captured, as most standardized tests try to do, by offering a few clever items posed after students have read each of several short, unrelated snippets of text.

Although reading theory has changed dramatically, reading tests have remained virtually unchanged since the 1920s (Farr and Carey, 1986). The result is that reading tests suffer from a number of weaknesses that are linked directly to differences between current interactive views of reading and reading instruction and the subskills approach that has dominated assessment and instruction for decades (Valencia and Pearson, 1987).

The discrepancy between current knowledge about reading and most existing reading tests creates an ironic situation for policymakers who hope to use tests as a lever to improve education. They want high quality education, but when they use outmoded reading tests to make important instructional, curricular, and policy decisions, the instructional validity of the information that is derived from the tests is questionable. It is unlikely that such efforts will improve the quality of educational practice because tests will drive the curriculum in an inappropriate direction.

The purpose of this chapter is to take an indepth look at how two states, Michigan and Illinois, used current theory and research to develop new statewide assessments of reading comprehension. The magnitude of the changes that have occurred in the Michigan and Illinois tests could not have taken place without the confluence of political, social, economic, and educational forces. It is important to understand the historical context at both the national and state level—the conditions that made these projects possible at this point in time.

In the first section of this chapter we present a brief historical review of testing in general and reading tests in particular. The emphasis is on the national political, social, economic, and educational events that set the stage for what took place in Michigan and Illinois. In the second part, a similar story is told for each state—what were the particular political, social, economic, and educational factors that shaped events in each state. In the third part we discuss the theoretical rationale for the new reading tests and describe the new tests in some detail. In the closing section, we discuss the lessons we have learned from these projects.

The National Context

Changes in the Nature and Uses of Tests

From the early 1900s to the late 1950s, testing in American education was predominantly a local phenomenon. While some testing was conducted at the state level for teacher and student certification, the emphasis at this time was not on the evaluation of school districts. Evaluation of individual students was still the responsibility of local districts (see Tyler, 1970). However, beginning in the early 1960s, local testing was augmented by externally mandated state and national tests that would play a central role in establishing and implementing educational policy (Madaus, 1985). Furthermore, as testing began to play a more prominent role in state and national policy, there was increasing concern about the nature and content of tests. This concern, combined with advances in thinking about learning and testing, resulted in changes in the types of tests used at the state and national levels.

The 1960s and 1970s

Various political, social, economic, and educational factors played a critical role in the emergence of the national and statewide testing phenomenon.

Among these were the Soviet Union's launching of Sputnik in 1957, the passage of the Elementary and Secondary Education Act of 1965 (ESEA), the publication of the first Coleman report (Coleman, et al., 1966), and the creation of the National Assessment of Educational Progress (NAEP) in 1963. The collective impact of these events was to move testing from backstage to centerstage in the political and educational decision-making arena.

Excellence and Equity.   One factor that played an influential role in the emergence of national and statewide testing was the push for excellence that began with the launching of Sputnik I in 1957. The perceived inability of the United States to compete internationally with the Soviet Union was attributed, in part, to the failure of the high school curriculum. This led the federal government to spend more than $100 million to fund curriculum development in science and mathematics under the auspices of the National Defense Educational Act. To evaluate whether their expenditures had paid off, federal policymakers relied on results from controlled studies to determine whether these new curricula were superior to conventional curricula; standardized tests were universally used as outcome measures in these studies (Madaus, 1985).

Concerns for equity in education also contributed to the shift from local testing to externally mandated state and national tests. The political desire for equality of educational opportunity across the social spectrum led to concern for equality in resources and access. This led to a preoccupation with equality in educational outcomes and a reliance on test scores as measures of educational and political success or failure (Salganik, 1985).

Equity issues led to two events that played a prominent role in the emergence of national and statewide testing. First, the Elementary and Secondary Education Act (ESEA) was passed in 1965 to create equal educational opportunity for all segments of society. To remedy problems of racial and economic inequality, the ESEA authorized nearly $1 billion for allocation to schools with a high concentration of children from low income homes. In return for assistance, the ESEA required each local district receiving funds to evaluate the effectiveness of its educational efforts using objective measures; additionally, the law permitted states to collect needs assessment data at the state level (Public Law 89–10, 1965), thus creating another opportunity for tests to be used.

The second event related to issues of equity was the Coleman report to the President and Congress on Equality of Educational Opportunity (Coleman et al., 1966). The purpose of the report was to examine the relations between school resources and student achievement. The primary effect of the Coleman report was, of course, to suggest that home factors played a more significant role than school factors in explaining achievement. But a secondary, more lasting, and perhaps unintended effect, was to establish a precedent for relying on test results to help settle the growing national debate about school effectiveness (Madaus, 1985). With this report, tests had secured a foothold in educational policy matters.

The increased use of test results for political purposes led to growing concern about the nature of the tests being used. For example, critics charged that there was a lack of congruence between the broad range of intended school outcomes and the narrow range of outcomes measured by the tests used for the Coleman report and other large-scale evaluations of compensatory education programs (Airasian and Madaus, 1983). The curricular reform generated by the reaction to Sputnik also focused attention on the need for tests that were more sensitive to particular instructional programs, as noted by Tyler (1969) in the National Society for the Study of Education's Sixty-eight Yearbook.

Since Sputnik, massive financial support has been given to projects concerned with the development of new courses in science and mathematics. Those supporting the construction of the new courses and teachers and administrators who are considering the use of them in their schools are asking for an evaluation of the effectiveness of the courses in comparison with other courses in the same fields. Most tests on the market were not constructed to furnish relative appraisals of different courses, and they have been found inadequate for the task. This need for evaluation of courses and curriculums is stimulating the development of new procedures, instruments, and theories that are designed to meet the need. (1−2)

An important event in changing the nature of national and state tests was the development of the National Assessment of Educational Progress (NAEP). In 1963, the U.S. Commissioner of Education, Francis Keppel, assembled a group of educators and laymen to discuss the need for dependable information about the educational attainment of our students. From this, NAEP was founded so that "necessary information might be periodically collected to furnish a basis for public discussion and broader understanding of educational progress and problems" (Tyler, 1970, 474). Although the initiative for NAEP came from the federal government, the initial project and first tests were funded by the Carnegie Corporation. In 1969, the funding of NAEP was returned to the federal government and NAEP was transferred to the Education Commission of the States (ECS), an agency chartered by Congress and funded by the individual states.

The NAEP project established several important precedents for national and statewide testing. First, the NAEP tests were objectives-referenced.

Prior to NAEP, there had been no attempt at matching tests and curriculum at a specific level (Haertel, 1988). Related to this was the development of NAEP objectives and tests through a broad-based consensus approach; the developers at ECS went to great lengths to gain input from all segments of the educational community. Second, NAEP was established with a recognition of the need for adequate time to develop, implement, and evaluate a national testing program.

Finally, the NAEP caretakers gave careful consideration to the likely impact of national test results on state boards of education and local school districts. Although many educators supported the idea of national testing, some were skeptical about how the results would be used and interpreted. The planning committee was concerned that if these issues were not addressed, national test results would become a political lever; and if this were to occur, the primary reason for collecting national data would dramatically shift information to control. By not releasing data in a manner that permitted comparison by schools, districts, or states, local anonymity was preserved.

Advances in Learning and Testing. During the same period of time that national and statewide testing was increasing, important advances in psychology and testing provided a new theoretical, procedural, and technological basis for test development. One of these advances was an influential instructional theory known as *mastery learning*. Mastery learning is based upon the premise that all, or at least most, students can learn most subjects provided that schools are willing to accommodate learners' needs (Bloom, 1968; Carroll, 1963). Students fail to learn not because of native limitations, but because schools fail to find appropriate instructional strategies.

Mastery learning appealed to reform-minded policymakers, educators, and test developers interested in promoting instructional equity. Traditionally, instruction had been defined in terms of group goals, so instruction was held constant and achievement was allowed to vary among individuals. Mastery learning holds that all individuals can achieve at a high level of proficiency if educators will accommodate them by varying instructional method, time on task, teacher feedback, and the like. In other words, achievement is held constant, and instruction is allowed to vary.

Mastery learning instruction is applied to specific subskill objectives rather than to global outcomes. Students are given some type of pretest to determine which skills they have or have not mastered, then instruction is provided for individual students on precisely those skills they need to learn; mastery is determined by some a priori criterion (usually 80 percent correct) for each of the objectives, and additional instruction is provided for those who have failed to master the objective or skill.

An advance in testing consistent with mastery learning that also took place during this same period was the development of criterion-referenced tests (CRTs). Instead of referencing individuals performance against the mean of a distribution, as is done for norm-referenced tests, CRTs establish an absolute standard (the criterion) for passing and failing any given test or subtest; it is this criterion to which individual scores are compared (the reference).

CRTs are based on the premise that test items should reflect actual behavior for the phenomenon being assessed, but they are neutral with respect to the issue of how the phenomenon is decomposed for testing. Since most school curricula break larger processes and bodies of content into subskills or subcomponents, the CRTs that were developed for school curricula tended to test curricula, skill by skill or component by component.

CRTs have had a significant impact on educational practice (Popham, 1981). First, because CRTs employed absolute standards, educational institutions and agencies had a simple index for determining success and failure for individuals, schools, states, or even curricula. Second, because CRTs were so often used in association with behavioral objectives, those objectives were used as a blueprint to specify both desired educational outcomes and test content. Third, once the basic objectives had been identified, their mastery could become the goal of instruction. Fourth, test results could be used to identify those with the greatest educational needs. Fifth, schools and teachers could be held accountable for educational progress within a very clear and allegedly rational system.

Criterion-referenced tests proliferated in the 1970s. In fact, Traub and Rowley (1980) described the 1970s as a decade "when the notion of criterion-referenced measurement captured and held the attention of the measurement profession unlike any other idea" (517). Criterion-referenced tests appeared in classrooms throughout the United States; even professional teacher organizations expressed support. In response to a survey conducted by Womer (1981), representatives of the National Education Association clearly stated their preference for criterion-referenced tests. Major test publishers also recognized the economic necessity of developing and marketing criterion-referenced tests.

Most importantly, perhaps, many legislators and state departments of education supported the development of statewide criterion-referenced tests (see Tyler and Wolf, 1974). The most notable example of this was the movement toward statewide minimum competency testing that flourished in the 1970s.

Minimum Competency Testing. By 1970 tests were starting to be used as political tools, but policymakers had not yet mandated test scores as the basis for direct sanctions against or rewards for individuals, schools, or districts (Lerner, 1981). The shift to these more direct political uses started in the late 1960s and prospered in the 1970s when compensatory funding for districts was linked to test scores, and as minimum competency testing gained a strong political foothold.

Minimum competency testing refers to a variety of educational programs and practices, most notably, the controversial use of test scores to determine grade-to-grade promotion or high school graduation. Airasian and Madaus (1983) conclude that minimum competency testing was born of a group of related concerns:

1. students' basic skills had seriously deteriorated;
2. students were being promoted from grade to grade without consideration for achievement;
3. students did not have the necessary skills to survive in society; and
4. the high school diploma had become devalued and was meaningless as a credential.

These perceptions grew out of reports of declining test scores and complaints from businesses, colleges, and the military that an alarming number of high school graduates lacked basic skills. As Pipho (1978) observed, minimum competency testing was a genuine grass roots movements that was clearly led, or pushed, by noneducators. Several Gallup polls on public attitudes towards education over more than a decade furnish ample evidence of the massive public support for the movement (Berk, 1986).

Underlying the perception that students were failing to acquire basic skills was the assumption that most students could and should master these skills and that they were being ill-served by the instructional system. Because policymakers could do little to reform instruction directly, they used minimum competency testing and associated sanctions as a means of improving instruction and achievement in the basic skills. From 1976 to 1980, the number of states requiring some form of minimum competency testing increased from eight to thirty-eight (Lerner, 1981).

The use of tests as enforcement mechanisms might not have been viewed as such as negative force by educators if the tests had been developed on the basis of a sound educational curriculum. However, statewide competency tests were often mandated in the absence of well-defined curricular goals (Airasian and Madaus, 1983; Calfee, 1983; Messick, 1980). In addition, the focus on minimum skills often narrowed the curriculum to a point at which the minimums became the maximums. For good or ill, by 1975 tests had become the vehicle for educational reform and would remain so on into the 1980s.

The Reform Movement of the 1980s

The early 1980s saw a flurry of influential reports decrying the impoverished state of American education. Student test scores had declined for nearly two decades, Americans trailed the rest of the world democracies in mathematics and science achievement, and young people were dropping out of high school at rates that had not improved since the mid-1960s (Wolf, 1988). Enduring the worst economic recession since the 1930s, the public worried about whether the nation possessed the intellectual talent to revitalize its industries and compete with the technological sophistication of the Far East (Kearns, 1988). The focus of reform shifted from the need to meet minimum standards to the need to improve higher-order skills and achievement in the sciences and mathematics (Linn, 1986).

The reports of the early 1980s set in motion a series of events that have caused this period to be called the decade of educational reform. Testing has played a prominent role in this reform movement. It has become both the means of identifying and solving educational problems. For example, in one of the best-known reports, *A Nation at Risk* (1983), the report of the National Commission on Excellence in Education, test results were used as indicators of the seriousness of problems in education. The report also pointed to tests as important instruments of change; tests should be used to certify student's credentials and to identify students who either need remedial intervention or deserve opportunities for advanced or accelerated work.

These concerns about the quality of education led to action at all levels of government and education (Chubb, 1988; Timar and Kirp, 1987; Tyler, 1987). States tried to gain greater control over local school districts. State governments cracked down on student underachievement by increasing graduation requirements, requiring regular testing, imposing sanctions for poor performance, and raising standards for teacher certification programs.

One of the major legislative attempts to increase government control over education was the national governors' report. In *Time for Results* (1986), the report of the National Governors' Association, the nation's governors announced a new educational reform agenda that extended states' efforts of the preceding years. This report, in conjunction with Secretary of Education Clarence Bell's use of ACT/SAT scores to compare states, led to increased demands by policymakers for relevant data that could be used to guide educational reform (Elliott and Hall, 1985). With this mandate the Chief State School Officers investigated the possibility of making state-by-state comparisons with national assessment data. In response to this initiative, Secretary of Education William Bennett appointed a national commission to explore this possibility. In March 1987, the commission recommended that NAEP be expanded to permit state-by-state comparisons (Selden, 1988).

One of the factors underlying the move toward state-by-state comparisons is the belief that a state's educational system must be ranked highly if it is to attract new business. States as varied as Arkansas, Mississippi, Massachusetts, and Texas see high-quality education as a key to economic success (Cohen, 1988). Thus, educational testing has become a high-stakes activity (Doyle and Haertel, 1985). This is nowhere more aptly demonstrated than in a recent New Jersey case where test scores were among the criteria used by the state board of education to declare a local district financially and educationally "bankrupt"and to begin proceedings for assuming control of the district (*New York Times*, May 1988). This high stakes pressure also operates at the local level where, for example, real estate agents use school and district test scores to attract buyers to particular neighborhoods or municipalities.

The political, social, and economic stakes in educational testing have become so high that local districts have been forced to teach to the test. Externally mandated testing programs have become the hidden curriculum (Darling, Hammond, and Wise, 1983; Porter, 1985). The recognition that tests have become the hidden curriculum in our schools has caused increasing concern about the nature and content of the tests themselves.

Recently, there has been a backlash to all this preoccupation with testing. Some groups have argued that tests should be outlawed altogether. Others have argued that since they have so much influence, they had better reflect what we really care about in education. Many of these concerns about the tests that are being used to influence curricula around the country arise from advances in thinking about learning and instruction that have occurred since the mid-1970s. Most large-scale tests are modeled after either the norm-referenced tests developed in the 1920s or the objective-referenced tests of the early and mid-1970s. However, current theory and research indicates that tests need to move beyond the product-oriented measures generated from principles of mastery learning to more process-oriented assessments derived from cognitive-based views of learning and instruction (Glaser, 1981; Linn, 1986). Therefore, concern about the directions in which tests are driving curriculum and instruction has combined with advances in knowledge about learning and instruction to create the conditions that are making changes in testing practices possible in the 1980s.

Reading Tests in the 1960s, 1970s, and 1980s

Reading tests provide a specific case in point of the changes observed in large-scale assessment practices between the 1960s and 1980s. The nature and use of large-scale reading tests in the 1960s was virtually the same as it was when these types of tests first appeared in the decade of 1910 and 1920 (Farr and Carey, 1986). These tests have been characterized by Pearson and Dunning (1985) as objective, machine-scorable, multiple-choice tests that exhibited high reliability. The issue of validity was considered, but usually through face validity (that is, the extent to which the test looks like what we define reading to be) or by establishing concurrent validity (the extent to which the test correlates with well-established, and usually highly regarded, tests of reading).

Although there were various theoretical views of the reading process during this period, both assessment and instruction were then and have continued to be dominated by a skills-based view of reading. This view was first articulated clearly in the National Society for the Study of Education's *Twenty-fourth Yearbook* (Whipple, 1925), which was devoted entirely to the subject of reading. The Yearbook Committee, chaired by William S. Gray, noted that a complete classification of attitudes, habits, and skills had never been made, but that a sufficient number could be distinguished to serve as a guide for teachers. Among the "habits of intelligent interpretation" listed in the 1925 *Yearbook* were: concentrating attention on the content, associating meanings with symbols, anticipating the sequence of ideas, associating ideas together accurately, recalling related experiences, recognizing the important elements of meaning, and deriving meanings from context and from pictures.

One need only examine the lists of skills in contemporary tests and instructional materials to understand the impact of the "habits" presented in the 1925 *Yearbook*. In her definitive review of American reading instruction, Smith (1925) indicated that "nearly every course of study and basal textbook in reading published after the *Twenty-fourth Yearbook* was issued, set up these same objectives as the ones which its method and materials were designed to achieve" (203). The impact was not limited to instruction, however, as the early test developers also assumed that there were separate skills that were worth measuring. For example, Gates's (1926) measure of comprehension included skills such as reading to appreciate general significance, to understand precise directions, to note details, and to predict outcomes of given events.

Although empirical evidence to refute the skills-based view of reading comprehension was available as early as 1944 (see, Davis, 1944; Thurstone, 1946), this research had little impact on either reading assessment or instruction. This is evident in Lohnes's review of the Sequential Tests of Educational Progress: Reading in the Buros's *Sixth Mental Measurements Yearbook* (1965) in which he remarked:

> It is admitted that tests measure a complex set of reading skills, but no evidence is forthcoming to support the contention that the chosen 'five major reading-for-comprehension skills' are major components of reading ability, or that the STEP reading tests do actually 'weight these five kinds of skills approximately equally.' All we know is that a committee of authorities agreed on this breakdown of reading into component skills. With due respect for the committee, it would be highly desirable to have their judgments tested and supported by empirical evidence. (327)

The changes described previously in the nature and uses of tests in the late 1960s and early 1970s were particularly evident in reading tests. Farr and Carey (1986) note that reading assessment was the subject of significant changes during this period as a result of major initiatives such as the National Right to Read Effort, Reading is Fundamental (RIF), the U.S. Office of Education's Basic Skills Program, "Sesame Street" and "The Electric Company", Head Start, Follow Through, the Elementary and Secondary Education Act (including Chapters I and III), and a host of other programs designed to eliminate illiteracy. With all of these programs came the mandate to evaluate their effectiveness and impact, often through the increased use of reading tests.

Changes in the uses of reading tests were accompanied by changes in the nature of reading tests fostered by the mastery learning and the criterion-referenced testing movements. These movements took the skills-based view of reading to an extreme, which resulted in tests that dissected reading into its most atomistic elements and provided an index of performance on each element (Pearson and Dunning, 1985). The dual appeal of skills or objectives-based tests as a means of promoting equity and accountability resulted in the use of criterion-referenced reading tests in externally mandated programs such as statewide competency testing.

Objectives-based, criterion-referenced reading tests were also used by individual cities and districts to create their own 'diagnostic-prescriptive' systems of instructional accountability (for example, Detroit Objective Referenced Tests; Chicago Mastery Learning). In addition, the publishers of basal reading programs began including criterion-referenced, skills management systems as part of their instructional materials. These systems were and still are used by many districts to determine promotion from one reading level to the next within the reading series used for instruction.

The result of all this is a circular process that has been relatively impervious to change and continues to have a major impact on the assessment and instruction of reading in today's schools. Specifically, textbook publishers look to statewide objectives and tests to guide them in selecting the skills for instruction. The developers of statewide tests often base their skills selection on the prevailing wisdom reflected by current instructional materials, and school districts seek those published instructional materials that reflect the skills evaluated on statewide tests. Thus, the goal of instruction has become mastery of the enabling skills evaluated on externally mandated tests. Unfortunately, the evidence suggests that skill mastery does not add up to reading ability (Anderson et al., 1985).

The 1980s brought great concern for the prevailing methods of assessment and instruction of reading. The failure, as evidenced by declining verbal SAT scores and results of NAEP of schools to provide the nation with a more literate populace, was a major focus of many of the previously mentioned national reports. At the same time, the research community expressed concern about the conceptualization of reading that was guiding current assessment and instruction in this area (see Curtis and Glaser, 1983; Guthrie and Kirsch, 1984; Linn, 1986). This concern led the National Academy of Education's Commission on Education and Public Policy to establish a Commission on Reading for the purpose of providing a synthesis of research findings "that can secure greater reliability in instruction and render educational outcomes more predictably beneficial" (Glaser, in Anderson et al., 1985, viii).

The report of the Commission on Reading was published in 1985 under the title *Becoming a Nation of Readers* (Anderson et al., 1985). The essence of this report was that reading is a holistic, constructive process rather than the aggregate of a series of isolated subskills. The report also indicated that "holding a reading teacher accountable for scores on a test of say dividing words into syllables is like holding a basketball coach accountable for the percentage of shots players make during the pre-game warm up" (Anderson et al., 1985, 100). One of the conclusions reached by the Commission was that "tests need to reflect the ultimate goals of reading instruction. If schools are to be held accountable for test scores, the test scores must be broad-gauged measures which reflect the goals of reading instruction as closely as possible" (101).

The combination of increased concern about the nature of reading tests being used for political purposes and advances in knowledge about reading and reading instruction has created the opportunity for change in reading assessment. One of the first large-scale tests constructed to be consistent with current theory and research was NAEP's literacy assessment of young adults in the United States. This assessment was basd on the recognition that "the complexity and diversity of literacy tasks in our society demand rejection of a simplistic single standard for literacy" and that a single measure or specific point on a scale can be used to separate the "literate" from the "illiterate" (Kirsch and Jungeblut, 1986, 1). The new statewide reading tests developed in Michigan and Illinois, which are the subject of this chapter, provide other examples of reconceptualized reading assessments.

Changing Reading Assessment in Michigan and Illinois

As described in the first section of this chapter, a series of national events ranging from the emphasis on scientific excellence in the late 1950s to the reform movement of the 1980s had a significant impact on state and national assessment. It was not simply the events themselves that shaped assessment, but the political, social, and economic forces of the times. These factors converged to provide the context for change at the national level, and they also provided the impetus for change in statewide assessment in Michigan and Illinois.

The Michigan Project

The national reform movement that led to the passage of the Elementary and Secondary Education Act (1965) and the issuance of the Coleman report (1966) heightened Michigan's awareness of the need for equality of educational opportunity across the social spectrum. The 1968–1969 session of the Michigan legislature followed the example set by the federal government and increased educational funding for local districts in need of supplemental funds. The two primary criteria for program effectiveness were how efficiently the schools were educating all of Michigan's children and how equitable the programs were for all students. However, state officials quickly discovered that it was impossible to evaluate these criteria with the available data.

Although performance data were available for local districts, these data could not be aggregated because testing programs were not uniform and the types of tests administered varied greatly from district to district. The policymakers' need for different data prompted the Michigan State Board of Education (MSBE) to begin searching for a solution. The Bureau of Research at Michigan Department of Education (MDE) developed a position paper that outlined the problems they had encountered in attempting to monitor the criteria set forth in the legislation and proposed some tentative solutions. These recommendations ultimately led to statewide assessment in the basic skill areas of reading and math (Kearney, Crowson, and Wilbur, 1970).

The formal MSBE recommendation for the collection of statewide assessment data came in January 1969. This recommendation was met with favorable approval by both the governor, who incorporated it into his educational reform package, and the legislature, which enacted the legislation (Public Act 307) (Kearney, 1970). The legislation directed MDE to begin planning and developing a comprehensive and periodic assessment of educational progress to be known as the Michigan Educational Assessment Program (MEAP). The second part of the legislation directed MDE to immediately undertake an annual assessment of basic skills at the fourth- and seventh-grade levels. This legislation mandated a shift in the state government's role in assessment: Michigan had gone from a voluntary to a mandatory statewide testing program.

The first statewide assessments in Michigan were norm-referenced tests designed to assess the basic skill areas of math and reading. In reading, the subtests consisted of vocabulary, language usage, and reading comprehension. Initially, the scores derived from these subtests were reported only by region. District scores were not made public because MDE believed that they would be used to make unwarranted comparisons among local school districts. However, the governor and legislature believed that district scores were essential for making informed decisions and asked the Attorney General to order MDE to release the scores. As a result, new legislation was adopted that required public disclosure of test scores as well as other related information.

Changes in the uses of statewide tests in Michigan also contributed to changes in the nature of the tests used for the MEAP. As test scores became more prominent and more closely aligned with policy decisions, educators throughout the state became increasingly concerned about perceived inconsistencies between the content of the tests and the curricula and instructional practices within schools. This resulted in pressure to develop assessments that were more curriculum-based. To assist with this, teachers and curriculum specialists were invited to review the tests and write better test items (Kearney, Crowson, and Wilbur, 1970).

A second factor contributing to changes in the nature of the statewide tests was Michigan's movement in 1971–1972 toward an accountability approach to education. John Porter (1976), the State Superintendent for Instruction during this period and an ardent advocate of accountability, indicated that the primary purpose of the state assessment program was to identify specific educational attainments and deficiencies in order to build upon the attainment and to reduce individual deficiencies. Porter also maintained that an accountability approach would help educators clarify their instructional intentions, thus making it possible for them to better respond to individual student needs.

Porter's concerns resulted in the Six-Step Michigan Accountability Process, which served as a partial framework for the development of new MEAP tests (Kearney, Donovan, and Fisher 1974). The six steps were:

1. to identify statewide goals for educational accountability
2. to translate the goals into objectives
3. to assess the needs in relation to the objectives
4. to test alternative delivery systems for the identification of innovative strategies for high-needs students
5. to foster the development of locally developed tests
6. to use the feedback from the accountability system to guide state and local educational policy.

The concerns of local educators regarding the nature of the MEAP tests in combination with other factors, such as the movement toward accountability, resulted in a change from norm-referenced tests to criterion-referenced tests based on a set of statewide goals and objectives. In fact, Michigan was the first state to use criterion-referenced tests in their statewide assessment program and implemented such tests in 1973 (Roeber, 1988, pers. com.). This change resulted in several practices that have become hallmarks of MDE's approach to the development, implementation, and revision of statewide tests.

First, the move to objective-based tests established the role of policy-makers and MDE in directing education that has become one of the cornerstones of test development in Michigan. Second, MDE established its commitment to using a consensus approach for the development of objectives and tests that relied on broad-based involvement of important educational groups within the state. For example, throughout the development and implementation of the first objective-referenced tests, there were provisions for the involvement of teachers, curriculum specialists, and administrators. MDE had modified NAEP's consensus approach by making it more heavily dependent on classroom teachers and curriculum specialists. Third, MDE contracted with professional organizations, such as the Michigan Reading Association (MRA), to review the objectives. By asking professional organizations such as MRA to become a formal part of the process, MDE hoped to foster a close working relationship, one that would be reciprocal in nature rather than antagonistic.

A fourth important hallmark of MDE's approach to test development was its use of external agencies for expertise in the development, administration, and analysis of the data. The California Test Bureau/McGraw Hill was granted the initial contract for development of the 1973 test instruments and data analyses of the project. During the revision begun in the mid-1970s the American Institute for Research did the technical editing and data analysis. What is important to recognize about these contracts is that while MDE used a variety of groups to help develop and implement the tests, they maintained full control over the entire process. These groups could recommend, but MDE had the responsibility for all the decisions.

The initial development of objectives and criterion-referenced tests in the early and mid-1970s was marked by four important factors that carried over into the 1980s: (1) MDE's willingness to change when there is a need; (2) MDE's willingness to involve the state reading organization (MRA) in all phases of test development; (3) MDE's willingness to use outside experts to inform the test development process; and (4) MDE's willingness to commit time and resources to the development, analysis, and implementation of the test.

The reform movement of the 1980s signalled a shift from an emphasis on minimum competency to a focus on excellence in education. Michigan's response to issues raised by national reports such as *A Nation at Risk* came in January 1984 when the State Board release a document entitled *Better Education for Michigan Citizens: A Blueprint for Action*. This document became the framework for educational reform in the state. It was followed in December by a report from the Governor's Educational Summit Task Force that outlined educational goals for Michigan. The governor's introduction to this document reinforced the educational emphasis within the state, stating that "education in Michigan is finally back where it belongs: at the top of our list of state priorities."

Reconceptualizing Reading. When the first performance objectives and objective-referenced tests were developed in the early 1970s, it was decided that periodic review and revision would be necessary. The most recent review of the reading objectives was initiated in 1982–1983 by the MDE Instructional Specialist in Reading. Even before the state's call for excellence, she and other leading reading educators in the state recognized the inconsistency that existed among the MDE objectives, the MEAP tests, and current knowledge about reading. Therefore, she initiated the review not with the objectives, but rather with an evaluation of the definition of reading implied by the objectives. With this as a point of departure, it was clear that research and theory would assume a more influential role in determining the nature of MDE reading objectives and MEAP tests than it had in the past.

In January 1983, the MDE Instructional Specialist in Reading convened a joint MDE/MRA committee whose charge was to revise the existing definition of reading. This revised definition would serve as the basis for new statewide reading objectives and new MEAP reading tests. During this review process, the committee developed a definition based on an interactive view of reading. Because the revised definition was a dramatic departure from the one implied by the existing objectives, it had major curricular and political implications that necessitated taking certain steps to insure its acceptance. A major revision in the conceptualization of reading could not be undertaken without the support of MRA, the most politically influential reading organization in the state. Therefore, the committee decided to submit the revised definition to the MRA Board of Directors first for its approval. With the MRA Board approval, the revised definition of reading would then be presented to the Michigan Board of Education.

Gaining approval from both MRA and the Michigan State Board of Education was not an easy task. Although theoretical and instructional knowledge had advanced, only a relatively small group of individuals within the state were familiar enough with these advances to understand their implications for assessment and instruction. This realization led to a series of presentations that were designed to familiarize the MRA Board and others with current knowledge about reading reflected in the proposed new definition.

The new definition of reading was approved by the MRA Board in 1984 and published as a position paper in the *Michigan Reading Journal* (Wixson and Peters, 1984). With MRA's support, the definition was presented to the Michigan State Board of Education to inform the members of the changes that were taking place in reading theory and instruction and the implications they would have for the state's reading objectives and tests. The State Board strongly suggested that before any approval of new objectives would be considered, it needed evidence that educators in the state supported the new definition and understood the implications it had for instruction and assessment.

This initial collaborative effort demonstrated three important points about MDE's ability to orchestrate change. First, by beginning with the definition and curricular goals, the entire test development process would be centered on the curriculum. This meant that each crucial decision pertaining to the test would have to address the question, how does assessment inform the instructional process? That is, how would the implementation of a particular objective or the inclusion of a particular set of items lead to better instruction? Second, MDE knew that the revised definition could not impact the test without support from the MRA. Third, the new tests could not be implemented unless the curriculum directors and reading specialists were prepared to accommodate the instructional shift implied by the revised definition.

Translating Theory into Practice. The next phase of the project involved translating the definition into a set of objectives that would serve as the basis for revising the MEAP reading tests. A subgroup of the joint MDE/MRA committee which possessed theoretical and practical knowledge related to the new definition began work on developing a new set of goals and objectives. This group, in conjunction with other knowledgeable educators throughout the state and nation, developed the initial set of new objectives based on the new definition of reading.

A draft document of the proposed new reading objectives was submitted to MDE and MRA for their reactions. It was clear to both groups that local educators would have a difficult time evaluating the proposed objectives without some information about how they were likely to be assessed. At this point MEAP contracted with MRA to produce a test blueprint that would serve two functions: to inform teachers of the proposed changes to the reading tests and to serve as a beginning point for test development. However, before a blueprint could be drafted, many issues had to be resolved. These included such topics as determining the type of passages to be used, identifying the type of procedures needed to select the passages, and developing the item types that were based on the new perspective of reading. To help address these, as well as many others issues, staff members from MDE and MEAP met jointly with the MRA team to work through these problems. In a series of meetings that took place over the course of more than a year this joint group explored and developed procedures that would ultimately form the foundation for the blueprint. It was this series of meetings that helped foster the trust that was essential for the remainder of this collaborative project.

As this group worked through the issues related to the development of the blueprint, it became evident that the original timeline for completion of the new test could not be met. To its credit, MEAP in the first of several adjustments, was willing to modify its timeline. In retrospect, MEAP's flexibility proved to be *critical* to the successful completion of the project. By recognizing the difficulty of the task, MEAP provided the needed time to think through each new phase of the project.

It became more apparent as work on the blueprint continued that if the revised definition and objectives were to be accepted by the state's reading teachers, they would have to become more knowledgeable about the theoretical and instructional shifts inherent in this new perspective. The job of educating Michigan teachers became the responsibility of the Curriculum Review Committee. This committee was organized by the MDE Instructional Specialist in Reading and was composed primarily of classroom teachers. One of its first tasks was to conduct a number of statewide workshops. The goal of these workshops was to provide local districts with a model for curriculum review that was based on the new definition. The purpose of this approach was to insure that the curriculum, not the test, became the focal point of the reform.

The curriculum review workshops were also designed to present the proposed new reading objectives to teachers and administrators from local districts. These presentations, as well as the earlier joint meeting between MEAP and MRA, made clear that a field review of the objectives would be needed before MSBE would approve them. The purpose of the field review was to provide local educators with the opportunity to evaluate the proposed reading objectives. Based in part on the favorable response from the field review, the Michigan State Board of Education approved the objectives in the spring of 1986.

Throughout this project, the Curriculum Review Committee assumed a major role in retraining many of the state's educators. At the core of this program of reeducation are numerous documents (for example, *What*

Research Says to the Classroom Teacher about Reading; New Decisions about Reading Instruction) and trainer-of-trainers workshops designed to provide teachers with the requisite knowledge for applying the new definition to a wide variety of important instructional topics. A key component in the training is a series of modules that were developed by the Curriculum Review Committee (for example, *Assessing Reading Comprehension, Assessing the Instructional Situation*, and *Metacognition*). What is important to note about these modules is that teachers not only developed them but also trained other teachers to use them. To date, close to ten thousand teachers have participated in these programs. As a result, there are significant numbers of educators who now understand and support the revised definition. In many instances, schools have implemented curricular reform based on the definition.

Test Development

Throughout the project, MEAP's ability to draw on a variety of internal and external sources proved useful in resolving many of the problems created by the development of an assessment consistent with the new definition and objectives. Following past precedents, MEAP entered into a series of contracts to obtain assistance from a variety of experts who possessed the requisite political, educational, theoretical, psychometric, and technical knowledge necessary to move reading assessment in a new direction. These resources were used to supplement MEAP's own expertise.

Three separate contractors were involved, each dealing with a different aspect of test development. For the item development and review, there were additional contracts with MRA, such as the one that produced the test blueprint. For the technical editing, data collection, and printing of the tryout test booklets, there were contracts with the test development firms, BETA Associates and NCS, which possessed the necessary personnel with technical expertise. For theoretical and research questions related to the development and implementation of the new test, there was a contract with the Center for Research on Learning and Schooling at the University of Michigan, which possessed the knowledge and research skills needed to address important theoretical and psychometric issues. The leadership provided by MEAP in coordinating these diverse resources was extremely important to the success of each of these contracts. In addition, conceptual continuity was provided throughout by the consultants who were involved in virtually every phase and element of the project.

MRA Contracts.   The primary purpose of the first two MRA contracts was the development of the test blueprint and item writing. Item development was the joint responsibility of MEAP and the item-writing teams that were selected as part of the MRA contract. One group of item writers was identified for each of the levels at which the test would be administered—at the beginning of grades four, seven, and ten. Each group was composed primarily of a member of the MEAP reading staff and reading teachers with experience at the appropriate grade levels. This was to insure that passage selection and item development were done by those who were most knowledgeable about reading instruction in Michigan. This procedure also served as a training ground for Michigan teachers and another vehicle for gaining support for the new conceptualization of reading.

The blueprint provided a starting point for training the item writers. First, item writers were shown how to select appropriate passages through the use of text mapping procedures that highlighted important information and the text's overall coherence and cohesiveness. Once an initial set of passages had been selected, the item writing teams were shown how to develop the new types of items. Careful consideration was given to the development of specifications for each new item type. These specifications were used by the teams to develop the new items for the new subtests.

Because the items were different from those in previous tests, a series of review procedures were established to maintain consistency within and across the various item subtypes. The MRA contract included the responsibility for the conceptual review of the items developed by the item-writing teams. The purpose of the conceptual review was to check for the theoretical integrity of each item—whether it contained the appropriate attributes and was consistent with good instructional practice. A second review was performed by the MEAP staff, which edited the items for structural and technical considerations. The items were subsequently reviewed by the technical contractor, and then reviewed once again by the MEAP staff before appearing in a tryout booklet.

In addition to the internal reviews, a number of external reviews were conducted under the MRA/MEAP contract. Over five-hundred teachers and administrators throughout the state were given an opportunity to evaluate the passages and items used in tryouts. Their comments were then used to inform the item-selection process. Content experts also were asked to evaluate the conceptual appropriateness of each selection, because social studies and science passages were the two types of informational passages used in the tryout tests. To insure the instructional integrity of the passages and items it was critical to represent adequately the domains of knowledge from which they were selected. In one case, for example, an entire passage was eliminated because the content experts found that it contained inaccurate information.

The most recent MRA contracts have maintained the item development and review responsibilities and have added the development of informal classroom assessment procedures that can be used in conjunction with the MEAP tests. Collectively, these contracts represent the continuation of a long-standing practice of cooperation and collaboration between the MDE and the MRA.

Technical Contracts. The primary responsibilities of the technical contractor for the item tryouts were technical editing, printing and distributing the tryout booklets to participating districts, and scoring the tryout data. Once the items had been reviewed by the MEAP staff, they were turned over to the technical contractor. However, before the technical editing could begin, the editors had to be trained in the procedures used for item development and item editing. For example, the manner in which the passages were selected and items developed prevented the technical editors from making changes in the reading selections as part of their editing.

When the technical editing was completed, the items were reviewed again by the MEAP staff to insure that technical editing had not changed the intent of the items. After the items had been revised as a result of the tryouts, they were again edited by the technical contractor. The technical contractors in charge of printing and distributing tryout and pilot tests and scoring and preliminary reporting of pilot data were NCS and BETA.

Research Contract. The unique nature of the project posed many new problems and questions concerning the psychometric integrity of the new tests. To address these issues, there was a need for systematic inquiry by individuals who were both knowledgeable about the conceptualization of reading used to develop the tests and who could conduct the relevant research. As a result, MEAP entered into a research contract with the Center for Research on Learning and Schooling at the University of Michigan to provide assistance with gathering the information necessary for making important decisions about the new tests.

The activities conducted as part of the research contract were designed to provide information regarding a variety of issues. Two of the central issues addressed by the research contract were the validity of the subtests and item subtypes and the relations between the new tests and the existing MEAP reading tests. Detailed analyses of tryout data were supplemented with interview data from over one thousand students to inform item selection and revision, the development of new item formats, and the design of subsequent tryouts and pilots. In addition, analyses were conducted for bias and to determine both bias and the developmental appropriateness of the reading selections.

Another major issue addressed by the research contract was the development of procedures for scoring and reporting. Detailed analyses of item subtypes were conducted to determine their appropriateness for use in scoring and reporting. Preliminary report formats consistent with the conceptual framework of the test were developed and field-tested. In addition the research contract provided assistance by convening panels of experts to assist in interpreting tryout and pilot data and to advise MEAP regarding such issues as scoring and equating passages. As part of this activity, representatives of the Michigan project met periodically with representatives of the Illinois project to share concerns and work through procedures for insuring the psychometric integrity of the new Michigan and Illinois reading tests. Additionally the Michigan and Illinois projects convened a national advisory panel that was comprised of reading educators, psychometricians, cognitive psychologists, and statisticians to advise them on matters ranging from subtest validity and data analysis to procedures for scoring and equating.

Tryouts and Piloting

The complexity of the test development process required multiple tryouts and pilots. The first item tryouts were conducted in the winter of 1987. The tryout data were scored by the technical contractor and analyzed under the research contract with the University of Michigan. The results of the data analyses, student interviews, and item statistics were used to select items for the item pilot in the fall of 1987. For this pilot twenty districts were selected to administer the pilot tests and participate in a series of workshops sponsored by MEAP and MRA. These workshops were designed both to disseminate information about the revised definition, objectives, and tests and to provide MDE with feedback about various aspects of the project, such as test administration procedures and the utility of proposed report formats.

A second set of passages and items underwent tryouts in the winter of 1988. Passages and items from this tryout were combined with passages and items from the fall 1987 pilot for use in the final test pilot that was administered in the fall of 1988.

An additional forty districts were added to the winter test pilot. This meant that a total of sixty districts would be part of the collaborative project that was designed to encourage each school district participating in the tryouts to examine its own curriculum in light of the changes suggested by the new test. A number of workshops were held to provide districts with resource materials that had been developed by the Curriculum Review Committee. The primary goal was to have districts link instructional practices to the results implied by the new test, thereby helping tie instructional improvement to testing.

All of the passages and items were administered simultaneously in the final test pilot to establish cut-scores and to equate for difficulty. This procedure allows different passages and items from the total pool to be administered in different years. The final test pilot also included a tryout of the proposed reporting formats.

The new MEAP reading tests are expected to come before the State Board of Education for approval in the winter of 1989. If approved, these tests are scheduled for full implementation in the fall of 1989.

The Illinois Project

Illinois's involvement in statewide assessment has gone through several stages of development. Prior to 1975, the Illinois State Board of Education did not conduct any form of assessment. In 1971 the State Superintendent in Illinois initiated "The Goals for the Seventies," an attempt to establish state leadership in an educational environment that was dominated by local control. Associated with this initial effort was the desire to make both local districts and schools more accountable. However, without a legislative mandate, statewide assessment would only be voluntary.

The stage of development from 1975 to 1980 included the collection of data, but without a link to student outcomes or to sanctions of any kind. There was involvement of local educators in the process, yet the low stakes of this assessment made the involvement and the impact of the assessment rather minimal.

The most recent stage of development began with the gradual shift toward identifying learner outcomes and developing a more valid assessment of reading comprehension. Yet, the link between curriculum and assessment continued to be missing until 1985, when the Illinois legislature placed its fiscal and conceptual support behind statewide and local objectives and assessment by enacting several laws which comprised the Educational Reform Package. Over the years the basis for valid, curriculum-based assessment had been evolving, and now it had the support it needed to gain credibility.

Initiating Statewide Assessment: 1975–1981

The first formal attempts at statewide assessment took place during 1975 to 1980 with the appointment of the first State Superintendent of Education by the seventeen-member State Board. (In Illinois this is the policymaking body.) During this time, student achievement began to emerge as a priority, and with this came a voluntary statewide assessment program. As the test was developed and implemented, three distinct but related factors became apparent: the impact of local control, the need for collaboration, and the changing nature of the content and format of the tests.

In 1975, the Illinois State Board of Education (ISBE), a separate group equivalent to the state department of education, issued its first Goal Statements, which committed the state to a "high-quality, fully integrated educational system" (ISBE, 1980). This document was the first call for the state to assess its educational goals. However, state assessment had to conform to concerns about local autonomy and collaboration. The State Board saw itself as providing guidance to local districts rather than circumventing their decision making, and the document frequently referred to the need for continual reassessment of the goals with the input of local districts and the public at large.

At the same time, the new state superintendent also combined two sections of the Illinois State Board of Education—Program Evaluation and Student Assessment. This merger represented the first time that student performance was linked with assessment; Illinois now had the structural alignment that would, in the future, help expedite statewide testing.

On the national level, the minimum competency movement was gaining momentum. The prevailing belief was that students' skills had deteriorated to the point that students were incapable of functioning effectively in society (Airasian and Madaus, 1983). Various states responded by instituting testing programs designed to assess minimum competencies in core skill areas, such as math and reading.

Illinois was no different. With the reorganization of its two assessment sections, ISBE was in a position to respond to the concerns about student performance in the basic skill areas. Accordingly, the new state superintendent issued a directive to begin collecting statewide data on achievement in reading and mathematics. Up to this point there had been no statewide student assessment in any subject area, either voluntary or mandated. This directive established the first Illinois Inventory of Education Progress (IIEP), a low-profile, voluntary data-gathering system.

From 1976 to 1978, the IIEP in reading and mathematics was patterned after the newly created NEAP. The reading assessment focused on minimum competency types of skills, such as reading signs, schedules, maps, and labels, as well as reading and answering questions about short, relatively easy passages. In keeping with a commitment to local input and following NAEP's consensus approach to test development, a committee of Illinois educators and ISBE personnel developed test objectives and selected items from the NAEP item pool for inclusion. Additional items were also written by the committee as needed. As further assurance of local autonomy, participation in the assessment was voluntary.

Data from these assessments were reported only by item: the percentage of students correctly responding, the predicted percentage of students responding correctly, and a critique and interpretation of each item developed by a representative committee of Illinois educators. No individual pupil, school, or district data were available (ISBE, 1979). This prevented state or local agencies from comparing results or using them for accountability.

Beginning in 1979, ISBE established a third goal of the assessment— publishing test results, which set the stage for public disclosure of test data and for public accountability (ISBE, 1981). In doing this, Illinois was responding to the pressure felt nationally for visibility and accountability. During this period, several provisions were made for Illinois educators to be involved in the assessment. Small committees of teachers, administrators, and university educators participated in decisions about the test objectives and test items and about the publication of results. Because statewide goals in reading were so broadly defined, these representative committees had to specify objectives and items for each assessment. This type of committee involvement reflected ISBE's recognition of the political and educational need for collaboration with educators in the field, and it continues today to be a hallmark of ISBE's approach to field involvement in state issues.

Under the guidance of the committees and ISBE staff, the content of the test moved from the tight focus on minimum competency tasks and multiple choice questions, to a preponderance of cloze items, to a combination of item types and more difficult paragraphs. However, common items from each year and each type were carried over to provide trend data.

Although the published reports often provided a theoretically based definition and discussion of the reading process that had been suggested by the committee, the experimentation with various item types suggests there was a lack of theoretical focus. The problem, however, was that as the committees changed, so did the objectives and items. Consequently, there was no clear, consistent theoretical focus for these tests (Kerins, 1987, pers. com.).

The apparent lack of theoretical focus also concerned some educators throughout the state. They believed that minimum competency skills and the kinds of items and tasks found on the test were devoid of "real reading." As a result, the assessment focus was inconsistent with what they thought a reading test should assess. What is important to realize is that, because there were no agreed upon statewide curricular objectives, the concerns were primarily focused on what a good reading test should look like rather than the implications the test had for instruction. In addition, this lack of concern for curricular implications can be partially attributable to the fact that the test was voluntary and, therefore, not associated with any distribution of funds or other legislative sanctions.

At the same time, consistent with the national scene, the legislature became concerned with whether it should become involved in minimum competency testing. To address this concern, the Illinois legislature in 1979 passed a bill requiring ISBE to conduct a study to ascertain whether minimum competency testing should be required by the State. The study included surveys of the status of minimum competency testing in Illinois and in the nation as a whole. ISBE concluded that: (1) minimum competency testing was limited in scope and that districts should use multiple methods of assessing student progress; (2) minimum competency testing was not necessary, but a sound evaluation procedure was imperative; and (3) districts should have regularly scheduled curriculum review, and school boards should develop policies on assessment. These recommendations were presented to the legislature; however, they were not accepted as part of the bill. Instead, minimum competency testing was not mandated and ISBE findings were simply recommended as 'best practice' to local districts.

These policy studies were conducted by the same section at ISBE involved in conducting the voluntary assessment (IIEP). This is a critical point because the overlap established a basis for communication and confidence between the assessment section of the ISBE and the seventeen-members of the Illinois State Board of Education. This strong working relationship carried over into the next stage of assessment development and provided an opportunity for the group to take a closer look at the existing assessment tools. Clearly, the results of the minimum competency studies suggested that Illinois should move beyond minimum competencies; this evidence provided the added focus and direction of the assessments of the 1980s.

By 1981, Illinois was experiencing the same dissatisfaction with the quality of schooling that was being felt at the national level (National Commission on Excellence in Education, 1983). In response, the Illinois State Board of Education took several actions which would later impact educational improvement efforts. First, ISBE authorized an intensive study of the state mandates which impacted local school districts. An initial focus of this study was on instructional programs. A major finding of this study was that secondary curricular areas, such as labor education and consumer education, had been mandated but that areas such as reading, language arts, math and science had not. Second, ISBE initiated the first requirement of an annual analysis and report of student achievement. This marked a dramatic shift from the laissez-faire assessments of the past to a more visible function of statewide assessment. Third, several other studies and programs were instituted that were aimed at finance, administration, and long-range planning. Fourth, ISBE began work on a definition of schooling which could be used as a template for ISBE consideration of various educational policy issues. These events marked the beginning of state-initiated studies regarding the quality of the educational system and the content, focus, and function of student assessment.

The Changing State Role in Education: 1982–1988

The next phase of assessment development was influenced by the results of several statewide studies, responses of ISBE to the commissioned reports, and the emphasis on excellence in education. Many of the initiatives begun in the last part of 1981 were completed or implemented during this time and several others were undertaken. For the first time in Illinois, the focus was on how well Illinois students performed, as compared with others across the nation, and on how school and student characteristics related to achievement. So, although there was still no official link between assessment and curriculum, Illinois saw the need to forge such a link.

Changes in State Thinking About Education and Accountability. Several political and educational movements in Illinois and the nation suggested that the existing educational situation in Illinois required attention. First, the results of studies of the instructional program mandates begun in 1981 were presented to ISBE and the Illinois legislature. The recommendations included a call for clearly stated learner outcomes in six content areas to be developed with the assistance of a representative ad hoc task force. Additionally legislation required local school districts to develop learner objectives and assessment systems consistent with those developed at the state level. As a result of these recommendations the Illinois General Assembly created the Illinois Commission on the Improvement of Elementary and Secondary Education, a bi-partisan legislative and citizen committee which conducted hearings around the state and eventually recommended measures for the improvement of elementary and secondary education that formed the basis for the Reform Package of 1985.

The ad hoc committee of Illinois educators recommended by the mandate studies was convened. This represented a recognition that there was to be a wide consensus process to determine what Illinois students should know and be able to do by the time they completed their schooling. It also pushed the balance of power to a more equal distribution between state and local educators by giving the state a more prominent role in determining student outcomes. This committee of over a hundred citizens and educators, the Corbally Committee, developed a list of outcome statements in each of six subjects areas. These outcome statements were shared with others through a series of meetings across the State, and then revised. In June 1984, ISBE approved these student learning outcomes, marking the first set of specific learner outcomes in Illinois educational history.

Second, in the foreword to the third annual report on student achievement (ISBE, 1984) the new State Superintendent of Education, Ted Sanders, suggested that the assessment data provided support for the establishment of learner outcomes at the state and local levels. He further suggested that it established the need for a statewide assessment system that would allow the state to hold schools accountable for the achievement of all students and provide a basis for program improvement. Together with the recommendations from the mandate studies, this statement marked the beginning of Illinois's efforts to establish a framework for student outcomes and to link those outcomes to an assessment system that would include all students.

There were many other reform studies, reports, and initiatives during 1984–1985 (for example, the Illinois Project for School Reform Education in a New Illinois, Education Reform Proposals of the Chicago Teachers' Union, and so on) that signified a concern for educational reform. The Governor also demonstrated unprecedented fiscal and conceptual commitment to improved education in his proposal of the Illinois Better Schools Program, and the legislature began work on several educational bills that would ultimately comprise a new educational reform package. As a result of testimony from community members, business people, educators, and ISBE personnel, several bills were proposed to amend the existing School Code of Illinois.

These political initiatives in some cases preceded the release of *A Nation at Risk* and in other cases moved forward from that work. The point is that Illinois policymakers and citizens had a firm vantage point from which to understand the problems facing the state's schools. It became evident during this period that Illinois must provide more specific expectations for its students and schools and that the assessments should provide information to assist with improving achievement. These events were reflected in the specific changes which occurred in the reading assessments.

Changes in the Statewide Reading Assessment. During 1982 to 1984, the focus of the asssessments was on multiple measures of achievement required by ISBE's 1980 student assessment policy (ISBE, 1983, 1984, 1985). For example, in reading and math, data were reported for the ACT, SAT, IIEP, and other specially conducted studies in an effort to obtain a more complete picture of the performance of students and, indirectly, of schools. This approach enabled state officials to maintain a commitment to local control and still provide national reference points against which to compare the achievement of Illinois students.

During this time there was also a shift in the format of the reading assessment. The impetus for this shift seemed to emerge from the leadership at ISBE, from the members of the Language Arts Assessment Committee, and from new research and practice regarding a process approach to writing. The wide acceptance of new instructional and assessment strategies in writing seemed to magnify the concerns about the reading tests identified in the late seventies and early eighties. As noted in the 1984 report, many of the questions in the 1976 to 1982 reading assessments were drawn from NAEP and "required short answers and reflected the 1970s testing philosophy of the separation of reading skills into such areas as 'word attack,' 'vocabulary,' and 'decoding.'"

In contrast, beginning in 1982, "There was an attempt to develop a reading assessment that could more adequately assess student achievement of reading comprehension" by using longer literature and science passages like those students would encounter in classes and by asking more inferential questions (Illinois State Board of Education, 1985). Once again, with the help of a representative committee of reading educators, teachers and university faculty, ISBE constructed new assessments for grades four, eight and eleven.

But there were several problems associated with this new assessment. The process of passage and item development was very costly and time-consuming and there was no state budget to support the assessment. New passages and items were developed by the small voluntary committee, Illinois educators, and one ISBE staff member and there was little financial support for such an enormous task in a voluntary assessment program. There was a recognition on the part of ISBE staff working collaboratively with a group of Illinois educators of a need for change in the reading assessment; they felt it did not reflect current theory and research. Yet these efforts would have relatively little impact on the state as a whole because the assessment touched very few people in the state: there were no mechanisms for dissemination of information; there was inadequate funding for this voluntary program; and there was no direct link with instruction.

An additional problem at this point was one of creating meaningful reports. The assessment produced results that focused on an overview, or snapshot, of the reading proficiency of the entire state. However, many school administrators wanted more specific data as a payoff for their voluntary participation in the assessment. Although ISBE reaffirmed its policy not to release results identifying specific schools (ISBE, 1985), it did agree to provide individual school data to individual schools to help them understand how their performance compared with schools with similar school factors, such as size, socioeconomic status, and location. Although the state had not provided the link with instruction, school personnel wanted to be able to use test results to guide instructional decisions.

These concerns led to a need for a more acceptable assessment of reading that could provide a national reference point. It led ISBE to a more tradional measure — a published norm-referenced test. In the fall of 1984, the State decided to administer the Degrees of Reading Power Test (ETS) to a voluntary sample of students in the spring of 1985. Their decision was guided by their belief that the Degrees of Reading Power had a stronger theoretical anchor than past assessments instruments and it would provide more specific information related to curricular material.

Unfortunately, the DRP was also problematic. Results revealed a ceiling effect for many Illinois students and a problem with the matching of test scores with scores calculated for reading materials (ISBE, 1986). Additionally, there was a concern about a mismach between the test objectives and the new learner outcomes adopted by ISBE, which led to the conclusion that the DRP could not be used.

The Educational Reform Package of 1985

In July 1985, the Illinois legislature passed a number of educational reforms that incorporated both the definition of schooling proposed by

ISBE and the concept of learner outcomes. This reform package brought into law the requirements of accountability, curriculum, and local control that had been gaining momentum since 1982. Among the components of the legislation were three mandates related to curriculum and assessment.

First, the law required ISBE to establish goals consistent with the legislated purpose of schooling. This resulted in the formal adoption of a series of Student Learning Outcomes proposed by the Corbally Committee. Thus, the law specified outcomes for all students in Illinois schools, stating what students "are expected to know and be able to do as a result of their schooling," rather than prescribing a specific class or a course of study. (See Appendix A for the Reading Learner Outcomes.)

Second, it mandated statewide assessment (Illinois Goal Assessment Program) in reading, mathematics, and language arts, beginning with reading in 1988 and gave the Board the authority to test in other areas as they deemed appropriate. Testing would be administered to all eligible students in the spring for grades three, six, eight, and ten, — a change in grade levels from the historical emphasis on grades four, eight and eleven (NAEP's assigned grades).

Third, the broadest emphasis of the legislation was a focus on local control of instruction, curriculum, and assessment. To achieve this end, local districts were to use the Learning Outcomes developed at the state level as a guide to help them develop their own individualized objectives that would meet or exceed the goals established by the State. Districts then were to develop Local Assessment Plans (LAP) to asses their local objectives. These objectives, along with a Local Assessment Plan, would be submitted to ISBE for approval. Notably, while this legislation signaled a move to more centralized accountability, in maintained a focus on locally determined curriculum, instruction, and assessment. Although this was to be the first state-mandated assessment in Illinois, the message was that local assessment was critical and, therefore, mandated as well.

Unfortunately, the educational reality was confounded by the rather short timelines for implementation. Local districts were to submit the first of their local objectives (language arts) and the first of their locally developed assessment plans (for the reading section of language arts) by September 1987, less than two years after the legislation was passed and seven months before local districts would see the statewide test. The first statewide assessment (in reading) was scheduled for April 1988, just two-and-a-half years after the legislation. Although curriculum compliance was required some time before the statewide test was administered, it is critical to recognize that both curricular and assessment changes were mandated at the same time. Unfortunately, what was not clear was whether curriculum or assessment should drive the curriculum.

This situation was further complicated by the broad nature of the Learner Outcomes. Local districts and ISBE felt that they needed examples of specific learning objectives that might emanate from such a broad state goal. As a result, later in October 1985, a second committee (Corbally 2) comprised of teachers, administrators, and teacher educators, was charged with the task of clarifying the learner outcome statements. The language arts subcommittee developed an introductory statement summarizing the current research-based interactive view of reading and, based upon this model, wrote seven interrelated general knowledge/skills that would help local districts understand and interpret the broad state goal in reading.

Both the state goals and the general knowledge/skills were stated deliberately in broad, general terms so that local districts could have greater latitude in developing their own objectives. However, many districts felt they needed more guidance than the knowledge/skills provided, so an extended group of the Corbally 2 Committee was reconvened to develop a list of sample learning objectives for grades three, six, eight and eleven. At every step of this very quick process, local districts made it clear that they needed more assistance to be able to carry out their tasks, and ISBE continually responded.

Over the next year, these knowledge/skills and sample learning objectives went through a series of consensus reviews and revisions until they were finally approved by the Board of Education and then disseminated to local districts in March of 1986, eight months prior to the deadline for districts to submit local objectives and assessment plans for reading. Although the objectives reflected the most current thinking in the reading field, they did not necessarily reflect the most common practices and beliefs of teachers in Illinois classrooms. It certainly was a logical extension of the work that had been occurring gradually and voluntarily at the state level and in many up-to-date districts, but there had been no widespread effort over time to familiarize the majority of teachers in the state with this information.

The final complicating factor was an economic one. Districts were promised funding to assist them with the development of local objectives and assessments. Although the fiscal support was promised for several years, declining budgets forced the legislature to suspend funding after 1986. This change in monetary support placed a great strain on many school districts trying to comply with mandated timelines and subsequently led to concern and resentment about the implementation of statewide assessment.

It is clear that the reform package grew out of years of study within Illinois, as well as concerns raised nationally about the quality of education.

There was also evidence of a need for a more careful and theoretically based definition of reading and a concern regarding the link between assessment and curriculum. Although the motivation for change and the input sought from educators and citizens across the state is noteworthy, the timelines imposed a very difficult situation on ISBE and local school districts. There was little time to work with all the teachers and administrators in the state, let alone prepare them for the first mandated statewide assessment.

Test Development

The Collaboration. The call for a state-mandated reading test combined with the new learner outcomes and the history of dissatisfaction with other reading assessment strategies led ISBE to the Center for the Study of Reading at the University of Illinois. At about this time, the State Superintendent of Education and the Directors of the Center for the Study of Reading began a series of informal dialogues that appeared to be fostered by several political, educational and economic factors.

Educationally, 1985 marked the publication of *Becoming a Nation of Readers* (Anderson *et al.*, 1985). This report was a summary of reading research and implications for educational practice. As part of a dissemination effort, a presentation to the seventeen member State Board was made. The Center extended an invitation to assist the state with the implementation of this research. The assessment section of ISBE decided this was a good opportunity to begin communication with the Center.

Additionally, in September 1985, the Center had begun a program of research in reading assessment. A temporary research position was created for investigation into alternative methods of reading assessment. Over the years there had been interest in reading assessment, but to this point there had not been the personnel available to head the project. Concurrently, there was an expectation at the federal level for more applied research from the federally funded centers. The Center for the Study of Reading was no exception. The Center was scheduled for re-competition in 1986, and the emphasis on applied research and collaboration with public institutions was clearly recognized.

Thus, in the fall of 1985, Illinois was presented with a unique set of circumstances: the educational reform legislation calling for the implementation of statewide curriculum and accountability; a nationally recognized reading research center located within the state that was concerned with applied research; and a state agency faced with the task of implementing the legislation under short timelines while recognizing its dissatisfaction with its past reading asssessment. In essence, there were two educational institutions with the common need to meet educational, political, and economic demands.

As a result of many discussions and negotiations, an agreement was reached in November 1985 between ISBE and the Center for the Study of Reading to join forces to provide prototypes of items for a test of reading achievement that, in comparison to conventional tests, better reflected the views of reading implicit in recent research and explicit in the new state goals and learner outcome statements. The aim was to evaluate the usefulness of several alternative item formats and strategies that might culminate in a unified perspective of reading theory, instruction, and assessment — the curriculum/assessment link. The assessment was not intended to report individual student data, but rather to report at the state, district, and school levels.

The Center for the Study of Reading and the Illinois State Board of Education entered into a contract on December 11, 1985 to develop and pilot prototypical reading passages and items. In addition to the contractual agreement, the project was assisted by the voluntary expertise of several University of Illinois psychometricians. The test items and administration design were to be turned over the ISBE by January 30, 1986. These tests were to be included as part of a larger state pilot in several subject areas in March 1986.

A contract for the printing and distribution of the new reading assessments, as well as the additional testing programs in science, math, and reading, was awarded to The Psychological Corporation. As part of that contract, The Psychological Corporation administered a subsection of the Metropolitan Reading Test and selected items from the last Illinois statewide reading assessment. Results from these two reading measures would be used to help evaluate the new piloted items.

Research and Development. The Illinois Reading Learner Outcomes and the accompanying rationale and goals provided the framework for the construction of the new reading assessment. These statements reflected current theory, research, and practice in reading, and together represented an interactive model of the reading process. Both the ISBE assessment staff and the statistical consultants to the project encouraged the development of an assessment tool that was theoretically sound rather than one shaped by traditional psychometric constraints.

Although seven "knowledge and skill" areas were identified under the

State Outcome for reading, these seven were understood to be inter-dependent. Thus, there was no attempt on the part of the Corbally 2 Committee, the test developers, or personnel within the ISBE assessment section to create discrete categories of items. In addition, the Corbally 2 Committee had designated these knowledge/skills to be identical for all grades, thus reflecting a common structure of the reading process. However, issues such as these were not as well understood initially throughout the ISBE agency. Several meetings were scheduled with ISBE administrators to discuss the interactive model of reading and to answer questions related to the learner outcomes and the assessment. Although those working closely to develop the project had established a framework for making decisions, many other people in the organization had not benefited from that close working relationship and required time to become familiar with a great deal of theory and research about reading and reading assessment.

This new approach to reading assessment required very careful piloting and in-depth research. Not only were the passages developed and items constructed specifically for this assessment, but it was a unique attempt to operationalize theoretical concepts into large-scale assessment strategies. For example, several new item formats were developed for each of the four components of the test—constructing meaning, topic familiarity, reading strategies, and literacy experiences. It was critical to be able to separate item difficulty from format difficulty and to assure the validity and reliability of each item and test component. The aim was to develop tests with formats and content that represented instructionally meaningful tasks to teachers and to students. Such a requirement demanded extensive piloting and research efforts.

In December 1985, reading passages and items formats were piloted with a small sample of students, and in March 1986, the full scale pilot was conducted. A random sample of schools and students within schools was drawn for the 1986 pilot. Tests were administered to approximately four thousand students across the state at each grade level (three, six, eight, and ten) in April 1986. In all, nine unique item formats were piloted in a modified matrix sampling design using twenty-six different test booklets. Tests were also administered to approximately seven hundred students at out-of-grade level to determine the grade appropriateness of the reading passages. Classroom teachers administered the tests and then completed feedback forms concerning the test items, format, and their observations of students during the examination period.

Following the written test, a representative sample of students from all grades was interviewed by staff of the Center for the Study of Reading.

Student interviews were an essential component of the 1985–1986 pilot test for two reasons: the first pertains to the issue of construct validity, the second to the novelty of the structure of the tests and of many of the new item formats.

It was imperative to obtain an independent measure of the validity of the new measure and carefully to review for potential difficulties associated with implementing novel formats, directions, and tasks. Although the Metropolitan Reading Test would provide a measure of concurrent validity, it was important to have an independent measure of validity more closely associated with the theory upon which the assessment was based.

The data were analyzed and a final report submitted to ISBE in September 1986. The paper-and-pencil measures, in-depth interviews, and teacher feedback forms were used to analyze the new assessment strategies. The advantages and disadvantages of the various formats were discussed and recommendations offered for the 1987 pilot.

During these eight months, ISBE staff members and researchers from CSR made a number of presentations at state and local meeting of the Illinois Reading Council. ISBE also sponsored a three day workshop for staff of the sixteen regional educational service centers across the state. Although the focus of this workshop was on how to assist local districts in implementing the recommendations from *Becoming a Nation of Readers*, and thus implementing the new Illinois Learner Outcomes in reading, one session of this workshop presented an update on the state reading assessment efforts.

It was during this period as well that Michigan and Illinois established a collaboration in an effort to share resources and ideas related to our respective reading assessments. Although the timelines were significantly different and the operationalization of concepts different, the theoretical basis and educational concerns were shared. This cooperative venture led to several meetings among the researchers and Board of Education staff and to shared costs for psychometric consultants. This cooperation was a critical factor in our efforts to rethink and reshape traditional assessment approaches and it continues to be a powerful force in our efforts today.

In October 1986, ISBE and CSR entered into a second contract: a three-year agreement to conduct and analyze the 1987 pilot, develop ten passages and accompanying items for each grade level to be used in the actual 1988 assessment, and to conduct two workshop to train Illinois educators to write items for future assessment. In addition to the continued statistical support of University of Illinois psychometricians, this contract included a subcontract to MetriTech, Inc. to print, disseminate, score, and analyze test results. The philosophy underlying this contract was that the Center would offer a maximum level of support in designing these tests in the first year but that gradually this responsibility would be transferred over to ISBE, which then would continue working with Illinois educators to select passages and write items for the next rounds of assessments. At the end of the third year of this contract, full responsibility would return to the state.

Between October 1986 and January 1, 1987, more than forty passages and two thousand items were developed for the April 1987 pilot involving approximately twelve thousand students in grades three, six, eight, and eleven. Once again, teacher feedback forms were distributed with every classroom testing package.

A unique testing design was developed for the tests; this was critical because every student would only respond to two passages and items and those results would be reported at the school level as well as the district and the state levels.

It was important to ensure that students were not unjustly penalized for having to respond to a particular passage. Included in the design was a contract with The Psychological Corporation to develop national norms through an equating process using the reading section of the Stanford Achievement Test. This was necessitated by another requirement of 1985 legislation, which required a national reference point to evaluate the progress of schools.

As part of the analyses of the 1987 pilot, several committees were asked to review the reading passages, items, statistical data, and pilot design. Included in this group was the State Board Bias Review Committee comprised of teachers, curriculum specialists, and university faculty representing every geographic region of the state. This group reviewed the statistical data on every item and also read every passage and item for content or syntactical bias. The Language Arts Advisory Committee reviewed all items as well and made recommendations for revisions. They approved the passages and items for inclusion in the actual 1988 assessment. The ISBE Technical Advisory Committee also reviewed statistical data, the pilot design, and the proposed 1988 design and offered suggestions. As report formats for the assessment were designed, another group of educators was convened to provide suggestions about the form the reports should take. Their feedback was consolidated with that of the technical advisors, test developers, and ISBE staff to create the reporting format for 1988.

Throughout this year, the assessment researchers at CSR and ISBE staff were involved in a number of outreach efforts designed to acquaint educators across Illinois with the new assessment. Several large group meetings were sponsored by ISBE to acquaint Educational Service Center personnel with the reading assessment and with strategies local school districts might use in their local assessment plans. These Service Centers were established and budgeted through the reform package to provide service and training to schools throughout the state. The focus of these outreach efforts was to try to help local districts develop locally appropriate assessments which paralleled, but were not identical to, the statewide assessment.

The emphasis continued to be on local adaptations of state guidelines. Two videotapes were also produced that discussed the Illinois Goal Assessment Program in reading and alternative assessment strategies local districts might consider when designing their individual local assessment plans. Additionally, several pamphlets and sample tests were widely distributed to familiarize teachers and administrators with the new reading assessment. All these efforts took place within one year.

Finally, the first of two item-writing workshops was conducted by the CSR development team during the summer of 1987. Fifteen teachers and Educational Service Center staff members from across the state spent three days in closely supervised workshops learning to write Constructing Meaning questions. The purpose of these workshops was to begin to prepare Illinois educators to assume the responsibility of developing items which might be included in subsequent pilot efforts.

A secondary purpose was to begin to acquaint educators with a process of assessment that might be used in local school districts. Again, the focus was on the alignment of local and statewide curriculum and assessment. Items developed in this workshop were reviewed and revised by the CSR assessment team and then submitted as pilot items to be included in the 1988 assessment. A second workshop was conducted during the summer of 1988.

Data from the 1987 workshop were analyzed along with the responses of all the advisory groups and the five hundred teachers who completed and returned feedback forms. From September to December 1987 the items and passages were revised and then submitted to National Computer Systems, the contractor with responsibility for printing, distributing, scanning, scoring, and reporting the 1988 Illinois Goal Assessment Program. From January to February 1988, an additional set of six passages and items were revised for piloting at each grade.

In April 1988, the first Illinois Goal Assessment Program in reading was administered to over 338,000 Illinois students in grades three, six, and eight.

Summary of Assessment History in Michigan and Illinois

The initial implementation of mandatory statewide asssessment in both states began as a response to political issues: in Michigan it was the desire for equity in educational funding and achievement; in Illinois it was a response to the national reform movement for excellence in education. This political context helped shape the process each state used as they sought to develop the new reading tests.

Michigan. The process that the Michigan Department of Education (MDE) used to revise its existing reading tests has evolved gradually over a twenty-year-period of experience with mandatory statewide assessment. Its cornerstone is a consensus approach, in which politically and educationally influential groups are involved from the beginning. Although MDE uses many groups throughout the consensus process, it has the sole responsibility for selecting items and passages, deciding on tests formats, and determining the scoring and reporting procedures used to implement the new test.

Some of the groups involved in the current effort are part of a network that was established during MDE's previous review cycles; other groups were added because of the unique nature of the project. One of the more influential groups was the MRA. Because of its political and educational ties throughout the state, MEAP contracted with MRA to develop a blueprint that established criteria for selecting passages and writing and reviewing items. This ensured that teachers and administrators would be intimately involved in many of the various stages of test development.

Curriculum development was of equal concern to test development in Michigan; therefore, the Curriculum Review Committee (CRC) was formed by MDE. Its primary responsibility was to update educators throughout the state on the changing views on reading and the implications this had for curriculum development, instruction, and assessment. The goal was to have local educators assume the responsibility for training their colleagues. By involving local educators in the training and dissemination process, the CRC provided a forum in which the new views on reading instruction and assessment could be discussed. This forum gave teachers an opportunity both to learn about and to react to the proposed changes. Through these discussions, teachers and administrators began to reach a consensus that provided important grassroots support for the new direction reading assessment was taking in Michigan.

Another important component in the concensus-building process was the research team from the Center for Research on Learning and Schooling (CRLS) at the University of Michigan. MEAP contracted with CRLS to provide assistance with important theoretical and psychometric issues that needed to be addressed during the various phases of test development. Not only did the research group provide technical support, but because this was a consensus process, it meant that the group had to work in close collaboration with other groups that were involved in the test development. For example, while the MRA identified passages and wrote items, it worked in conjunction with the University of Michigan group to collect tryout data from students and teachers; that data would be used by MEAP to determine the appropriateness of passages and items.

Illinois. Because Illinois had a strong preference for locally controlled testing and no history of mandatory statewide assessment in reading, its procedures for test development unfolded differently. With the legislation for mandatory statewide assessment in 1985, the Illinois State Board of Education (ISBE) was given two and a half years to have a test in place. Because the ISBE wanted to develop a test that was consistent with current theory and research and its new learner outcomes, it turned to the Center for the Study of Reading (CSR) at the University of Illinois at Champaign-Urbana for assistance. CSR entered into a contractual arrangement with ISBE whereby CSR assumed primary responsibility for the development and piloting of the first two editions of the new tests. This collaborative arrangement was politically and educationally beneficial for both organizations; ISBE would get a test that was theoretically and psychometrically sound and CSR would have an important collaborative arrangement with a major public educational agency. Notably, during the initial stages of test development the process was not constrained by political pressures from outside groups. As a result, Illinois was able to be more innovative in its development of item types and formats. Later on, this early isolation would prove to be a difficult political situation.

In addition, since it was a major research institution, CSR had the resources to conduct important validity studies that were used to inform both the item-writing and passage-selection process as well as the scoring and reporting procedures. Thus, throughout the test development phase, Illinois was able to use research in important ways that influenced the content and format of its tests. These data were shared with Michigan as part of a joint collaborative project.

Because there was a short timeline, ISBE did not have the opportunity to disseminate information about the new test as widely as it would have liked. Consequently, most educators first learned there was a new test during either the various stages of item tryouts or when the test was administered for the first time on a statewide basis in the spring of 1988. This lack of communication, coupled with the fact that other newly mandated tests were also being implemented during this period, intensified the reaction to the new test.

These reactions caused ISBE to make substantive changes in the structure of the test. While the initial test development process was controlled by research considerations, the final implementation was controlled by educational and political considerations. In some cases the two conflicted with one another.

The framework for initial test development and dissemination efforts were shaped largely by limited time and experience with statewide assessment. By giving most of the responsibility for these activities to the CSR test developers and the small group of ISBE staff, the task could be accomplished in a very short period of time. However, once the mechanisms were in place, ISBE's role grew quickly and CSR's role gradually decreased. The newly legislated Educational Service Centers also began to assume responsibility for more large-scale dissemination and assistance.

Overview of Michigan and Illinois Reading Test Projects

One of the most interesting aspects of the Michigan and Illinois projects was translating a theory of reading into a new type of reading comprehension test. At the time Michigan and Illinois embarked on these projects, reading comprehension testing had not significantly changed since the 1920s (Farr and Carey, 1986). To help understand the differences that exist between the traditional and the new types of tests, we begin by reviewing the theory on which the new tests are based. While the Michigan and Illinois' tests share a common theoretical framework, there are differences in how each state operationalized individual test components and testing procedures. Therefore, in the subsequent sections each component will be presented, sample items provided, and testing procedures described.

The Theory

The first step in the Michigan and Illinois projects was specifying the conceptualization of reading that would serve as the basis for statewide reading goals and objectives and the new reading tests. Significant changes in theoretical views of reading emerged in the 1970s and 1980s. There was a shift from theoretical premises and unexamined assumptions to a theoretical perspective predicated on extensive research relevant to an interactive view of reading.

At the core of an interactive view of reading is the constructivist assumption that comprehension consists of representing or organizing information in terms of one's previously acquired knowledge. This view assumes that readers collect evidence about what the text might mean as they are reading. Some of this evidence comes from information in the text. But as ideas enter working memory, they trigger associations, causing readers to invoke knowledge that is already a part of their memory. Therefore, reading comprehension depends on readers' ability to appropriately interrelate their previously acquired knowledge and the information suggested by the text (Mason, 1984).

A synthesis of current research suggests that reading is the process of constructing meaning through the dynamic interaction among the reader, the text, and the context of the reading situation (Anderson et al., 1985; Wixson and Peters, 1984). This perspective suggests that readers construct meaning when they comprehend much the same way writers construct meaning when they compose. Accordingly, meaning is not in the text to be extracted through a series of analyses. Rather, it is built in the mind of the reader on the basis of information from the reader, the text, and the reading context. Each adds significantly to the construction of a coherent "text."

The Reader.   An interactive view of reading suggests that a variety of reader factors interact with each other and with factors outside the reader to influence reading. Prior knowledge, knowledge about reading, and attitudes and motivation are among the reader factors that are most important in determining learning and performance in reading.

It has been known for many years that the nature and extent of a reader's prior knowledge or schema has a significant effect on the meaning that is constructed for a given text (Ausubel, 1963; Barlett, 1932; Bransford and Johnson, 1972; Anderson, Spiro, and Montague, 1977). Numerous studies with adults have demonstrated that texts are interpreted within the context of the reader's past experiences and prior knowledge (see, for example, Anderson, Reynolds, Schallert, and Goetz, 1977). Similarly, studies with school-aged children indicate that higher levels of accurate prior knowledge result in increased comprehension, particularly the ability to draw inferences from the text (see, Lipson, 1982, 1983; Pearson, Hansen, and Gordon, 1979).

Johnston's (1984) research indicates that prior knowledge is an important source of test bias and independent of the effects of intelligence. He concludes that it is neither possible nor desirable to eliminate the prior knowledge factor. Rather, it should be measured and taken into account as a valuable source of information for test interpretation.

Research also suggests that readers' metacognitive knowledge about the process of reading influences performance. Skilled readers know a great deal about the reading process, and this knowledge influences their ability to select and use appropriate strategies and skills in different reading situations (Myers and Paris, 1978). Specifically, skilled readers have knowledge about the purposes of reading, the various text and task factors that influence reading, the different skills and strategies used for reading, and when, why, and how to use different reading strategies (Brown, Armbruster, and Baker, 1984; Garner and Reis, 1981).

The most persuasive evidence for the relation between metacognitive abilities and reading skills comes from the numerous instructional studies that have demonstrated that various forms of metacognitive training result in improved performance on a wide variety of comprehension measures (for example, Palincsar and Brown, 1984; Paris, Cross, and Lipson, 1984; Hansen and Pearson, 1983; Raphael and Pearson, 1985). These studies suggest that readers learn more efficiently and effectively when they have metacognitive skills, such as the ability to accurately determine the complexity of certain tasks, formulate a plan for reading, select the appropriate strategies, judge the quality of their performance, and develop corrective action if needed.

Reader's attitudes toward reading are also a central factor affecting reading performance. Good readers generally have more positive attitudes toward reading than poor readers (Alexander and Filler, 1976). Attitudes, beliefs, and expectancies become more negative with failure; they result in less effort, which in turn maintains a cycle of failure (Dweck and Bempechat, 1983). A related finding is that high interest in reading materials results in greater desire to read and in increased comprehension (Asher, 1980).

Research also indicates that positive self-perceptions promote achievement-oriented behavior, whereas low self-perceptions lead to decreased motivation (Harter, 1981). Positive attitudes and self-perceptions are associated with one's sense of control over their successes and failures. The debilitating effect of a perceived lack of control has been demonstrated in studies of learned helplessness (Seligman, 1975) and causal attributions

(Weiner, 1979). According to learned helplessness theory, repeated and prolonged failure leads to perceptions that outcomes are unrelated to an individual's actions. This results in a general expectation that all events that happen to oneself are uncontrollable, which in turn produces passive behavior.

The Text. Current research suggests that there are a number of text factors that have a significant effect on both how much and what readers understand and learn from a text. This has lead to current descriptions of texts as being either "considerate" or "inconsiderate" (Armbruster, 1984). Considerate texts are designed to enable the reader to gather appropriate information with minimal effort; in contrast, inconsiderate texts require the reader to put forth extra effort to compensate for the inadequacies of the text. Among the factors that determine if a text will be considerate or not are text type and organization, text structure, and text coherence.

A major factor in determining students' reading performance is the type of text being read. Research in this area suggests that major differences exist between narrative and expository text. Narrative text is often characterized by specific elements of information such as problem, conflict, and resolution. Expository text, by contrast, is generally described in terms of organizational or rhetorical structures such as causal (what started the civil war), comparative (how Russian and U.S. governments differ), or descriptive (the stages of photosynthesis). Not only are there important differences between narrative and informational texts, but these differences affect reading performance (Berkowitz and Taylor, 1981; Olson, 1985).

There are also important differences within text types. The various types of narrative texts — fables, adventure stories, and mysteries — all have different organizational patterns. Expository materials also have a variety of organizational patterns including causal, comparative, problem/solution (Meyer and Rice, 1984). In addition, different types of expository text reflect the domain of knowledge or discipline they represent (Anderson and Armbruster, 1984). A physics text may use a causal organization to describe laws that explain natural phenomenon in a predictable manner, however, a causal organization may be used quite differently in a history text, since the past does not predict the future for a historian.

Hierarchical text structure is another factor that influences how readers derive meaning from text. Most texts are structured around a small set of topics that have clearly discernible levels of information (Kintsch and van Dijk, 1978; Lorch and Lorch, 1985). One point that research seems to be relatively clear about is that information located at the top levels of the hierarchy is recalled and retained better than information at lower levels.

In other words, hierarchical structure influences what and how much is learned from reading.

A third factor that influences meaning construction is text coherence, or how clearly the information is presented. Research suggests that the quality and type of information recalled is influenced by how well a text is organized (Beck et al., 1984; Lorch, Lorch, and Mathews, 1985). It has been demonstrated that readers comprehend and recall a text better when topic sentences are present rather than absent (see, for example, Bridge et al., 1984; Lorch and Lorch, 1985; Schwarz and Flammer, 1981). In addition, comprehension of major ideas is enhanced when they are stated explicitly at the beginning of paragraphs or text sections, and when they are highlighted or cued (see, Aulls, 1975; Baumann, 1986; Williams, Taylor, and Ganger, 1981). Finally, texts with logically ordered paragraphs are better recalled than texts with less well-ordered paragraphs (Brooks and Dansereau, 1983; Kintsch, Mandel, and Kozminsky, 1977).

The Context. Reading performance also varies as a function of contextual factors such as the purposes for reading and the tasks that are associated with reading. It has been demonstrated that children are better able to identify the main idea of simple expository paragraphs when they are asked to choose the best title than when they are asked to write a summary sentence (Williams, Taylor, and deCani, 1984; Williams et al., 1981). In addition, research suggests that the type and content of questions readers are asked subsequent to reading can influence the nature of their comprehension and learning (Drum, Calfee, and Cook, 1981; Langer, 1985; Wixson, 1983, 1984).

The various dimensions of the setting in which reading takes place can also affect reading performance. Researchers have found differences in readers' performance on a task depending on whether it is administered as part of an informal instruction lesson or as part of a formal testing situation (Mosenthal and Na, 1980). It has been demonstrated that the instructions provided to students' prior to reading influence the information they remember from text (Frederiksen, 1975).

In summary, an interactive view of reading suggests that reading is a constructive process in which meaning is generated from the interaction among the reader, the text, and the context of the reading situation. This means that reading is not a static process; rather, it is a dynamic process that changes as a function of many different reader, text, and contextual factors. This view stands in direct contrast to the view of reading currently dominating reading assessment and instruction in American schools. The traditional view implies that students can be taught or tested on specific skills under one set of reading conditions and that their learning or performance will generalize to all reading conditions. The newer view suggests that things are not that simple and demands assessment and instruction that reflect the true complexity of reading processes.

The Objectives

Following the specification of the conceptual framework the next step was to develop a set of essential goals and objectives that reflected current interactive theory and research about reading. Although the final products look somewhat different (see Appendix A), both sets of goals are designed to describe, as closely as possible, the characteristics of skilled readers as we know them today.

The important characteristics of skilled readers reflected in the reading goals that serve as the basis for the new Michigan and Illinois reading tests are as follows: *First*, good readers are able to integrate their knowledge and skills as they construct meaning for different text under a variety of reading conditions; *Second*, good readers have knowledge about the various purposes for reading, about how different reader, text, and contextual factors influence their reading, and about the skills and strategies they can use in their reading; *Third*, good readers have positive reading habits and attitudes about reading and positive perceptions of themselves as readers.

Constructing meaning, knowledge about the reading process, and reading habits and attitudes are presented as separate goals and objectives; however, they actually function interactively rather than independently. In fact, it is precisely this concept that distinguishes an interactive view of reading from those of the past.

Previous conceptualizations maintained that students needed to achieve competence in each of several skill components (specific decoding and comprehension skills) to read successfully; the whole was not complete without the aggregation of the many identified parts. In contrast, an interactive view acknowledges the possibility of "compensation." Some readers may succeed because they have such well-developed knowledge about the topics they are asked to read about; others, because they are especially good at solving problems; still others, because they have highly positive expectations about themselves.

The Test Components

Once the goals and objectives for reading were completed, the next task for the Michigan and Illinois projects was to develop an assessment instrument that accurately reflected the holistic, interactive view of reading evident in the new goals and objectives. The basic components of the new tests are (1) the reading selections; (2) constructing meaning items; (3) items evaluating metacognitive knowledge about the reading process; (4) reading habits and attitudes items; and (5) items assessing students' familiarity with the topics of the reading selections. The Constructing Meaning subtests reflect the overall goal of reading instruction—holistic understanding of naturally occurring materials. The other three subtests are designed as an aid to the interpretation of performance on Constructing Meaning.

Text Selection and Analysis

The selection and analysis of the reading materials were critical steps in the Michigan and Illinois test projects. The research on the characteristics of text that influence comprehension provided the basis for both the selection criteria and the mapping procedures used for identifying and analyzing passages for the new reading tests.

Selection Criteria. The research on text type, structure, and coherence led both Michigan and Illinois to develop several criteria to assist with text selection. Texts were selected if they were hierarchically structured and coherent and if they accurately reflected domain knowledge.

In addition to the research rationale for text selection, there were a number of instructionally based criteria. First, the test passages had to be representative of the materials students at the tested grade levels were likely to encounter in their classrooms. Second, there would be two types of test passages—thematic narratives and subject area textbook selections. Although there were numerous other types of texts that might be selected, because of the limited number of passages that were to be used at each level, only those that were the most widely used in the curriculum were selected. The final instructional criterion called for intact stories and content selections from five hundred to two thousand words in length. These selection criteria contrast sharply with the criteria of efficiency and readability that dominate text selection processes in currently available tests.

Text Mapping. Procedures for mapping both narrative and expository texts were developed (1) to provide a holistic representation of the text, (2) to provide a systematic method for distinguishing between important and unimportant information in a selection, and (3) to identify and highlight important organizational features of a selection, (for example, important concepts, causal relationships, and adjunct aids such as maps, graphs, and literary devices). These mapping procedures provided the basis for text selection and item development. They also have the potential to provide a model for how to analyze texts in preparation for instruction consistent with the content of the new tests.

The procedures for mapping stories were based on research and analysis from the fields of linguistics, literary theory, and cognitive psychology. The key elements of the story maps are themes, problem, resolution, major events, setting, and major characters. Appendix B presents the map for a third grade story, "Making Friends" (Fladland, 1984), which is used as an example throughout the description of the test items. As revealed by the map, this is a story about a young boy who has just moved to a new neighborhood and how he tries to make a new friend.

Story maps are designed to emphasize the interrelations among ideas in a story. Rather than treating setting as merely a locational feature, it is related to the other elements of the plot and the themes. Similarly, the category of character development provides information about how the characters are portrayed in the major events of the story, their various roles, and how they function in relation to the themes. Collectively, the elements of information on the story map provide a holistic representation of the text and the processes involved in constructing meaning for narratives.

The structural differences between narrative and expository texts required the development of separate procedures for mapping expository or informational materials. Concepts and the relations among concepts comprise the basis for constructing a holistic representation of informational text. This is done by producing a diagram of the text to highlight important relations among superordinate, coordinate and subordinate concepts. An example of a concept map for a tenth grade selection, "French Revolution" (Leinwand, 1974), that is used throughout the description of the test items is provided in Appendix B. As revealed by the map, this selection is about the problems created by the old regime that set in motion a series of events that ultimately led to the French Revolution.

The information that is most important to the author's central points is placed at the top of the map. Importance is determined by following the structure of the text (for example, titles, subtitles, ideas within the body of the text). As the map indicates, "French Revolution" is organized according to the reasons for the revolution. By organizing information hierarchically it is possible to identify the various levels of information within a given text. Concept maps identify three levels of information: central purpose, major ideas, and supporting ideas.

Relations among ideas within a text are specified on the concept map by "links" (that is, reasons, results, examples, and characteristics) that reveal the overall clarity and interrelatedness of the ideas. The relational links also make clear some of the structural differences the exist within the across various disciplines. The map of French Revolution does not merely reflect a causal organization, but more importantly, it organizes information into categories representative of how historians analyze and interpret historical events.

The procedures for mapping narrative and informational texts developed for the Michigan and Illinois reading tests proved effective in aiding the selection and analysis of test passages. If the various story map categories proved difficult to identify or were missing, or if the relational links were difficult to determine or concepts hard to place within the map, the passages were rejected. Despite these procedures, however, it should be noted that not all test passages could be classified as considerate texts.

Mapping also served as the basis for developing test questions focused on the information central to understanding the texts. Finally, the mapping procedures developed for these tests have instructional implications for a variety of practices, such as evaluating group discussions or individual summaries, analyzing the questions provided in teachers' manuals, and developing comprehension activities focused on important content and process goals.

Constructing Meaning

The Constructing Meaning subtests are designed to evaluate students' ability to generate an integrated understanding of both narrative and informational texts. Constructing Meaning questions are developed from text maps that highlight the important elements of information and the relations among them within each text. These questions require students to integrate information across large segments of text; they also require students to engage in the complex reasoning and inferential elaboration that are the essence of constructive processing.

In keeping with the research, the map became the stimulus for the development of Construction Meaning questions for the new Michigan and Illinois tests. There were no attempts to impose a prespecified ratio for types of questions (for example, 30 percent literal, 40 percent inferential, and the like). Instead, questions focus on the understanding of important ideas and their relations within a text.

Another goal was to develop Constructing Meaning questions that are consistent with good instructional practice. Test questions are designed to reflect the constructive processing that occurs when readers reason their way through text, rather than focusing on either isolated skills or unimportant elements of information. Instructionally, these types of items imply that students should be learning how to problem-solve their way through well-developed materials rather than be drilled on isolated skill exercises.

The Constructing Meaning questions on the Illinois and Michigan tests focus on the categories of information on the text maps (themes, major ideas). In addition, the multiple choice questions on the Michigan tests are classified by the type of processing required to answer each question correctly: intersentence questions require the reader to construct meaning from information provided within one to three contiguous sentences in the text; text questions require the reader to integrate information within sections of text larger than several sentences as well as across an entire text; and beyond-text questions require readers to rely heavily on information from their own experiences in addition to information in the text.

Although the Illinois items reflect these three levels of processing, they cannot be classified in this manner because of the question format used on the Illinois tests. The format permits the reader to select one, two, or three correct responses for each multiple choice question. Thus, answers to a given question often represent more than one level of reasoning.

In the interest of space, sample items are provided for only one type of passage from each state test. The sample items for the story, "Making Friends," are modeled after the Illinois tests, and the sample items for the informational selectio, "French Revolution," are modeled after the Michigan tests. However, it is important to remember that both states employ both narrative and informational reading selections.

Sample Items for Narrative Texts. The sample questions presented below are taken from the third grade story, "Making Friends." These items are representative of the fifteen Constructing Meaning questions developed for each narrative selection on the Illinois tests. The first question focuses on the problem in the story, that of making a new friend. This item requires readers to understand the motivation for the actions of the main character, Andy, and the unfolding of events in the story.

Why did Andy start building a friend?

*a.   He misunderstood what his father said.
 b.   He wanted to get rid of old boxes.
*c.   He was lonely in his new home.
 d.   He wanted to practice giving things away.
*e.   He wanted to surprise his parents.

Rather than asking readers to simply identify the character's behavior, this question requires an understanding of the problem that precipitated it. In this particular case, the reader must understand the literal problem as well as the more subtle inferential problem — that Andy misunderstood what his father meant by "making a friend."

Some questions require readers to use the information throughout the text along with their knowledge of the main theme, "friendship," to go beyond text-based information or inferences. The beyond-text transfer question below is an example of one that requires the reader to use the text as a basis for a prediction.

What will probably happen to Andy and Carla after the story ends?

 a.   Andy and Carla will never speak to one another again.
 b.   Andy will move away in a few weeks and never see Carla again.
*c.   Andy and Carla will play together tomorrow.
 d.   Andy and Carla will go to Disneyland together.
 e.   Carla will introduce Andy to some of her friends.

Character questions ask about character traits or motivations that influence major events or the resolution of the story problem. Unlike typical character questions, these go beyond simple character identification to an understanding of how the character contributes to the story. This question requires the reader to focus on one key event in the story and the main character's motivation for his action.

Why did Andy accept Carla's offer to help him build his friend?

*a.   He needed glue and she had some.
*b.   He was secretly hoping that Carla would become his real friend.
 c.   He knew that Carla was good at gluing.
 d.   He needed a bigger block of wood.
 e.   His mother told him that Carla was a nice person.

Questions about major events in a story focus on the events that form a "causal chain," or a related set of events and consequences. Such questions require more than an understanding of the sequence of events, they require an understanding of how each event advances the progress toward the development of the plot and resolution of the problem.

Why didn't Andy want to ask his mom for glue?

a.   His mom probably didn't have any.
*b.   He was afraid his mom would tell his dad about the surprise.
*c.   He wanted to surprise his mom with the friend he was making.
d.   His mother would want to put his friend together for him.
e.   Because he thought his mom was too busy to help.

Sample Items for Informational Texts. The following examples for the tenth grade French Revolution passage are representative of the twenty Constructing Meaning items that follow each informational selection on the Michigan tests.

The first example is a central purpose question. Central purpose questions for the French Revolution passage focus on the causal relations between the top levels of information on the concept map. These relations provide the top-level structure of the text and reflect both the content of the text and the structure of the discipline represented by the text.

The example provided here is a central purpose, beyond-text question. This question requires readers to restructure the top-level information in the text into conceptual categories that are consistent with the way historians interpret many historical events. One way to reorganize the information is by social and economic causes. Because these terms are not directly mentioned in the text, readers must use their knowledge of history to restructure the information, making it a beyond-text question.

The two major causes of the French Revolution can be categorized as

*a.   social and economic.
b.   reactionary and revolutionary.
c.   liberal and conservative.
d.   judicial and legislative.

Major-idea questions ask readers to identify the relations between and within the second and third levels of information on the concept map. To answer the following question readers have to synthesize information that is located within one of the major sections of the text. It requires them to identify an important event that led to the French Revolution, the demand by the Third Estate for additional rights.

What happened when the Estates General was called by Louis XVI?

    a. The First Estate protested the issuing of the cahiers.
    b. Louis XVI received the money he needed.
    c. The Estates General voted to support the American Revolution.
  *d. The Third Estate demanded additional rights.

Supporting-idea questions focus on information depicted in the relations between and within the third and lower levels on the concept map. Supporting-idea questions are not focused on any details, as is often the case in existing reading tests, but are about ideas that support the understanding of the major ideas and central purposes of the text. For example, a supporting-idea intersentence question for the French Revolution asks the reader to identify an important weakness within King Louis XVI's personality that contributed to the outbreak of the revolution.

Some of King Louis XVI's problems came about because he

    a. refused to listen to Marie Antoinette.
    b. wanted to expand the power of the monarchy.
  *c. ignored the advice of this financial advisors.
    d. gave new power to the National Assembly.

Knowledge about Reading

The metacognitive components of these tests are designed to measure students' knowledge about how various reader, text, and contextual factors influence their reading and about strategy usage in different reading situations. In other words, this component measures what students know about how to read different materials.

Several important issues had to be addressed in developing metacognitive items. First, it is impossible to directly assess, with a paper-and-pencil test, students' monitoring of interrelations among purpose, text, task, and strategy. Therefore, the metacognitive test questions are limited to knowledge or understanding of the reading process, and strategic processing must be inferred from the ability to respond to different types of questions.

Second, it is important for the knowledge questions to provide a good model for instruction. We were concerned that the generic items commonly used in metacognitive measures (What is reading? What's hard about reading?) would lead to what we called "silly coaching," rather than meaningful instruction. For example, if a question asked about the various organizational patterns used by authors (description, causation, comparison), it would be possible to drill students on the answers to these types of question and for students to answer them correctly without learning anything that is likely to improve their reading.

To avoid this problem and to provide examples of how this type of information should be taught/learned, the knowledge items are constructed to accompany each of the test passages. So, when students are asked questions such as how the author organized a particular section of a test passage to provide certain information, the best preparation for answering these types of questions is repeated experience recognizing authors' use of different organizational patterns to communicate their ideas in "real" texts. These types of questions also ensure that students have a common reference point for answering knowledge questions.

Illinois Items. The Illinois Reading Strategy items are placed immediately after the Constructing Meaning questions and are specific to the passage read. These items were developed to assess students' knowledge within two metacognitive domains: (1) useful strategies to solve potential problems encountered while reading; and (2) the discrimination among important, or central, ideas and less important, or less central, ideas presented in the text.

Responses to Strategy items are scored using a discrepancy from-expert model. Data from three groups of "experts" (students placed two to three grade levels above the targeted grade, adults, and test developers) were used to develop the answer key. Students are given full credit for answers that match the expert key exactly and partial credit for those that approximate the key. This procedure acknowledges the evolving expertise in reading strategies that have been indicated from research.

One of three types of problems readers might encounter are posed in items evaluating students' knowledge of the problem-solving domain: answering a question, understanding an ambiguous figure of speech, word, or section of text, or having limited time to study for an exam about the passage. Five strategies for solving the problem are presented and students are asked to rate the helpfulness of each of the strategies. By posing the metacognitive problem in this way, readers can demonstrate their flexibility and sensitivity to various reading tasks. For example,

You have just read "Making Friends." Imagine that one of the questions you have to answer is,

What did Andy do when he couldn't find anything to use as the legs for his friend?

How much would it help if you were to...

start to reread the story from the beginning

  a. won't help at all
*b. will help a little bit
  c. will help quite a bit
  d. will help a lot

reread the part of the story where Andy looks in the backyard

  a. won't help at all
  b. will help a little bit
  c. will help quite a bit
*d. will help a lot

look quickly through the paragraphs

  a. won't help at all
  b. will help a little bit
*c. will help quite a bit
  d. will help a lot

look up the meaning of "legs" in the dictionary

*a. won't help at all
  b. will help a little bit
  c. will help quite a bit
*d. will help a lot

reread the part of the story where Andy shows his dad what he made

*a. won't help at all
  b. will help a little bit
  c. will help quite a bit
  d. will help a lot.

The second domain, centrality, is also presented in one of three possible scenarios: summarizing the passage, note taking, and understanding the author's message. Each of these requires the reader to discern important information from less important information, a strategy used by skilled readers. For example,

You have just read "Making Friends," but two of your classmates have not read it. Imagine that you are asked to tell them what the story is mainly about.
How much would it help them understand what the story is mainly about if you said,
"It is about Andy looking in the kitchen and finding a paper towel roll. He was thinking that he would cut it in half to make arms for his friend."

    a. won't help at all
    b. will help a little bit
    c. will help quite a bit
  *d. will help a lot

"It is about Andy finding a roll from paper towels and a cottage cheese bowl. He was looking for buttons to help his mother with the unpacking."

    a. won't help at all
    b. will help a little bit
    c. will help quite a bit
  *d. will help a lot

"It is about a boy who meets a real friend while building a pretend friend."

    a. won't help at all
    b. will help a little bit
    c. will help quite a bit
  *d. will help a lot

"It is about Andy moving into a new neighborhood. He found an owl, some buttons, and a branch from a tree."

  *a. won't help at all
    b. will help a little bit
    c. will help quite a bit
    d. will help a lot

"It is about a boy who searches for odds and end to help him build a pretend friend. A girl helps him put the parts together and he learns what a real friend is."

   *a. won't help at all
   b. will help a little bit
   c. will help quite a bit
   d. will help a lot

Michigan Items. The fourteen knowledge items for each passage are administered immediately following the Constructing Meaning items. There are several types of knowledge items. However, there was no attempt to construct an item of each type for each passage. Rather, items were constructed to reflect the most important types of metacognitive knowledge associated with each passage.

The first type of knowledge question focuses on readers' awareness of the influence that their own knowledge, experiences, and interests have on their reading comprehension. In narrative material, readers use their world knowledge to construct a fictional world, so they can understand the characters, their situations, and actions. Similarly, informational materials require the use of domain-specific information about a particular topic.

The following question for the "French Revolution" is intended to determine if students are aware of the type of knowledge they need to interpret the selection.

Which of the following would help you MOST in understanding this story?

   a. knowing that revolutions are often violent
   b. understanding how a monarchy and feudalism differ
   *c. knowing that revolutions can change governments
   d. understanding how the French and English revolutions are different

The second category of knowledge questions focuses on readers' understanding of different dimensions of text and how they influence their comprehension. Consistent with the research, these types of knowledge questions focus on text type and location, text structure—for example, the function of organizational patterns within text, and text features such as linguistic devices, adjunct aids, and literary devices.

The questions on knowledge of text type and location focus on basic distinctions (for example, narrative versus informational text) at the elementary level, and finer distinctions (for example, mystery versus science fiction) at the upper-grade levels. The purpose of these questions is not merely to name different types of literary genre, but more importantly to communicate the importance of teaching students about the features of different types of texts.

Questions about text structure focus on both the larger or macro-level organization of the texts — that is, the relations among story components in narratives and the dominant organization pattern, if any, in informational texts, and the smaller or micro-level organizational patterns that occur within small sections or subsections of the texts. These questions are designed to evaluate students' awareness of text structure and the role it plays in understanding important textual information. The first question below examines readers' knowledge of the top-level structure of the "French Revolution," and the second question examines readers' understanding of how a particular section of the text is organized to explain a specific concept.

The author of this chapter helps you to understand the French Revolution by

   a.   analyzing historical documents from the French Revolution.
  *b.   explaining cause and effect relationships among historical events.
   c.   comparing important historical ideas.
   d.   providing biographical information about key figures.

Section 2 of this passage describes the Old Regime by

  *a.   listing different groups.
   b.   comparing different groups.
   c.   linking sequences of events.
   d.   outlining a series of causes.

The questions about knowledge of text features focus on adjunct aids and linguistic and literary devices. Questions are constructed only for text features that are significant to the understanding of important textual information, as determined by the text map. Questions about adjunct aids focus on readers' awareness of features such as illustrations, figures, charts, headings, subheadings, marginal notes, italics, political cartoons, introductions, summaries, and inserted questions and the role they play in helping the reader understand important textual information. The following example from the French Revolution section focuses on the function of a particular question that has been inserted in the text.

The primary purpose of question 6 on page 377 is to help the reader understand

  a. the primary cause of the French Revolution.
  b. the major reason for the French Revolution.
 *c. the French Revolution in light of a specific issue.
  d. the two major views of the French Revolution.

Questions about linguistic devices evaluate readers' awareness of text features such as the use of connectives or referential terms (so, because, then, next, he, it, this, that, there) and how these devices influence comprehension. This example from the "French Revolution" evaluates readers' understanding of the author's use of specific connective terms.

In Section 3, the author uses the words "yet" and "but" to

 *a. contrast the Third Estate's power and functions.
  b. clarify the privileges of the Third Estate.
  c. contrast the influence of the First and Third Estates.
  d. describe the influence of the monarchy.

Knowledge questions have also been constructed that focus on reader knowledge of the use and function of literary devices such as figurative language, imagery, or techniques (as flashback and foreshadowing). Again, it is not the goal to find a literary device in every selection; instead, it is to ask questions about them when they are important to a holistic understanding of the text.

The final category of knowledge questions focuses on readers' knowledge about strategies and their use under different reading conditions. For example, in the French Revolution passage, students are asked to determine the best way to find the answer to a particular question.

How could you BEST answer the question under the timeline on page 363?

  a. Skim the subtitles in the passage.
  b. Study the figure on page 362.
  c. Reread Section 5 of this passage.
 *d. Read the next section of this chapter.

Attitudes and Habits

The new Michigan and Illinois reading tests are also designed to assess students' literacy habits, attitudes, and self-perceptions. The items on these subtests are intended to communicate that students' habits and attitudes toward reading have an important influence on their reading behavior and that they must be taken into consideration in planning instruction and in interpreting performance.

Items on the Michigan tests are tied directly to each of the test passages and focus on students' interest in each of the reading selections, their perceptions of how well they understood each passage and answered the accompanying questions, and the amount of effort they put forward in reading the selection and answering the questions. Items on the Illinois tests are general, rather than specific to each test passage, and focus on students' reading and writing behaviors in school and the various ways in which students use reading and writing in their lives.

Michigan Items.   The attitude items are a standard set of twelve questions asked in relation to each of the passages on the tests. Students at all grade levels are asked to indicate if they strongly agree, agree, disagree, or strongly disagree with each statement.

The first four attitude items evaluate students' perceptions of their own ability to understand the selection and answer questions, such as, "It was easy for me to answer the questions for the French Revolution," "I had a hard time understanding the main ideas in the French Revolution."

The middle four attitude items are designed to determine the amount of effort students put forth in reading the selection and answering the questions. Examples of these items are statements such as "I worked carefully so I would do well on the test questions for the French Revolution," and "I put very little effort into understanding the main ideas of the French Revolution."

The last four attitude items examine the students' level of interest in the selection. The following are examples of these items: "I would like to tell someone else about the ideas in the French Revolution" and "Reading more passages like the French Revolution would be boring."

Illinois Items.   The literacy items are similar for all grade levels. They assess literacy habits and attitudes in four reading and writing areas shown to have an influence on achievement: in-school activities, out-of-school activities, strategies used while reading and writing, and uses of reading and writing. Students are asked to indicate how often they read for enjoyment, use a reference book in school, read something for homework, write in a journal at home, or use reading to learn new information. Information gathered from these items helps provide an understanding of the student behaviors that may be influencing reading achievement and it may suggest interventions to increase the amount and type of literacy activities students experience.

Topic Familiarity

The prior knowledge components of the new Michigan and Illinois tests assess students' familiarity with the important concepts that underlie the central focus of each test passage. These subtests are designed to evaluate both the breadth and depth of students' knowledge about specific concepts rather than general background knowledge. Level of prior knowledge is used neither to penalize nor to reward students, but rather to help interpret students' comprehension of each of the test passages.

The concepts evaluated on the topic familiarity subtests are selected from the themes and central purposes identified on the story and concepts maps. Concepts selected for inclusion may not even appear in the text itself but are important to understand the text. The procedures used to select concepts and the formats of the topic familiarity items provide a model for teachers to use in designing prereading assessment and instruction for the classroom.

Michigan Items. The fifteen topic familiarity items for each passage are administered together in the first session. The three types of items are characteristics, examples, and relations. The key concept in the samples below from the French Revolution section is "independence."

The first type of question asks the reader to identify the characteristics or critical attributes of a target concept. The attributes used in these items are selected to reflect a range of understanding. For example,

Does self-governing help to tell about *independence*?

*a. yes   b. no

Does giving in to others help to tell about *independence*?

a. yes   *b. no

The second type of question asks the reader to identify examples of the target concept. Again, examples were designed to reflect a range of understanding.

Is Canada's separation from England an example of *independence*?

*a. yes   b. no

The third type of item focuses on the relations among key concepts. An understanding of the relations evaluated in these items is important for understanding the themes or central purposes of the passages.

Protest can be used to gain independence.

*a. yes   b. no

Relational items are also important because they suggest to teachers the importance of helping students build an integrated knowledge base as the basis for understanding new concepts.

Illinois Items. Prior to reading each passage, students are presented with fifteen topic familiarity items designed to activate and assess their knowledge of the concepts important to understanding the passage. At the third-grade level, this section is read aloud to the students to minimize the influence of reading ability; at the other grade levels, students read independently but are permitted to ask for help as needed.

The question prompt directs readers to think about what they know about the topic, storyline, theme, or type of text and then to predict what ideas might be encountered as they read the passage. The purpose is not to predict precisely what will be presented in the passage, but rather to use prior knowledge to anticipate what might likely be included.

The predictions are presented as fifteen multiple choice questions representing three levels of knowledge: expert, average, and novice. Students respond to these questions by indicating how likely it is that the ideas might be included in such a passage by answering; yes, maybe, or no. This three-by-three matrix for item generation permits the assessment of both the depth and breadth of the students knowledge. As in the reading strategy items, these items are scored using a discrepancy model, giving readers partial credit for responses that approach those of expert readers. The example below is from the Making Friends story.

"Today you are going to read a story like the stories you read in your reading books at school. This story is about a boy who has just moved to a new neighborhood and how he tries to make a new friend. Think about what the boy might do, how the boy might feel and what might happen in such a story. Below are several ideas. For each idea, decide whether or not you might find it in this kind of story. Then fill in the bubble below the answer that tells what you think. Your choices are:

YES   = I think the idea would probably be in a story like this.
MAYBE = The idea could be in a story like this.
NO   = I don't think the idea would be in a story like this.

1. He misses his old friends.
   YES*   MAYBE   NO
2. He asks the boy next door to walk to school with him.
   YES   MAYBE*   NO
3. He calls the fire department.
   YES   MAYBE   NO*
4. Some children playing ball do not ask him to play.
   YES   MAYBE*   NO

Testing Procedures

Administration

Michigan. State reading tests are administered each year to every pupil at the beginning of grades four, seven, and ten. All students within each grade-level receive the same sets of passages and items within a given year. However, it is expected that the sets of passages and items for the new tests will never be reused more than once, if at all.

Each test consists of two passages, one narrative and one informational selection. The topic familiarity items for both passages are administered first, followed by the passages and the constructing meaning, knowledge, and attitude items. Each passage is followed by forty-six items — twenty constructing meaning, fourteen knowledge about reading, and twelve attitude items.

Illinois. The original administration design called for each student to read and respond to questions from one narrative passage and one expository passage. Using a pool of approximately six passages per grade level, passages were randomly assigned to students within classrooms for grades six, eight, and eleven. Because the grade-three test requires the teachers to read aloud, passages were randomly assigned to classrooms rather than students. However, due to classroom time constraints, the Illinois State Board of Education decided that each student would respond to one rather than two passages.

The first statewide census testing was implemented in April 1988. With the exception of identified special education students and those of limited English proficiency, all Illinois students in grades three, six, and eight took the test. Implementation of the grade eleven test is scheduled for Spring 1990.

Scoring and Reporting

Michigan. The MEAP reports scores at the individual, classroom, school, and district levels. Proposed scoring and reporting procedures were being piloted at the time of this writing for possible use with the approved tests in the fall of 1989. Although pass/fail cutoff scores had not been determined yet, it was anticipated that students would have to meet some minimum criterion on the constructing meaning items for each passage in order to pass the test.

The constructing meaning scores are primary and are reported in numbers. The scores from the other three subtests (topic familiarity, knowledge about reading, and attitudes and self-perceptions) are to be used to interpret constructing meaning scores and are reported as either high, moderate, or low. In the case of attitudes and self-perceptions, a high score indicates that the students believed in their ability to read the passage and answer the questions correctly, tried hard to do well, and were interested in the reading selection. The pilot individual report form uses a bar graph to depict the constructing meaning scores for each of the two passages. These bar graphs are also subdivided to reveal the proportion of different types of questions (that is, inter-sentence, text, and beyond-text) that were answered correctly for each passage. The level of perform-ance (high, moderate, low) on the interpretive subtests for each passage (topic familiarity, knowledge about reading, and attitudes and self-perceptions) is reported directly under the bar showing the constructing meaning score for each passage. The individual report also indicates the student's status with regard to passing each passage, the total test, and their category of achievement.

The pilot class report form provides detailed information for each student in a class on individual performance on the total test (passing and category of achievement) and individual performance on each passage. Scores on each of the subtests are provided for each passage. In addition, constructing meaning scores are reported for each passage in terms of question type, total, and passing. The class report also provides summary information regarding the total number and percentage of students passing the entire test and each passage, and the number and percentage of students scoring high, moderate, and low on the interpretive subtest who passed each passage.

The pilot school summary report provides summary charts showing the percentage of students falling in each category of achievement and comparing the current year's performance with previous years. This report also provides a frequency distribution of Constructing Meaning scores for each selection and summary information on the percentage of students scoring high, moderate, or low on each interpretive subtest for each passage.

Illinois. Scores on the Illinois Goal Assessment Program in Reading are reported at the school, district, and state levels; no reports are available for individual students or for individual classrooms (unless, of course, there is only one classroom of the targeted grade level in the school or the district). Because of the sampling design, school and district scores are adjusted for differences in the difficulty level of each passage. At the third-grade level there is some teacher pacing of the test and therefore all students in a class receive the same test. Estimations are calculated on the basis of classes within schools and districts.

The primary assessment outcome is the constructing meaning score and the other scores (topic familiarity, reading strategies and literacy experiences) are reported as a means to help interpret the constructing meaning score.

Constructing meaning scores are reported as scaled scores (and score bands) to enable the comparison with the aggregate score obtained by those in the same school district, the state, or the nation; since these scaled scores are anchored in terms of 1988 performance, they may be used to evaluate progress for these different aggregate units across time. The national scaled score is a predicted score based on an equating study of the Illinois test with a nationally normed test of reading comprehension, thus providing information about Illinois students compared with national performance standards.

Reading strategy and topic familiarity results are reported in terms of their distribution and their relationship to constructing meaning. Scores are divided into three categories: those falling in the lowest 25 percent, those in the middle 50 percent, and those in the top 25 percent of the distribution. The percentage of students falling into each reading strategy or topic familiarity category is reported along with the average constructing meaning score for students in each category. These scores are reported for students at the school, district, and state levels. This combination of scores helps educators understand not only how much students know in each of these areas but, more importantly, how well they are able to use these strategies and knowledge to construct meaning.

The literacy experiences section of the report provides descriptive data about various reading and writing activities which have been found to correlate positively with constructing meaning. Results are reported as the percentage of students in each school who engage in selected activities.

What We Have Learned

The Michigan and Illinois projects are by no means perfect. However, they do represent real breakthroughs and examples of how change can occur. In this section, we reflect on what we have learned from these projects about the nature of change in the development of statewide objectives and assessments. The point we wish to make is that ultimately the process works, but it is not easy and it does not result in universal satisfaction. This is due in part to the highly political context that to a larger extent dictates the procedures one must adopt to implement change. It would be naive to assume that projects similar to these could or should operate outside this highly charged political context. One cannot influence change in a political setting without entering that arena. From our experiences we have developed one common insight: while all politics is not assessment, all assessment is politics. This discussion focuses on three factors that are inextricably linked to the process of change undertaken in these projects. They are collaboration, compromise, and resources.

The Need for Collaboration

The political nature of the process for changing statewide assessment makes collaboration at many levels essential. Collaboration begins with a willingness on the part of individuals in influential positions to take the risks associated with innovative projects. Too many of us are willing to accept the status quo either because people like it or because they know what to expect from it. The State Departments of Education provide one of the few places where new ideas can be explored and implemented. The changes to the Michigan and Illinois reading tests would not have occurred without the initiative of individuals in influential positions who were willing to take risks and who were knowledgeable about dealing with resistance to change.

When a State Department of Education is interested in and willing to change, it is essential that collaboration occur between curriculum specialists and assessment personnel. Our experience suggests that assessment must be tied closely to curriculum and that assessment and curriculum personnel within the state must work together to guide both development and dissemination. Without this collaboration there is the risk that the assessment will not reflect meaningful curricular goals or, worse, that it may be at odds with them. This can result in inappropriate interpretations of the test data and misguided instruction on the part of local districts.

There must also be collaboration among state department personnel and knowledgeable, influential individuals and groups in the profession. This collaboration is important on two counts. First, professionals provide the expertise that is necessary to develop objectives and tests. Second, professional groups provide the "grass roots" support needed to convince other educators that the innovation is worthwhile. Without grass roots support, change becomes a top down process that is likely to produce disharmony and hostility at the local district level.

Collaboration at these levels brings about a sense of ownership on the part of everyone involved, from classroom teachers to state department personnel. When the details have been worked out together, everyone understands how decisions were made and is comfortable with explaining and defending those decisions when necessary. Ownership at the state level is important because state personnel ultimately are responsible for both the process and the products of the project. If there is little ownership on the part of state personnel, they are more likely to succumb to external pressure and make arbitrary changes in the final products.

Ownership among practitioners in the field is also necessary for acceptance of and efforts toward change. If there is little ownership on the part of the constituents of the test, they are more likely to lobby against the changes and undermine efforts at implementation.

Although ownership at many levels is desirable and necessary, it can also create problems. If individuals at all levels and from all areas feel a strong sense of ownership, there can be problems with territoriality and recognition. If, for example, the test is perceived by districts as more important than the curricular objectives, there may be undesirable tension between curriculum and assessment personnel at the state level. Similarly, if the individuals doing the conceptual work on the project are more visible than the individuals behind the scene who manage and implement the project, there may be hard feelings among the team members. These situations can also threaten the success of the project.

The Need for Compromise

An inevitable outgrowth of collaboration is the need for compromise. In the context of changing statewide assessment, compromise is influenced by the political nature of the change process. Advisory groups and development teams are formed first to satisfy the political need for broad representation and second to reflect professional expertise. Although this practice helps develop widespread support for the project, it often means compromise in the nature of the final product in areas such as passage selection, passage and item difficulty, item content and format, and scoring and reporting procedures. These can be reasonable compromises that enhance the acceptability of the products, or they can be compromises that threaten the integrity of the project.

Another compromise that often results from the political nature of the process is the amount of time available for development and research. The political exigencies of the process often require short timelines and which are insufficient for research and development. The bottom line for researchers involved in this process is that they have much less control over their work than usual. In essence, the political concerns make the process of change a giant juggling act designed to satisfy the needs and desires of numerous individuals and groups, including policymakers, state level curriculum and measurements specialists, psychometricians, researchers, professionals in the field, administrators, teachers, and the public.

The Need for Resources

The last point in this discussion concerns the area of resources. Two of the most important resources in these types of projects are time and state personnel with test-development experience. Major changes cannot be expected to happen overnight. Time is needed for people to learn to work together and trust each other, to conceptualize and become knowledgeable in new areas, and to develop and field test new materials. This is particularly true when change occurs through the processes of collaboration and concensus that is so important for the success of these projects.

Time is also important for dissemination of information during project development. School personnel need to be informed in time to prepare for proposed changes in conceptualization that have implications for curriculum and instruction. Without sufficient time, changes may not have been adequately evaluated, nor constituents adequately prepared. This can lead to serious difficulties in the implementation of the new assessment.

Staffs and departments within the state experienced in developing and implementing statewide curricular objectives and assessments are another important resource for projects aimed at major changes. Individuals and departments with this type of experience know how to facilitate change in ways that anticipate and accommodate potential problems. Without this experience, it is difficult to make innovations while trying to learn the business of developing and implementing statewide objectives and tests.

Conclusion

Collectively, the observations discussed here have implications for future projects aimed at making major changes in statewide assessments. The following are offered as guidelines for future projects such as those undertaken in Michigan and Illinois:

- Start with curriculum; build in collaboration between curriculum and measurement specialists at the state level and between state personnel and knowledgeable, influential professionals in the field.
- Provide for sufficient resources, especially time for development and dissemination, and experienced personnel.
- Provide for research and evaluation of new procedures.
- Develop and implement plans for large-scale dissemination prior to implementation.

These guidelines are derived from our experiences in Michigan and Illinois. Although these guidelines have some general applicability, every state that undertakes a project of this type is likely to have a different experience based on its own unique set of circumstances. As other states embark on projects similar to those in Michigan and Illinois, we look to them to supplement this list of guidelines. Also, there is much more to be learned as these and other similar objectives and tests are implemented.

The final point we would like to make is that, despite all of the difficulties, the importance of statewide objectives and tests in decision making at the state and local district levels makes this is an activity worth pursuing. If even a small number of districts or teachers improve their instructional practice as a result of changes in statewide goals and assessments, then these projects have accomplished something worthwhile.

Epilogue

It's been four years since we wrote this paper, and another five years since much of the thinking behind these tests began. Nine years is an eternity in the recent frantic pace of change in assessment. The national scene has changed dramatically, including almost unanimous support from educators, policy-makers, and commercial testing publishers to alter the ways in which we think about and implement assessment (e.g., American Educational Research Association, National Council on Educational Standards and Testing, International Reading Association, National Council of Teachers of English, National Council of Teachers of Mathematics). In many ways, we believe that the efforts to alter large-scale literacy assessment in Michigan and Illinois, set the stage for the authentic assessment movement and, specifically, for many of the changes we are now witnessing in literacy assessment. These tests demonstrated that large scale assessment could change.

Our framework for reconceptualizing reading assessment reflected a commitment to the alignment of curriculum, practice, research, and assessment as well as a commitment to more authentic reading passages and more meaningful, higher level questions, all of which continue to be powerful forces in the development of new assessments. Indeed, the National Assessment of Educational Progress, other state assessments, and commercially published tests now incorporate many of the conceptual underpinnings, development procedures, and features introduced in Michigan and Illinois. Obviously, the Michigan and Illinois tests only touched the surface of possibilities. We were still constrained by multiple choice formats, short testing times, and the limitations of our own thinking at the time. Other assessments have since gone far beyond our hopes and even our undefined dreams. Today, concepts such as performance-based assessments, open-ended response formats, and the integration of reading and writing assessment are being considered in the development of large-scale literacy assessments and issues of time, format, validity, and reliability are being reconsidered (e.g. Linn, Baker, Dunbar).

Just as the world has moved forward since 1988, so too have Michigan and Illinois. An update is useful.

Michigan. Our recent experiences in Michigan are in many respects similar to those of the newly emerging nations of Central Europe; once a revolution begins, it is hard to control. In some situations we have watched carefully agreed upon procedures for maintaining the theoretical and psychometric integrity of the test give way to the political pressures of the time. Several examples illustrate the on-going tension.

Passages that have gone through field testing and numerous reviews were removed without input from any group. MDE unilaterally deleted passages they thought were "inappropriate". When topic familiarity items were subjected to political criticism, MDE gave serious consideration to dropping them from the test despite their instructional validity. The tenth grade reading test is currently being considered for use as part of the new high school proficiency examination. This would require altering the current cut scores. The problem is that neither the test nor the procedures used to establish the cut scores were created with this purpose in mind. Hopefully, reason will prevail and other assessment alternatives will be found. On the positive side, local school districts continue to support the theoretical views that underlie the test. Many districts have realigned their curricula and modified their instructional practices so they are more consistent with the theoretical constructs embedded in the test. The lesson continues to be, politics is an important part of large scale assessment.

Illinois. The Illinois Goal Assessment Program in Reading for grades 3, 6 and 8 has continued to be administered every year since 1988, and as scheduled, the grade 11 test was added in 1990. Two major changes are scheduled, or have taken place, since 1988—one involving changes in the format of the test and one a result of new legislation.

The general procedures for passage selection and item development have remained the same. However, the format of the prior knowledge and the metacognitive sections have been changed to parallel the more than one correct answer multiple choice constructing meaning items. Concern about the different item formats within the test prompted ISBE personnel to make this change rather than theoretical or instructional considerations. Plans are also underway to pilot the integration of the reading and writing assessment, and to use reading passages that are thematically linked so that students can answer questions across passages.

The second, and more major change, is part of new legislation which is scheduled to be implemented in 1993. It requires the state to return individual test scores and establishes an accreditation system for schools based on outcomes rather than compliance. The reporting for individual scores will have dramatic implications for the length, structure, administration, and psychometric qualities of the test. The original test design was formulated to assess groups of students—it deliberately did not provide sufficient sampling of student abilities or the psychometric properties for individual reporting. Instead of a matrix sampling design in which students read and answer questions about one passage out of six, all students will be required to read the same three passages. The Constructing Meaning scores will be reported for individuals but limited reliability will require that the other sections of the test (prior knowledge, metacognitive strategies, and habit & attitudes) be reported only at the district and state levels. The accreditation legislation requires the implementation of both a local assessment system as well as the state test, forcing districts to assume more responsibility for on-going assessment of their students and placing an emphasis on multiple indicators of accountability.

The lessons we learned during the development and implementation of the Michigan and Illinois tests remain pertinent today. In fact, the national political visibility of assessment and the move to more classroom-based assessment make the need for collaboration, compromise, and resources even more powerful. There will be new lessons as well, particularly related to implementation of new classroom-based assessments in which teacher knowledge of content, instruction, and assessment is critical, especially if the information is used for accountability. As we experiment with more innovative formats we will need to be careful that assessment does not move faster than curricular and instructional changes and that new assessments meet standards of validity, reliability, and equity before they are used for high-stakes purposes.

The models we developed a mere five years ago are now on their way to obsolescence. However, our experiences, and those of others before us, will be useful reminders of the processes and principles that enabled change to take place. We continue to believe that despite the challenges, efforts to grapple with curricular goals, instruction, and assessment are critical to the improvement of education. We must take an active role in the dialogue and the development of new assessments to assure that they promote high quality teaching and learning.

Acknowledgments

The development and implementation of the Michigan and Illinois state assessment projects have truly been a collaborative endeavor. We are only a small part of a much larger team of people, agencies, and organizations who began work as far back as 1983 on these projects. Without the dedicated commitment of each and everyone of them the projects would not have been possible. Ultimately, these projects would not have been initiated or completed without the support of the policy making bodies of each state.

While there are too many people to mention individually, we would like to thank those key individuals and groups who devoted many long and arduous hours to the completion of these projects:

Michigan. From the Michigan Department of Education: Edward Roeber, Peggy Dutcher, Caroline Kirby, Sharif Shakrani, Robert Smith, and Elaine Weber.

From the Michigan Reading Association several of its past presidents who provided important leadership roles: Mary Bigler, Nancy Seminoff, Karen Urbschat, Helen Johncock, Betty Anne Rowlands, Gwen O'Donnell, and Jerri Hansen.

All the members of the Michigan Reading Association Contract Team, especially Sandy Schwartz.

From the Center for Research on Learning and Schooling at the University of Michigan, Scott Paris, and all the members of the Curriculum Review Committee.

Illinois. Test co-authors: Robert Reeve and Timothy Shanahan; psychometric consultants: Robert Linn and Samuel Krug.

From the Illinois State Broad of Education: Thomas Kerins, Carmen Chapman, Eunice Greer, Jack Fyans, Carolyn Ferrara, and Mervin Brennan.

In addition, we would like to thank Edward Roeber and Thomas Kerins for their helpful comments on this chapter.

This document represents the views of its authors and no way represents an official position of the personnel in either state.

Appendix A: State Goals and Objectives

Illinois

State Goals for Learning and Sample Learning Objectives

There are three levels of specificity presented below. First is the State Goal in Language Arts that relates to specifically to reading. This goal was developed by the State Board of Education with the assistance of the

Corbally Committee which was comprised of educators, business people and the general public. As with all the State Goals, it was intended to be a relatively timeless statement of what students should be expected to know and be able to do when they complete their education.

Second, is a list of seven knowledge/skills developed by a second representative group of Illinois educators (Corbally 2 Committee) to help local districts understand and interpret the broad state goals. Both the state goals and the general knowledge/skills were deliberately stated in broad, general terms so that local districts could have greater latitude in developing their own objectives. The Corbally 2 Committee also added an introductory section to the knowledge/skills because it wanted to provide some theoretical background for teachers and administrators to help them understand an interactive view of the reading process.

Finally, there is list of sample learning objectives developed by an extended group of the Corbally 2 Committee in response to a request to define more explicitly the general knowledge/skills. Although the state goals for learning and the general knowledge/skills in each area were intended to be general, many districts asked for more specific guidance before embarking on their own. Local districts were advised to use these objectives as a guide rather than as a blueprint. These sample district-level objectives provide one of the many possible sets of objectives which are consistent with the state goals for learning. Districts could choose to adopt these sample objectives as their own, although we would assume that none would do so without due consideration of local conditions and needs and an appropriate process of thoughtful review. Districts could also adapt these sample objectives to correspond to their own views. The approach we suggest is for school districts to use this sample set of leaning objectives as a guide to assist them in their efforts to develop local district learning objectives. (p. v, Illinois State Board of Education, 1987). The sample objectives developed are identical for all grade levels, just as the knowledge/skills are. As described in the introductory section above, the reading process across developmental levels remains relatively constant with the task difficulty becoming more complex in increasing grades.

Learning Outcome Statement

As a result of their schooling, students will be able to read, comprehend, interpret, evaluate, and use written material.
General Knowledge/Skill Statements:

    a.   Recognize, recall, and summarize information from material read.

    b.   Generate questions and predictions and give rationales for each prior to, during, and after reading.

    c.   Understand the various purposes for reading and identify text to accomplish each purpose.

    d.   Be sensitive to difficulties of the text, requirements of the task, and their own abilities and motivation.

    e.   Draw inferences appropriate to achieving a full understanding of the text.

    f.   Integrate information from more than one text.

    g.   Justify and explain answers to questions about material read.

Sample Learning Objectives for Goal 1:
By the end of grade (3, 6, 8, 11), given the readers' prior knowledge and reading material with appropriate vocabulary demands, sentence complexity, organizational plan, and concept load, students should be able to:

*a*1)   Locate information that is explicitly stated in the text.

*a*2)   Remember the information that is explicitly stated in the text and restate this information in their own words.

*a*3)   Summarize the important ideas of the text and the important supporting details.

*b*1)   Ask questions and make predictions about a passage prior to reading, based upon prior knowledge and the limited information about the passage contained in the title, pictures or other introductory material.

*b*2)   Ask questions and make predictions about a passage while reading, taking into account all of the important information available up to that point in the reading.

*b*3)   Ask questions after reading that take into account the entire text read and are used to clarify and to review the information.

*c*1)   Understand a variety of reasons for reading such as learning of new information, use of text to accomplish the readers' goals, social interaction, entertainment, and self-exploration.

*c*2)   Use appropriate texts such as fiction, nonfiction, poetry, letters, directions, and reference material to accomplish the various purposes for reading.

*d*1)   Understand the difficulties of the text (vocabulary, demands, content, organization, author's purpose), requirements of the task (what is expected as a result of reading), and their own knowledge, abilities and motivation.

*d*2)   Adjust their strategies for reading and understanding, using de-
        coding skills, context clues, self-questioning, predicting, use of
        reference materials, rereading, and adjustment of reading speed
        based on the demands of the reading situation.

*e*1)   Make inferences about the text such as unknown vocabulary,
        causal relationships, author's purpose, characters' emotions and
        motives, mood and tone using information from the text and prior
        knowledge.

*e*2)   Explain the rationale for inferences made using the information
        from the text and from the readers' knowledge.

*f*1)   Use, synthesize, and analyze information from a variety of sources
        to enhance understanding (for example, form opinions based upon a
        variety of information, to compare/contrast, to verify information
        and to expand knowledge).

*g*1)   Explain and verify answers to questions about what has been
        read.

The Michigan Reading Objectives

The Reading Objectives address three major areas: constructing meaning;
knowledge about reading; and attitudes and self-perceptions.

Constructing Meaning

This category is the first and the major category among the three segments.
It follows directly from the philosophy of reading that describes reading
as a process of constructing meaning. There are two sections of objectives
under this category: interactive reading; and skills. The interactive reading
section presents objectives that guide the development of the constructive, interactive nature of reading. The skills section identifies those
classic skills that are an aid to this process.

Developmental Progression.   The developmental progression takes place
not so much as a function of differences in goals across grade levels, but
in terms of complexity of the reading situations to which these objectives
are applied. It is expected that students in each level will be able to apply
these skills to situations that are appropriate for their grade level. For
example, third grade students are expected to be able to integrate information within an uncomplicated story for the purpose of answer-

ing workbook questions about the story. Students in the sixth grade, are expected to integrate information within selections from social studies or science textbooks to prepare for a test, and students in the ninth grade are expected to integrate information within reference material to write a report.

Knowledge about Reading

The second category of objectives is subdivided into three areas: purposes and goals; reader, text, and contextual factors that influence reading; and strategies. These objectives focus on readers' awareness of these features of the reading process, and on their knowledge about how these aspects of the reading process influence their reading.

Developmental Progression. The developmental progression within the knowledge objectives is evident in two ways. First, while third grade readers are expected simply to be aware of many of these aspects of reading, the older students are expected not only to be aware of these facets of the reading process, but also to understand how these characteristics of the reading process are likely to influence their reading (See objective 14 under reader, text, and contextual factors that influence reading).

Second, it is expected that students' knowledge of these various features of the reading process will become more sophisticated as they progress through the grades. For example, while it is expected that third grade students understand the differences between narrative and informational text, it is expected that sixth grade students will have knowledge about different types of narrative and informational texts (such as adventure storices, folk tales, biography, social studies texts) and that ninth grade students will be aware of even finer distinctions among text types (such as editorials, allegories, and content texts for specific disciplines).

The third category of objectives focuses on those aspects of readers' attitudes about reading and perceptions of themselves as readers that influence reading.

Developmental Progression. As with the other categories of objectives, differences in expectations across grade levels are more a matter of level or dc~cc than of differences in the objectives themselves. So, for example, students at the ninth grade level are expected to have a greater, more refined understanding of their competencies and limitations as readers than students at the sixth and third grade levels.

The Essential Objectives for Reading Education

Third Grade

The specific component of each category for each of the three grade levels (third, sixth and ninth) follows:

Constructing Meaning

Interactive Reading

1. ability to construct meaning under a variety of different reader, text, and contextual conditions
   a. ability to identify and use text factors (that is, text types, structures, and features) as an aid in constructing meaning
   b. ability to select, employ, monitor, and regulate appropriate strategies under varying reader, text, contextual conditions
   c. ability to integrate textual information within sentences, within a whole text, with information outside the text and with information from the reader's knowledge

The objectives at this grade level will be applied to text types, structures, and features as well as to instructional tasks that are developmentally appropriate. For example, at the third grade level this might involve reading an adventure story, a historical biography, or an article from a children's magazine and be asked to identify major events in the story, recognize the importance of certain illustrations, or answer questions that are similar to those that appear in workbooks.

Skills for Constructing Meaning

1. ability to use a variety of strategies to recognize words, for example, predictions, context clues, phonics, and structural analysis
2. ability to use contextual clues to aid vocabulary and concept development

3. ability to recall/recognize text based information
4. ability to integrate information writing a text
5. ability to integrate information from more than one text
6. ability to evaluate and react critically to what has been read
7. ability to construct a statement of a central purpose or theme
8. ability to identify major ideas/events and supporting information within and across texts

Knowledge About Reading

Goals and Purposes

1. knowing that the goal of reading is constructing meaning
   a. knowing that reading skills are tools for achieving the goal of constructing meaning
2. knowing that reading is communication
   a. knowing that what is read was written by someone who was trying to say something
   b. knowing that authors have different intentions and knowing what they are, for example, entertain, persuade, inform
   c. knowing that the reader's adopted purpose(s) influence(s) comprehension
   d. knowing that social context influences reading, for example, peers, home, subculture

Reader—Text—Contextual: Factors that Influence Reading

1. knowing about READER characteristics (for example, prior knowledge, purpose, interest, attitudes, word recognition and comprehension strategies)
2. knowing about TEXT factors
   a. knowing about different types of texts, for example, narrative and informational
   b. knowing about different text structures, for example, elements of story structure, patterns of organization
   c. knowing about different text features, for example, illustrations, connecting words, figurative language
3. knowing about CONTEXTUAL FACTORS
   a. knowing about the different settings in which reading takes place in and out of school

    b. knowing about different reading tasks, for example, workbook assignments, discussion questions

4. knowing that constructing meaning involves an interaction among READER, TEXT, and CONTEXTUAL factors

Strategies*

1. knowing about a variety of strategies for identifying words, for example, predictions, context clues, phonics, and structural analysis
2. knowing about a variety of strategies to aid comprehension, for example, summarizing, self-questioning, predicting
3. knowing when and why to use certain word recognition and comprehension strategies
4. knowing that it is important to monitor and regulate comprehension
5. knowing that strategies are employed flexibly, that is they are differentiated by reader, text, contextual factors

Attitudes and Self-perceptions

- developing a positive attitude toward reading
- choosing to read often in their free time both at home and in school
- choosing to read a variety of materials for a variety of purposes
- developing an understanding of their competencies and limitations in reading
- developing a positive attitude (image) toward themselves as readers

* Strategies and Skills are used interchangeably throughout this document.

Sixth Grade

Constructing Meaning

Interactive Reading

1. ability to construct meaning under a variety of different reader, text, and contextual conditions
    a. ability to identify and use text factors (text types, structures, and features) as an aid in constructing meaning

b. ability to select, employ, monitor and regulate appropriate strategies under varying reader, text, and contextual conditions
c. ability to read in a nucnt manner, for example, phrasing, automaticity
d. ability to integrate textual information within sentences and within a whole text with information outside the text and with information from the reader's knowledge

The objectives at this grade level will be applied to text types, structures, and features as well as to instructional tasks that are developmentally appropriate. For example, at the sixth-grade level this might involve reading a science fiction story, material from a geography or science book and be asked to identify the theme or central purpose of the selection, interpret graphs and charts, or summarize any type of material that is read.

Skills for Constructing Meaning

1. ability to use a variety of strategies to recognize words, for example, predictions, context clues, phonics, and structural analysis
2. ability to use contextual clues to aid vocabulary and concept development
3. ability to recall/recognize text based information
4. ability to integrate information within a text
5. ability to integrate information from more than one text
6. ability to evaluate and react critically to what has been read
7. ability to construct a statement of a central purpose or theme
8. ability to identify major ideas/events and supporting information within and across texts

Knowledge About Reading

Goals and Purposes

1. knowing that the goal of reading is constructing meaning
   a. knowing that reading skills are tools for achieving the goal of constructing meaning
2. knowing that reading is communication
   a. knowing that what is read was written by someone who was trying to say something

b. knowing that authors have different intentions and knowing what they are, for example, fantasize, analyze, explain
c. knowing how the reader's adopted purpose(s) influence(s) comprehension
d. knowing how social context influences reading, for example, peers, home, subculture

Reader — Text Contextual: Factors that Influence Reading

1. knowing about READER characteristics influence reading, for example, prior knowledge, purpose, interest, attitudes, word recognition and comprehension strategies
2. knowing about TEXT factors
   a. knowing about how different types of texts influence reading, for example, adventure, mystery, historical, social studies, science
   b. knowing about how different text structures influence reading, for example, descriptive and casual relationships
   c. knowing about how different text features influence reading, for example, charts, headings/subheadings, metaphors
3. knowing about CONTEXTUAL Factors
   a. knowing about how different settings influence reading, for example, library, scout meetings, readings class
   b. knowing about different reading tasks influence reading, for example, written questions, book reports, class discussion
4. knowing about READER, TEXT, and CONTEXTUAL factors interact to influence reading

Strategies*

1. knowing about a variety of strategies for identifying words, for example, predictions, context clues, phonics, and structural analysis
2. knowing about a variety of strategies to aid comprehension, for example, outlining, skimming, detailed reading
3. knowing when and why to use certain word recognition and comprehension strategies
4. .knowing that it is important to monitor and regulate comprehension
5. knowing that strategies are employed flexibly that is, they are differentiated by reader, text, contextual factors

Attitudes and Self-perceptions

- developing a positive attitude toward reading
- choosing to read often in their free time both at home and in school
- choosing to read a variety of materials for a variety of purposes
- developing an understanding of their competencies and limitations in reading
- developing a positive attitude (image) toward themselves as readers

* Strategies and Skills are used interchangeably throughout this document.

Ninth Grade

Constructing Meaning

Interactive Reading

1. ability to construct meaning under a variety of different reader, text, and contextual conditions
   a. ability to identify and use text factors (that is, text types, structures, and features) as an aid in constructing meaning
   b. ability to select, employ, monitor, and regulate appropriate strategies* under varying reader, text, and contextual conditions
   c. ability to read in a fluent manner, for example, phrasing, automacity
   d. ability to integrate textual information within sentences, within a whole text, with information outside the text and with information from the reader's knowledge

The objectives at this grade level will be applied to text types, structures, and features as well as to instructional tasks that are developmentally appropriate. For example, at the ninth-grade level this might mean reading an American history or biology text and being asked to interrelate the important concepts in the selection, integrate information from more than one selection or interpret graphs and tables. With literary materials it might mean recognizing metaphoric language, imagery, or comparing major characters in the selection.

Skills for Constructing Meaning

1. ability to use a variety of strategies to recognize words, for example, predictions, context clues, phonics, and structural analysis
2. ability to use contextual clues to aid vocabulary and concept development
3. ability to recall recognize text based information
4. ability to integrate information within a text
5. ability to integrate information from more than one text
6. ability to evaluate and react critically to what has been read
7. ability to construct a statement of a central purpose or theme
8. ability to identify major ideas/events and supporting information within and across texts

Knowledge About Reading

Goals and purposes

1. knowing that the goal of reading is constructing meaning
   a. knowing that reading skills are tools for achieving the goal of constructing meaning
2. knowing that reading is communication
   a. knowing that what is read was written by someone who was trying to say something
   b. knowing that authors have different intentions and knowing what they are, for example, criticize, satirize, synthesize, editorialize
   c. knowing that the reader's adopted purpose(s) influence(s) comprehension
   d. knowing how social context influences reading, for example, peers, home, subculture

Reader—Text Contextual: Factors that Influence Reading

1. knowing about how READER characteristics influence reading (for example, prior knowledge, purpose, interest, attitudes, word recognition and comprehension strategies)
2. knowing about TEXT factors

    a. knowing about how different text structures influence reading (for example, essays, editorials, history, government, ecology, biology)

    b. knowing about how different text structures influence reading (for example, problem solution, superordinate/subordinate)

    c. knowing about how different text features influence reading (for example, graphs, marginal notations, imagery, flashback)

3. knowing about CONTEXTUAL FACTORS

    a. knowing about how different settings influence reading (for example, library, club meetings, work place)

    b. knowing about how different reading tasks influence reading (for example, library research, test preparation, lab reports)

4. knowing how READER, TEXT, and CONTEXTUAL factors interact to influence reading.

Strategies*

1. knowing about a variety of strategies for identifying words (for example, predictions, context clues, phonics, and structural analysis)

2. knowing about a variety of strategies to aid comprehension (for example, notetaking, conceptual mapping, memorizing)

3. knowing when and why to use a certain word recognition and comprehension strategies

4. knowing that it is important to monitor and regulate comprehension

5. knowing that strategies are employed flexibly, that is, they are differentiated by reader, text, contextual factors

Attitudes and Self-perceptions

A. developing a positive attitude toward reading

B. choosing to read often in their free time both at home and in school

C. choosing to read a variety of materials for a variety of purposes

D. developing an understanding of their competencies and limitations in reading

E. developing a positive attitude (image) toward themselves as readers

* Strategies and Skills are used interchangeably throughout this document

Appendix B

Text Maps
Narrative Map
149
Map for "Making Friends"

Theme: There is more than one way to make a friend
Problem: Andy wants to please his dad and make a new friend but he doesn't know how.
Resolution: He constructs a pretend friend and makes a real friend in the process.
Setting: A new neighborhood Events:

1. Family moves
   Need — Wants to please father
   Plan — Make a friend
   Action — Unsure how to make a friend
   Outcome — Decides to try

2. Collects material
   Need — Build a friend
   Plan — Find possible material
   Action — Collects material
   Outcome — Has all the parts

3. Put friend together
   Need — Complete the project
   Plan — Find glue
   Action — Carla brings glue
   Outcome — Friend is completed

4. Dad comes home
   Need — Share project
   Plan — Show father his pretend friend
   Action — Father likes the pretend friend and meets Carla
   Outcome — Father is happy with both friends

Informational Map

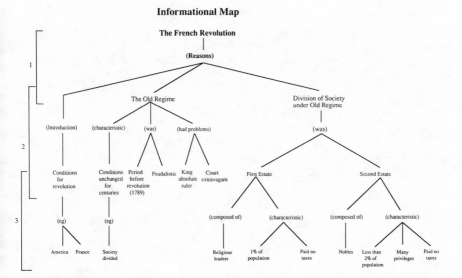

The French Revolution

(Reasons)

1 - Central ideas
2 - Major ideas
3 - Supporting ideas

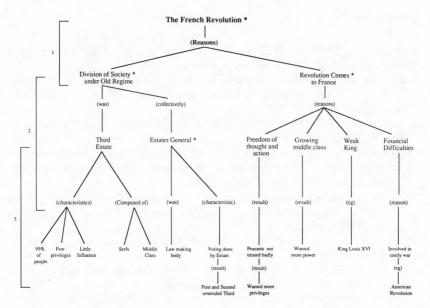

The French Revolution *

(Reasons)

* Adjunct Aid

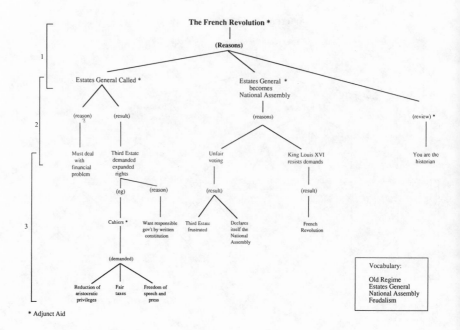

* Adjunct Aid

References

Airasian, P. W. and G. F. Madaus. (1983) Linking testing and instruction: Policy issues, *Journal of Educational Measurement*, 20, 103–18.

Armbruster, B. B. (1984) The problem of "inconsiderate text". In G. G. Duffy, L. R. Roehler & J. Mason (eds.), *Comprehension instruction*, New York: Longman, 202–220.

Alexander, J. and R. Filler. (1976) *Attitudes and reading.* Newark: International Reading Association.

Anderson, R. C., Hiebert, E., Scott, J. A. and A. G. Wilkinson. (1985) *Becoming a nation of readers: The report of the commission on reading.* Washington, D.C.: The National Institute of Education.

Anderson, R. C., Reynolds, R. E., Schallert, D. L. and E. T. Goetz. (1977) Frameworks for comprehending discourse, *American Educational Research Journal*, 14, 367–381.

Anderson, R. C., Spiro, R. and W. E. Montague. (1977) *Schooling and the acquisition of knowledge.* Hillsdale: Erlbaum.

Anderson, T. H. and B. B. Armbruster. (1984) Content area textbooks. In R. C. Anderson, J. Osborn & R. J. Tierney (eds.), *Learning to read in American schools: Basal readers and content texts.* Hillsdale: Lawrence Erlbaum Associates, Inc., 193–226.

Asher, S. (1980) Topic interest and children's reading comprehension. In R. J. Spiro, B. C. Bruce & W. F. Brewer (eds.) *Theoretical issues in reading comprehension*. Hillsdale: Erlbaum.

Aulls, M. W. (1975) Expository paragraph properties that influence literal recall, *Journal of Reading Behavior*, 7, 391–400.

Ausubel, D. P. (1963) *The psychology of meaningful verbal learning*. NY: Grune & Stratton.

Bartlett, F. C. (1932) *Remembering*. Cambridge: Cambridge University Press.

Baumann, J. F. (1986) Effect of rewritten content textbook passages on middle grade students' comprehension of main ideas: Making the inconsiderate considerate, *Journal of Reading Behavior*, 28, 1–21.

Beck, I. L., McKeown, M. G., Omanson, R. C. and M. T. Pople. (1984) Improving the comprehensibility of stories: The effects of revisions that improve coherence, *Reading Research Quarterly*, 19, 263–277.

Berk, R. A. (1986) Minimum competency testing: Status and potential. In B. S. Plake and J. C. Witt (eds.) *The future of testing*. Hillsdale: Erlbaum, 89–144.

Berkowitz, S. and B. Taylor. (1981) The effects of text type and familiarity on the nature of information recalled by readers. In M. L. Kamil (ed.), *Directions in reading: Research and instruction* (30th Yearbook of the National Reading Conference) Washington, D.C.: National Reading Conference, 157–161.

Bloom, B. S. (1968) Learning for mastery, *Evaluation Comment*, 1, 1–22.

Bransford, J. D. and M. K. Johnson. (1972) Contextual prerequisites for understanding: Some investigations of comprehension and recall, *Journal of Verbal Learning and Verbal Behavior*, 11, 717–726.

Bridge, C. A., Belmore, S. M., Moskow, S. P., Cohen, S. S. and P. D. Matthews. (1984) Topicalization and memory for main ideas in prose, *Journal of Reading Behavior*, 16, 61–80.

Brooks, L. W. and D. F. Dansereau. (1983) Effects of structural schema training and organization on expository prose processing, *Journal of Educational Psychology*, 75, 811–820.

Brown, A. L., Armbruster, B. B. and L. Baker. (1984) The role of metacognition in reading and studying. In J. Oransanu (ed.) *A decade of reading research: Implications for practice*. Hillsdale: Erlbaum.

Buros, O. K. (1965) *The sixth mental measurement yearbook*. New Brunswick: Rutgers University Press.

Calfee, R. (1983) Establishing instructional validity for minimum competency programs. In G. F. Madaus (ed.), *The courts, validity and minimum competency testing*. Hingham: Kluwer-Nijhoff Publishing.

Carroll, J. B. (1963) A model of school learning, *Teachers College Record*, 64, 723–733.

Chubb, J. E. (1988) Why the current wave of school reform will fail, *The Public Interest*, 90, 28–49.

Cohen, M. (1988) Designing state assessment systems, *Phi Delta Kappan*, 69, 583–588.

Coleman, J. S., Campbell, E. G., Hobson, C. J., McPartland, J., Mood, A. M.,

Weinfeld, F. D. and R. L. York. (1966) *Equality of educational opportunity*. Washington, D.C.: Office of Education, Department of Health, Education, and Welfare.

Curriculum Review Committee. (1986) *New decisions about reading instruction*. Grand Rapids: Michigan Reading Association.

Curriculum Review Committee. (1986) *What research says to the classroom teacher about reading*. Grand Rapids: Michigan Reading Association.

Curriculum Review Committee. (1987) *Metacognition*. Lansing, MI.

Curriculum Review Committee. (1988) *Assessing reading comprehension*. Lansing, MI.

Curriculum Review Committee. (1988) Assessing the instructional situation. Lansing, MI.

Curtis, M. E. and R. Glaser. (1983) Reading theory and the assessment of reading achievement, *Journal of Educational Measurement*, 20, 133–148.

Darling-Hammond, L. and A. Wise. (1983) Beyond standardization: State standards and school improvement, *Elementary School Journal*, 85, 315–36.

Davis, F. B. (1944) Fundamental factors of comprehension in reading, *Psychometrika*, 9, 185–197.

Doyle, D. P. and T. W. Haertle. (1985) *Excellence in education: The states take charge*. Washington, D.C.: American Enterprise Institution.

Drum, P. A., Calfee, R. C. and L. K. Cook. (1981) The effects of surface structure variables on performance in reading comprehension tests, *Reading Research Quarterly*, 16, 486–514.

Dweck, C. S. and J. Bempechat. (1983) Children's theories of intelligence: Consequences for learning. In S. G. Paris, G. M. Olson & H. S. Stevenson (eds.) *Learning and motivation in the classroom*. Hillsdale: Erlbaum.

Elliott, E. J. and R. Hall. (1985) Indicators of performance: Measuring the educators, *Educational Measurement: Issues and Practice*, 4, 6–9.

Farr, R. and R. F. Carey. (1986) *Reading: What can be measured?* (Second Edition) Newark: International Reading Association.

Fiske, E. B. (1988) America's test mania. *The New York Times*, Section 12, 16–20.

Fladland, K. (1984) Making friends. *Highlights for children*. Columbus: Highlights for Children, Inc.

Frederiksen, C. H. (1975) Effects of context-induced processing operations on semantic information acquired from discourse, *Cognitive Psychology*, 7, 139–166.

Garner, R. and R. Reis. (1981) Monitoring and resolving comprehension obstacles: An investigation of spontaneous text lookbacks among upper-grade good and poor comprehenders, *Reading Research Quarterly*, 16, 569–582.

Gates, A. I. (1926) A series of tests for the measurement and diagnosis of reading ability in grades 3 to 8, *Teacher College Record*, 28, 1–23.

Glaser, R. (1981) The future of testing: A research agenda for cognitive psychology and psychometrics, *American Psychologist*, 36, 923–936.

Guthrie, J. T. and I. Kirsch. (1984) The emergent perspective on literacy, *Phi Delta Kappa*, 65, 351–355.

Haertel, E. (1985) Construct validity and criterion referenced testing, *Review of Educational Research*, 55, 23–46.

Haertel, E. (1988) Personal communication.

Haney, W. (1984) Testing reasoning and reasoning about testing. *Review of Educational Research*, 54, 597–654.

Haney, W. (1985) Making testing more educational. *Educational Leadership*, 55, 4–13.

Hansen, J. and Pearson, P. D. (1983) An instructional study Improving the inferential comprehension of fourth grade good and poor readers, *Journal of Educational Psychology*, 75, 821–829.

Harter, S. (1981) A model of mastery motivation in children: Individual differences and developmental change. In W. A. Colliers (ed.), *Aspects of the development of competence: The Minnesota symposium on child psychology* (Vol. 14, pp. 215–255) Hillsdale: Erlbaum.

Illinois State Board of Education. (1981) Illinois inventory of educational progress, reading results of the 1979 and 1980 IIEP. Springfield.

Illinois State Board of Education. (1983) Student achievement in Illinois: An analysis of student progress–1982. Springfield: Illinois State Board of Education.

Illinois State Board of Education. (1984) Student achievement in Illinois: An analysis of student progress–1983. Springfield.

Illinois State Board of Education. (1985) Student achievement in Illinois: An analysis of student progress–1984. Springfield.

Illinois State Board of Education. (1986) Student achievement in Illinois: An analysis of student progress in language arts–1985. Springfield.

Illinois State Board of Education. (1985) Excellence in the making. Springfield: Illinois Commission on the Improvement of Elementary and Secondary Education.

Illinois State Board of Education. (1983) Phase I mandate studies, final staff recommendations. Springfield.

Illinois State Board of Education. (1980) Illinois State Board of Education goals statement. Springfield.

Illinois State Board of Education. (1987) State goals for learning and sample learning objectives–Language arts. Springfield.

Johnston, P. H. (1984) Prior knowledge and reading comprehension test bias, *Reading Research Quarterly*, 19, 219–239.

Kearns, D. T. (1988) An educational recovery plan for America. *Phi Delta Kappan*, 69, 565–570.

Kearney, C. P., Crowson, R. L. and T. P. Wilbur. (1970) The Michigan educational assessment of education. *Michigan Journal of Secondary Education*, 11, 15–27.

Kearney, C. P. (1970) The politics of educational assessment in Michigan, *Planning and Changing*, 1, 71–82.

Kearney, C. P., Donovan, D. L. and T. H. Fisher. (1974) In defense of Michigan's accountability program, *Phi Delta Kappan*, 56, 14–19.

Kerins, C. T. (1987) Personal communication.

Kintsch, W. and T. A. van Dijk. (1978) Toward a mode of discourse comprehension and production, *Psychological Review*, 85, 363–394.

Kintsch, W., Mandel, T. S. and E. Kozminsky. (1977) Summarizing scrambled stories, *Memory & Cognition*, 5, 547–552.

Kirsch, I. S. and A. Jungeblut. (1986) *Literacy: Profiles of America's young adults.* Princeton: National Assessment of Educational Progress.

Langer, J. A. (1985) Levels of questioning: An alternative view, *Reading Research Quarterly*, 20, 586–602.

Lapointe, A. (1988) Reading results of the national assessment of educational progress: Results and implications. Presentation at the International Reading Association, Toronto, Canada.

Lerner, B. (1981) The minimum competence testing movement: Social, scientific, and legal implications, *American Psychologist*, 36, 1057–1066.

Leinwand, G. (1974) *The pageneant of world history.* Boston: Allyn and Bacon, Inc., Ch. 19, 359–364.

Linn, R. L. (1986) Educational testing and assessment: Research needs and policy issues, *American Psychologist*, 41, 1153–1160.

Linn, R. L. (1987) A linear equating procedure for estimating a total test score from paired subtest scores. Champaign-Urbana: University of Illinois (unpublished manuscript)

Lipson, M. Y. (1982) Learning new information from text: The role of prior knowledge and reading ability, *Journal of Reading Behavior*, 14, 243–262.

Lipson, M. Y. (1983) The influence of religious affiliation on children's memory for text information, *Reading Research Quarterly*, 18, 448–457.

Lorch, R. F. and E. P. Lorch. (1985) Topic structure representation and text recall, *Journal of Educational Psychology*, 77, 137–148.

Lorch, R. F., Lorch, E. P. and P. D. Mathews. (1985) On-line processing of the topic structure of a text, *Journal of Memory and Language*, 24, 350–362.

Madaus, G. F. (1985) Test scores as administrative mechanisms in educational policy, *Phi Delta Kappan*, 66, 611–617.

Mason, J. M. (1984) A schema-theoretic view of the reading process as a basis for comprehension instruction. In G. G. Duffy, L. R. Roehler & J. Mason (eds.), *Comprehension instruction.* New York: Longman, 26–38.

Messick, S. (1980) *Constructs and their vicissitudes in educational and psychological measurement: Proceedings of a colloquium on theory and application in education and employment.* Princeton: U.S. Office of Personnel Management and Educational Testing Service.

Meyer, B. J. F. and E. Rice. (1984) The structure of text. In P. D. Pearson, R. Barr, M. Kamil and P. Mosenthal (eds.), *Handbook of reading research.* New York: Longman, 319–352.

Michigan State Board of Education. (1984) *Better education for Michigan citizens: A blueprint for action.* Lansing.

Mosenthal, P. and T. Na. (1980) Quality of children's recall under two classroom testing tasks: Towards a sociopsycholinguistic model of reading comprehension, *Reading Research Quarterly*, 15, 504–528.

Myers, M. and S. G. Paris. (1978) Children's metacognitive knowledge about reading. *Journal of Educational Psychology*, 70, 680–690.

National Commission on Excellence in Education. (1983) *A nation at risk: The imperative for educational reform.* Washington, D.C.: U.S. Government Printing Office.

National Governors' Association. (1986) *Time for results: The governors' 1991 report on education.* Washington, D.C.: National Governors' Association.

New York Times. (1988) New Jersey takes over local district. May 12, 9.

Olson, M. W. (1985) Text type and reader ability: The effects of paraphrase and text-based inference questions, *Journal of Reading Behavior*, 17, 199–214.

Palincsar, A. S. and A. L. Brown. (1984) Reciprocal teaching of comprehension fostering and monitoring activities, *Cognition and Instruction*, 1, 117–175.

Paris, S. G., Cross, D. and M. Y. Lipson. (1984) Informed strategies for learning: A program to improve children's reading awareness and comprehension, *Journal of Educational Psychology*, 76, 1239–1252.

Pearson, P. D., Hansen, J. and C. Gordon. (1979) The effect of background knowledge on young children's comprehension of explicit and implicit information, *Journal of Reading Behavior*, 11, 201–209.

Pearson, P. D. and D. Dunning. (1985) The impact of assessment on reading instruction, *Illinois Reading Council Journal*, 13, 19–28.

Pipho, C. (1978) Minimum competency testing in 1978: A look at state standards, *Phi Delta Kappan*, 59, 585–588.

Popham, W. J. (1981) The case for minimum competency testing, *Phi Delta Kappan*, 63, 89–91.

Popham, W. J. (1983) Task-teaching versus test-teaching, *Educational Measurement: Issues and Practice*, 2, 10–11.

Porter, A. C. (1985) The role of testing in effective schools, *American Education*, January/February, 25–28.

Porter, J. W. (1976) The virtues of a state assessment program, *Phi Delta Kappan*, 57, 667–668.

Public Law 89–10, 89th Congress, H.R. 2362, April 11, 1965, Sec. 205 (a) (5)

Raphael, T. E. and Pearson, P. D. (1985) Increasing students' awareness of source of information for answering questions, *American Educational Research Journal*, 22, 217–236.

Roeber, E. (1988) Personal communication.

Rumelhart, D. E. (1977) Understanding and summarizing brief stories. In D. LaBerge & S. J. Samuels (eds.) *Basic processing in reading: Perception and comprehension.* Hillsdale: Erlbaum, 265–303.

Salganik, L. H. (1985) Why testing reforms are so popular and how they are changing education, *Phi Delta Kappan*, 66, 607–610.

Sanders, T. (1986) A state responds: The Illinois story. Paper presented to the National Commission on Excellence on Education. Salt Lake City.

Schwarz, M. N. K. and A. Flammer. (1981) Text structure and title effects on comprehension and recall, *Journal of Verbal Learning and Verbal Behavior*, 20, 61–66.

Selden, R. (1988) Teacher assessment. Presentation, International Reading Association, Toronto, Canada.

Seligman, M. E. P. (1975) *Helplessness: On depression, development, and death.* San Francisco: Freeman.

Smith, N. B. (1965) *American reading instruction.* Newark: International Reading Association.

Thurstone, L. L. (1946) Note on a reanalysis of Davis' reading tests. Psychometrika, 11, 185–188.

Timar, T. B. and D. L. Kirp. (1987) Educational reform and institutional competence, *Harvard Educational Review,* 57, 308–330.

Traub, R. E. and G. L. Rowley. (1980) Reliability of test scores and decisions. *Applied Psychological Measurement,* 4, 517–545.

Tyler, R. W. (1965) Assessing the progress of education, *Phi Delta Kappan,* 47, 13–16.

Tyler, R. W. (1969) Introduction. *Educational evaluation: New roles, new means, sixty-eighth yearbook of the National Society for the Study of Education, Part II.* Chicago: University of Chicago Press.

Tyler, R. W. (1970) National assessment: A history and sociology, *School and Society,* 98, 471–477.

Tyler, R. W. (1987) Educational reforms, *Phi Delta Kappan,* 69, 277–280.

Tyler, R. W. and R. M. Wolf. (eds.) (1974) *Crucial issues in testing.* Berkeley: McCutchan Publishing Company.

Valencia, S. and P. D. Pearson. (1987) Reading assessment: Time for change, *The Reading Teacher,* 40, 726–32.

Weiner, B. (1979) A theory of motivation for some classroom experiences, *Journal of Educational Psychology,* 71, 3–25.

Whipple, G. M. (1925). Reading tests—Standardized and informal. In G. M. Whipple (Ed.), *Report of the National Committee on Reading* (Twenty-fourth Yearbook of the National Society for the Study of Education, Part I). Bloomington, IL: Public School Publishing.

Williams, J. P., Taylor, M. B., and S. Ganger. (1981). Text variations at the level of the individual sentence and the comprehension of simple expository paragraphs. *Journal of Educational Psychology,* 73, 851–865.

Williams, J. P., Taylor, M. B., and J. S. deCani. (1984). Constructing macro structure for expository text. *Journal of Educational Psychology,* 76, 1065–1075.

Wixson, Karen K. (1983). Postreading question-answer interactions and children's learning from text. *Journal of Educational Psychology,* 30, 413–423.

Wixson, Karen K. (1984). Level of importance of postquestions and children's learning from text. *American Educational Research Journal,* 21, 419–434.

Wixson, Karen K. and Charles W. Peters (1984). Reading redefined: A Michigan Reading Association position paper. *Michigan Reading Journal,* 17, 4–7.

Wolf, Richard M. (1988). The NAEP and international comparisons. *Phi Delta Kappan,* 69, 580–582.

Womer, Frank B. (1970). *What is national assessment*. Ann Arbor, MI: National Assessment of Educational Progress.

Womer, Frank B. (1981). State-level testing: Where we have been may not tell us where we are going. *New Directions for Testing and Measurement*, 10, 1–12.

INDEX